Chalice Hymnal

CHALICE PRESS
ST. LOUIS, MISSOURI

CHALICE HYMNAL

Copyright © 1995 Chalice Press

First Printing, 1995

ISBN 0-8272-8029-7   Pew Edition
ISBN 0-8272-8030-0   Gift Edition
ISBN 0-8272-8031-9   Keyboard Edition
ISBN 0-8272-8032-7   Large Print Edition

Printed in the United States of America

Preface

In 1987, the General Assembly of the Christian Church (Disciples of Christ) approved a resolution, initiated by the Association of Disciple Musicians, that called for the development of a new hymnbook for Disciples worshipers. After preliminary explorations, work began in earnest in the spring of 1991 with the establishment of a fifteen-member hymnal development committee under the joint auspices of Christian Board of Publication and the Division of Homeland Ministries. *Chalice Hymnal* is the product of that endeavor.

The committee held fourteen meetings over a three-year period, both in plenary session and as two subcommittees: Language, Theology, and Worship; and Texts, Tunes, and Service Music. A denomination-wide survey was conducted that established the broad range of hymns that Disciples sing and generated the core of the new hymnal. Extensive research into the recent hymn explosion and the hymnody of Christians around the globe brought thousands of items to the attention of the committee. Every resource in the *Chalice Hymnal* was approved by a two-thirds majority of committee members, and every stanza of every hymn was sung before voting.

Like a mosaic, in which pieces of all shapes, shades, and sizes come together to form a beautiful whole, this hymnal brings together old favorite hymns and new discoveries that reflect the rich diversity of Disciples. It is a user-friendly hymnal, with singable tunes and comfortable keys. A variety of ethnic traditions is included, especially African-American, Hispanic, and Asian. Twenty-one hymns are in Spanish as well as English, offering opportunities for bilingual singing in multicultural worship.

With great care and pastoral sensitivity, some hymn texts have been amended to eliminate or reduce archaic language, generic masculine references for humanity, and the negative use of metaphors about darkness or physical disabilities. Language in the hymnal expands the imaging of God in a rich and empowering way.

God is the central focus of our worship and of this hymnal, as can be seen in the major sections into which it is divided: God beyond all name and form; God known in Jesus Christ; God present in the Holy Spirit; God's church; and God's world. Of particular assistance to worship planners is the organizing of a large body of material around the basic components of Sunday worship, from gathering to going forth.

Recognizing the centrality of the Lord's Supper in Christian worship, the *Chalice Hymnal* lives up to its name by incorporating forty communion hymns. Worship material and service music are interspersed throughout the hymnal, for use by the entire congregation. A selection of psalms with sung responses is provided, with its own introduction and guidelines for use (p. 726f.). A separate worship section at the back contains a brief order of worship for elders and others serving communion to the confined and a model order of Sunday worship with basic resources.

To assist accompanists in setting appropriate tempos, metronome markings for newer and less familiar tunes are provided, but only as general guidelines. Tempos naturally will vary according to custom and the acoustics of the worshiping space.

A special feature of the hymnal is a three-year cycle of daily worship incorporating a psalm, a scripture text, and the words of one of the hymns in this collection. There was a time when each Christian individual or family owned a personal hymnbook, for use as a devotional guide second in importance only to the Bible. *Chalice Hymnal* provides an opportunity for recovering that vital spiritual tradition.

Many individuals contributed to the production of this resource. Gratitude is expressed to the members of the "Hymnal Hundred" who served as consultants to the process, providing useful feedback to the committee's work. Volunteers from the Association of Disciple Musicians contributed the proofing of music entries. An initial hymnal revision committee was blessed by the contributions of Kim Cornish, Tom Fountain, Dorothy Lester, James Osuga, McNeil Robinson, James Todd, and Tom Wood. Richard Gorsuch collated and interpreted the hymns survey. Al Graves diligently set all the hymns in this book on computer. Lisa Cripe served valuably as hymnal project assistant.

The editors wish to thank our colleagues on the hymnal development committee in an especially heartfelt way. They served selflessly and tirelessly in a task that was daunting at times, but never overwhelming. Their multiple and varied gifts, from poetry to musicianship to extraordinary graciousness, are reflected in these pages. They are:

Gayle Schoepf, Chair, *Chalice Hymnal* Development Committee
Colbert S. Cartwright, Chair, Language, Theology, and Worship
Susan L. Adams, Chair, Texts, Tunes, and Service Music
Ronald J. Allen, Secretary
Ruth C. Duck
David L. Edwards
Luis E. Ferrer
Gertrude S. Fujii

O. I. Cricket Harrison
Floyd Knight, Jr.
Peter M. Morgan
Larry Sivis
Brent Stratten

Chalice Hymnal is prayerfully offered to God and to the church in support of faithful worship and praise to the living God. May it be an instrument of grace and teaching through which God speaks to the church and the church communes with God, well into the twenty-first century.

Daniel B. Merrick
Editor

David P. Polk
Project Director and Co-Editor

Organization of the Hymnal

GOD Beyond All Name and Form

Praising God of Many Names   1

O burning Mountain, O chosen Sun,
    O perfect Moon, O fathomless Well,
O unattainable Height, O Clearness beyond measure,
    O Wisdom without end, O Mercy without limit,
O Strength beyond resistance, O Crown beyond all majesty:
    The humblest thing you created sings your praise.

—Mechthild of Magdeburg, 13th-century Christian mystic and reformer

Joyful, Joyful, We Adore Thee

Descant

4. Mor-tals, join the hap-py cho-rus; stars of morn-ing, take your part;

1. Joy-ful, joy-ful, we a-dore thee, God of glo-ry, Lord of love;
2. All thy works with joy sur-round thee, earth and heaven re-flect thy rays,
3. Thou art giv-ing and for-giv-ing, ev-er bless-ing, ev-er blest,
4. Mor-tals, join the hap-py cho-rus stars of morn-ing, take your part;

love di-vine is reign-ing o'er us, bind-ing those of ten-der heart. So

hearts un-fold like flowers be-fore thee, open-ing to the sun a-bove.
stars and an-gels sing a-round thee, cen-ter of un-bro-ken praise.
well-spring of the joy of liv-ing, o-cean depth of hap-py rest!
love di-vine is reign-ing o'er us, bind-ing those of ten-der heart.

sing-ing, move we on-ward, vic-tors in the midst of strife;

Melt the clouds of sin and sad-ness, drive our fear and doubt a-way;
Field and for-est, vale and moun-tain, flow-ery mead-ow, flash-ing sea,
Thou our Fa-ther, Christ our Broth-er, all who live in love are thine;
Ev-er sing-ing, move we on-ward, vic-tors in the midst of strife,

WORDS: Henry van Dyke, 1907, alt.
MUSIC: Ludwig van Beethoven, 1824; arr. Edward Hodges, 1864;
desc. Susan Adams, 1995

HYMN TO JOY
87.87D

joy-ful mu-sic leads us sun-ward in the tri-umph song of life.

giv-er of im-mor-tal glad-ness, fill us with the light of day.
chant-ing bird and flow-ing foun-tain, call us to re-joice in thee.
teach us how to love each oth-er, lift us to the joy di-vine.
joy-ful mu-sic leads us sun-ward in the tri-umph song of life.

The Sun Is on the Sea and Shore 3

1. The sun is on the sea and shore, a new day has be-gun;
2. Your love is ev-er in our view, like shin-ing stars by night;
3. We do not know what grief and care each com-ing day may bring;

with morn-ing hymns we will a-dore the bless-ed Three-in-One;
your gifts are ev-ery morn-ing new, O God of love and light;
the heart shall find some glad-ness there that trusts you in each thing;

and we shall praise you ev-er more un-til the day is done.
your mer-cy, like the heav-en's blue, fills all our daz-zled sight.
the life that serves you ev-ery-where will nev-er cease to sing.

WORDS: Louis F. Benson, 1897; adapt. Austin C. Lovelace, 1991, alt.
MUSIC: J. L. Macbeth Bain, 1915, alt.
Adapt. © 1991 Austin C. Lovelace

BROTHER JAMES' AIR
86.86.86

4 Holy, Holy, Holy! Lord God Almighty!

Descant

4. Ho - ly, God Al - might - y!

1. Ho - ly, ho - ly, ho - ly! Lord God Al - might - y!
2. Ho - ly, ho - ly, ho - ly! all the saints a - dore thee;
3. Ho - ly, ho - ly, ho - ly! though the dark - ness hide thee,
4. Ho - ly, ho - ly, ho - ly! Lord God Al - might - y!

Thy works praise thee in earth and sky and sea;

Ear - ly in the morn - ing our song shall rise to thee;
cast - ing down their gold - en crowns a - round the glass - y sea;
though the sin - ful hu - man eye thy glo - ry may not see;
All thy works shall praise thy name in earth and sky and sea;

God most ho - ly, mer - ci - ful and might - y!

ho - ly, ho - ly, ho - ly! Mer - ci - ful and might - y,
cher - u - bim and ser - a - phim fall - ing down be - fore thee,
on - ly thou art ho - ly; there is none be - side thee,
ho - ly, ho - ly, ho - ly! Mer - ci - ful and might - y;

WORDS: Reginald Heber, 1826, alt.
MUSIC: John B. Dykes, 1861; desc. O. I. Cricket Harrison, 1994

NICAEA
11 12.12 10

Desc. © 1995 Chalice Press

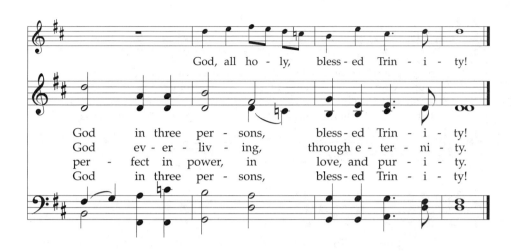

God, all ho - ly, bless - ed Trin - i - ty!

God in three per - sons, bless - ed Trin - i - ty!
God ev - er - liv - ing, through e - ter - ni - ty.
per - fect in power, in love, and pur - i - ty.
God in three per - sons, bless - ed Trin - i - ty!

O for a Thousand Tongues to Sing 5

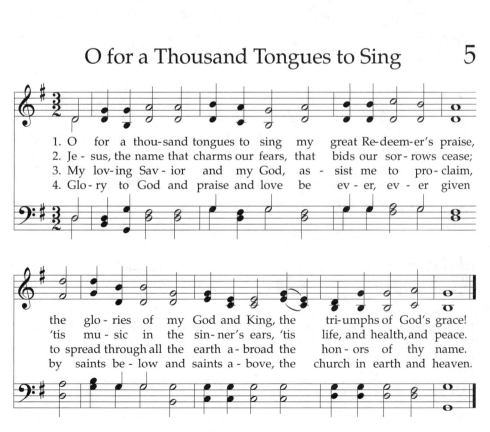

1. O for a thou-sand tongues to sing my great Re-deem-er's praise,
2. Je - sus, the name that charms our fears, that bids our sor - rows cease;
3. My lov-ing Sav - ior and my God, as - sist me to pro-claim,
4. Glo - ry to God and praise and love be ev - er, ev - er given

the glo - ries of my God and King, the tri-umphs of God's grace!
'tis mu - sic in the sin-ner's ears, 'tis life, and health, and peace.
to spread through all the earth a - broad the hon - ors of thy name.
by saints be - low and saints a - bove, the church in earth and heaven.

WORDS: Charles Wesley, 1739, alt.
MUSIC: Carl Gotthelf Gläser, 1828; arr. Lowell Mason, 1839

AZMON
CM

6 Sing Praise to God Who Reigns Above

1. Sing praise to God who reigns a - bove, the God of all cre - a - tion, the God of power, the God of love, the God of our sal - va - tion. With heal - ing balm my soul is filled and ev - ery faith - less mur - mur stilled: to God all praise and glo - ry.

2. Our God is nev - er far a - way, but through all grief dis - tress - ing, an ev - er pres - ent help and stay, our peace and joy and bless - ing. As with a moth - er's ten - der hand, God gent - ly leads the cho - sen band: to God all praise and glo - ry.

3. Then all my glad - some way a - long, I sing a - loud your prais - es, that all may hear the grate - ful song my voice un - wea - ried rais - es. Be joy - ful in the Lord, my heart, both soul and bod - y bear your part: to God all praise and glo - ry.

4. Let all who name Christ's ho - ly name give God all praise and glo - ry; let all who own God's power pro - claim a - loud the won - drous sto - ry! Cast each false i - dol from its throne, for Christ is Lord, and Christ a - lone: to God all praise and glo - ry.

WORDS: Johann J. Schütz, 1675; tr. Frances E. Cox, 1864, alt.
MUSIC: Bohemian Brethren's *Kirchengesänge*, 1566; harm. Maurice F. Bell, 1906

MIT FREUDEN ZART
87.87.887

♩=62-68

When in Our Music God Is Glorified
7

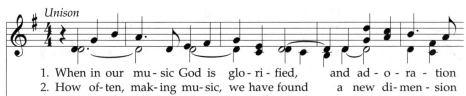

1. When in our mu-sic God is glo-ri-fied, and ad-o-ra-tion
2. How of-ten, mak-ing mu-sic, we have found a new di-men-sion
3. So has the church, in lit-ur-gy and song, in faith and love, through
4. And did not Je-sus sing a psalm that night when ut-most e-vil
5. Let ev-ery in-stru-ment be tuned for praise! Let all re-joice who

1. leaves no room for pride, it is as though the whole cre-a-tion cried,
2. in the world of sound, as wor-ship moved us to a more pro-found
3. cen-tu-ries of wrong, borne wit-ness to the truth in ev-ery tongue:
4. strove a-gainst the Light? Then let us sing, for whom he won the fight:
5. have a voice to raise! And may God give us faith to

1. "Al - le-lu-ia!"
2. "Al - le-lu-ia!"
3. "Al - le-lu-ia!"
4. "Al - le-lu-ia!"
5. sing al-ways: "Al - le-lu-ia!"

WORDS: Fred Pratt Green, 1971
MUSIC: Charles V. Stanford, 1904

ENGELBERG
10 10 10 w. alleluias

$\mathbf{o}$=54-60

8 All Praise to God for Song God Gives

1. All praise to God for song God gives, for music
2. The word gives both the life and light, and guides us
3. In song let God be glo - ri - fied, for God is
4. All praise to God, whose sa - cred word has brought good

and a hope that lives; God's sa - cred word is
through the shades of night, so let the mu - sic
a - ble to pro - vide the mu - sic for the
news to all who heard. We wor - ship God and

so pro - found, we sing and let the truth re - sound.
sound God's praise as hymns bring glad - ness to our days.
sing - ers' art as song God plac - es in the heart.
sing with joy, and in - stru - ments of praise em - ploy.

Refrain

God gave us mu - sic, gave us voice; sing

Ped.

WORDS: Carlton C. Buck, 1986
MUSIC: Dale Wood, 1986

SACRED SONG
LM w. refrain

♩=96-104

al - le - lu - ia and re - joice! We lift in faith se - cure and strong the sa - cred word through sa - cred song.

Church Musicians' Prayer 9

God of Glory, around whose eternal throne
   all the heavenly powers offer their ceaseless songs of praise:
Grant that we may overhear these songs,
   and with our own lips and lives interpret them to all
   in whose presence we play or sing;
That your church may behold the beauty of God,
   and see with mortal eyes the land that is afar off,
   where all your promises are celebrated,
   and where all your love in every sight and sound
   is the theme of eternal rejoicing;
   through Jesus Christ our Lord. **Amen.**

—Erik Routley, 20th-century English pastor and hymnologist

10

Bring Many Names

1. Bring man-y names, beau-ti-ful and good,
2. Strong moth-er God, work-ing night and day,
3. Warm fa-ther God, hug-ging ev-ery child,
4. Old, ach-ing God, grey with end-less care,
5. Young, grow-ing God, ea-ger, on the move,
6. Great, liv-ing God, nev-er ful-ly known,

1. cel-e-brate, in par-a-ble and sto-ry, ho-li-ness in
2. plan-ning all the won-ders of cre-a-tion, set-ting each e-
3. feel-ing all the strains of hu-man liv-ing, car-ing and for-
4. calm-ly pierc-ing e-vil's new dis-guis-es, glad of good sur-
5. say-ing no to false-hood and un-kind-ness, cry-ing out for
6. joy-ful dark-ness far be-yond our see-ing, clos-er yet than

1. glo-ry, liv-ing, lov-ing God. Hail and Ho-
2. qua-tion, gen-i-us at play: Hail and Ho-
3. giv-ing till we're re-con-ciled: Hail and Ho-
4. pris-es, wis-er than de-spair: Hail and Ho-
5. jus-tice, giv-ing all you have: Hail and Ho-
6. breath-ing, ev-er-last-ing home: Hail and Ho-

WORDS: Brian Wren, 1987
MUSIC: Carlton R. Young, 1987

WESTCHASE
9 10.11 9

♩=56-60

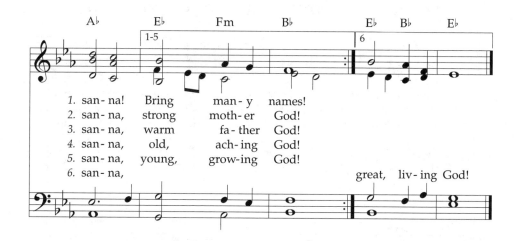

1. san- na! Bring man- y names!
2. san- na, strong moth- er God!
3. san- na, warm fa- ther God!
4. san- na, old, ach- ing God!
5. san- na, young, grow- ing God!
6. san- na,   great, liv- ing God!

Names of God Litany   11

O God, because you are the source of all life and love and being,
We call you Creator;
Because we know the history of your presence among your covenanted people
 and honor their tradition,
We call you Lord;
Because our Savior, Jesus Christ, your obedient child,
 knew you intimately and spoke of you so,
We call you Father;
Because you are present in the act of birth
 and because you shelter, nurture, and care for us,
We call you Mother;
Because you hold us up and give us strength and courage
 when we are weak and in need,
We call you Sustainer;
Because we have known you in our pain and suffering,
We call you Comforter;
Because beyond pain lies your promise of all things made new,
We call you Hope;
Because you are the means of liberation and the way to freedom,
We call you Redeemer.
 **Confident that you will hear, we call upon you with all the names that
make you real to us, the names that create an image in our minds and hearts,
an image that our souls can understand and touch. And yet, we know that
you are more than all of these.**
 Blessing and power, glory and honor be unto you, our God. Amen.

—Second National Meeting of United Church of Christ Women

12 Source and Sovereign, Rock and Cloud

1. Source and Sov-ereign, Rock and Cloud, For-tress, Foun-tain, Shel-ter, Light,
2. Word and Wis-dom, Root and Vine, Shep-herd, Sav-ior, Ser-vant, Lamb,
3. Storm and Still-ness, Breath and Dove, Thun-der, Tem-pest, Whirl-wind, Fire,

Judge, De-fend-er, Mer-cy, Might, Life whose life all life en-dowed:
Well and Wa-ter, Bread and Wine, Way who leads us to I AM:
Com-fort, Coun-selor, Pres-ence, Love, En-er-gies that nev-er tire:

May the church at prayer re-call that no sin-gle ho-ly name

but the truth be-hind them all is the God whom we pro-claim.

WORDS: Thomas H. Troeger, 1987
MUSIC: Joseph Parry, 1879

ABERYSTWYTH
77.77D

God of Many Names

Unison

1. God of man-y names, gath-ered in-to One,
   God of hov-ering wings, womb and birth of time,

2. God of Jew-ish faith, ex-o-dus and law,
   God of Je-sus Christ, rab-bi of the poor,

3. God of wound-ed hands, web and loom of love,
   God of man-y names, gath-ered in-to One,

in your glo-ry come and meet us, mov-ing, end-less-ly be-com-ing;
joy-ful-ly we sing your prais-es, breath of life in ev-ery peo-ple,

in your glo-ry come and meet us, joy of Mir-i-am and Mo-ses;
joy-ful-ly we sing your prais-es, cru-ci-fied, a-live for-ev-er,

in your glo-ry come and meet us, car-pen-ter of new cre-a-tion;
joy-ful-ly we sing your prais-es, mov-ing end-less-ly be-com-ing,

Refrain (Harmony)

Hush, hush, hal-le-lu-jah, hal-le-lu-jah! Shout, shout, hal-le-lu-jah, hal-le-lu-jah!

Sing, sing, hal-le-lu-jah, hal-le-lu-jah! Sing God is love, God is love! love!

WORDS: Brian Wren, 1985
MUSIC: William P. Rowan, 1985

MANY NAMES
55.88 w. refrain

© 1986 Hope Publishing Co.

♩=56-60

14 Womb of Life, and Source of Being

1. Womb of life, and source of be-ing, home of ev-'ry
2. Word in flesh, our bro-ther Je-sus, born to bring us
3. Brood-ing Spir-it, move a-mong us; be our part-ner,
4. Moth-er, Broth-er, ho-ly Part-ner; Fath-er, Spir-it,

rest-less heart, in your arms the worlds a-wak-ened; you have
sec-ond birth, you have come to stand be-side us, know-ing
be our friend. When our mem-'ry fails, re-mind us whose we
On-ly Son: we would praise your name for-ev-er, one-in-

loved us from the start. We, your chil-dren, gath-er
weak-ness, know-ing earth. Priest who shares our hu-man
are, what we in-tend. La-bor with us, aid the
three, and three-in-one. We would share your life, your

'round you, at the ta-ble you pre-pare. Shar-ing sto-ries,
strug-gles, Life of Life, and Death of Death, ris-en Christ, come
birth-ing of the new world yet to be, free of ser-vant,
pas-sion, share your word of world made new, ev-er sing-ing,

WORDS: Ruth Duck, 1986, 1990
MUSIC: Traditional Dutch melody; arr. Julius Roentgen, 1906

IN BABILONE
87.87D

tears, and laugh-ter, we are nur-tured by your care.
stand a - mong us, send the Spir - it by your breath.
lord, and mas - ter, free for love and u - ni - ty.
ev - er prais-ing, one with all, and one with you.

Psalm 33:1–3

Rejoice, You Pure in Heart   15

1. Re - joice, you pure in heart; lift prais-es to the sky;
2. Bright youth and snow-crowned age, strong souls and spir - its meek,
3. With voice as full and strong as o-cean's surg-ing praise,
4. Yes, on through life's long path, still sing-ing as you go,
5. Praise God who rules all worlds; the ris - en Christ a - dore.

1. your fes - tive ban-ner wave with joy, the cross of Christ raise high!
2. raise high your free, ex - ult - ing song, God's won-drous prais-es speak.
3. send forth the hymns the saints have loved, the psalms of an - cient days.
4. from youth to age, by night and day, in glad-ness and in woe.
5. Praise God the Spir-it, Ho - ly Fire, one God for ev - er - more!

Refrain

Re - joice, re - joice, re - joice, give thanks and sing.

Re - joice, re - joice,

WORDS: Edward H. Plumptre, 1865, alt.; st. 5 Ruth Duck, 1981
MUSIC: Arthur H. Messiter, 1883

MARION
SM w. refrain

St. 5 © 1981 Ruth Duck

16 Come, Thou Fount of Every Blessing

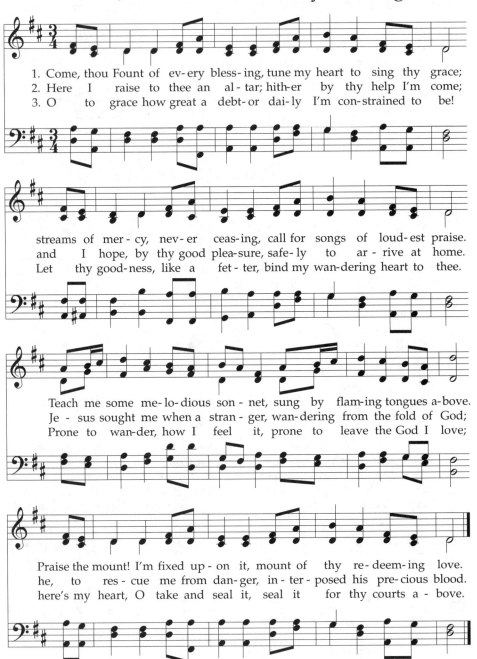

1. Come, thou Fount of ev-ery bless-ing, tune my heart to sing thy grace;
2. Here I raise to thee an al-tar; hith-er by thy help I'm come;
3. O to grace how great a debt-or dai-ly I'm con-strained to be!

streams of mer-cy, nev-er ceas-ing, call for songs of loud-est praise.
and I hope, by thy good plea-sure, safe-ly to ar-rive at home.
Let thy good-ness, like a fet-ter, bind my wan-dering heart to thee.

Teach me some me-lo-dious son-net, sung by flam-ing tongues a-bove.
Je-sus sought me when a stran-ger, wan-dering from the fold of God;
Prone to wan-der, how I feel it, prone to leave the God I love;

Praise the mount! I'm fixed up-on it, mount of thy re-deem-ing love.
he, to res-cue me from dan-ger, in-ter-posed his pre-cious blood.
here's my heart, O take and seal it, seal it for thy courts a-bove.

WORDS: Robert Robinson, 1758, alt.
MUSIC: Wyeth's *Repository of Sacred Music, Part Second*, 1813

NETTLETON
87.87D

O Worship the King

1. O wor ship the King, all glo - rious a - bove,
2. How great is your might! How stead - fast your grace!
3. The earth with its store of won - ders un - told,
4. Your boun - ti - ful care what tongue can re - cite?
5. Frail chil - dren of dust, and fee - ble as frail;

1. and grate - ful - ly sing God's won - der - ful love,
2. Your robe is the light; your can - o - py, space;
3. Al - might - y, your power has found - ed of old,
4. It breathes in the air, it shines in the light;
5. in you do we trust, nor find you to fail;

1. our Shield and De - fend - er, the An - cient of Days,
2. your char - iots of wrath the deep thun - der - clouds form,
3. es - tab - lished it fast by a change - less de - cree,
4. it streams from the hills, it de - scends to the plain
5. your mer - cies, how ten - der, how firm to the end,

1. pa - vil - ioned in splen - dor and gird - ed with praise.
2. in ma - jes - ty rid - ing the wings of the storm.
3. and round it has cast, like a man - tle, the sea.
4. and sweet - ly dis - tills in the dew and the rain.
5. our Mak - er, De - fend - er, Re - deem - er and Friend!

WORDS: Robert Grant, 1833, alt.
MUSIC: Attr. Johann Michael Haydn (18th century); arr. William Gardiner, 1815

LYONS
10 10.11 11

18 All People That on Earth Do Dwell

1. All peo - ple that on earth do dwell, sing
2. Know that there is one God, in - deed, who
3. En - ter the sa - cred gates with praise, with
4. Pro - claim a - gain that God is good, whose

out your faith with cheer - ful voice; de - light in God whose
fash - ions us with - out our aid, who claims us, gives us
joy ap - proach the tem - ple walls. Ex - tol and bless our
mer - cy is for - ev - er sure, whose truth at all times

praise you tell, whose pres - ence calls you to re - joice.
all we need, whose ten - der care will nev - er fade.
God al - ways as peo - ple whom the Spir - it calls.
firm - ly stood, and shall from age to age en - dure.

WORDS: William Kethe, 1561, alt.
MUSIC: Louis Bourgeois, 1551

OLD HUNDREDTH
LM
Alt. tune: OLD HUNDREDTH (altered rhythm)

19 Prayer of an African Girl

O great Chief, light a candle within my heart that I may see what is therein and sweep the rubbish from your dwelling place.

—Anonymous

I'll Praise My Maker

20

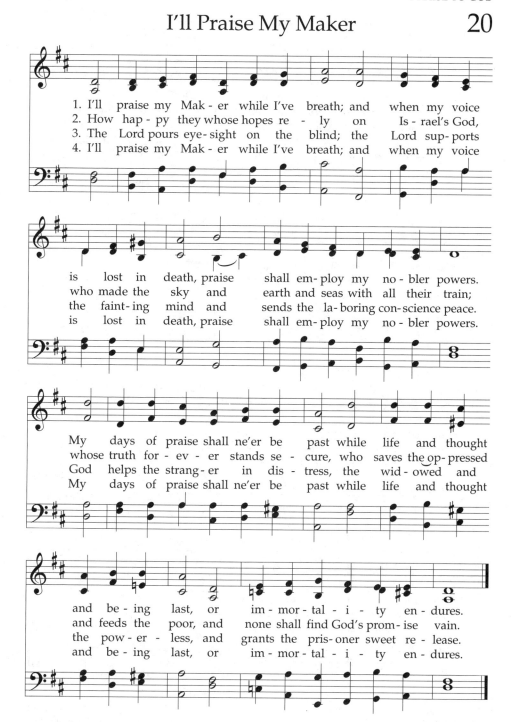

1. I'll praise my Mak-er while I've breath; and when my voice
2. How hap-py they whose hopes re - ly on Is - rael's God,
3. The Lord pours eye-sight on the blind; the Lord sup-ports
4. I'll praise my Mak-er while I've breath; and when my voice

is lost in death, praise shall em-ploy my no - bler powers.
who made the sky and earth and seas with all their train;
the faint-ing mind and sends the la-boring con-science peace.
is lost in death, praise shall em-ploy my no - bler powers.

My days of praise shall ne'er be past while life and thought
whose truth for - ev - er stands se - cure, who saves the op-pressed
God helps the strang-er in dis - tress, the wid - owed and
My days of praise shall ne'er be past while life and thought

and be - ing last, or im - mor - tal - i - ty en - dures.
and feeds the poor, and none shall find God's prom-ise vain.
the pow - er - less, and grants the pris-oner sweet re - lease.
and be - ing last, or im - mor - tal - i - ty en - dures.

WORDS: Isaac Watts, 1719; adapt. John Wesley, 1736; alt.
MUSIC: Attr. Matthäus Greiter, 1525; harm. V. Earle Copes, 1963

OLD 113th
888.888

♩=58-62

21 Let the Whole Creation Cry

1. Let the whole cre - a - tion cry,
2. All who strive to serve the Lord, Al - le - lu - ia!
3. Men and wom - en, young and old,

"Glo - ry be to God on high!"
Proph - ets burn - ing with God's word, Al - le - lu - ia!
Raise the an - them man - i - fold,

Sun and moon, lift up your voice,
Those to whom the arts be - long, Al - le - lu - ia!
Join with chil - dren's songs of praise,

Night and stars, in God re - joice,
Add your voic - es to the song, Al - le - lu - ia!
Wor - ship God through all your days,

Words: Stopford A. Brooke, 1881, alt.
Music: Robert Williams, 1817

LLANFAIR
77.77 w. alleluias

All Creatures of Our God and King **22**

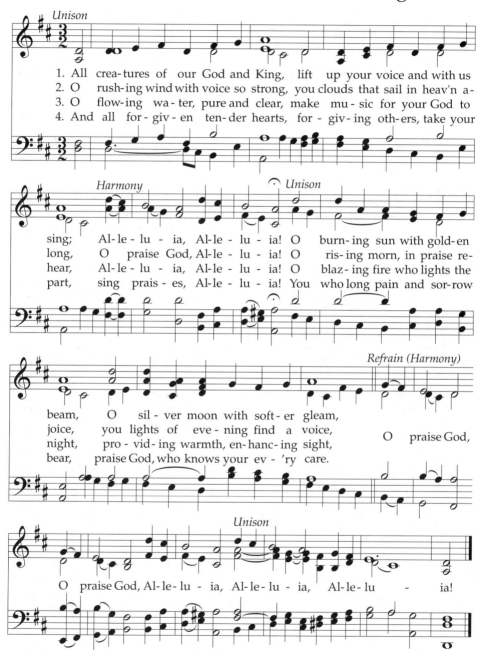

1. All crea-tures of our God and King, lift up your voice and with us
2. O rush-ing wind with voice so strong, you clouds that sail in heav'n a-
3. O flow-ing wa-ter, pure and clear, make mu-sic for your God to
4. And all for-giv-en ten-der hearts, for-giv-ing oth-ers, take your

sing; Al-le-lu-ia, Al-le-lu-ia! O burn-ing sun with gold-en
long, O praise God, Al-le-lu-ia! O ris-ing morn, in praise re-
hear, Al-le-lu-ia, Al-le-lu-ia! O blaz-ing fire who lights the
part, sing prais-es, Al-le-lu-ia! You who long pain and sor-row

beam, O sil-ver moon with soft-er gleam,
joice, you lights of eve-ning find a voice,
night, pro-vid-ing warmth, en-hanc-ing sight,
bear, praise God, who knows your ev-'ry care.

O praise God,

O praise God, Al-le-lu-ia, Al-le-lu-ia, Al-le-lu-ia!

WORDS: Francis of Assisi, 1225; tr. William H. Draper, 1925, alt.
MUSIC: *Geistliche Kirchengesänge*, 1623; harm. Ralph Vaughan Williams, 1906

LASST UNS ERFREUEN
88.44.88 w. refrain

23 Praise, My Soul, the God of Heaven

1. Praise, my soul, the God of heav - en, glad of heart your
2. Praise to God for grace and fav - or shown to all who
3. Moth - er - like, God tends and spares us, know - ing well our
4. Frail as sum - mer's flower we flour - ish: blows the wind, and
5. An - gels, teach us ad - o - ra - tion you who see God

1. car - ols raise; ran - somed, healed, re - stored, for - giv - en,
2. are op - pressed. God shows stead - fast love for - ev - er,
3. frag - ile frame. Fath - er - like, God gent - ly bears us,
4. it is gone. But, while mor - tals rise and per - ish,
5. face to face; sun and moon and all cre - a - tion,

1. who, like me, should sing God's praise? Al - le - lu - ia!
2. slow to chide, and swift to bless. Al - le - lu - ia!
3. ten - der - heart - ed, slow to blame. Al - le - lu - ia!
4. God's com - pass - ion still lives on. Al - le - lu - ia!
5. dwell - ers all in time and space, Al - le - lu - ia!

1. Al - le - lu - ia! Praise the Mak - er all our days.
2. Al - le - lu - ia! Glo - rious is God's faith - ful - ness!
3. Al - le - lu - ia! All with - in me praise God's name!
4. Al - le - lu - ia! Praise the high e - ter - nal One!
5. Al - le - lu - ia! Praise with us the God of grace!

WORDS: Henry F. Lyte, 1834; adapt. Ecumenical Women's
Center and Ruth Duck, 1974
MUSIC: John Goss, 1869

LAUDA ANIMA
87.87.87

♩=108-116

The God of Abraham Praise 24

1. The God of A-braham praise. All prais-ed be the Name,
2. God's spir-it flow-ing free, high surg-ing where it will—
3. God has e-ter-nal life im-plant-ed in the soul.

who was, and is, and is to be, is still the same;
in proph-et's word it spoke of old— is speak-ing still.
God's love shall be our strength and stay, while a-ges roll.

the one e-ter-nal God, ere all that now ap-pears,
Es-tab-lished is God's law, and change-less it shall stand,
Praise to the liv-ing God! All prais-ed be the Name,

the First, the Last, be-yond all thought through time-less years!
deep writ up-on the hu-man heart, on sea, or land.
who was, and is, and is to be, is still the same!

WORDS: Daniel ben Judah (14th century); tr. Max Landsberg and Newton Mann, 1885; alt.
MUSIC: Hebrew melody, transcribed by Meyer Leoni c. 1770

LEONI
66.84D

25 Praise to the Lord, the Almighty

Descant

5. Praise to the Lord! O let all of earth's peo-ples and

1. Praise to the Lord, the Al-might-y, who rules all cre-
2. Praise to the Lord, who o'er all things so won-drous-ly
3. Praise to the Lord, who doth pros-per thy work and de-
4. Praise to the Lord, who doth nour-ish thy life and re-
5. Praise to the Lord! O let all of earth's peo-ples and

rac - es, all that hath life and breath, give thanks for man-i-fold

1. a - tion. O my soul, wor-ship the well-spring of health and sal-
2. reign - eth, who, as on wings of an ea-gle up-lift-ed, sus-
3. fend thee. Sure-ly God's good-ness and mer-cy here dai-ly at-
4. store thee, fit-ting thee well for the tasks that are ev-er be-
5. rac - es, all that hath life and breath, give thanks for man-i-fold

WORDS: Joachim Neander, 1680; tr. Catherine Winkworth, 1863, alt.;
st. 4 tr. Rupert E. Davies, 1983
MUSIC: *Erneuerten Gesangbuch*, 1665; desc. Craig Sellar Lang, 1953

LOBE DEN HERREN
14.14.478

grac - es. Let the A - men sound from God's peo - ple a-

1. va - tion. All ye who hear, now to God's tem- ple draw
2. tain - eth. Hast thou not seen? All that is need- ful hath
3. tend thee. Pon- der a - new what the Al- might- y can
4. fore thee. Then to thy need God as a moth- er doth
5. grac - es. Let the A - men sound from God's peo- ple a -

gain. Glad - ly for - ev - er sing prais - es.

1. near. Join me in glad ad - o - ra - tion.
2. been grant- ed in what God or - dain - eth.
3. do, who with great love doth be - friend thee.
4. speed, spread- ing the wings of grace o'er thee.
5. gain. Glad- ly for - ev - er sing prais - es.

God, We Give You Thanks and Praise   26

God, we give you thanks and praise, God, we give you

thanks and praise, mer- cy and love you show us dai - ly,

bless - ed al - ways be your name.

May be sung as a round

WORDS: Timothy Tan, Taiwan (20th century)
MUSIC: Nai-chen Tai, Taiwan (20th century)

TENG-SAN
Irr.

Used by permission of Asian Institute for Liturgy and Music

♩=84-88

27 Come, Thou Almighty King

Descant

4. To thee, One in Three, e - ter - nal prais - es be, hence ev-er-more! Thy maj - es - ty may we in glo - ry see,

1. Come, thou al - might - y King, help us thy name to sing; help us to praise: one God, all glo - ri - ous, o'er all vic - to - ri - ous,
2. Come, thou in - car - nate Word, gird on thy might - y sword; our prayer at - tend: come, and thy peo - ple bless, and give thy word suc - cess;
3. Come, ho - ly Com - fort - er, thy sa - cred wit - ness bear in this glad hour! Thou who al - might - y art, now rule in ev - ery heart,
4. To thee, great One in Three e - ter - nal prais - es be hence ev - er - more! Thy sov - ereign maj - es - ty may we in glo - ry see,

WORDS: Anonymous, c. 1760
MUSIC: Felice de Giardini, 1769; desc. Charles H. Webb

ITALIAN HYMN
664.6664

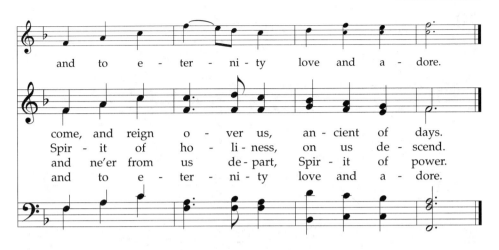

and to e - ter - ni - ty love and a - dore.

come, and reign o - ver us, an - cient of days.
Spir - it of ho - li - ness, on us de - scend.
and ne'er from us de - part, Spir - it of power.
and to e - ter - ni - ty love and a - dore.

In the Name of the Lord 28

There is strength in the name of the Lord; there is pow'r in the name of the Lord; there is hope in the name of the Lord!

Bless - ed is he who comes in the name of the Lord!

WORDS: Phill McHugh, Gloria Gaither, and Sandi Patty, 1986
MUSIC: Sandi Patty, 1986

IN THE NAME OF THE LORD
Irr.

29

Alabaré
(Oh, I Will Praise)

WORDS: Latin America (20th century); tr. Luis Ferrer and O. I. Cricket Harrison, 1994
MUSIC: Latin America (20th century)

ALABARÉ
Irr.

♩=108-116

to - dos a - la - ba - ban al Se - ñor.
glo - ria y a - la - ban - zas al Se - ñor.
Tú nos has cre - a - do por a - mor.

all of them were prais - ing God's name;
ing praise and glo - ry to our God.
have cre - a - ted us in love.

U - nos o - ra - ban, o - tros can - ta - ban y
Glo - ria al Pa - dre, glo - ria al Hi - jo y
Te a - do - ra - mos, te ben - de - ci - mos, y

some were pray - ing, oth - ers were sing - ing, but
Glo - ry to Fath - er, glo - ry to Son, and
We will a - dore you. We give you bless - ing and

F   *D.C. al Fine*

to - dos a - la - ba - ban al Se - ñor.
glo - ria al Es - pí - ri - tu de a - mor.
to - dos can - ta - mos en tu ho - nor.

all of them were prais - ing God's name.
glo - ry to the Spir - it of love.
al - ways sing your hon - or and your praise!

30

Masithi
(Sing Amen)

(Ma - si - thi:)   A - men,   si - ya - ku - du - mi - sa. (Ma - si - thi:)
(Sing a - men:)   A - men,   we praise your name, O   God. (Sing a - men:)

A - men,   si - ya - ku - du - mi - sa. (Ma - si - thi:)   A - men, Ba - wo,
A - men,   we praise your name, O   God. (Sing a - men:)   A - men, Ba - wo,

a - men, Ba - wo,   a - men,   si - ya - ku - du - mi - sa.
a - men, Ba - wo,   a - men,   we praise your name, O   God.

WORDS: South African hymn
MUSIC: Attr. S. C. Molefe

MASITHI
Irr.

Used by permission of Lumko Institute

♩=112-120

31   Prayer of St. Augustine

Eternal God, you are the light of the minds that know you,
     the joy of the hearts that love you, and
     the strength of the wills that serve you.
Grant us so to know you that we may truly love you, and
     so to love you that we may fully serve you,
     whom to serve is perfect freedom.

—Augustine of Hippo, 5th-century bishop and theologian (adapt.)

Sing Hallelujah

Descant

Sing hal-le-lu-jah to the Lord.

Unison

Sing hal-le-lu-jah to the Lord. Sing hal-le-

Sing hal-le-lu-jah, hal - le - lu-

lu-jah to the Lord. Sing hal-le-lu - jah, sing hal-le-

jah; sing hal-le-lu-jah to the Lord.

lu-jah. Sing hal-le-lu-jah to the Lord.

WORDS and MUSIC: Linda Stassen-Benjamin, 1974

SING HALLELUJAH
Irr.

♩=72-80

33 How Great Thou Art

1. O Lord my God! when I in awe-some won-der
2. When through the woods and for-est glades I wan-der,
3. And when I think that God, his Son not spar-ing,
4. When Christ shall come with shout of ac-cla-ma-tion

con-sid-er all the worlds thy hands have made,
and hear the birds sing sweet-ly in the trees;
sent him to die, I scarce can take it in;
and take me home, what joy shall fill my heart.

I see the stars, I hear the roll-ing thun-der,
when I look down from loft-y moun-tain gran-deur
that on the cross, my bur-den glad-ly bear-ing,
Then I shall bow in hum-ble ad-o-ra-tion,

thy power through-out the un-i-verse dis-played.
and hear the brook, and feel the gen-tle breeze;
he bled and died to take a-way my sin;
and there pro-claim, my God, how great thou art!

WORDS and MUSIC: Stuart K. Hine, 1953, based on a Swedish folk melody
and a poem by Carl Gustav Boberg, 1885

O STORE GUD
11 10.11 10 w. refrain

Luke 2:14

Glory to God

34

Glo - ri - a, glo - ri - a, in ex - cel - sis De - o!
Glo - ry to God, glo - ry to God, glo - ry in the high - est!

Glo - ri - a, glo - ri - a, al - le - lu - ia, al - le - lu - ia!
Glo - ry to God, glo - ry to God, al - le - lu - ia, al - le - lu - ia!

May be sung as a round

WORDS: Luke 2:14
MUSIC: Jacques Berthier and the Community of Taizé, 1979

GLORY TO GOD
Irr.

Music © 1979 Les Presses de Taizé; used by permission of GIA Publications, Inc.

♩·=66-70

35 Glory Be to the Father

Glo - ry be to the Fa - ther, and to the Son, and to the Ho - ly Ghost; as it was in the be - gin - ning, is now, and ev - er shall be, world with - out end. A - men. A - men.

WORDS: Lesser Doxology (3rd-4th centuries)
MUSIC: Henry W. Greatorex, 1851

GREATOREX
Irr.

36 Glory Be to the Father

Glo - ry be to the Fa - ther, and to the Son, and to the

WORDS: Lesser Doxology (3rd-4th centuries)
MUSIC: Charles Meineke, 1844

MEINEKE
Irr.

Ho - ly Ghost; as it was in the be - gin - ning, is
now, and ev - er shall be, world with - out end. A - men. A - men.

Glory Be to God 37

Glo - ry be to God and to the Christ and to the Ho - ly Ghost;
as it was in the be - gin - ning, is now, and ev - er shall be,
world with - out end. A - men. A - men.

WORDS: Lesser Doxology (3rd-4th centuries), alt.
MUSIC: Elaine Clemens Berkenstock, 1991

CLEMENS
Irr.

Music © 1995 Elaine Clemens Berkenstock

38   Clap Your Hands

May be sung as a round

WORDS: Jimmy Owens, 1972 (para. Psalm 47:1)
MUSIC: Jimmy Owens, 1972; harm. Dale Grotenhuis, 1986
© 1972 Communiqué Music, Inc., a div. of The Sparrow Corp.

CLAP YOUR HANDS
Irr.

♩=124-132

My Tribute

To God be the glo - ry, to God be the glo - ry,

to God be the glo - ry for the things you have done.

With his blood Christ has saved me; with your power you have raised me;

to God be the glo - ry for the things you have done.

WORDS and MUSIC: Andraé Crouch, 1971

MY TRIBUTE
Irr.

♩=92-100

40 Alleluiah! Alleluiah!

bubu na wo = honor to you

WORDS: Traditional, from Togo; tr. I-to Loh
MUSIC: Togo melody, arr. Michee Abouandjinou

Tr. used by permission of I-to Loh

TOGO ALLELUIAH
Irr.

♩=100-106

Halle-Halle-Halleluja 41

Hal - le-Hal - le-Hal - le - lu - ja. Hal - le-Hal - le-Hal - le - lu - ja.

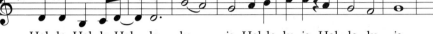

Hal - le-Hal - le-Hal - le - lu - ja. Hal - le-lu - ja. Hal - le - lu - ja.

MUSIC: Caribbean

Sing and Rejoice 42

Sing and re - joice, sing and re - joice,
Al - le - lu - ia, al - le - lu - ia,

let all things liv - ing now sing and re - joice!
peace and good - will to all, peace and good - will!

May be sung as a round

WORDS: Traditional, alt.
MUSIC: William B. Bradbury (19th century)

SING AND REJOICE
Irr.

All Praise to You, Creator God 43

All praise to you, Cre - a - tor God,

for all your bless - ings giv'n with love; for friends and food,

for life re - newed, we give you thanks, O God.

May be sung as a round

WORDS and MUSIC: Margery Maple, 1993
© 1995 Chalice Press

ADM BLESSING
88.86

44 Bless the Lord, O My Soul

Leader: All works of God: bless the Living God;
praise and magnify God forever.

People: Bless the Lord,

O my soul, bless-ed art thou, O God.

Leader: Servants of God: bless the
Living God; praise and
magnify God forever.

People: Bless the Lord, O

my soul, and all that is with-in me bless God's ho - ly name.

WORDS: Psalm 103:1
MUSIC: M. Ippolitof-Ivanoff (19th and 20th century)

BLESS THE LORD
Irr.

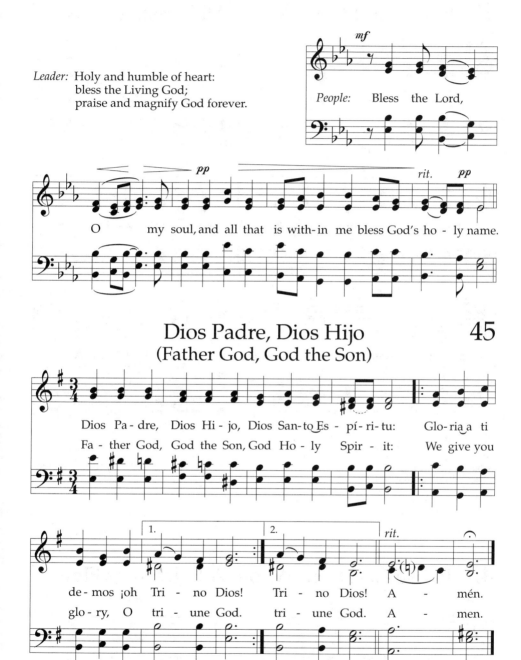

Leader: Holy and humble of heart:
bless the Living God;
praise and magnify God forever.

People: Bless the Lord,

O my soul, and all that is with-in me bless God's ho - ly name.

Dios Padre, Dios Hijo
(Father God, God the Son)

45

Dios Pa - dre, Dios Hi - jo, Dios San - to Es - pí - ri - tu: Glo - ria a ti
Fa - ther God, God the Son, God Ho - ly Spir - it: We give you

1.
de - mos ¡oh Tri - no Dios! Tri - no Dios! A - mén.
glo - ry, O tri - une God. tri - une God. A - men.

WORDS and MUSIC: Pablo Fernández Badillo (20th century)

DIOS PADRE
Irr.

Used by permission of Pablo Fernández Badillo

♩=132-148

46 Praise God from Whom All Blessings Flow

Praise God from whom all bless - ings flow; praise him,* all crea - tures here be - low; praise him* a - bove, ye heaven - ly host: Praise Fa - ther, Son, and Ho - ly Ghost. A - men.

*Or: God

WORDS: Thomas Ken, 1674
MUSIC: Louis Bourgeois, 1551

OLD HUNDREDTH
LM (altered rhythm)

47 Praise God from Whom All Blessings Flow

Praise God from whom all bless - ings flow; praise

WORDS: Thomas Ken, 1674, alt.
MUSIC: Louis Bourgeois, 1551

OLD HUNDREDTH
LM

Alt. tune: OLD HUNDREDTH (altered rhythm)

God, all crea-tures here be-low; praise God a-bove, ye heaven-ly hosts: Cre-a-tor, Christ, and Ho-ly Ghost. A-men.

Praise God from Whom All Blessings Flow 48

Praise God from whom all bless-ings flow; praise Christ, all crea-tures here be-low; praise Ho-ly Spir-it ev-er-more; one God, tri-une, whom we a-dore. A-men.

WORDS: Thomas Ken, 1674, alt.
MUSIC: Thomas Tallis, c. 1561

TALLIS' CANON
LM

49   From All That Dwell Below the Skies

From all that dwell be-low the skies let the Cre-a-tor's praise a-rise: Al-le-lu – ia! Al-le-lu – ia! Let the Re-deem-er's name be sung through ev-ery land, in ev-ery tongue. Al – le-lu – ia! Al – le lu – ia! Al-le-lu – ia! Al – le-lu – ia! Al-le-lu – ia!

WORDS: Isaac Watts, 1719, alt.
MUSIC: *Geistliche Kirchengesänge*, 1623;
   harm. Ralph Vaughan Williams, 1906

LASST UNS ERFREUEN
88.44.88 w. refrain

Praise God, from Whom All Blessings Flow 50

Praise God, from whom all blessings flow;
   praise God, all creatures here below:
     Alleluia! Alleluia!
Praise God, the source of all our gifts!
Praise Jesus Christ, whose power uplifts!
Praise the Spirit, Holy Spirit!
     Alleluia! Alleluia! Alleluia!

WORDS: Thomas Ken, 1674; adapt. Gilbert H. Vieira, 1978

Adapt. © 1989 The United Methodist Publishing House

Recommended tune:
LASST UNS ERFREUEN
(88.44.88 w. refrain)

Isaiah 6:3

Holy, Holy, Holy, Lord God of Hosts! 51

Ho - ly, ho - ly, ho - ly, Lord God of hosts! Heav'n and earth are

full of thee! Heav'n and earth are prais-ing thee, O God most high!

WORDS: Mary A. Lathbury, 1877
MUSIC: William F. Sherwin, 1877

CHAUTAUQUA (Refrain only)
Irr.

Fire of the Spirit 52

Fire of the Spirit, life of the lives of creatures,
   spiral of sanctity, bond of all natures,
goal of charity, lights of clarity,
   taste of sweetness to sinners, be with us and hear us.

Composer of all things, light of all the risen,
   key of salvation, release from the dark prison,
hope of all unions, scope of chastities,
   joy in the glory, strong honor, be with us and hear us.

—Hildegard of Bingen, 12th-century Benedictine abbess

53 Morning Has Broken

1. Morn-ing has bro - ken like the first morn - ing, black-bird has
2. Sweet the rain's new fall sun-lit from heav - en, like the first
3. Mine is the sun - light! Mine is the morn - ing born of the

spo - ken like the first bird. Praise for the sing-ing! Praise for the
dew - fall on the first grass. Praise for the sweet-ness of the wet
one light E - den saw play! Praise with e - la - tion, praise ev-ery

morn - ing! Praise for them, spring - ing fresh from the Word!
gar - den, sprung in com - plete - ness where God's feet pass.
morn - ing, God's re - cre - a - tion of the new day!

WORDS: Eleanor Farjeon, 1931
MUSIC: Gaelic melody; arr. Dale Grotenhuis, 1985

BUNESSAN
55.54D

The First Day of Creation

54

1. The first day of creation is dawn-ing in the soul,
2. Yet God is re-cre-at-ing more than our in-ner world:
3. All life in Christ is com-passed by that trans-form-ing grace

up - on the deep God hov-ers where fear and cha-os roll.
look up be-yond the plan-ets where gal-ax-ies are swirled.
which spins new worlds and won-ders in ev-ery time and place.

The in-ward dark is part-ing. The seas make room for land.
Look out and see how of-ten sur-pris-ing love is shown.
O Twirl-er of the star-dust, O Light no dark-ness rims,

Great shore-lines are e-merg-ing a new world is at hand!
Christ is at work re-shap-ing both stars and hearts of stone.
your new cre-a-tion pul-ses with wor-ship, praise and hymns.

WORDS: Thomas H. Troeger, 1985
MUSIC: Carol Doran, 1985

NEW CREATION
76.76D

♩=126

Alt. tune: LLANGLOFFAN

55 O God of Every Shining Constellation

1. O God of ev-'ry shin-ing con-stel-la-tion
2. You have de-signed the at-om's hid-den forc-es,
3. You have im-pressed your im-age on your crea-tures,

that wheels in splen-dor through the mid-night sky,
your laws its might-y en-er-gies ful-fill;
and though they mar that im-age, love them still;

grant us your Spir-it's true il-lu-mi-na-tion
teach us, to whom you give such rich re-sourc-es,
o-pen our eyes to Christ, whose gra-cious fea-tures

to read the se-crets of your work on high.
in all we use, to serve your ho-ly will.
help us dis-cern the beau-ty of your will.

WORDS: Albert F. Bayly, 1950, alt.
MUSIC: V. Earle Copes, 1963

VICAR
11 10.11 10

♩=104-112

For the Beauty of the Earth 56

1. For the beau-ty of the earth, for the glo-ry of the skies,
2. For the beau-ty of each hour of the day and of the night,
3. For the joy of ear and eye, for the heart and mind's de-light,
4. For the joy of hu-man love, broth-er, sis-ter, par-ent, child,
5. For thy church that ev-er-more lift-eth ho-ly hands a-bove,

1. for the love which from our birth o-ver and a-round us lies,
2. hill and vale, and tree and flower, sun and moon, and stars of light,
3. for the mys-tic har-mo-ny link-ing sense to sound and sight,
4. friends on earth, and friends a-bove, for all gen-tle thoughts and mild,
5. of-fering up on ev-ery shore one pure sa-cri-fice of love,

Lord of all, to thee we raise this our hymn of grate-ful praise.

WORDS: Folliot S. Pierpoint, 1864
MUSIC: Conrad Kocher, 1838; arr. William Henry Monk, 1861

DIX
77.77.77

Feast of a Hundred Hills 57

I enjoyed the feast of a hundred hills, all lying in the quietude of the infinite, who had formed them a feature of his own power. For a moment I retreated to the back of the mountain, that I might enjoy the sweets of solitude, that I might hold converse for a moment with the great sentiment of power that impressed itself on the surrounding scene. With the multitude of hills lying all around me, I could not but lift up my hat as being in the presence of God.

—*Walter Scott, 19th-century Disciples frontier evangelist*

58   Many and Great, O God

1. Man-y and great, O God, are thy things, Mak-er of
earth and sky. Thy hands have set the heav-ens with stars;
thy fin-gers spread the moun-tains and plains. Lo, at thy
word the wa-ters were formed; deep seas o - bey thy voice.

2. Grant un-to us com - mu - nion with thee, thou star a -
bid - ing one; come un-to us and dwell with us;
with thee are found the gifts of life. Bless us with
life that has no end, e - ter-nal life with thee.

Suggested percussion part for hand drum or tom - tom:

WORDS: Joseph R. Renville, c. 1846; para. Philip Frazier, 1929
MUSIC: Native American melody; harm. Richard Proulx, 1986

LACQUIPARLE
Irr.

Harm. © 1986 GIA Publications, Inc.

♩=76-80

This Is My Father's World

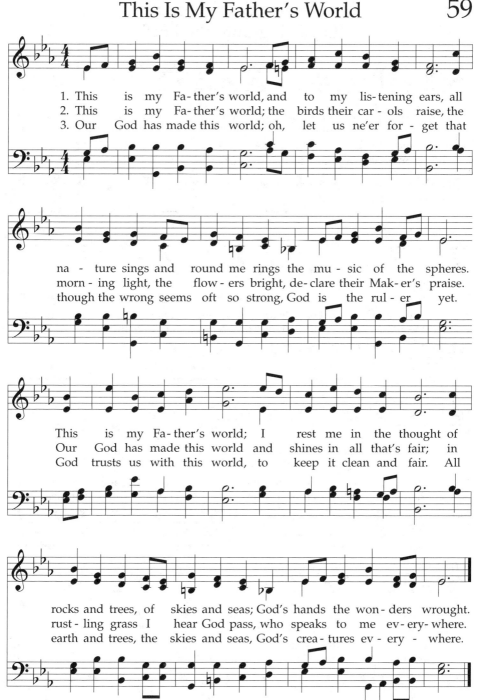

1. This is my Fa-ther's world, and to my lis-tening ears, all
2. This is my Fa-ther's world; the birds their car - ols raise, the
3. Our God has made this world; oh, let us ne'er for - get that

na - ture sings and round me rings the mu - sic of the spheres.
morn - ing light, the flow - ers bright, de - clare their Mak-er's praise.
though the wrong seems oft so strong, God is the rul - er yet.

This is my Fa-ther's world; I rest me in the thought of
Our God has made this world and shines in all that's fair; in
God trusts us with this world, to keep it clean and fair. All

rocks and trees, of skies and seas; God's hands the won - ders wrought.
rust - ling grass I hear God pass, who speaks to me ev - ery- where.
earth and trees, the skies and seas, God's crea - tures ev - ery - where.

WORDS: Maltbie D. Babcock, 1901, alt.
MUSIC: Traditional English melody; adapt. Franklin L. Sheppard, 1915

TERRA BEATA
SMD

60 Cantemos al Señor
(Let's Sing unto the Lord)

Unísono (Unison)

1. Can - te - mos al Se - ñor un him - no de a - le -
2. (Can-) te - mos al Se - ñor un him - no de a - la -

1. Let's sing un - to the Lord a hymn of glad re -
2. (Let's) sing un - to the Lord a hymn of ad - o -

grí - a, un cán - ti - co de a - mor al na -
ban - za que ex - pre - se nues - tro a - mor, nues - tra

joic - ing. Let's sing a hymn of love, at the
ra - tion, which shows our love and faith and the

cer el nue - vo dí - a. Él hi - zo el cie - lo, el
fe y nues - tra es - pe - ran - za. En to - da la crea -

new day's fresh be - gin - ning. God made the sky a -
hope of all cre - a - tion. Through all that has been

mar, el sol y las es - tre - llas y
ción pre - go - na su gran - de - za, a -

bove, the stars, the sun, the o - ceans; and
made, the Lord is praised for great - ness, and

WORDS: Carlos Rosas, 1976; tr. Roberto Escamilla, Elise S. Eslinger,
    and George Lockwood, 1983, 1987
MUSIC: Carlos Rosas, 1976; arr. Raquel Mora Martinez

ROSAS
67.68D w. refrain

♩.=68-76

61 All Things Bright and Beautiful

All things bright and beau - ti - ful, all crea - tures great and small,

all things wise and won - der - ful, in love God made them all.

1. Each lit - tle flower that op - ens, each lit - tle bird that sings,
2. The pur - ple - head - ed moun - tain, the riv - er run - ning by,
3. The cold wind in the win - ter, the pleas - ant sum - mer sun,

WORDS: Cecil F. Alexander, 1848
MUSIC: English melody (17th century); adapt. Martin Shaw, 1915

ROYAL OAK
76.76 w. refrain

♩=112-120

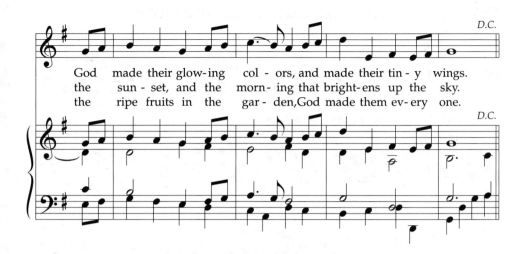

D.C.

God made their glow-ing col - ors, and made their tin - y wings.
the sun - set, and the morn - ing that bright-ens up the sky.
the ripe fruits in the gar - den, God made them ev - ery one.

Creator God, Creating Still 62

1. Cre - a - tor God, cre - at - ing still, by will and word and deed,
2. Re - deem - er God, re-deem-ing still, with o - ver-flow-ing grace,
3. Sus - tain - er God, sus-tain-ing still, with strength for ev - ery day,
4. Great Trin - i - ty, for this new day we need your pres - ence still.

cre - ate a new hu-man - i - ty to meet the pres - ent need.
pour out your love on us, through us, make this a ho - ly place.
em - power us now to do your will. Cor - rect us when we stray.
Cre - ate, re - deem, sus - tain us now to do your work and will.

WORDS: Jane Parker Huber, 1977
MUSIC: Attr. William Croft, 1708

ST. ANNE
CM

63 How Majestic Is Your Name

WORDS and MUSIC: Michael W. Smith, 1981

HOW MAJESTIC
Irr.

♩=128-136

We Sing Your Mighty Power, O God 64

1. We sing your might-y power, O God, that made the moun-tains rise,
2. We sing your good-ness, sov-ereign God, who filled the earth with food;
3. There's not a plant or flower be-low, but makes your glo-ries known;

that spread the flow-ing seas a-broad, and built the loft-y skies.
you formed the crea-tures with your word, and then pro-nounced them good.
and clouds a-rise, and tem-pests blow, by or-der from your throne.

We sing the wis-dom that or-dained the sun to rule the day.
Oh! how your won-ders are dis-played, wher-e'er we turn our eyes:
While all that bor-rows life from you is ev-er in your care,

The moon shines full at your com-mand, and all the stars o-bey.
if we sur-vey the ground we tread, or gaze up-on the skies.
and ev-ery-where that we can be, you, God, are pres-ent there.

WORDS: Isaac Watts, 1715, alt.   ELLACOMBE
MUSIC: *Gesangbuch der H. W. k. Hofkapelle*, 1784   CMD

65 A Mighty Fortress Is Our God

1. A might-y for-tress is our God, a bul-wark nev-er fail-ing,
2. Did we in our own strength con-fide, our striv-ing would be los-ing,
3. And though this world with dev-ils filled, should threat-en to un-do us,
4. God's word a-bove all earth-ly powers, no thanks to them, a-bid-eth.

our pres-ent help a-mid the flood of mor-tal ills pre-vail-ing.
but there is one who takes our side, the one of God's own choos-ing.
we will not fear for God has willed the truth to tri-umph through us.
The Spir-it and the gifts are ours, through Christ, who with us sid-eth.

For still our an-cient foe doth seek to work us woe, with craft and
You ask who that may be? Christ Je-sus, it is he with might-y
The powers of dark-ness grim, we trem-ble not for them; their rage we
Let goods and kin-dred go, this mor-tal life al-so. The bod-y

pow-er great, and armed with cru-el hate, on earth with-out an e-qual.
pow'r to save, vic-to-rious o'er the grave, Christ will pre-vail tri-um-phant!
can en-dure, for lo, their doom is sure: One lit-tle word shall fell them.
they may kill, God's truth a-bid-eth still, God's reign en-dures for-ev-er.

WORDS: Martin Luther, c. 1529; tr. Frederick H. Hedge, 1852;
  adapt. Ruth Duck, 1981, 1990
MUSIC: Martin Luther, c. 1529; harm. from *The New Hymnal for American Youth*, 1930

EIN' FESTE BURG
87.87.66.667

Immortal, Invisible, God Only Wise 66

1. Im - mor - tal, in - vis - i - ble, God on - ly wise,
2. Un - rest - ing, un - hast - ing, and si - lent as light,
3. To all, life thou giv - est, to both great and small;
4. Thou reign - est in glo - ry; thou dwell - est in light,

in light in - ac - ces - si - ble hid from our eyes,
nor want - ing, nor wast - ing, thou rul - est in might;
in all life thou liv - est, the true life of all;
thine an - gels a - dore thee, all veil - ing their sight;

most bless - ed, most glo - rious, the An - cient of Days,
thy jus - tice like moun - tains high soar - ing a - bove
we blos - som and flour - ish as leaves on the tree,
all prais - es we ren - der: O help us to see

al - might - y, vic - to - rious, thy great name we praise.
thy clouds which are foun - tains of good - ness and love.
and with - er and per - ish, but naught chang - eth thee.
that on - ly the splen - dor of light hid - eth thee.

WORDS: Walter Chalmers Smith, 1867, alt.
MUSIC: Welsh folk melody
ST. DENIO
11 11.11 11

67 O God, Our Help in Ages Past

Descant

6. O God, our help in a - ges past, our hope for years to come,

1. O God, our help in a - ges past, our hope for years to come,
2. Un - der the shad - ow of thy throne still may we dwell se - cure;
3. Be - fore the hills in or - der stood, or earth re - ceived its frame,
4. A thou-sand a - ges, in thy sight, are like an eve - ning gone;
5. Time, like an e - ver - roll - ing stream, soon bears us all a - way;
6. O God, our help in a - ges past, our hope for years to come,

be thou our guide while life shall last, and our e - ter - nal home.

1. our shel - ter from the storm - y blast, and our e - ter - nal home!
2. suf - fi - cient is thine arm a - lone, and our de - fense is sure.
3. from ev - er - last - ing, thou art God, to end - less years the same.
4. short as the watch that ends the night be - fore the ris - ing sun.
5. we fly for - got - ten, as a dream dies at the o - pening day.
6. be thou our guide while life shall last, and our e - ter - nal home.

WORDS: Isaac Watts, 1719, alt.
MUSIC: Attr. William Croft, 1708; desc. Donald P. Hustad, 1989

ST. ANNE
CM

68 Ancient Jewish Prayer

You, O God, are mighty for ever. You cause the wind to blow and the rain to fall.
You sustain the living, give life to the dead, support the falling, loose those who
are bound, and keep your faith to those that sleep in the dust. Who is like unto
you, O God of mighty acts?

—Traditional Jewish prayer, adapt.

How Like a Gentle Spirit

69

Unison

1. How like a gen - tle spir - it deep with - in
2. Let God be God wher - ev - er life may be;
3. God like a moth - er ea - gle hov - ers near
4. When in our vain pre - ten - sions we con - spire
5. Through all our fret - ful claims of sex and race

1. God reins our fer - vent pas - sions day by day,
2. let ev - ery tongue bear wit - ness to the call;
3. on might - y wings of pow - er man - i - fest;
4. to shape God's im - age as we see our own,
5. the un - i - ver - sal love of God shines through,

1. and gives us strength to chal - lenge and to win
2. all hu - man - kind is one by God's de - cree;
3. God like a gen - tle shep - herd stills our fear,
4. hark to the voice a - bove our base de - sire;
5. for God is love tran - scend - ing style and place

1. de - spite the per - ils of our cho - sen way.
2. let God be God, let God be God for all.
3. and com - forts us a - gainst a peace - ful breast.
4. God is the sculp - tor, we the bro - ken stone.
5. and all the i - dle op - tions we pur - sue.

WORDS: C. Eric Lincoln, 1987
MUSIC: Alfred Morton Smith, 1941

SURSUM CORDA
10 10.10 10

♩=104-112

70 God of the Sparrow God of the Whale

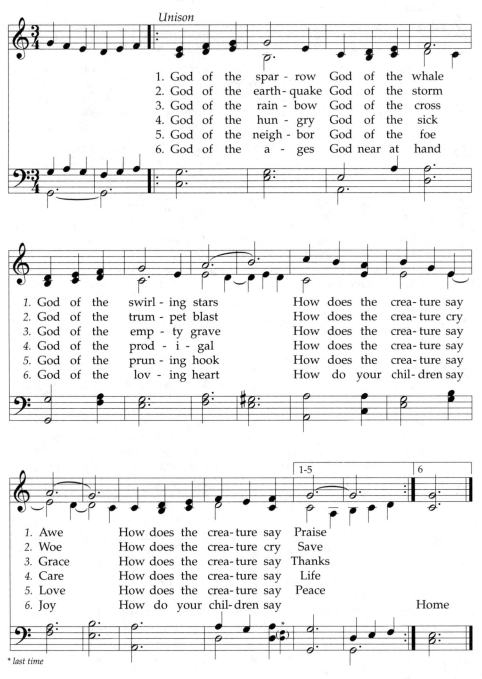

Unison

1. God of the spar - row God of the whale
2. God of the earth- quake God of the storm
3. God of the rain - bow God of the cross
4. God of the hun - gry God of the sick
5. God of the neigh - bor God of the foe
6. God of the a - ges God near at hand

1. God of the swirl - ing stars   How does the crea-ture say
2. God of the trum - pet blast   How does the crea-ture cry
3. God of the emp - ty grave   How does the crea-ture say
4. God of the prod - i - gal   How does the crea-ture say
5. God of the prun - ing hook   How does the crea-ture say
6. God of the lov - ing heart   How do your chil-dren say

1-5 | 6

1. Awe   How does the crea-ture say Praise
2. Woe   How does the crea-ture cry Save
3. Grace   How does the crea-ture say Thanks
4. Care   How does the crea-ture say Life
5. Love   How does the crea-ture say Peace
6. Joy   How do your chil-dren say   Home

* *last time*

WORDS: Jaroslav J. Vajda, 1983
MUSIC: Carl F. Schalk, 1983

ROEDER
546.77

Words © 1983 Jaroslav J. Vajda; music © 1983 GIA Publications, Inc.

♩.=44-48

Your Love, O God

WORDS: Anders Frostenson, 1968; tr. Fred Kaan, 1972
MUSIC: V. Earle Copes, 1963

VICAR
11 10.11 10

♩=104-112

72   To God Be the Glory

1. To God be the glo - ry, great things he hath done! So loved he the
2. O per - fect re-demp- tion, the pur-chase of blood, to ev - ery be -
3. Great things he hath taught us, great things he hath done, and great our re -

world that he gave us his Son, who yield - ed his life an a -
liev - er the prom-ise of God; the vil - est of-fend- er who
joic - ing thru Je - sus the Son; but pur - er, and high- er, and

tone-ment for sin, and o-pened the life-gate that all may go in.
tru - ly be - lieves, that mo- ment from Je - sus a par-don re - ceives.
great - er will be our won-der, our trans-port, when Je - sus we see.

Refrain

Praise the Lord, praise the Lord, let the earth hear his voice! Praise the

WORDS: Fanny J. Crosby, 1875
MUSIC: William H. Doane, 1875

TO GOD BE THE GLORY
11 11.11 11 w. refrain

Lord, praise the Lord, let the peo-ple re-joice! O come to the Fa-ther thru

Je-sus the Son, and give him the glo-ry, great things he hath done!

There's a Wideness in God's Mercy 73

1. There's a wide-ness in God's mer-cy like the wide-ness of the sea;
2. There is wel-come for the sin-ner, and more grac-es for the good!
3. For the love of God is broad-er than the meas-ure of our mind;
4. If our love were but more sim-ple, we should rest up-on God's word;

there's a kind-ness in God's jus-tice, which is more than lib-er-ty.
There is mer-cy with the Sav-ior; there is heal-ing in his blood.
and the heart of the E-ter-nal is most won-der-ful-ly kind.
and our lives would be il-lu-mined by the pres-ence of our Lord.

WORDS: Frederick W. Faber, 1854
MUSIC: Lizzie S. Tourjee, 1877; harm. Charles H. Webb, 1988

WELLESLEY
87.87

74 A Woman and a Coin

1. A wo-man and a coin— the coin is
2. (A) shep-herd and a sheep— the sheep is
3. (A) par-ent and a child— the child is
4. (Dear) God, you sought us when— the world was

lost! How much it means to her, what time and
lost! Far from the flock, the one in hun-dred
lost! The par-ent feeds on mem-o-ries and
lost, you gave Your on-ly Son at what a

toil, what part it was to play in her bright
cries, then— risk-ing life— the shep-herd's voice and
hope, the pro-di-gal on husks and one last
cost; your Spir-it wel-comes home the tem-pest-

WORDS: Jaroslav J. Vajda, 1990
MUSIC: Carl F. Schalk, 1990

NYGREN
10 10 10.10 10

♩=64-68

dreams!   Am I that treas-ured coin worth search-ing
staff!   Am I that treas-ured sheep worth dy - ing
chance.   Am I that treas-ured child worth wait - ing
tossed;   now we can be all you were dream-ing

for?   I'm found, and you re - joice! What love! What
for?   I live, and you re - joice! What love! What
for?   I'm home, and you re - joice! What love! What
of.   We're safe, and you re - joice! What love! What

1, 2, 3   4.

love!   2. A
love!   3. A
love!   4. Dear

love!

75 I Was There to Hear Your Borning Cry

1. I was there to hear your born-ing cry, I'll be
3. When you heard the won-der of the word I was
5. In the mid-dle a-ges of your life, not too
7. I was there to hear your born-ing cry, I'll be

there when you are old. I re-joiced the day you
there to cheer you on; you were raised to praise the
old, no long-er young, I'll be there to guide you
there when you are old. I re-joiced the day you

were bap-tized, to see your life un-fold.
liv-ing God, to whom you now be-long.
through the night, com-plete what I've be-gun.
were bap-tized, to see your life un-fold.

Fine

2. I was there when you were but a child, with a
4. If you find some-one to share your time and you
6. When the eve-ning gen-tly clos-es in and you

WORDS and MUSIC: John Ylvisaker, 1985

WATERLIFE
97.96

♩=92-96

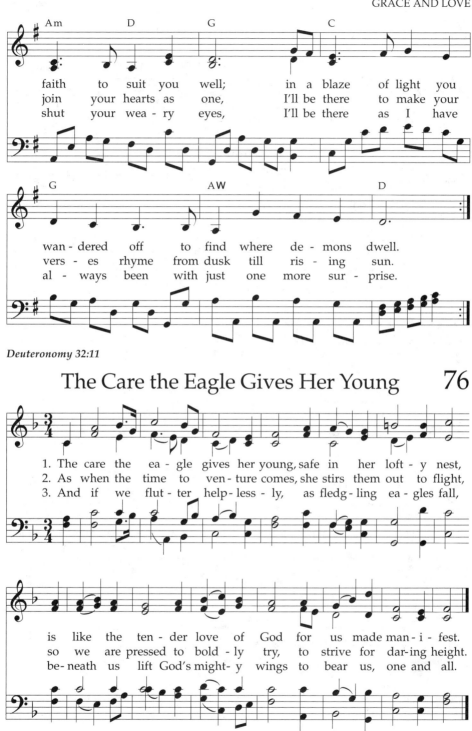

faith   to   suit   you   well;   in a   blaze   of light   you
join   your   hearts as   one,   I'll be   there   to make   your
shut   your   wea - ry   eyes,   I'll be   there   as   I   have

wan - dered   off   to   find   where   de - mons   dwell.
vers - es   rhyme   from dusk   till   ris - ing   sun.
al - ways   been   with just   one   more   sur - prise.

Deuteronomy 32:11

The Care the Eagle Gives Her Young   76

1. The care the ea - gle gives her young, safe in her loft - y nest,
2. As when the time to ven - ture comes, she stirs them out to flight,
3. And if we flut - ter help - less - ly, as fledg - ling ea - gles fall,

is like the ten - der love of God for us made man - i - fest.
so we are pressed to bold - ly try, to strive for dar - ing height.
be - neath us lift God's might - y wings to bear us, one and all.

WORDS: R. Deane Postlethwaite (20th century)   CRIMOND
MUSIC: Jesse Seymour Irvine, 1872; harm. TCL Pritchard, 1929   CM

Harm. © Oxford University Press

77 On Eagle's Wings

1. You who dwell in the shel-ter of the Lord, who a-
bide in God's shad-ow for life, say to the Lord: "My
ref - uge, my rock in whom I trust!"

Refrain

"And I will raise you up on ea - gle's wings,
bear you on the breath of dawn, make you to shine like the
sun, and hold you in the palm of my hand."

WORDS and MUSIC: Michael Joncas, 1979

ON EAGLE'S WINGS
Irr.

After last refrain

And hold you, hold you in the palm of my hand.

2. The snare of the fowl-er will nev-er cap-ture you, and fam-ine will bring you no fear: un-der God's wings your ref-uge, God's faith-ful-ness your shield.

3. You need not fear the ter-ror of the night, nor the ar-row that flies by day; though thou-sands fall a-bout you, near you it shall not come.

4. For to God's an-gels is giv-en a com-mand to guard you in all of your ways; up-on their hands they will bear you up, lest you dash your foot a-gainst a stone.

78 The Lord's My Shepherd

WORDS: *Scottish Psalter*, 1650, alt.
MUSIC: Jessie Seymour Irvine, 1871; arr. David Grant,
1872; desc. W. Baird Ross (20th century)

CRIMOND
CM

God Is My Shepherd

79

1. God is my shep-herd, I'll not want, I feed in pas-tures green.
2. Re - stored to life each morn-ing new, I rise up from the dust
3. When I must pass through shad-owed vale, where loss and death a-wait,
4. No en-e-my can o-ver-come, no power on earth de-feat
5. Good-ness and mer-cy all my days will sure-ly fol-low me;

1. God grants me rest and bids me drink from wa-ters calm and clean.
2. to fol-low God whose pres-ence gives me con-fi-dence and trust.
3. I will not fear for God is there, my shep-herd strong and great,
4. the ones a-noint-ed by God's grace and fed with man-na sweet.
5. and where God reigns in heaven and earth, my dwell-ing place will be.

1. Through dai-ly tasks, I'm blessed and led by one I have not seen.
2. I praise the name of God to-day; in God I put my trust.
3. whose rod and staff will com-fort me and all my fears a-bate.
4. My cup is filled and o-ver-flows as I my Sav-ior greet.
5. My shep-herd bless-es, cares, and leads through all e-ter-ni-ty.

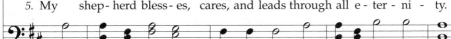

WORDS: *Scottish Psalter*, 1650; adapt. Lavon Bayler, 1992
MUSIC: J. L. Macbeth Bain, 1915; harm. Gordon Jacob, 1934,
   adapt. Walter W. Felton, 1955

BROTHER JAMES' AIR
86.86.86

80 My Shepherd, You Supply My Need

1. My Shep - herd, you sup - ply my need; most ho - ly
2. When through the shades of death I walk, your pres - ence
3. Your sure pro - vi - sions, gra - cious God, at - tend me

is your name; in pas - tures fresh you make me feed, be -
is my stay; one word of your sup - port - ing breath drives
all my days; O may your house be my a - bode, and

side the liv - ing stream. You bring my wand - 'ring spir - it
all my fears a - way. Your hand, in sight of all my
all my work be praise. Here would I find a set - tled

back, when I for - sake your ways; you lead me,
foes, does still my ta - ble spread; my cup with
rest, while oth - ers go and come; no more a

WORDS: Para. Isaac Watts, 1719, alt.
MUSIC: *Southern Harmony*, 1835

RESIGNATION
CMD

for your mer - cy's sake, in paths of truth and grace.
bless - ings o - ver - flows, your oil a - noints my head.
stran - ger, nor a guest, but like a child at home.

Knee-bowed and Body-bent   81

To be read by leader, with the congregation responding by singing portions of "My Shepherd, You Supply My Need."

O Lord, we come this morning knee-bowed and body-bent
before your throne of grace.

My Shepherd, you supply my need; most holy is your name.

O Lord—this morning—bow our hearts beneath our knees,
and our knees in some lonesome valley.

In pastures fresh you make me feed, beside the living stream.

We come this morning like empty pitchers to a full fountain,
with no merits of our own.

You bring my wand'ring spirit back, when I forsake your ways.

O Lord, open up a window of heaven,
and lean out far over the battlements of glory, and listen this morning.

You lead me, for your mercy's sake, in paths of truth and grace.

—James Weldon Johnson, 20th-century African-American educator

Luke 12:6–7

82 His Eye Is on the Sparrow

1. Why should I feel dis-cour-aged, why should the
2. "Let not your heart be trou-bled," his ten-der
3. When-ev-er I am tempt-ed, when-ev-er

shad-ows come, why should my heart be lone-ly
word I hear, and rest-ing on his good-ness,
clouds a-rise, when song gives place to sigh-ing,

and long for heaven and home, when Je-sus is my
I lose my doubts and fears; though by the path he
when hope with-in me dies, I draw the clos-er

por-tion? My con-stant friend is he: his eye is
lead-eth but one step I may see: his eye is
to him, for care he sets me free: his eye is

WORDS: Civilla D. Martin, 1905
MUSIC: Charles H. Gabriel, 1905

SPARROW
Irr. w. refrain

83 Mothering God, You Gave Me Birth

1. Moth-er-ing God, you gave me birth in the bright
2. Moth-er-ing Christ, you took my form, of-fer-ing
3. Moth-er-ing Spir-it, nur-t'ring one, in arms of

morn-ing of this world. Cre-a-tor, Source of
me your food of light, grain of life, and
pa-tience hold me close, so that in faith I

ev-'ry breath, you are my rain, my wind, my
grape of love, your ver-y bod-y for my
root and grow un-til I flow'r, un-til I

sun; you are my rain, my wind, my sun.
peace; your ver-y bod-y for my peace.
know; un-til I flow'r, un-til I know.

WORDS: Jean Janzen, 1991, based on the writings of Julian of Norwich (14th century)
MUSIC: Brent Stratten, 1994

JULIAN
LM w. repeat

Words © 1991 Jean Janzen; music © 1995 Chalice Press

♩.=52-58

The God of Us All

1. The God of us all is our Fa - ther, he guides us when we are in dan - ger, he calls us to hon - or the stran - ger.
2. The God of us all is our Moth - er, she teach - es us her truth and beau - ty, she shows us a love be - yond du - ty.
3. Our God is a Fa - ther and Moth - er, sur - round - ing us all with pro - tec - tion, to give to the world new di - rec - tion.

Great is the Lord, ev - er a - dored!

Alto xylophone (optional)

Soprano xylophone (optional)

Drum (optional)

WORDS: Ron O'Grady (20th century)
MUSIC: I-to Loh, Taiwan (20th century); arr. Susan Adams, 1995

SANTA MESA
999.44

♩=72-80

85 Eternal Father, Strong to Save

1. E - ter - nal Fa - ther, strong to save, whose arm has bound the
2. O Sav - ior, whose al - might - y word the wind and waves sub -
3. O Ho - ly Spir - it, who did brood up - on the cha - os
4. O Trin - i - ty of love and power, all trav - elers guard in

rest - less wave, who bid the might - y o - cean deep its
mis - sive heard, who walked up - on the foam - ing deep, and
wild and rude, and bid its an - gry tu - mult cease, and
dan - ger's hour; from rock and tem - pest, fire and foe, pro -

own ap - point - ed lim - its keep: O hear us when we
calm a - mid its rage did sleep: O hear us when we
gave, for fierce con - fu - sion, peace: O hear us when we
tect them where - so - e'er they go; thus ev - er - more shall

cry to thee for those in per - il on the sea.
cry to thee for those in per - il on the sea.
cry to thee for those in per - il on the sea.
rise to thee glad praise from air and land and sea.

WORDS: William Whiting, 1860, alt.
MUSIC: John B. Dykes, 1861

MELITA
88.88.88

Great Is Thy Faithfulness

86

1. Great is thy faith-ful-ness, O God my Fa-ther, there is no shad-ow of
2. Sum-mer and win-ter, and spring-time and har-vest, sun, moon and stars in their
3. Par-don for sin and a peace that en-dur-eth, thy own dear pres-ence to

turn-ing with thee; thou chang-est not, thy com-pas-sions, they fail not;
cours-es a-bove, join with all na-ture in man-i-fold wit-ness
cheer and to guide; strength for to-day and bright hope for to-mor-row,

Refrain

as thou hast been thou for-ev-er wilt be. Great is thy faith-ful-ness!
to thy great faith-ful-ness, mer-cy and love.
bless-ings all mine, with ten thou-sand be-side!

Great is thy faith-ful-ness! Morn-ing by morn-ing new mer-cies I see; all I have

need-ed thy hand hath pro-vid-ed—Great is thy faith-ful-ness, Lord, un-to me!

WORDS: Thomas O. Chisholm, 1923
MUSIC: William M. Runyan, 1923

FAITHFULNESS
11 10.11 10 w. refrain

87 I Will Sing of the Mercies of the Lord

I will sing of the mer-cies of the Lord for - ev - er, I will

sing, I will sing; I will sing of the mer-cies of the

Lord. With my mouth will I make known thy

faith-ful-ness, thy faith-ful-ness; with my mouth will I make

known thy faith-ful-ness to all gen-er - a - tions. I will

WORDS and MUSIC: James H. Fillmore (early 20th century)

FILLMORE
Irr.

All My Hope on God Is Founded 88

1. All my hope on God is found-ed, who does still my
2. Hu - man pride and earth - ly glo - ry, sword and crown be -
3. But in ev - ery time and sea - son, out of love's a -

trust re - new. Safe through change and chance God guides me,
tray our trust; though with care and toil we build them,
bun - dant store, God sus - tains the whole cre - a - tion

ev - er faith - ful, ev - er true. God un - known,
tower and tem - ple fall to dust. But God's power,
fount of life for - ev - er - more. We who share

God a - lone, seeks to claim my heart as home.
hour by hour, is my tem - ple and my tower.
earth and air count on God's un - fail - ing care.

WORDS: Joachim Neander, 1680, alt.; st. 3 tr. Fred Pratt Green, 1986
MUSIC: Joachim Neander, 1680 (from chorale *Unser Herrscher*)

NEANDER
87.87.67

St. 3 © 1989 Hope Publishing Co.

GOD Known In Jesus Christ

89   Christ Comes as One Unknown

Christ comes to us as one unknown, without a name, as of old by the lakeside he came to those who knew him not. He speaks to us the same word: "Follow thou me," and sets us to the tasks which he has to fulfill for our time. He commands. And to those who obey him, whether they be wise or simple, he will reveal himself in the toils, the conflicts, the sufferings which they shall pass through in his fellowship, and as an ineffable mystery they shall learn in their own experience who he is.

—Albert Schweitzer, 20th-century theologian and missionary

Come, Christians, Join to Sing

1. Come, Chris-tians, join to sing: Al - le - lu - ia! A - men!
2. Come lift your hearts on high: Al - le - lu - ia! A - men!
3. Praise yet our Christ a - gain: Al - le - lu - ia! A - men!

Loud praise to Christ we bring: Al - le - lu - ia! A - men!
Let prais-es fill the sky: Al - le - lu - ia! A - men!
Life shall not end the strain: Al - le - lu - ia! A - men!

Let all with heart and voice, be - fore his throne re - joice;
Christ is our Guide and Friend on whom we can de - pend;
On heav-en's bliss-ful shore his good-ness we'll a - dore,

praise we with grate-ful choice: Al - le - lu - ia! A - men!
his love shall nev - er end: Al - le - lu - ia! A - men!
sing - ing for - ev - er-more: Al - le - lu - ia! A - men!

WORDS: Christian Henry Bateman, 1843, alt.
MUSIC: Traditional Spanish melody; harm. David Evans, 1927

MADRID
66.66D

♩=112-120

Harm. used by permission of Oxford University Press

Philippians 2:9–11

91 All Hail the Power of Jesus' Name!

1. All hail the power of Je-sus' name! Let an-gels pros-trate
2. Ye seed of Is-rael's cho-sen race, ye ran-somed of the
3. O sin-ners, who can ne'er for-get the worm-wood and the
4. Let ev-ery kin-dred, ev-ery tribe, on this ter-res-trial
5. O that with yon-der sac-red throng we at his feet may

1. fall; bring forth the roy - al di - a - dem, and
2. fall, hail him who saves you by his grace, and
3. gall, go spread your tro - phies at his feet, and
4. ball, to him all maj - es - ty as - cribe, and
5. fall! We'll join the ev - er - last - ing song, and

1. crown him Lord of all; bring forth the roy - al
2. crown him Lord of all; hail him who saves you
3. crown him Lord of all; go spread your tro - phies
4. crown him Lord of all; to him all maj - es -
5. crown him Lord of all; we'll join the ev - er -

1. di - a - dem, and crown him Lord of all.
2. by his grace, and crown him Lord of all.
3. at his feet, and crown him Lord of all.
4. ty as - cribe, and crown him Lord of all.
5. last - ing song, and crown him Lord of all.

WORDS: Edward Perronet, 1779; alt. John Rippon, 1787
MUSIC: Oliver Holden, 1792

CORONATION
CM

All Hail the Power of Jesus' Name!   92

1. All hail the power of Je - sus' name! Let an - gels pros-trate
2. Ye cho - sen seed of Is - rael's race, ye ran-somed from the
3. Let ev - 'ry kin - dred, ev - 'ry tribe, on this ter - res - trial
4. Oh, that with yon - der sa - cred throng we at his feet may

fall, let an - gels pros-trate fall. Bring forth the roy - al
Fall, ye ran-somed from the Fall, hail him who saves you
ball, on this ter - res-trial ball, to him all maj - es -
fall, we at his feet may fall! We'll join the ev - er -

di - a - dem, and crown him,
by his grace,
ty as - cribe,
last - ing song,

crown him, crown him, crown him, crown him,

crown

crown him, crown him, crown him; and crown him Lord of all!

him, and crown him Lord of all!

WORDS: Edward Perronet, 1779; alt. John Rippon, 1787
MUSIC: James Ellor, 1838

DIADEM
86.68 w. refrain

93

Praise Him! Praise Him!

1. Praise him! praise him! Je - sus, our bless - ed Re - deem - er!
2. Praise him! praise him! Je - sus, our bless - ed Re - deem - er!
3. Praise him! praise him! Je - sus, our bless - ed Re - deem - er!

Sing, O Earth, his won - der - ful love pro - claim!
For our sins he suf - fered, and bled and died;
Heaven - ly por - tals loud with ho - san - nas ring!

Hail him! hail him! high - est arch - an - gels in glo - ry;
he our Rock, our hope of e - ter - nal sal - va - tion,
Je - sus, Sav - ior, reign - eth for - ev - er and ev - er;

strength and hon - or give to his ho - ly name!
hail him! hail him! Je - sus the cru - ci - fied.
crown him! crown him! Proph - et and Priest and King!

WORDS: Fanny J. Crosby, 1869
MUSIC: Chester G. Allen, 1869

JOYFUL SONG
12 10.12 10.11 10.11 10

Like a shep - herd Je - sus will guard his chil - dren,
Sound his prais - es! Je - sus who bore our sor - rows;
Christ is com - ing! o - ver the world vic - to - rious,

in his arms he car - ries them all day long:
love un - bound - ed, won - der - ful, deep and strong:
power and glo - ry un - to the Lord be - long:

Refrain

Praise him! praise him! tell of his ex - cel - lent great - ness;

praise him! praise him ev - er in joy - ful song!

Christians Only

94

We are not the only Christians; we are Christians only.

—early Disciples slogan

95 Jesus Shall Reign Where'er the Sun

Descant

Let ev - ery crea - ture rise with song;

1. Je - sus shall reign wher - e'er the sun
2. To Christ shall end - less prayer be made,
3. Peo - ple and realms of ev - ery tongue
4. Bless - ings a - bound wher - e'er he reigns;
5. Let ev - ery crea - ture rise with song;

hon- or and praise to Christ be - long

1. does its suc - ces - sive jour - neys run;
2. and end - less prais - es crown his head;
3. dwell on his love with sweet - est song;
4. all pris - oners leap to lose their chains,
5. hon - or and praise to Christ be - long;

an- gels de - scend with songs a - gain, and

1. his love shall spread from shore to shore
2. his name like sweet per - fume shall rise
3. and in - fant voic - es shall pro - claim
4. the wea - ry find e - ter - nal rest,
5. an - gels de - scend with songs a - gain,

WORDS: Isaac Watts, 1719, alt.
MUSIC: John Hatton, 1793; desc. Erik Routley, alt.

DUKE STREET
LM

Desc. © 1985 Wm. B. Eerdmans Publishing Co.

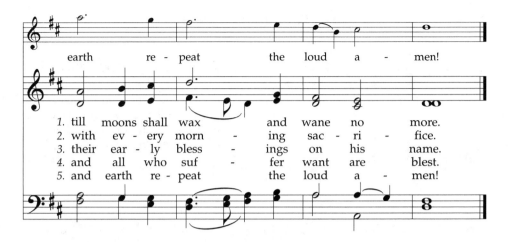

earth re - peat the loud a - men!

1. till moons shall wax and wane no more.
2. with ev - ery morn - ing sac - ri - fice.
3. their ear - ly bless - ings on his name.
4. and all who suf - fer want are blest.
5. and earth re - peat the loud a - men!

Song of Christ's Obedience   96

RESPONSE

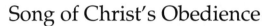

At the name of Je - sus ev - ery knee shall bend.

R

Let the same mind be in you that was in Christ Jesus,
who, though he was in the form of God,
   did not regard equality with God
   as something to be exploited,
but emptied himself,
   taking the form of a servant,
   being born in human likeness.
And being found in human form, he humbled himself
   and became obedient to the point of death—
   even death on a cross.
Therefore God also highly exalted him
   and gave him the name that is above every name,
so that at the name of Jesus every knee should bend,
   in heaven and on earth and under the earth,
   and every tongue should confess that Jesus Christ is Lord,
      to the glory of God the Father.   **R**

WORDS: Philippians 2:5–11; Response, Philippians 2:10a
MUSIC: Benedictine plainsong (13th century)

97 Fairest Lord Jesus

1. Fair - est Lord Je - sus, rul - er of all na - ture,
2. Fair are the mead - ows, fair - er still the wood - lands,
3. Fair is the sun - shine, fair - er still the moon - light,

O thou of God to earth come down; thee will I cher - ish,
robed in the bloom-ing garb of spring: Je - sus is fair - er,
and all the twink-ling, star - ry hosts: Je - sus shines bright- er,

thee will I hon - or, thou, my soul's glo - ry, joy, and crown.
Je - sus is pur - er, who makes the woe - ful heart to sing.
Je - sus shines pur - er, than all the an - gels heaven can boast.

WORDS: *Münster Gesangbuch*, 1677; tr. *Church Chorals and Choir Studies*, 1850, alt.   ST. ELIZABETH
MUSIC: *Schlesische Volkslieder*, 1842   568.558

98 Our Union with Christ

In our union with Christ we will be
    clouds with life-giving rain,
    trees bearing luscious fruit
    and fountains of cold stream-water for thirsty travelers.

—*Robert Richardson, 19th-century Disciples writer and editor*

O, How I Love Jesus

1. There is a name I love to hear, I love to sing its worth;
2. It tells me of a Sav-ior's love, who died to set me free;
3. It tells of one whose lov-ing heart can feel my deep-est woe,

it sounds like mu-sic in my ear, the sweet-est name on earth.
it tells me of his pre-cious blood, the sin-ner's per-fect plea.
who in each sor-row bears a part, that none can bear be-low.

Refrain

O, how I love Je-sus, O, how I love Je-sus,

O, how I love Je-sus, be-cause he first loved me!

WORDS: Frederick Whitfield, 1855; refrain anon.
MUSIC: Traditional American melody (19th century)

O, HOW I LOVE JESUS
CM w. refrain

100 When Morning Gilds the Skies

1. When morn ing gilds the skies, my heart a - wak - ing cries,
2. Dis - cord - ant hu - man - kind, in this your con - cord find,
3. Sing, suns and stars of space, sing, all that see his face;
4. Be this, while life is mine, my can - ti - cle di - vine;

may Je - sus Christ be praised! A - like at work and prayer
may Je - sus Christ be praised! Let all the earth a - round
may Je - sus Christ be praised! God's whole cre - a - tion o'er,
may Je - sus Christ be praised! Be this the e - ter - nal song,

to Je - sus I re - pair; may Je - sus Christ be praised!
ring joy - ous with the sound, may Je - sus Christ be praised!
both now and ev - er - more: may Je - sus Christ be praised!
through all the a - ges long: may Je - sus Christ be praised!

WORDS: German hymn (early 19th century); tr. Edward Caswall, 1858, alt.
MUSIC: Joseph Barnby, 1868

LAUDES DOMINI
666.666

Jesus, Thou Joy of Loving Hearts 101

1. Je - sus, thou joy of lov - ing hearts, thou fount of
2. Thy gra - cious word hath ev - er stood: thou sav - est
3. We taste thee, O thou liv - ing bread, and long to
4. Our rest - less spir - its yearn for thee, wher - e'er our
5. O Je - sus, ev - er with us stay; make all our

1. life, thou light of light, great - er than plea - sure
2. those that on thee call; to them that seek thee,
3. feast up - on thee still; we drink of thee, the
4. change - ful lot is cast: glad when thy gra - cious
5. mo - ments calm and bright; ban - ish the sin of

1. earth im - parts, thy love is true and pure de - light.
2. thou art good; to them that find thee, all in all.
3. foun - tain - head, and thirst our souls from thee to fill.
4. smile we see; blest when our faith can hold thee fast.
5. earth, we pray; shed o'er the world thy ho - ly light.

WORDS: Latin (12th century); tr. Ray Palmer, 1858, alt.
MUSIC: Henry Baker, 1854

QUEBEC
LM

102   Jesus, the Very Thought of Thee

1. Je - sus, the ver - y thought of thee,
2. No voice can sing, no heart can frame,
3. O hope of ev - ery con - trite heart,
4. Je - sus, our on - ly joy be thou,

with sweet-ness fills my breast; but sweet - er far thy
nor can the mind re - call a sweet - er sound than
O joy of all the meek, to those who ask, how
as thou our prize wilt be; Je - sus, be thou our

face to see, and in thy pres - ence rest.
thy blest name, O Sav - ior of us all.
kind thou art! How good to those who seek!
glo - ry now, and through e - ter - ni - ty.

WORDS: Attr. Bernard of Clairvaux (12th century); tr. Edward Caswall, 1849
MUSIC: John B. Dykes, 1866

ST. AGNES
CM

103   Prayer of St. Anselm

And you, Jesus, sweet Lord, are you not also a mother?
Truly, you are a mother, the mother of all mothers,
who tasted death in your desire to give life to your children.

—Anselm, 1033-1109, Archbishop of Canterbury

Of the Father's Love Begotten   104
(Of Eternal Love Begotten)

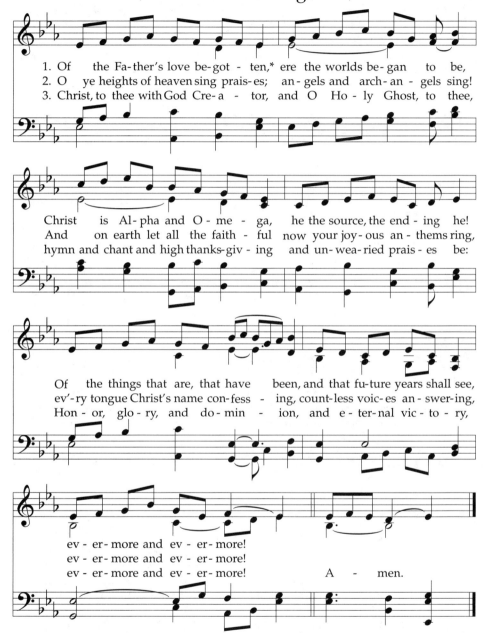

1. Of the Fa-ther's love be-got - ten,* ere the worlds be-gan to be,
2. O ye heights of heaven sing prais- es; an- gels and arch- an - gels sing!
3. Christ, to thee with God Cre-a - tor, and O Ho - ly Ghost, to thee,

Christ is Al- pha and O - me - ga, he the source, the end - ing he!
And on earth let all the faith - ful now your joy- ous an - thems ring,
hymn and chant and high thanks-giv - ing and un- wea-ried prais- es be:

Of the things that are, that have been, and that fu-ture years shall see,
ev'- ry tongue Christ's name con-fess - ing, count-less voic- es an - swer-ing,
Hon - or, glo - ry, and do- min - ion, and e- ter-nal vic - to- ry,

ev - er - more and ev - er - more!
ev - er - more and ev - er - more!
ev - er - more and ev - er - more! A - men.

*Of eternal love begotten

DIVINUM MYSTERIUM
87.87.877

WORDS: Aurelius Clemens Prudentius (4th century); st. 1, 3 tr. John Mason
Neale, 1854, and Henry W. Baker, 1859, alt.; st. 2 tr. R. F. Davis, 1906, alt.
MUSIC: Plainsong, Mode V (13th century); harm. C. Winfred Douglas, 1940

105 O Morning Star

1. O Morn-ing Star, how fair and bright! You shine with God's own
2. Come, heav'n-ly bright-ness, light di-vine, and deep with-in our
3. Christ, when you look on us in love, at once there falls from

truth and light, a - glow with grace and mer - cy! Come
hearts now shine; there light a flame un - dy - ing! In
God a - bove a ray of pur - est plea - sure. Your

shine on us, O heav-en's sun; our on - ly Sav - ior,
your one bod - y let us be as liv - ing branch - es
Word and Spir - it, flesh and blood re - fresh our souls with

you have won our hearts to serve you on - ly!
of a tree, your life our lives sup - ply - ing.
heav'n - ly food. You are our dear - est trea - sure!

WORDS: Philipp Nicolai, 1599; tr. *Lutheran Book of Worship*, 1978, alt.
MUSIC: Philipp Nicolai, 1599

WIE SCHÖN LEUCHTET
87.78.87.48.48

Low - ly, ho - ly! Great and glo - rious, all vic - to - rious, rich in
Now, though dai - ly earth's deep sad - ness may per - plex us and dis -
Let your mer - cy warm and cheer us! Oh, draw near us! For you

bless - ing! Rule and might o'er all pos - sess - ing!
tress us, yet with heav'n - ly joy you bless us.
teach us God's own love through you has reached us.

Alleluia 106

1. Al - le - lu - ia, al - le - lu - ia, al - le - lu - ia, al - le - lu - ia,

al - le - lu - ia, al - le - lu - ia, al - le - lu - ia, al - le - lu - ia.

2. Christ is risen.   3. I will praise you.

WORDS: Jerry Sinclair, 1972, alt.   ALLELUIA
MUSIC: Jerry Sinclair, 1972   44.44D

Philippians 2:9–11

107

Jesucristo Es el Señor
(Jesus Christ Is Lord of All)

Je - su - cris - to es el Se - ñor, el Se - ñor, el Se - ñor.
Je - sus Christ is Lord of all, Lord of all, Lord of all.

Je - su - cris - to es el Se - ñor; Glo - ria sea a El.
Je - sus Christ is Lord of all. Glo - ry to his name.

Ya de mi vi - da es el Se - ñor; de su ig - le - sia es el Se - ñor;
O - ver my life Je - sus is the Lord; ov - er the church Je - sus is the Lord;

del u - ni - ver - so es el Se - ñor. Glo - ria sea a El.
o - ver the u - ni - verse he is Lord. Glo - ry to his name.

WORDS: Jorge Himitián (20th century); tr. Luis Ferrer, 1994
MUSIC: Jorge Himitián (20th century)

HIMITIÁN
Irr.

Tr. © 1995 Chalice Press

♩·=64-68

Lift High the Cross

Refrain (Unison)

Lift high the cross, the love of Christ pro - claim

till all the world a - dore his sa - cred name.

Fine

Harmony

1. Come, Chris-tians, fol - low this tri - um-phant sign. The
2. Each new-born ser - vant of the Cru - ci - fied bears
3. O Lord, once lift - ed on the glo - rious tree, your
4. So shall our song of tri - umph ev - er be: praise

D.C.

hosts of God in u - ni - ty com - bine.
on the brow the seal of Christ who died.
death has brought us life e - ter - nal - ly.
to the cru - ci - fied for vic - to - ry.

WORDS: George William Kitchin and Michael Robert Newbolt, 1916, alt.　　　　　CRUCIFER
MUSIC: Sydney H. Nicholson, 1916　　　　　　　　　　　　　　　　　　　　10.10 w. refrain

© 1974 Hope Publishing Co.　　　　　　　　　　　　　　　　　　　　　　　𝅗𝅥=56-60

109

Jesús Es Mi Rey Soberano
(O Jesus, My King and My Sovereign)

WORDS: Vicente Mendoza, 1921; tr. Esther Frances,
1982, and George Lockwood, 1988
MUSIC: Vicente Mendoza, 1921

MI REY Y MI AMIGO
Irr.

♩.=52-56

Tr. © 1982, 1989, The United Methodist Publishing House

110   You Servants of God

Descant

4. Then let us a - dore and ren - der God's right,

1. You ser - vants of God, your Sav - ior pro - claim,
2. God's truth reach - es high, al - might - y to save,
3. Sal - va - tion to God who sits on the throne!
4. Then let us a - dore and ren - der God's right,

all glo - ry and power, all wis - dom and might,

and pub - lish a - broad that won - der - ful name:
and yet re - mains nigh: God's pres - ence we have.
Let all cry a - loud for what God has done.
all glo - ry and power, all wis - dom and might,

all hon - or and bless - ing with an - gels a - bove,

the name, all vic - to - rious, of Je - sus ex - tol;
The great con - gre - ga - tion God's tri - umphs shall praise,
The prais - es of Je - sus the an - gels pro - claim;
all hon - or and bless - ing with an - gels a - bove,

WORDS: Charles Wesley, 1744, alt.
MUSIC: Attr. William Croft, 1708; desc. John Wilson

HANOVER
10 10.11 11

Text revisions © 1993 The Pilgrim Press; desc. used by permission of
Oxford University Press

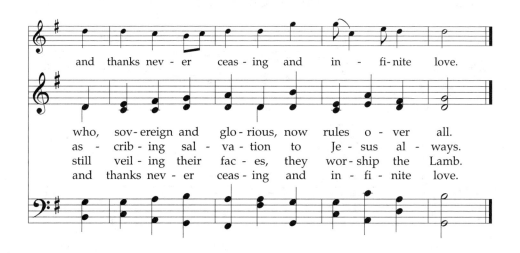

and thanks nev - er ceas - ing and in - fi - nite love.

who, sov - ereign and glo - rious, now rules o - ver all.
as - crib - ing sal - va - tion to Je - sus al - ways.
still veil - ing their fac - es, they wor - ship the Lamb.
and thanks nev - er ceas - ing and in - fi - nite love.

Santo, Santo, Santo
(Holy, Holy, Holy)

111

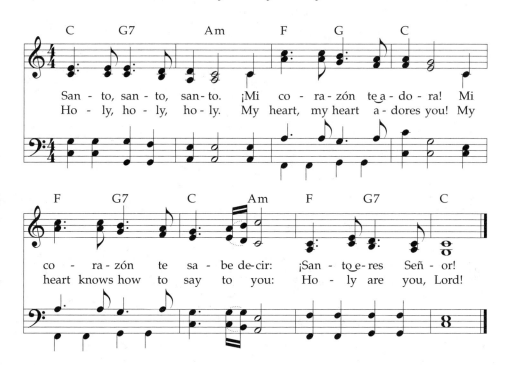

San - to, san - to, san - to. ¡Mi co - ra - zón te a - do - ra! Mi
Ho - ly, ho - ly, ho - ly. My heart, my heart a - dores you! My

co - ra - zón te sa - be de - cir: ¡San - to e - res Señ - or!
heart knows how to say to you: Ho - ly are you, Lord!

WORDS: Latin America (20th century)
MUSIC: Latin America (20th century); arr. 1990 Iona Community

SANTO
67.67

♩=96

112

Holy Ground

WORDS and MUSIC: Geron Davis, 1983

HOLY GROUND
Irr.

♩=88-100

Mark 10:13–16

Jesus Loves Me!

113

1. Je - sus loves me! This I know, for the Bi - ble tells me so.
2. Je - sus loves me! This I know, as he loved so long a - go,
3. Je - sus loves me still to - day, walk - ing with me on my way,

Lit - tle ones to him be - long; they are weak, but he is strong.
tak - ing chil - dren on his knee, say - ing, "Let them come to me."
want - ing as a friend to give light and love to all who live.

Refrain

Yes, Je - sus loves me! Yes, Je - sus loves me!

Yes, Je - sus loves me! The Bi - ble tells me so.

WORDS: St. 1, Anna B. Warner, 1860; st. 2, 3, David R. McGuire, c. 1970
MUSIC: William B. Bradbury, 1862

JESUS LOVES ME
77.77 w. refrain

114 Thou Art Worthy

Thou art wor-thy, thou art wor-thy, thou art wor-thy, O Lord,

to re-ceive glo-ry, glo-ry and hon-or, glo-ry and hon-or and

power; for thou hast cre-at-ed, hast all things cre-at-ed,

thou hast cre-at-ed all things; and for thy plea-sure

they are cre-at-ed, for thou art wor-thy, O Lord.

WORDS and MUSIC: Pauline Michael Mills, 1963

WORTHY
Irr.

♩=116-126

There's Something About That Name 115

Jesus, Jesus, Jesus! There's just some-thing a-bout that name! Master, Sav-ior, Je-sus! Like the fra-grance af-ter the rain. Je-sus, Je-sus, Je-sus! Let all heav-en and earth pro-claim: kings and king-doms will all pass a-way, but there's some-thing a-bout that name!

WORDS: Gloria Gaither and William J. Gaither, 1970
MUSIC: William J. Gaither, 1970

© 1970, 1995, William J. Gaither

THAT NAME
Irr.

♩=116-126

116 I Thank You, Jesus

1. I thank you, Je-sus, thank you, Je-sus,
2. You've been my fa-ther, been my moth-er,

(Thank you, Je-sus,) (thank you, Je-sus,)
(Been my fa-ther,) (been my moth-er,)

thank you, Je-sus, my Sav-ior God, for you brought me, yes, you
been my sis-ter, my broth-er, too, for you brought me, yes, you

brought me from a might-y a might-y long way, a might-y long
brought me from a might-y, a might-y long way, a might-y long

I thank you, Je-sus, thank you, Je-sus,
You've been my fa-ther, been my moth-er,

way.
way.

(Thank you, Je-sus,) (thank you, Je-sus,)
(Been my fa-ther,) (been my moth-er,)

WORDS: Kenneth Morris, 1948
MUSIC: Kenneth Morris, 1948; adapt. and arr. Joyce F. Johnson, 1992, alt.

I THANK YOU
Irr.

thank you, Je-sus, my Sav-ior God, for you brought me, yes, you
been my sis-ter, my bro-ther, too, for you brought me, yes, you

brought me from a might-y, a might-y long way. (a might-y long way.)
brought me from a might-y, a might-y long way. (a might-y long way.)

Philippians 2:9–11

He Is Lord

117

He is Lord, he is Lord! He is ris-en from the

dead and he is Lord! Ev-ery knee shall bow,

ev-ery tongue con-fess that Je - sus Christ is Lord.

WORDS: Philippians 2:9–11, adapt.
MUSIC: Traditional melody; arr. Tom Fettke, 1986

HE IS LORD
Irr.

118 Glorious Is Your Name, O Jesus

Glo - rious is your name, O Je - sus, prais - es to your

name. Oh, glo - rious and righ - teous and

ho - ly is your name. Oh, glo - ri - ous is your

name. I feel your pres - ence

WORDS and MUSIC: Robert J. Fryson, 1982, alt.

GLORIOUS IS YOUR NAME
Irr.

♩=108-116

119 O Come, O Come, Emmanuel

1. O come, O come, Em- man - u - el, and ran-som cap-tive
2. O come, thou Day-spring, come and cheer our spir-its by thine
3. O come, thou Wis-dom from on high, and or-der all things,
4. O come, De-sire of na - tions, bind all peo-ples in one

Is - ra - el, that mourns in lone-ly ex - ile here,
ad - vent here; dis-perse the gloom-y clouds of night,
far and nigh; to us the path of knowl-edge show,
heart and mind; bid en-vy, strife and quar - rels cease;

un - til the Son of God ap - pear.
and death's deep shad-ows put to flight.
and cause us in her ways to go. Re - joice, re - joice!
fill the whole world with heav - en's peace.

Em-man - u - el shall come to thee, O Is - ra - el!

WORDS: Latin hymn (12th century); st. 1-2 tr. John Mason Neale, 1851;
st. 3-4 tr. Henry Sloane Coffin, 1916
MUSIC: French melody (15th century); arr. and harm. Thomas Helmore, 1854

VENI EMMANUEL
LM

Advent Antiphons

Antiphon 1   O Emmanuel, our King and giver of the law,
the people await you, their Savior:
Come and save us, O Lord our God.

Antiphon 2   O Wisdom, you came from the lips of God most high,
and you reach from one end of the universe to the other,
powerfully and gently ordering all things:
Come to teach us the way of prudence.

Antiphon 3   O Adonai and Leader of the house of Israel,
you appeared to Moses in the flame of a burning bush
and at Sinai you gave him the law:
Come with your outstretched arm to save us.

Antiphon 4   O Root of Jesse, you stand as a sign to the peoples;
before you kings are silent and the Gentiles pray with longing:
Come now and set us free.

Antiphon 5   O Key of David and ruler of the house of Israel,
you open and none can shut; you shut and none can open:
**Come and lead out of the prison house the captives
who sit in darkness and in the shadow of death.**

Antiphon 6   O Morning Star, you are the splendor of eternal life;
you are the dawning sun, the Sun of justice:
**Come and enlighten those who sit in darkness
and in the shadow of death.**

Antiphon 7   O King of the nations and the fulfillment of their longing,
you are the Cornerstone and you make all one;
you formed us from primeval clay:
Come and save us.

Used by permission of the Church of the Province of Southern Africa (Anglican)

Isaiah 40:3; 52:10

Prepare the Way of the Lord
121

Pre - pare the way of the Lord. Pre - pare the way of the Lord,

and all peo - ple will see the sal - va - tion of our God. Pre -

WORDS: Isaiah 40:3; 52:10
MUSIC: Jacques Berthier and the Community of Taizé, 1984

PREPARE THE WAY
Irr.

Music © 1984 Les Presses de Taizé; used by permission of GIA Publications, Inc.

♩·=72-80

Isaiah 40:1–8

122 Comfort, Comfort You My People

1. Com - fort, com - fort you my peo - ple, tell of peace, thus says our God;
2. For the her - ald's voice is call - ing in the des - ert far and near,
3. Make you straight what long was crook - ed, make the rough-er plac - es plain;

com - fort those who sit in dark - ness bowed be-neath op-pres-sion's load.
bid - ding us to make re - pent - ance since the reign of God is here.
let your hearts be true and hum - ble, as be-fits God's ho - ly reign.

Speak you to Je - ru - sa - lem of the peace that waits for them;
O that warn - ing cry o - bey! Now pre - pare for God a way;
For the glo - ry of our God now o'er earth is shed a - broad;

tell them that their sins I cov - er, and their war-fare now is o - ver.
let the val - leys rise in meet - ing and the hills bow down in greet - ing.
and all flesh shall see the to - ken that God's word is nev - er bro - ken.

WORDS: Johannes G. Olearius, 1671; tr. Catherine Winkworth, 1863, alt.
MUSIC: Louis Bourgeois, 1551; harm. Claude Goudimel, 1564

GENEVA 42
87.87.77.88

♩=140-148

The Coming of God

RESPONSE

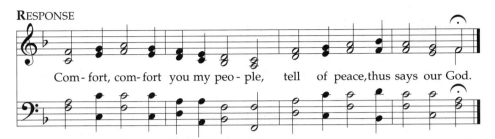

Com - fort, com - fort you my peo - ple, tell of peace, thus says our God.

R
 Comfort, O comfort my people,
  says your God.
 Speak tenderly to Jerusalem,
  and cry to them
 that they have served their term,
  that their penalty is paid,
 that they have received from the LORD's hand
  double for all their sins.   **R**

 A voice cries out:
 "In the wilderness prepare the way of the LORD,
  make straight in the desert a highway for our God.
 Every valley shall be lifted up,
  and every mountain and hill be made low;
 the uneven ground shall become level,
  and the rough places a plain.
 Then the glory of the LORD shall be revealed,
  and all people shall see it together,
  for the mouth of the LORD has spoken."
 Get you up to a high mountain,
  O Zion, herald of good tidings;
 lift up your voice with strength,
  O Jerusalem, herald of good tidings,
  lift it up, do not fear;
 say to the cities of Judah,
  "Here is your God!"   **R**

WORDS: Isaiah 40:1–5, 9; Response, Johannes G. Olearius, 1671
MUSIC: Louis Bourgeois, 1551

124 Let All Mortal Flesh Keep Silence

Unison

1. Let all mor - tal flesh keep si - lence, and with fear and
2. Tru - ly God, yet born of Mar - y, as of old on
3. Rank on rank the host of heav - en spreads its van - guard
4. At his feet the six - winged ser - aph; cher - u - bim, with

trem - bling stand; pon - der noth - ing earth - ly mind - ed,
earth he stood, word of God, in hu - man ves - ture,
on the way, as the Light of light de - scend - eth
sleep - less eye, veil their fac - es to the Pres - ence,

for with bless - ing in his hand Christ our God to earth de -
in the bod - y and the blood, Christ will give to all the
from the realms of end - less day, that the powers of hell may
as with cease - less voice they cry, "Al - le - lu - ia, Al - le -

scend - eth, our full hom - age to de - mand.
faith - ful his own self for heaven - ly food.
van - ish as the shad - ows clear a - way.
lu - ia, Al - le - lu - ia, God most high!"

WORDS: *Liturgy of St. James* (4th century); tr. Gerard Moultrie, 1864
MUSIC: French carol (17th century); harm. *The English Hymnal*, 1906

PICARDY
87.87.87

Come, O Long-expected Jesus 125

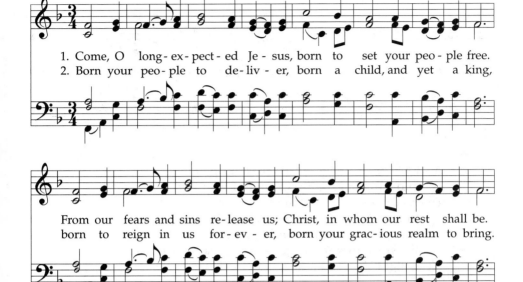

1. Come, O long-ex-pect-ed Je-sus, born to set your peo-ple free.
2. Born your peo-ple to de-liv-er, born a child, and yet a king,

From our fears and sins re-lease us; Christ, in whom our rest shall be.
born to reign in us for-ev-er, born your grac-ious realm to bring.

You, our strength and con-so-la-tion, come sal-va-tion to im-part;
By your own e-ter-nal Spir-it rule in all our hearts a-lone;

dear de-sire of man-y a na - tion, joy of man-y a long-ing heart.
by your all - suf - fi - cient mer - it raise us to your glo-rious throne.

WORDS: Charles Wesley, 1744
MUSIC: Rowland H. Prichard, 1830; harm. *The English Hymnal*, 1906

HYFRYDOL
87.87D

126   The Peaceful Realm

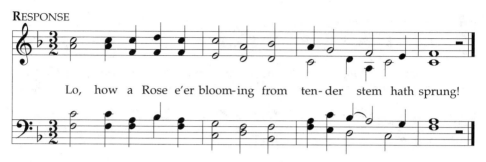

Lo, how a Rose e'er bloom-ing from ten-der stem hath sprung!

R

A shoot shall come out from the stump of Jesse,
   and a branch shall grow out of his roots.
The spirit of the LORD shall rest on him,
   the spirit of wisdom and understanding,
   the spirit of counsel and might,
   the spirit of knowledge and the fear of the LORD.
His delight shall be in the fear of the LORD.
He shall not judge by what his eyes see,
   or decide by what his ears hear;
but with righteousness he shall judge the poor,
   and decide with equity for the meek of the earth;
he shall strike the earth with the rod of his mouth,
   and with the breath of his lips he shall kill the wicked.
Righteousness shall be the belt around his waist,
   and faithfulness the belt around his loins.   **R**

The wolf shall live with the lamb,
   the leopard shall lie down with the kid,
the calf and the lion and the fatling together,
   and a little child shall lead them.
The nursing child shall play over the hole of the asp,
   and the weaned child shall put its hand on the adder's den.
They will not hurt or destroy
   on all my holy mountain;
for the earth will be full of the knowledge of the LORD
      as the waters cover the sea.   **R**

WORDS: Isaiah 11:1–6, 8–9; Response, German carol (15th century),
  tr. Theodore Baker, 1894
MUSIC: Traditional melody; arr. Michael Praetorius, 1609

Creator of the Stars of Night

Unison

1. Cre - a - tor of the stars of night, your peo - ple's ev - er - last - ing light, O Christ, re - deem - er of us all, we pray you, hear us when we call.
2. To you the deep tra - vail was known that made the whole cre - a - tion groan. You came, O Sav - ior, to set free your own in glo - rious lib - er - ty.
3. When this old world drew on toward night, you came, but not in splen - dor bright, not as a mon - arch, but the child of Mar - y, blame-less moth - er mild.
4. At your great name, O Je - sus, now all knees must bend, all hearts must bow: all things on earth with one ac - cord, like those in heaven shall call you Lord.

WORDS: Latin hymn (9th century); tr. as in *The Hymnal*, 1940, alt.   CONDITOR ALME
MUSIC: Plainsong, Mode IV; harm. C. Winfred Douglas, 1943, alt.   LM

Alt. tune: PUER NOBIS NASCITUR

128 One Candle Is Lit

Unison

1. Come sure - ly, Lord Je - sus, as dawn fol - lows night,
2. Come quick - ly, sha - lom, teach us how to pre - pare
3. Come, fes - tive - ly sing while a - wait - ing the birth,
4. Come, wan - der where li - on and lamb gent - ly play,
5. Come, lis - ten, the sounds of God - with - us ring clear,

1. our hearts long to greet you, as ros - es, the light.
2. for a gift that com - pels us with jus - tice to care.
3. join an - gels in danc - ing from heav - en to earth.
4. where e - vil is ban - ished and faith takes the day,
5. and signs of a cross in the dis - tance ap - pear.

1. Sal - va - tion, draw near us, our vi - sion en - gage.
2. Our spir - its are rest - less till sin and war cease.
3. Wave ban - ners of good news, lift high thank - ful praise.
4. a babe in a man - ger to fool the world's eyes.
5. The Word once made flesh, yet the Word ev - er near.

WORDS: Mary Anne Parrott, 1988
MUSIC: William J. Kirkpatrick, 1895

CRADLE SONG
11 11.11 11

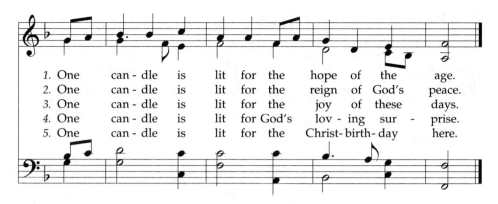

1. One can - dle is lit for the hope of the age.
2. One can - dle is lit for the reign of God's peace.
3. One can - dle is lit for the joy of these days.
4. One can - dle is lit for God's lov - ing sur - prise.
5. One can - dle is lit for the Christ- birth- day here.

Lift Up Your Heads, O Mighty Gates   129

1. Lift up your heads, O might- y gates; be - hold the glo - rious
2. Fling wide the por - tals of your heart; make it a tem - ple,
3. Re - deem- er, come! We o - pen wide our hearts to you; here,
4. So come, our Sov - ereign; en - ter in! Let new and no - bler

Rul - er waits! The Sov - ereign One is draw - ing
set a - part from earth - ly use for heav-en's em -
Christ, a - bide! Let us your in - ner pres - ence
life be - gin; your Ho - ly Spir - it guide us

near; the Sav - ior of the world is here.
ploy, a - dorned with prayer and love and joy.
feel, your grace and love in us re - veal.
on, un - til the glo - ri - ous crown be won.

WORDS: Georg Weissel, 1642; tr. Catherine Winkworth, 1855, alt.   TRURO
MUSIC: *Psalmodia Evangelica*, 1789   LM

Text revisions courtesy of United Church Board for Homeland Ministries/The Pilgrim Press

Luke 1:46b–55

130 My Soul Gives Glory to My God

1. My soul gives glo - ry to my God. My
2. My God has done great things for me: yes,
3. From age to age, to all who fear, such
4. Love casts the might - y from their thrones, pro -
5. Praise God, whose lov - ing cov - e - nant sup -

1. heart pours out its praise. God lift - ed up my
2. ho - ly is her name. All peo - ple will de -
3. mer - cy love im - parts, dis - pens - ing jus - tice
4. motes the in - se - cure, leaves hun - gry spir - its
5. ports those in dis - tress, re - mem - ber - ing past

1. low - li - ness in man - y mar - ve - lous ways.
2. clare me blessed, and bless - ings they shall claim.
3. far and near, dis - miss - ing self - ish hearts.
4. sat - is - fied, the rich seem sud - den - ly poor.
5. prom - is - es with pres - ent faith - ful - ness.

Guitar and keyboard should not sound together.

WORDS: Miriam Therese Winter, 1978, 1987
MUSIC: Wyeth's *Repository of Sacred Music, Part Second*, 1813;
  harm. Charles H. Webb, 1988

MORNING SONG
CM

♩=88-96

Song of Mary

131

(Magnificat)

RESPONSE

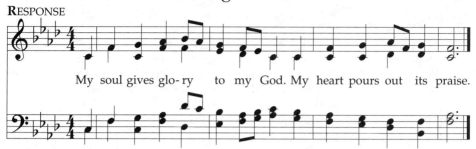

My soul gives glo-ry to my God. My heart pours out its praise.

R

My soul proclaims the greatness of the Lord,
my spirit rejoices in God my Savior,
   who has looked with favor on me, a lowly servant.
From this day all generations shall call me blessed:
the Almighty has done great things for me
   and holy is the name of the Lord,
   whose mercy is on those who fear God
   from generation to generation.   **R**

The arm of the Lord is strong,
   and has scattered the proud in their conceit.
God has cast down the mighty from their thrones
   and lifted up the lowly.
God has filled the hungry with good things,
   and sent the rich away empty.
God has come to the aid of Israel, the chosen servant,
   remembering the promise of mercy,
   the promise made to our forebears,
   to Abraham and to his children forever.   **R**

WORDS: Luke 1:46b–55, ICET, rev. ELLC; Response, Miriam Therese Winter, 1978, 1987
MUSIC: Wyeth's *Repository of Sacred Music, Part Second*, 1813; harm. Charles H. Webb, 1988

132 When God Is a Child

Unison

1. Hope is a star that shines in the night,
2. Peace is a ribbon that cir - cles the earth,
3. Joy is a song that wel - comes the dawn,
4. Love is a flame that burns in our heart.

lead - ing us on till the morn-ing is bright.
giv - ing a prom - ise of safe - ty and worth.
tell - ing the world that the Sav - ior is born.
Je - sus has come and will nev - er de - part.

Refrain

When God is a child there's joy in our song. The last shall be
first and the weak shall be strong, and none shall be a - fraid.

WORDS: Brain Wren, 1985
MUSIC: Joan Collier Fogg, 1987

MOON BEAMS
Irr. w. refrain

♩=112

like a child

WORDS and MUSIC: Dan Damon, 1992

© 1993 Hope Publishing Co.

LIKE A CHILD
3333.333D

♩=88-96

134 Emmanuel, Emmanuel

WORDS and MUSIC: Bob McGee, 1976

McGEE
Irr.

♩=84-92

Blessed Be the God of Israel 135

Unison

1. Blessed be the God of Is - rael, who comes to set us free,
2. Now from the house of Da - vid a child of grace has come,
3. On all by death im - pris - oned the sun be - gins to rise,

who vis - its and re - deems us, and grants us lib - er - ty.
a Sav - ior who will lead us to our e - ter - nal home.
the dawn - ing of for - give - ness up - on the sin - ner's eyes,

The proph - ets spoke of mer - cy, of free - dom and re - lease;
Be - fore him goes the her - ald, fore - run - ner in the way,
to guide the feet of pil - grims a - long the paths of peace;

God shall ful - fill the prom - ise to bring our peo - ple peace.
the proph - et of sal - va - tion, the har - bin - ger of day.
O bless our God and Sav - ior with songs that nev - er cease!

WORDS: Michael Perry, 1973
MUSIC: Hal H. Hopson, 1983

MERLE'S TUNE
76.76D

♩=112-120

136 Christians All, Your Lord Is Coming

1. Chris-tians all, your Lord is com-ing, draw-ing near in
2. Chris-tians all, your Lord is com-ing, call-ing you to
3. Chris-tians all, your Lord is com-ing, he will rise up
4. Chris-tians all, your Lord is com-ing, hope for peace is

ho - ly birth. Ring the bells and sound the trum-pets,
serve in deed. See the ones who hurt and suf - fer,
from the dead. Lift the cup, of sin for - giv - en;
now at hand. Let there be no hes - i - ta - tion,

let your mu - sic fill the earth. Dance and move to
hear their cry and act with speed. Set all self - ish
bless the host and eat his bread. Mend the ways where
walk in faith where life de - mands. Bear the word that

show God's glo - ry; kneel and pause to hear God's word.
ways be - hind you. Purge your hearts of sin - ful greed.
peace is bro - ken, give your - selves to true Sha - lom.
God has giv - en; share the birth that stirs your soul.

WORDS: Jim Miller, 1993
MUSIC: Joshua Leavitt's *Christian Lyre*, 1830

PLEADING SAVIOR
87.87D

Words © 1995 Chalice Press

♩=104-108

Al - le - lu - ia! Al - le - lu - ia! Rise and let your songs be heard.
Al - le - lu - ia! Al - le - lu - ia! Christ in you will meet their need.
Al - le - lu - ia! Al - le - lu - ia! Dwell as one in church and home.
Al - le - lu - ia! Al - le - lu - ia! Christ will come and make you whole.

Song of Zechariah 137

RESPONSE

Blessed be the God of Is - rael, who comes to set us free.

R

Blessed be the Lord, the God of Israel,
who has come to set the chosen people free.
God has raised up for us
a mighty savior from the house of David.
Through the holy prophets, God promised of old
to save us from our enemies,
from the hands of all who hate us;
to show mercy to our forebears,
and to remember the holy covenant.
This was the oath God swore to our ancestor Abraham,
to set us free from the hands of our enemies,
free to worship without fear,
holy and righteous in God's sight,
all the days of our life.   R

And you, child, shall be called the prophet of the Most High,
for you will go before the Lord to prepare the way,
to give God's people knowledge of salvation
by the forgiveness of their sins.
In the tender compassion of our God,
the dawn from on high shall break upon us,
to shine on those who dwell in darkness and the shadow of death,
and to guide our feet into the way of peace.   R

WORDS: Luke 1:68–79 (ICET, rev. ELLC, alt.); Response, Michael Perry, 1973
MUSIC: Hal H. Hopson, 1983

138 Awake! Awake, and Greet the New Morn

1. A - wake! a - wake, and greet the new morn, for
2. In deep - est night his com - ing shall be, when
3. Re - joice, re - joice, take heart in the night, though

an - gels her - ald its dawn-ing, sing out your joy, for
all the world is de - spair-ing, as morn - ing light so
dark the win - ter and cheer-less, the ris - ing sun shall

soon he is born, be - hold! the Child of our long - ing.
qui - et and free, so warm and gen - tle and car - ing.
crown you with light, be strong and lov - ing and fear - less;

WORDS and MUSIC: Marty Haugen, 1983

REJOICE, REJOICE
98.98.87.89

© 1983 GIA Publications, Inc.

♩·=50-54

139 All Earth Is Waiting

Unison

1. All earth is wait-ing to see the Prom-ised One,
2. Thus says the proph-et to those of Is - ra - el,
3. Moun-tains and val-leys will have to be made plain;
4. In low-ly sta - ble the Prom-ised One ap-peared,

and o - pen fur-rows, the sow-ing of our God. All the
"A vir-gin moth-er will bear Em-man-u-el": one whose
o - pen new high-ways, new high-ways for our God, who is
yet feel that pres-ence through-out the earth to - day, for Christ

world, bound and strug-gling, seeks true lib-er-ty; it
name is "God with us," our Sav-ior shall be, through
now com-ing clos-er, so come all and see, and
lives in all Chris-tians and is with us now; a -

cries out for jus-tice and search-es for the truth.
whom hope will blos-som once more with-in our hearts.
o - pen the door-ways as wide as wide can be.
gain, on ar-riv-ing Christ brings us lib-er-ty.

WORDS: Alberto Taulé, 1972; tr. Gertrude C. Suppe, 1987, alt.
MUSIC: Alberto Taulé, 1972; harm. Skinner Chávez-Melo, 1988

TAULÈ
11 11.12 12

♩=70-76

Hail to the Lord's Anointed

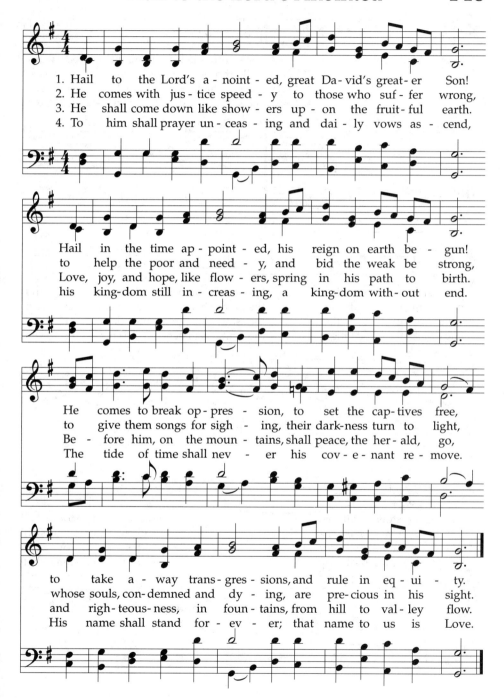

1. Hail to the Lord's a-noint-ed, great Da-vid's great-er Son!
2. He comes with jus-tice speed-y to those who suf-fer wrong,
3. He shall come down like show-ers up-on the fruit-ful earth.
4. To him shall prayer un-ceas-ing and dai-ly vows as-cend,

Hail in the time ap-point-ed, his reign on earth be-gun!
to help the poor and need-y, and bid the weak be strong,
Love, joy, and hope, like flow-ers, spring in his path to birth.
his king-dom still in-creas-ing, a king-dom with-out end.

He comes to break op-pres-sion, to set the cap-tives free,
to give them songs for sigh-ing, their dark-ness turn to light,
Be-fore him, on the moun-tains, shall peace, the her-ald, go,
The tide of time shall nev-er his cov-e-nant re-move.

to take a-way trans-gres-sions, and rule in eq-ui-ty.
whose souls, con-demned and dy-ing, are pre-cious in his sight.
and righ-teous-ness, in foun-tains, from hill to val-ley flow.
His name shall stand for-ev-er; that name to us is Love.

WORDS: James Montgomery, 1822   SHEFFIELD
MUSIC: Traditional English melody   76.76D

Luke 19:39–40

141 A Stable Lamp Is Lighted

1. A sta - ble lamp is light - ed whose
2. (This) child through Da - vid's cit - y shall
3. (Yet) he shall be for - sak - en, and
4. (But) now, as at the end - ing, the

glow shall wake the sky; the stars shall bend their voic - es, and
ride in tri - umph by; the palm shall strew its branch - es, and
yield - ed up to die; the sky shall groan and dark - en, and
low is lift - ed high; the stars shall bend their voic - es, and

ev - 'ry stone shall cry. And ev - 'ry stone shall
ev - 'ry stone shall cry. And ev - 'ry stone shall
ev - 'ry stone shall cry. And ev - 'ry stone shall
ev - 'ry stone shall cry. And ev - 'ry stone shall

WORDS: Richard Wilbur, 1959
MUSIC: David Hurd, 1984

ANDUJAR
76.76.66.76

♩.=64-70

cry, and straw like gold shall shine; a barn shall har-bor
cry, though hea-vy, dull, and dumb, and lie with-in the
cry, for hearts made hard by sin: God's blood up-on the
cry, in prais-es of the child by whose de-scent a-

1, 2, 3

heav - en, a stall be-come a shrine. This
road - way to pave his king-dom come. Yet
spear - head, God's love re-fused a - gain. But
mong us the worlds are rec - on-ciled.

4

142 People, Look East

1. Peo - ple, look east, the time is near of the
2. Fur - rows, be glad. Though earth is bare, one more
3. Stars, keep the watch. When night is dim, one more
4. An - gels an - nounce with shouts of mirth him who

crown - ing of the year. Make your house fair as you are
seed is plant - ed there. Give up your strength the seed to
light the bowl shall brim, shin - ing be - yond the frost - y
brings new life to earth. Set ev - ery peak and val - ley

a - ble, trim the hearth and set the ta - ble.
nour - ish, that in course the flower may flour - ish.
weath - er, bright as sun and moon to - geth - er.
hum - ming with the word, the Lord is com - ing.

Peo - ple, look east and sing to - day:

Peo - ple, look east:

Love, the Guest, is on the way.
Love, the Rose, is on the way.
Love, the Star, is on the way.
Peo - ple, look east: Love, the Lord, is on the way.

WORDS: Eleanor Farjeon, 1928
MUSIC: Traditional French carol; harm. Martin Shaw, 1928

BESANÇON
87.98.87

♩.=62-70

Joy to the World

143

1. Joy to the world, the Lord is come! Let earth re-
2. Joy to the world, the Sav - ior reigns! Let all their
3. He rules the world with truth and grace, and makes the

ceive her King; let ev - ery heart pre - pare him room,
songs em - ploy; while fields and floods, rocks, hills, and plains
na - tions prove the glo - ries of his right - eous - ness,

and heaven and na - ture sing, and heaven and na - ture
re - peat the sound-ing joy, re - peat the sound-ing
and won-ders of his love, and won-ders of his

And heaven and na - ture sing, and
Re - peat the sound-ing joy, re -
And won-ders of his love, and

sing, and heaven, and heaven and na - ture sing.
joy, re - peat, re - peat the sound-ing joy.
love, and won - ders, won - ders of his love.

heaven and na - ture sing,
peat the sound-ing joy,
won-ders of his love,

WORDS: Isaac Watts, 1719
MUSIC: Attr. George Frederick Handel, 1741; arr. Lowell Mason, 1848

ANTIOCH
CM w. repeat

144 O Little Town of Bethlehem

1. O lit-tle town of Beth-le-hem, how still we see thee lie!
2. For Christ is born of Ma - ry, and gath-ered all a - bove
3. How si - lent - ly, how si - lent - ly the won-drous gift is given!
4. O ho - ly Child of Beth-le-hem, de-scend to us, we pray;

A - bove thy deep and dream-less sleep the si - lent stars go by.
while mor-tals sleep, the an - gels keep their watch of won-dering love.
So God im - parts to hu - man hearts the joys of high - est heaven.
cast out our sin, and en - ter in; be born in us to - day.

Yet in thy dark streets shin - eth the ev - er - last - ing Light;
O morn-ing stars, to - geth - er pro-claim the ho - ly birth.
No ear may hear Christ com - ing, but in this world of sin,
We hear the Christ-mas an - gels the great glad tid - ings tell;

the hopes and fears of all the years are met in thee to - night.
Your voic - es raise to God in praise; and peace to all on earth.
where meek souls will re - ceive him still, the dear Christ en - ters in.
O come to us, a - bide with us, our God, Em - man - u - el.

WORDS: Phillips Brooks, 1868, alt.
MUSIC: Lewis H. Redner, 1868

ST. LOUIS
86.86.76.86

Silent Night, Holy Night

1. Si - lent night, ho - ly night, all is calm, all is bright
2. Si - lent night, ho - ly night, shep-herds quake at the sight,
3. Si - lent night, ho - ly night, Son of God, love's pure light
4. Si - lent night, ho - ly night, won-drous star, lend thy light;

round yon vir - gin moth-er and child, ho - ly in-fant so ten-der and mild,
glo - ries stream from heav-en a - far, heaven-ly hosts sing al - le - lu - ia;
ra - diant beams from thy ho-ly face, with the dawn of re-deem - ing grace,
with the an - gels let us sing, al - le-lu - ia to our King;

sleep in heav - en-ly peace, sleep in heav - en-ly peace.
Christ, the Sav - ior, is born! Christ, the Sav - ior, is born!
Je - sus, Lord, at thy birth, Je - sus, Lord, at thy birth.
Christ, the Sav - ior, is born, Christ the Sav - ior, is born.

WORDS: Joseph Mohr, 1818; tr. John F. Young, 1863
MUSIC: Franz Gruber, 1818

STILLE NACHT
Irr.

146　　　From Heaven Above

1. From heaven above to earth I come to
2. To you this night is born a child of
3. This is the Christ, God's Son most high, who
4. "Glo - ry to God in high - est heaven, who

bring good news to ev - ery - one! Glad tid - ings of great
Ma - ry, cho - sen vir - gin mild; this new - born child of
hears your sad and bit - ter cry; he will him - self your
un - to us the Christ has given." With an - gels sing the

joy I bring to all the world, and glad - ly sing:
low - ly birth shall be the joy of all the earth.
Sav - ior be and from all sin will set you free.
Sav - ior's birth, a glad new year to all the earth.

WORDS: Martin Luther, 1535; tr. *Lutheran Book of Worship*, 1978, alt.　　　　VOM HIMMEL HOCH
MUSIC: Valentin Schumann's *Geistliche Lieder*, 1539　　　　　　　　　　　　　LM

Away in a Manger

Unison

1. A - way in a man - ger, no crib for a bed, the lit - tle Lord
2. The cat - tle are low - ing, the ba - by a - wakes, but lit - tle Lord
3. Be near me, Lord Je - sus, I ask thee to stay close by me for -

Je - sus laid down his sweet head. The stars in the sky looked
Je - sus, no cry - ing he makes. I love thee, Lord Je - sus, look
ev - er, and love me, I pray. Bless all the dear chil - dren in

down where he lay, the lit - tle Lord Je - sus, a - sleep on the hay.
down from the sky, and stay by my cra - dle till morn - ing is nigh.
thy ten - der care, and fit us for heav - en to live with thee there.

WORDS: Anonymous (19th century)
MUSIC: Attr. James R. Murray, 1887; harm. LBW, 1978

AWAY IN A MANGER
11 11.11 11

Alt. tune: CRADLE SONG

148 O Come, All Ye Faithful

WORDS: John Francis Wade, 1743; tr. Frederick Oakeley, 1841, and others
MUSIC: John Francis Wade, 1743; desc. David Willcocks, 1961

ADESTE FIDELES
Irr. w. refrain

let us a - dore him, Christ, the Lord!

O come, let us a - dore him, Christ, the Lord!

Angels, from the Realms of Glory 149

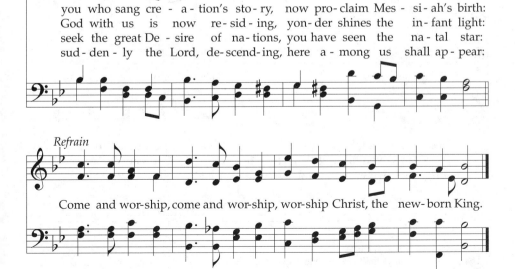

1. An - gels, from the realms of glo - ry, wing your flight o'er all the earth;
2. Shep - herds, in the fields a - bid - ing, watch - ing o'er your flocks by night,
3. Sag - es, leave your con - tem - pla - tions bright - er vi - sions beam a - far;
4. Saints be - fore the al - tar bend - ing, watch - ing long in hope and fear,

you who sang cre - a - tion's sto - ry, now pro - claim Mes - si - ah's birth:
God with us is now re - sid - ing, yon - der shines the in - fant light:
seek the great De - sire of na - tions, you have seen the na - tal star:
sud - den - ly the Lord, de - scend - ing, here a - mong us shall ap - pear:

Refrain

Come and wor - ship, come and wor - ship, wor - ship Christ, the new - born King.

WORDS: James Montgomery, 1816
MUSIC: Henry T. Smart, 1867

REGENT SQUARE
87.87.87

Luke 2:10–14

150 Hark! the Herald Angels Sing

Descant

3. All hail the Sun of

1. Hark! the her - ald an - gels sing,
2. Christ, by high - est heaven a - dored;
3. Hail the heaven - born Prince of Peace!

"Glo - ry to the
Christ, the ev - er -
Hail the Sun of

Righ - teous - ness!

He is risen with heal-ing

new - born King; peace on earth, and mer - cy mild,
last - ing Lord! Late in time be- hold him come,
Righ-teous- ness! Light and life to all he brings,

God and sin - ners
off- spring of the
risen with heal - ing

in his wings.

His glo - ry by,

rec - on - ciled!"
Vir - gin's womb.
in his wings,

Joy - ful, all ye
Veiled in flesh the
mild he lays his

na - tions, rise,
God - head see;
glo - ry by,

WORDS: Charles Wesley, 1739, alt.
MUSIC: Felix Mendelssohn, 1840; arr. William H. Cummings, 1856;
desc. Paul Liljestrand

MENDELSSOHN
77.77D w. refrain

151 The First Noel

1. The first No - el, the an - gel did say, was to
2. They look - ed up and saw a star shin - ing
3. And by the light of that same star three
4. This star drew nigh to the north - west, o'er
5. Then en - tered in those wise men three, full

1. cer - tain poor shep-herds in fields as they lay; in fields where
2. in the east, be - yond them far, and to the
3. wise men came from coun - try far; to seek for a
4. Beth - le - hem it took its rest, and there it
5. rev - erent - ly up - on their knee, and of - fered

1. they lay keep - ing their sheep, on a cold win - ter's
2. earth it gave great light, and so it con -
3. king was their in - tent, and to fol - low the
4. did both stop and stay, right ov - er the
5. there, in his pres - ence, their gold and

WORDS: Traditional English carol (17th century)
MUSIC: Traditional English melody; desc. Healey Willan, 1926

THE FIRST NOEL
Irr. w. refrain

Desc. used by permission of Oxford University Press

Descant

No - el, No - el, No-

Refrain

1. night that was so deep.
2. tin- ued both day and night.
3. star wher - ev - er it went. No - el, No - el, No -
4. place where Je - sus lay.
5. myrrh and frank - in - cense.

el, No - el, born is the King of Is - ra - el.

el, No - el, born is the King of Is - ra - el.

The Birth of Jesus 152

Joseph went from the town of Nazareth in Galilee to Judea, to the city of David called Bethlehem, because he was descended from the house and family of David. He went to be registered with Mary, to whom he was engaged and who was expecting a child. While they were there, the time came for her to deliver her child. And she gave birth to her firstborn son and wrapped him in bands of cloth, and laid him in a manger, because there was no place for them in the inn.

In that region there were shepherds living in the fields, keeping watch over their flock by night. Then an angel of the Lord stood before them, and the glory of the Lord shone around them, and they were terrified. But the angel said to them, "Do not be afraid; for see—I am bringing you good news of great joy for all the people: to you is born this day in the city of David a Savior, who is the Messiah, the Lord. This will be a sign for you: you will find a child wrapped in bands of cloth and lying in a manger." And suddenly there was with the angel a multitude of the heavenly host, praising God and saying, "Glory to God in the highest heaven, and on earth peace among those whom he favors!"

Luke 2:4–14

153 It Came upon the Midnight Clear

1. It came up-on the mid-night clear, that glo-rious song of old,
2. Still through the clo-ven skies they come, with peace-ful wings un-furled,
3. And you be-neath life's crush-ing load whose forms are bend-ing low,
4. For lo, the days are has-tening on, by proph - et seen of old,

from an-gels bend-ing near the earth to touch their harps of gold;
and still their heaven-ly mu-sic floats o'er all the wea-ry world;
who toil a-long the climb-ing way, with pain-ful steps and slow,
when with the ev - er - cir-cling years shall come the time fore-told;

"Peace on the earth, good will to all, from heaven's all gra-cious King."
a - bove its sad and low-ly plains they bend on hover-ing wing,
look now, for glad and gold-en hours come swift-ly on the wing;
when peace shall o - ver all the earth its an - cient splen-dors fling,

The world in sol - emn still-ness lay to hear the an - gels sing.
and ev - er o'er its Ba-bel sounds the bless - ed an - gels sing.
O rest be-side the wea-ry road, and hear the an - gels sing!
and the whole world send back the song which now the an - gels sing.

WORDS: Edmund H. Sears, 1849
MUSIC: Richard S. Willis, 1850

CAROL
CMD

While Shepherds Watched Their Flocks 154

1. While shep-herds watched their flocks by night, all seat-ed on the ground, the mes-sen-ger of God camedown, and glo-ry shone a-round, and glo-ry shone a-round.

2. "Fear not," the an-gel said— for dread had seized their trou-bled mind, "Glad ti-dings of great joy I bring to all of hu-man-kind, to all of hu-man-kind.

3. "To you, in Da-vid's town this day, is born of Da-vid's line, a Sav-ior, who is Christ, the Lord, and this shall be the sign: and this shall be the sign:

4. "The heaven-ly Babe you there shall find to hu-man view dis-played, all mean-ly wrapped in swath-ing bands, and in a man-ger laid, and in a man-ger laid."

5. Thus spake the ser-aph, and forth-with ap-peared a shin-ing throng of an-gels prais-ing God, who thus ad-dressed their joy-ful song: ad-dressed their joy-ful song:

6. "All glo-ry be to God on high and on the earth be peace; good-will hence-forth from heaven to earth be-gin and nev-er cease, be-gin and nev-er cease."

WORDS: Nahum Tate, 1700, alt.
MUSIC: George Frederick Handel, 1728

CHRISTMAS
CM

155 Angels We Have Heard on High

Descant

4. See with-in a man-ger laid, Christ, whom choirs of

1. An - gels we have heard on high, sweet - ly sing - ing
2. Shep - herds, why this ju - bi - lee? Why your joy - ous
3. Come to Beth - le - hem and see Christ, who comes in
4. See with - in a man - ger laid, Christ, whom choirs of

an - gels praise; Ma - ry, Jo - seph, lend your aid,

o'er the plains, and the moun - tains in re - ply
strains pro - long? What the glad - some tid - ings be
low - ly birth. Come a - dore on bend - ed knee
an - gels praise; Ma - ry, Jo - seph, lend your aid,

Refrain

while our hearts in love we raise. Ah!

ech - o - ing their joy - ous strains.
which in - spire your heav'n - ly song? Glo
Je - sus, joy of heav'n and earth.
while our hearts in love we raise.

WORDS: Traditional French carol; tr. *Crown of Jesus*, 1862, alt.
MUSIC: French carol melody; arr. Edward Shippen Barnes, 1937;
 harm. Austin C. Lovelace, 1964, alt.; desc. Richard E. Gerig, 1956

GLORIA
77.77 w. refrain

Song of Simeon
(Nunc Dimittis)

156

RESPONSE

Now let us sing our Sav-ior's praise, and tell God's good-ness all our days.

R

Lord, now let your servant in peace;
your word has been fulfilled:
my own eyes have seen the salvation
which you have prepared in the presence of all people,
a light to reveal you to the nations
and the glory of your people Israel.   **R**

WORDS: Luke 2:29–32, ICET, rev. ELLC; Response, Ruth Duck, 1978
MUSIC: Adapt. from Robert Schumann, 1839

157   For All Who Give You a Face

For all who give you a face, Lord Jesus,
by spreading your love in the world, we praise you.

For all who give you hands,
by doing their best toward their sisters and brothers, we praise you.

For all who give you a mouth, Lord Jesus,
by defending the weak and the oppressed, we praise you.

For all who give you eyes,
by seeing every bit of love in the heart of man and woman, we praise you.

For all who give you a heart, Lord Jesus,
by preferring the poor to the rich, the weak to the strong, we praise you.

For all who give to your poverty the look of hope for your Reign,
we praise you.

For all who reveal you simply by what they are, Lord Jesus,
because they reflect your beauty in their lives, we praise you.

You who are the God of a thousand faces,
yet whom nothing can reveal completely
except the face of the child of Bethlehem, we pray to you:

Continue in our lives the mystery of Christmas.
Let your Son become flesh in us
so that we may be for all our brothers and sisters the revelation of your love.

Lucien Deiss, 20th-century French Catholic liturgist

158   Her Baby, Newly Breathing

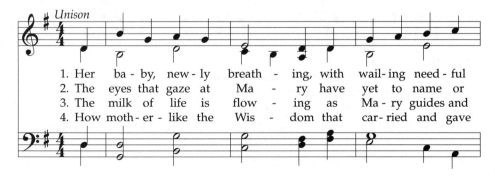

1. Her ba-by, new-ly breath - ing, with wail-ing need-ful
2. The eyes that gaze at Ma - ry have yet to name or
3. The milk of life is flow - ing as Ma-ry guides and
4. How moth-er-like the Wis - dom that car-ried and gave

WORDS: Brian Wren, 1987
MUSIC: Hal H. Hopson, 1983

MERLE'S TUNE
76.76D

♩=112-116

cry, by Ma - ry kissed and cra - dled, is
trace the world of shape and col - or, or
feeds her word - less Word, em - bod - ied in
birth to all things, seen and un - seen, and

lulled in lul - la - by. Long months of hope and
rec - og - nize a face; yet Ho - li - ness E -
in - fant joys and needs. E - nor - mous, form - less
nur - tured in - fant earth: un - stint - ing, un - pro -

wait - ing, the thrill and fear of birth, are
ter - nal is per - fect - ly ex - pressed in
striv - ings, and yearn - ings deep and wide, be -
tect - ed, pre - pared for nail and thorn, con -

crowned with ex - ul - ta - tion, and God is on the earth.
hands that clutch un - think - ing, and lips that tug the breast.
cra - dled in com - mun - ion, are fed and sat - is - fied.
strict - ed in - to male - ness, and of a wom - an born.

159 There's a Song in the Air!

1. There's a song in the air! There's a star in the sky!
2. There's a tu-mult of joy o'er the won-der-ful birth,
3. We re-joice in the light, and we ech-o the song

There's a moth-er's deep prayer and a ba-by's low cry!
for the Vir-gin's sweet boy is the Lord of the earth.
that comes down through the night from the heav-en-ly throng,

And the star rains its fire while the an-gel choirs sing,
See, the star rains its fire while the an-gel choirs sing,
and we wel-come the glo-ri-ous gos-pel they bring,

for the man-ger of Beth-le-hem cra-dles a king!
for the man-ger of Beth-le-hem cra-dles a king!
and we greet in the cra-dle our sav-ior and king.

WORDS: Josiah G. Holland, 1879, alt.
MUSIC: Karl P. Harrington, 1904

CHRISTMAS SONG
66.66.12 12

Lo, How a Rose E'er Blooming

160

1. Lo, how a rose e'er bloom - ing from ten - der stem
2. I - sa - iah 'twas fore - told it, the rose I have

hath sprung, of Jes - se's lin - eage com - ing by
in mind; with Mar - y we be - hold it, the

faith - ful proph - ets sung; it came a flow'r - et bright,
vir - gin moth - er kind. To show God's love a - right

a - mid the cold of win - ter when half spent was the night.
she bore to us a Sav - ior when half spent was the night.

WORDS: German carol (15th century); tr. Theodore Baker, 1894
MUSIC: Traditional melody; arr. Michael Praetorius, 1609

ES IST EIN ROS
76.76.676

161 I Wonder as I Wander

1. I wonder as I wander, out under the sky, how
2. When Mary birthed Jesus, 'twas in a cow's stall, with
3. If Jesus had wanted for any wee thing, a
4. I wonder as I wander, out under the sky, how

Jesus the Savior did come for to die for
wise men and farmers and shepherds and all, but
star in the sky or a bird on the wing, or
Jesus the Savior did come for to die for

poor ordinary people like you and like I; I
high from God's heaven a star's light did fall, the
all of God's angels in heaven for to sing, he
poor ordinary people like you and like I; I

wonder as I wander, out under the sky.
promise of ages it then did recall.
surely could have it, 'cause he was the King.
wonder as I wander, out under the sky. Out under the sky.

WORDS: Traditional Appalachian carol; coll. John Jacob Niles, 1934
MUSIC: Traditional Appalachian melody; coll. John Jacob Niles, 1934; arr. Donald P. Hustad, 1984

I WONDER AS I WANDER
Irr.

What Child Is This

1. What Child is this who, laid to rest, on Ma-ry's lap is sleep-ing?
2. Why lies he in such mean es-tate where ox and ass are feed-ing?
3. So bring him in-cense, gold, and myrrh, come, rich and poor, to own him,

Whom an-gels greet with an-thems sweet, while shep-herds watch are keep-ing?
Good Christ-ian, fear: for sin-ners here the si-lent Word is plead-ing.
the King of kings sal-va-tion brings, let lov-ing hearts en-throne him.

Refrain

This, this is Christ the King, whom shep-herds guard and an-gels sing:

haste, haste to bring him laud, the Babe, the Son of Ma-ry.

WORDS: William C. Dix, c. 1865
MUSIC: English melody (16th century)

GREENSLEEVES
87.87 w. refrain

163 Infant Holy, Infant Lowly

WORDS: Polish carol; tr. Edith M. G. Reed, 1925
MUSIC: Polish folk melody; adapt. A. E. Rusbridge

W ZLOBIE LEZY
87.87.88.77

Adapt. used by permission of Rosalind Rusbridge

Good Christian Friends, Rejoice

1. Good Chris-tian friends, re - joice with heart and soul and voice!
2. Good Chris-tian friends, re - joice with heart and soul and voice!
3. Good Chris-tian friends, re - joice with heart and soul and voice!

Lis - ten now to what we say: News! News! Je- sus Christ is born to- day.
Now you hear of end- less bliss: Joy! Joy! Je- sus Christ was born for this!
Now you need not fear the grave: Peace! Peace! Je- sus Christ was born to save!

Ox and ass be - fore him bow, and he is in the man- ger now.
He has o- pened heav- en's door, and we are blest for ev- er- more.
Calls you one and calls you all, to gain the ev - er - last- ing hall.

Christ is born to - day! Christ is born to - day!
Christ was born for this! Christ was born for this!
Christ was born to save! Christ was born to save!

WORDS: Latin (14th century); tr. John Mason Neale, 1853, alt.
MUSIC: German melody (14th century); harm. David Hugh Jones, 1953

IN DULCI JUBILO
Irr.

Luke 2:7

165 Once in Royal David's City

1. Once in roy-al Da-vid's cit-y stood a low-ly
2. Christ came down to earth from hea-ven, love in-car-nate
3. Je-sus is our child-hood's pat-tern; day by day like
4. And our eyes at last shall see him, through his own re-

cat-tle shed, where a mo-ther laid her ba-by
for us all, and his shel-ter was a sta-ble,
us he grew, he was lit-tle, weak, and help-less,
deem-ing love; for that child who seemed so help-less

in a man-ger for his bed: Ma-ry was that mo-ther
and his cra-dle was a stall; with the poor, the scorned, the
tears and smiles like us he knew. Thus he feels for all our
lives and reigns in heaven a-bove; and he leads his chil-dren

mild, Je-sus Christ her lit-tle child.
low-ly, lived on earth our Sav-ior ho-ly.
sad-ness, and he shares in all our glad-ness.
on to the place where he is gone.

WORDS: Cecil F. Alexander, 1848, alt.
MUSIC: Henry John Gauntlett, 1849; harm. Arthur H. Mann, 1919

IRBY
87.87.77

'Twas in the Moon of Wintertime

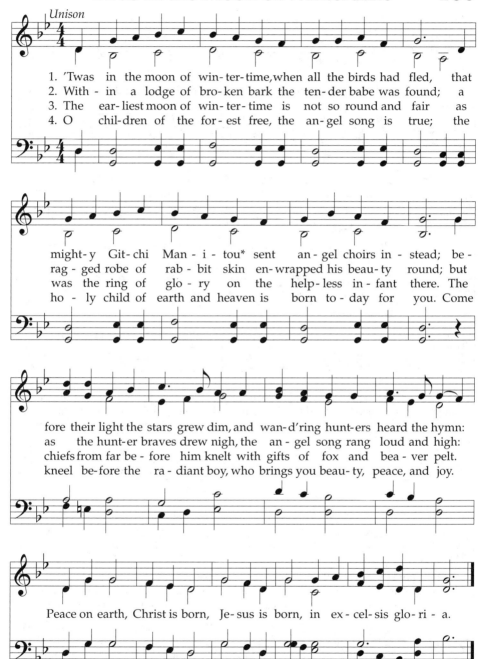

Unison

1. 'Twas in the moon of win-ter-time, when all the birds had fled, that
2. With-in a lodge of bro-ken bark the ten-der babe was found; a
3. The ear-liest moon of win-ter-time is not so round and fair as
4. O chil-dren of the for-est free, the an-gel song is true; the

might-y Git-chi Man-i-tou* sent an-gel choirs in-stead; be-
rag-ged robe of rab-bit skin en-wrapped his beau-ty round; but
was the ring of glo-ry on the help-less in-fant there. The
ho-ly child of earth and heaven is born to-day for you. Come

fore their light the stars grew dim, and wan-d'ring hunt-ers heard the hymn:
as the hunt-er braves drew nigh, the an-gel song rang loud and high:
chiefs from far be-fore him knelt with gifts of fox and bea-ver pelt.
kneel be-fore the ra-diant boy, who brings you beau-ty, peace, and joy.

Peace on earth, Christ is born, Je-sus is born, in ex-cel-sis glo-ri-a.

Gitchi Manitou = Great God

WORDS: Jean de Brébeuf, c. 1643; tr. Jesse E. Middleton, 1926, alt.
MUSIC: French Canadian melody; harm. Frederick F. Jackisch, 1978

JESOUS AHATONHIA
86.86.88 w. refrain

𝅗𝅥=54-60

167 Go Tell It on the Mountain

Refrain

Go, tell it on the moun-tain, o-ver the hills and ev-ery-where;

go, tell it on the moun-tain, that Je-sus Christ is born.

1. While shep-herds kept their watch-ing o'er si-lent flocks by night,
2. The shep-herds feared and trem-bled, when lo! a-bove the earth,
3. Down in a low-ly man-ger the hum-ble Christ was born,

be-hold through-out the heav-ens there shown a ho-ly light.
rang out the an-gel cho-rus that hailed the Sav-ior's birth.
and God sent us sal-va-tion that bless-ed Christ-mas morn.

WORDS: African-American spiritual; adapt. John W. Work, Jr., 1907
MUSIC: African-American spiritual; arr. William Farley Smith, 1986

GO TELL IT ON THE MOUNTAIN
Irr. w. refrain

Down to Earth

Unison

1. Down to earth as a dove, came to all,
2. This is love come to light, now is fear
3. Je - sus Christ comes to feed hun-gry ones

ho - ly love; Je-sus Christ from a - bove bring-ing great sal - va - tion,
put to flight. God de-feats ev - il's blight; giv - ing for our sor - rows,
in their need; in the house there is bread: Je - sus in a sta - ble,

Refrain

meant for ev - ery na - tion.
hope of new to-mor - rows. Let us sing, sing, sing, dance and spring,
in the church a ta - ble.

spring, spring. Christ is here, ev - er near! Glo - ria in ex - cel - sis.

WORDS: Fred Kaan, 1968
MUSIC: *Piae Cantiones*, 1582; arr. Gustav Holst, 1925

PERSONENT HODIE
666.66 w. refrain

Words © 1968 Hope Publishing Co.; arr. © 1924, renewed, J. Curwen & Sons

♩=72-80

169

O Thou Joyful
(¡Oh Santísimo!)

1. O thou joy - ful, O thou won-der-ful grace-re - veal-ing
2. O thou joy - ful, O thou won-der-ful love - re - veal-ing

1. ¡Oh san - tí - si - mo, fe - li - cí - si - mo, Gra - to tiem-po de
2. ¡Oh san - tí - si - mo, fe - li - cí - si - mo, Gra - to tiem-po de

Christ - mas - tide! Je - sus came to win us from all sin with-
Christ - mas - tide! Loud ho - san - nas sing - ing and all prais-es

Na - vi - dad! A es - te mun-do he - ri - do, Cris - to le ha na-
Na - vi - dad! Co - ros ce - les - tia - les O - yen los mor-

in us; glo - ri - fy the ho - ly child!
bring - ing: may Thy love with us a - bide!

ci - do: ¡A - le - grí - a, a - le - grí - a, cris - tian - dad!
ta - les: ¡A - le - grí - a, a - le - grí - a, cris - tian - dad!

WORDS: Johannes D. Falk; Eng. tr. Henry Katterjohn, 1919;
Span. tr. Federico Fliedner
MUSIC: Tattersall's *Psalmody*, 1794

O SANCTISSIMA
457.667

♩=96

How Great Our Joy!

1. While by the sheep we watched at night, lo, there ap-peared an
2. Born is the Child, in man-ger small, whom God has sent to
3. Go you this night, and you shall find the Sav-ior born for
4. Je-sus, the gift from heav'n a-bove fills all our hearts with

an - gel bright:
save us all.
hu - man - kind.
joy and love.

How great our joy! Great our joy!

Joy, joy, joy! Joy, joy, joy! Glo-ry to God who

reigns on high! Glo-ry to God who reigns on high!

WORDS: Traditional German carol, alt.
MUSIC: Traditional German melody; arr. Hugo Jüngst, c. 1890

JUNGST
Irr.

171 God's Love Made Visible!

Play small notes in absence of string bass.
Claves
Maracas

1. God's love made vis-i-ble! In-com-pre-hen-si-ble!
2. God gave the Son to us to dwell as one of us—

Christ is in-vin-ci-ble! His love shall reign! From love so boun-ti-ful,
a bless-ing un-to us! His love shall reign! To him all hon-or bring,

bless-ings un-count-a-ble make death sur-mount-a-ble! His love shall reign!
heav-en and earth will sing, prais-ing our Lord and King! His love shall reign!

WORDS: Iola Brubeck, 1975
MUSIC: Dave Brubeck, 1975

POSADA
12 10.12 10.99.12 10

♩=140-150

Joy - ful - ly pray for peace and good will! All of our yearn-ing
O - pen all doors this day of his birth, all of good will in-

he will ful - fill. Live in a lov-ing way! Praise him for ev-ery day!
her - it the earth. His star will al-ways be guid-ing hu-man-i-ty

O - pen your hearts and pray. His love shall reign!
through - out e - ter - ni - ty! His love shall reign!

Matthew 2:1–12

172   We Three Kings

All: 1. We three kings of O - ri - ent are; bear - ing
Opt. Solo: 2. Born a King on Beth - le - hem's plain, gold I
Opt. Solo: 3. Frank - in - cense to of - fer have I; in - cense
Opt. Solo: 4. Myrrh is mine; its bit - ter per - fume breathes a
All: 5. Glo - rious now be - hold him a - rise; Christ and

1. gifts we tra - verse a - far, field and foun - tain,
2. bring to crown him a - gain, King for - ev - er,
3. owns a De - i - ty nigh; prayer and prais - ing,
4. life of gath - er - ing gloom; sor - rowing, sigh - ing,
5. God and sac - ri - fice: al - le - lu - ia,

1. moor and moun - tain, fol - low - ing yon - der star.
2. ceas - ing nev - er, o - ver us all to reign.
3. voic - es rais - ing, wor - ship - ing God on high.
4. bleed - ing, dy - ing, sealed in the stone - cold tomb.
5. al - le - lu - ia, sounds through the earth and skies.

Refrain (after 1 & 5 only)

O star of won - der, star of light, star with roy - al beau - ty bright,

WORDS and MUSIC: John H. Hopkins, Jr., 1857

KINGS OF ORIENT
88.446 w. refrain

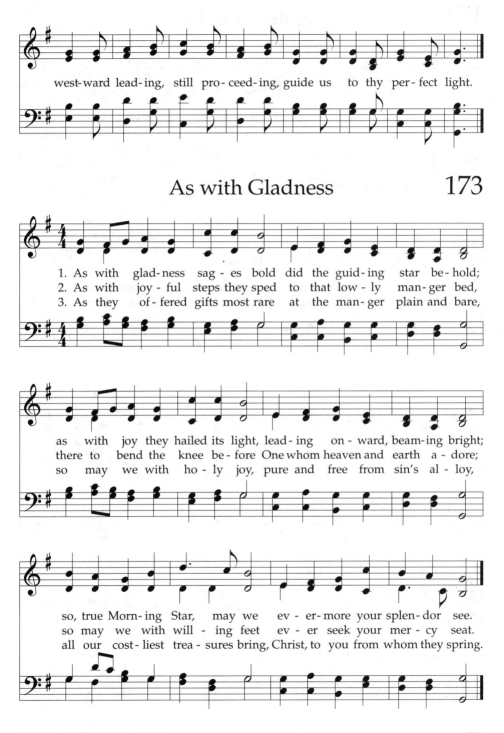

As with Gladness 173

1. As with glad-ness sag-es bold did the guid-ing star be-hold;
2. As with joy-ful steps they sped to that low-ly man-ger bed,
3. As they of-fered gifts most rare at the man-ger plain and bare,

as with joy they hailed its light, lead-ing on-ward, beam-ing bright;
there to bend the knee be-fore One whom heaven and earth a-dore;
so may we with ho-ly joy, pure and free from sin's al-loy,

so, true Morn-ing Star, may we ev-er-more your splen-dor see.
so may we with will-ing feet ev-er seek your mer-cy seat.
all our cost-liest trea-sures bring, Christ, to you from whom they spring.

WORDS: William C. Dix, 1861, alt.
MUSIC: Conrad Kocher, 1838; arr. William Henry Monk, 1861

DIX
77.77.77

174 Brightest and Best

WORDS: Reginald Heber, 1811, alt.
MUSIC: *Southern Harmony*, 1835; harm. Marty Haugen, 1987

STAR IN THE EAST
11 10.11 10D

Harm. © 1987 GIA Publications, Inc.

175 Lovely Star in the Sky

Unison

1. Love-ly star in the sky, ban-ish-ing the night,
2. Roy-al child ly-ing there, man-ger for a bed,
3. What can we do to show our de-vo-tion true?
4. None of these things of price would give Je-sus joy;

shine down and hal-low us, light up our path.
with all the an-i-mals sleep-ing in hay;
Shall we pre-sent to him sweet-smell-ing gifts:
how then will we ex-press thanks for his birth?

Star shin-ing in the East, be our true guide;
an-gels sing rev-'rent-ly, wor-ship the child,
far moun-tain's frank-in-cense, san-dal-wood myrrh?
One pres-ent, one a-lone, Christ would de-sire:

lead us to Beth-le-hem, where the child lies.
low-ly in maj-es-ty, rul-er of all.
Shall it be pre-cious gold, pearls from the sea?
love from our deep-est heart, our own best love.

WORDS: Adapted from a Korean hymn by Reginald Heber
MUSIC: Un-Yung La (Korea)

HANURE BINNANUN
Irr.

♩=88-92

Sing of God Made Manifest

176

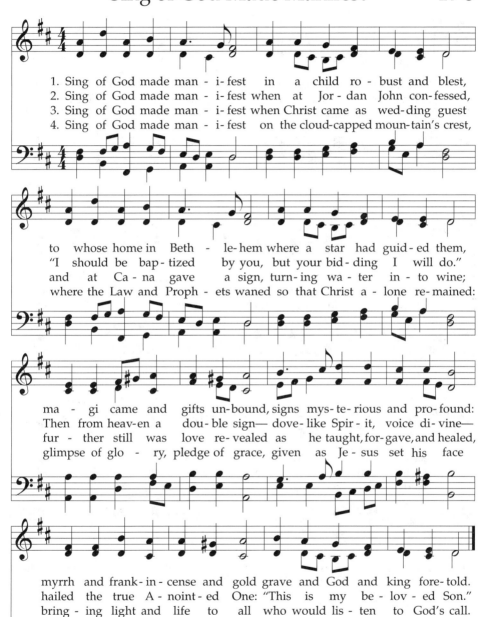

1. Sing of God made man - i-fest in a child ro - bust and blest,
2. Sing of God made man - i-fest when at Jor - dan John con-fessed,
3. Sing of God made man - i-fest when Christ came as wed-ding guest
4. Sing of God made man - i-fest on the cloud-capped moun-tain's crest,

to whose home in Beth - le-hem where a star had guid-ed them,
"I should be bap - tized by you, but your bid-ding I will do."
and at Ca - na gave a sign, turn-ing wa - ter in - to wine;
where the Law and Proph - ets waned so that Christ a - lone re-mained:

ma - gi came and gifts un-bound, signs mys-te-rious and pro-found:
Then from heav-en a dou - ble sign— dove-like Spir - it, voice di - vine—
fur - ther still was love re-vealed as he taught, for-gave, and healed,
glimpse of glo - ry, pledge of grace, given as Je - sus set his face

myrrh and frank-in-cense and gold grave and God and king fore-told.
hailed the true A - noint - ed One: "This is my be - lov - ed Son."
bring - ing light and life to all who would lis - ten to God's call.
toward the wait-ing cross and grave, sign of hope that God would save.

WORDS: Carl P. Daw, Jr., 1989
MUSIC: Jacob Hintze, 1678; harm. Johann Sebastian Bach (18th century)

SALZBURG
77.77D

177   What Was Your Vow and Vision

1. What was your vow and vi - sion, re - vealed and rec - og -
2. Was this God's call, the crown - ing of all you had be -
3. We meet you at the wa - ter and pon - der why and

nized, Christ, when you came to Jor - dan and
come: "Go, show and tell my com - ing, my
how, in hope that we may fol - low where

asked to be bap - tized? Was there a sud - den
own, my cho - sen one"? Did scrip - ture join with
God is go - ing now, a - noint - ed by your

WORDS: Brian Wren, 1975, rev. 1994
MUSIC: *Southern Harmony*, 1835; harm. Hal H. Hopson, 1986

COMPLAINER
76.76D

Words © 1975, harm. © 1986, Hope Publishing Co.

♩=100-108

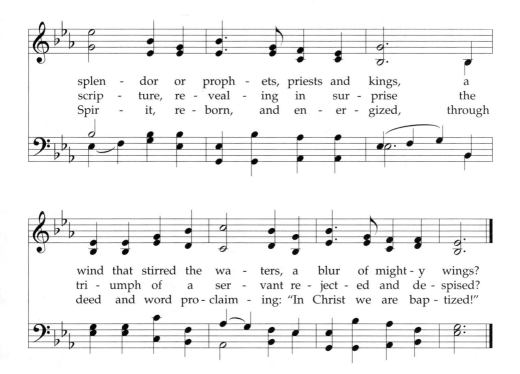

splen - dor or proph - ets, priests and kings, a
scrip - ture, re - veal - ing in sur - prise the
Spir - it, re - born, and en - er - gized, through

wind that stirred the wa - ters, a blur of might - y wings?
tri - umph of a ser - vant re - ject - ed and de - spised?
deed and word pro - claim - ing: "In Christ we are bap - tized!"

You Were Like Me, Jesus   178

You were like me, Jesus—
you walked uncertain in vacillation
between the yes and the no;
I know it, for I read it in your human look.

It comforts me knowing that I am not alone
in this human valley,
for I saw your footprints in it.

—*Luis F. del Pilar, 20th-century Puerto Rican Disciples executive*

179   Forty Days and Forty Nights

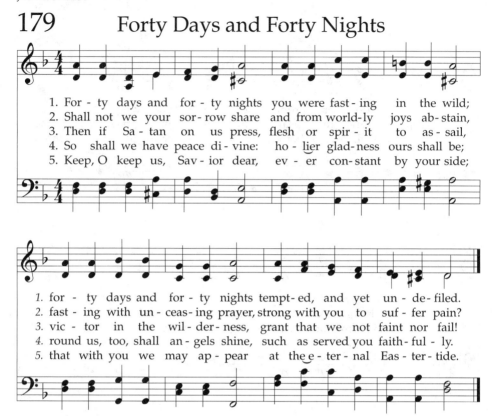

1. For-ty days and for-ty nights you were fast-ing in the wild;
2. Shall not we your sor-row share and from world-ly joys ab-stain,
3. Then if Sa-tan on us press, flesh or spir-it to as-sail,
4. So shall we have peace di-vine: ho-lier glad-ness ours shall be;
5. Keep, O keep us, Sav-ior dear, ev-er con-stant by your side;

1. for-ty days and for-ty nights tempt-ed, and yet un-de-filed.
2. fast-ing with un-ceas-ing prayer, strong with you to suf-fer pain?
3. vic-tor in the wil-der-ness, grant that we not faint nor fail!
4. round us, too, shall an-gels shine, such as served you faith-ful-ly.
5. that with you we may ap-pear at the e-ter-nal Eas-ter-tide.

WORDS: George H. Smyttan, 1856, alt.
MUSIC: Attr. Martin Herbst, 1676

HEINLEIN
77.77

♩=50-54

180 Lord, Who Throughout These Forty Days

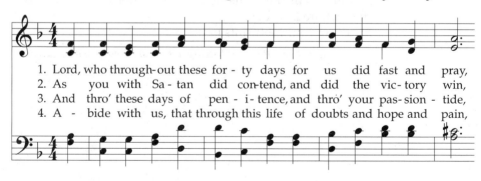

1. Lord, who through-out these for-ty days for us did fast and pray,
2. As you with Sa-tan did con-tend, and did the vic-tory win,
3. And thro' these days of pen-i-tence, and thro' your pas-sion-tide,
4. A-bide with us, that through this life of doubts and hope and pain,

WORDS: Claudia F. Hernaman, 1873, alt.
MUSIC: Adapt. from John Day's *English Psalter*, 1562

ST. FLAVIAN
CM

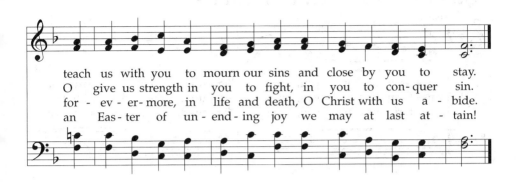

teach us with you to mourn our sins and close by you to stay.
O give us strength in you to fight, in you to con-quer sin.
for - ev - er-more, in life and death, O Christ with us a - bide.
an Eas-ter of un-end-ing joy we may at last at - tain!

Mark 4:35–41

The Storm Is Strong

181

1. The storm is strong; we face the wind. The wa - ter
2. But you, Christ, you are with us here. We turn to
3. Who can you be? What power your say that ev - en

ris - es; waves crash in. Where are we now? Where
you in all our fear. The sin - gle word you
winds and sea o - bey? Re - move our fear of

will we be? There is no mer - cy on this sea.
say is "peace," and wind and waves and storm all cease.
death and harm. Give us your faith and still our storm.

WORDS: Sylvia Dunstan, 1989
MUSIC: Griffith Hugh Jones, 1890

LLEF
LM

Words © 1991 GIA Publications, Inc.

♩=76-88

Luke 9:28–36

182 Transform Us

Unison

1. Trans-form us as you, trans - fig-ured, stood a-part on
2. Trans-form us as you, trans - fig-ured, once spoke with those
3. Trans-form us as you, trans - fig-ured, would not stay with-

Ta - bor's height. Lead us up our sa - cred moun-tains,
ho - ly ones. We, sur-round-ed by the wit - ness
in a shrine. Keep us from our great temp - ta - tion—

search us with re - veal-ing light. Lift us from where we have
of those saints whose work is done, live in this world as your
time and truth we quick-ly bind. Lead us down those dai - ly

fall - en, full of ques-tions, filled with fright.
Bod - y, cho - sen daugh-ters, cho - sen sons.
path - ways where our love is not con - fined.

WORDS: Sylvia Dunstan, 1989
MUSIC: Traditional French melody (17th century); harm. *The English Hymnal*, 1906

PICARDY
87.87.87

Words © 1991 GIA Publications, Inc.

We Meet You, O Christ

183

Unison

1. We meet you, O Christ, in man-y a guise;
   your im-age we see in sim-ple and wise.
   You live in a pal-ace, ex-ist in a shack;
   we see you, the gar-dener, a tree on your back.

2. In mil-lions a-live, a-way and a-broad;
   in-volved in our life, you live down the road.
   Im-pris-oned in sys-tems, you long to be free;
   we see you, O Je-sus, still bear-ing your tree.

3. In hu-man dis-tress we still hear you cry;
   for free-dom you march, in ri-ots you die.
   Your face in the pa-pers we read and we see.
   The tree must be plant-ed by hu-man de-cree.

4. You choose to be made at one with the earth;
   the dark of the grave pre-pares for your birth.
   Your death is your ris-ing, cre-a-tive your word;
   the tree springs to life and our hope is re-stored.

WORDS: Fred Kaan, 1966
MUSIC: Carl F. Schalk, 1987

STANLEY BEACH
10 10.11 11

♩=108-116

184 Sing of Mary, Pure and Lowly

1. Sing of Ma-ry, pure and low-ly, maid-en moth-er, wise and mild. Sing of God's own Son most ho-ly, who be-came her lit-tle child. Fair-est child of fair-est moth-er, God in-car-nate come to earth, Word made flesh, our

2. Sing of Je-sus, son of Ma-ry, in the home at Naz-a-reth. Toil and la-bor can-not wea-ry love en-dur-ing un-to death. Con-stant was the love he gave her, though it drove him from her side, forth to preach, and

3. Joy-ful moth-er, full of glad-ness, in your arms your Lord was borne. Mourn-ful moth-er, full of sad-ness, all your heart with pain was torn. Glo-rious moth-er, now re-ward-ed with a crown at Je-sus' hand, age to age your

WORDS: Roland Ford Palmer, 1938
MUSIC: Joshua Leavitt's *Christian Lyre*, 1831

PLEADING SAVIOR
87.87D

♩=88-96

ver - y broth - er, takes our na - ture by his birth.
heal, and suf - fer, till on Cal - va - ry he died.
name re - cord - ed shall be blest in ev - ery land.

The Beatitudes 185

RESPONSE

Bless-ed are the poor in spir-it, tru-ly heav-en is their re-ward.

R

When Jesus saw the crowds, he went up the mountain;
    and after he sat down, his disciples came to him.
Then he began to speak, and taught them, saying:
"Blessed are the poor in spirit,
    for theirs is the kingdom of heaven.
Blessed are those who mourn,
    for they will be comforted.
Blessed are the meek,
    for they will inherit the earth.
Blessed are those who hunger and thirst for righteousness,
    for they will be filled.
Blessed are the merciful,
    for they will receive mercy.   R

Blessed are the pure in heart,
    for they will see God.
Blessed are the peacemakers,
    for they will be called children of God.
Blessed are those who are persecuted for righteousness' sake,
    for theirs is the kingdom of heaven.
Blessed are you when people revile you and persecute you
    and utter all kinds of evil against you falsely on my account.
Rejoice and be glad, for your reward is great in heaven,
    for in the same way they persecuted the prophets
        who were before you."   R

WORDS: Matthew 5:1–12; Response, Matthew 5:3, alt.
MUSIC: French carol (17th century)

186 Silence, Frenzied, Unclean Spirit!

1. "Si - lence, fren - zied, un - clean spir - it!" cried God's heal - ing
2. Lord, the de - mons still are thriv - ing in the gray cells
3. Si - lence, Lord, the un - clean spir - it in our mind and

Ho - ly One. "Cease your rant - ing! Flesh can't bear it;
of the mind: ty - rant voic - es, shrill and driv - ing,
in our heart; speak your word that when we hear it,

flee as night be - fore the sun." At Christ's words the de - mon
twist - ed thoughts that grip and bind, doubts that stir the heart to
all our de - mons shall de - part. Clear our thought and calm our

trem - bled, from its vic - tim mad - ly rushed, while the crowd that
pan - ic, fears dis - tort - ing rea - son's sight, guilt that makes our
feel - ing; still the frac - tured, war - ring soul. By the pow - er

WORDS: Thomas H. Troeger, 1984
MUSIC: Carol Doran, 1984

AUTHORITY
87.87D

© 1984 Oxford University Press

♩=100-108

alt. tune: EBENEZER

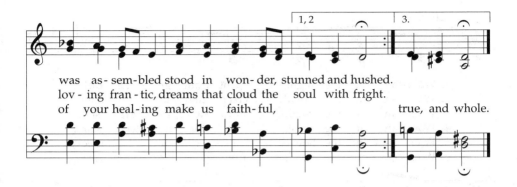

was as-sem-bled stood in won-der, stunned and hushed.
lov-ing fran-tic, dreams that cloud the soul with fright.
of your heal-ing make us faith-ful, true, and whole.

Matthew 5:1–12

Blessed Are the Persecuted 187

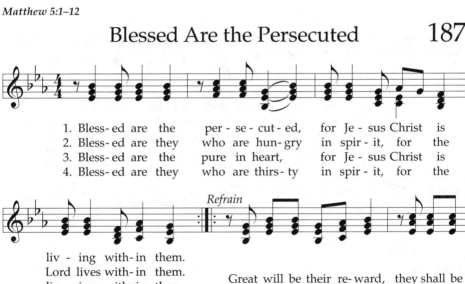

1. Bless-ed are the per-se-cut-ed, for Je-sus Christ is
2. Bless-ed are they who are hun-gry in spir-it, for the
3. Bless-ed are the pure in heart, for Je-sus Christ is
4. Bless-ed are they who are thirs-ty in spir-it, for the

Refrain

liv-ing with-in them.
Lord lives with-in them.
liv-ing with-in them.
Lord lives with-in them.

Great will be their re-ward, they shall be

giv'n a crown, when the Lord comes from heav'n to meet them.

WORDS: Adapt. Esther C. Bergen, 1990
MUSIC: Tonga melody (Zambia)

TONGA
Irr. w. refrain

Words © 1990 Mennonite World Conference

♩=88-96

188 Woman in the Night

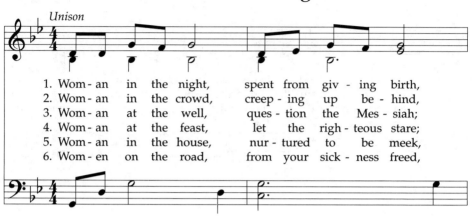

Unison

1. Wom-an in the night, spent from giv-ing birth,
2. Wom-an in the crowd, creep-ing up be-hind,
3. Wom-an at the well, ques-tion the Mes-siah;
4. Wom-an at the feast, let the righ-teous stare;
5. Wom-an in the house, nur-tured to be meek,
6. Wom-en on the road, from your sick-ness freed,

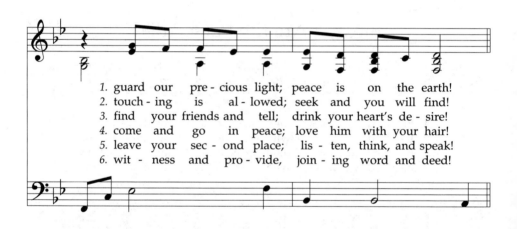

1. guard our pre-cious light; peace is on the earth!
2. touch-ing is al-lowed; seek and you will find!
3. find your friends and tell; drink your heart's de-sire!
4. come and go in peace; love him with your hair!
5. leave your sec-ond place; lis-ten, think, and speak!
6. wit-ness and pro-vide, join-ing word and deed!

Refrain

Come and join the song, wom-en, chil-dren, men;

WORDS: Brian Wren, 1982, rev. 1994
MUSIC: Jim Stanton, 1993

ELIZABETH
55.55 w. refrain

♩=80-88

Je - sus makes us free to live a - gain!

7. Women on the hill,
   stand when men have fled!
   Christ needs loving still,
   though your hope is dead!
   Refrain

8. Women in the dawn,
   care and spices bring;
   earliest to mourn;
   earliest to sing!
   Refrain

Love One Another
189

This is my commandment: Love one another.

Dwell in me, as I in you.
Those who dwell in me, and I in them, bear much fruit.

This is my commandment: Love one another.

As the Father has loved me, so I have loved you.
Dwell in my love.

This is my commandment: Love one another.

If you heed my commands, you will dwell in my love,
as I have heeded the Father's commands and dwell in his love.
This is my commandment: love one another, as I have loved you.

This is my commandment: Love one another.

No one has greater love than this,
to lay down one's life for one's friends.
You are my friends if you do what I command you.

This is my commandment: Love one another.

—Adapted from John 15:4–5, 9–14

190 Tell Me the Stories of Jesus

Unison (Optional S.A.)

1. Tell me the sto-ries of Je-sus I love to hear;
2. First let me hear how the chil-dren stood round his knee,
3. In-to the cit-y I'd fol-low the chil-dren's band,

things I would ask him to tell me if he were here:
and I shall fan-cy his bless-ing rest-ing on me;
wav-ing a branch of the palm tree high in my hand;

scenes by the way-side, tales of the sea,
words full of kind-ness, deeds full of grace,
one of his her-alds, yes, I would sing

sto-ries of Je-sus, tell them to me.
all in the love-light of Je-sus' face.
loud-est ho-san-nas, "Je-sus is King!"

WORDS: William H. Parker, 1885
MUSIC: Frederick A. Challinor, 1903

STORIES OF JESUS
84.84.54.54

Ride On, Ride On in Majesty!   191

1. Ride on, ride on in ma-jes-ty! As all the crowds ho-san-na cry; through wav-ing branch-es slow-ly ride, O Sav-ior, to be cru-ci-fied.

2. Ride on, ride on in ma-jes-ty! In low-ly pomp ride on to die; O Christ, your tri-umph now be-gin o'er cap-tive death and con-quered sin.

3. Ride on, ride on in ma-jes-ty! The an-gel ar-mies of the sky look down with sad and won-dering eyes to see the ap-proach-ing sac-ri-fice.

4. Ride on, ride on in ma-jes-ty! Your last and fierc-est foe de-fy; bow your meek head to mor-tal pain, then take, O God, your power and reign.

WORDS: Henry H. Milman, 1827, alt.
MUSIC: Adapt. from Robert Schumann, 1839

CANONBURY
LM

192 All Glory, Laud, and Honor

Descant

3. Ho - san - na! Sing prais-es! Ho - san - na!

1. All glo - ry, laud, and hon - or, to you, Re-deem-er, King,
2. The com - pa - ny of an - gels are prais - ing you on high,
3. To you be - fore your pas - sion they sang their hymns of praise;

Ho - san - na! Sing prais-es! Our ho - san - nas raise!

to whom the lips of chil - dren made sweet ho - san - nas ring!
and we with all cre - a - tion in cho - rus make re - ply.
to you, now high ex - alt - ed, our mel - o - dy we raise.

You heard their prais - es now hear us as we pray.

You are a child of Is - rael, Great Da-vid's great-er son;
The peo - ple of the He - brews with palms be-fore you went;
As you re-ceived their prais - es, now hear us as we pray.

WORDS: Theodulph of Orleans c. 821; tr. John Mason Neale, 1854, alt.
MUSIC: Melchior Teschner, 1615; harm. William Henry Monk, 1861;
  desc. O. I. Cricket Harrison, 1994

ST. THEODULPH
76.76D

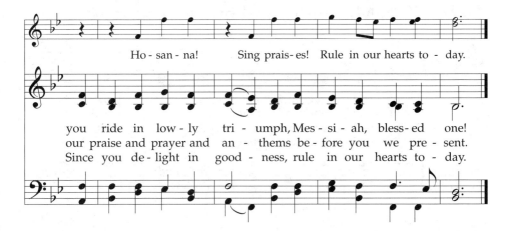

Ho - san - na!   Sing prais- es! Rule in our hearts to - day.

you   ride   in   low - ly   tri - umph, Mes - si - ah, bless- ed   one!
our praise and prayer and   an - thems be - fore you   we   pre - sent.
Since you de - light in   good - ness, rule   in   our   hearts to - day.

Mark 11:1–11

A Cheering, Chanting, Dizzy Crowd   193

A cheering, chanting, dizzy crowd
had stripped the green trees bare,
and hailing Christ as king aloud,
waved branches in the air.

They laid their garments in the road
and spread his path with palms
and vows of lasting love bestowed
with royal hymns and psalms.

When day dimmed down to deep'ning dark
the crowd began to fade
'til only trampled leaves and bark
were left from the parade.

Lest we be fooled because our hearts
have surged with passing praise,
remind us, God, as this week starts
where Christ has fixed his gaze.

Instead of palms a winding sheet
will have to be unrolled,
a carpet much more fit to greet
the king a cross will hold.

WORDS: Thomas H. Troeger, 1985

Recommended tune:
MORNING SONG
(CM)

194 'Tis Midnight, and on Olive's Brow

1. 'Tis mid-night, and on Ol-ive's brow the
2. 'Tis mid-night, and, from all re-moved, the
3. 'Tis mid-night, and, for oth-ers' guilt, the
4. 'Tis mid-night, and from heaven-ly plains is

star is dimmed that late-ly shone; 'tis mid-night, in the
Sav-ior wres-tles lone with fears; e'en that dis-ci-ple
Man of Sor-rows weeps in blood; yet he that has in
borne the song that an-gels know; un-heard by mor-tals

gar-den now the suf-fering Sav-ior prays a-lone.
whom he loved heeds not the Sav-ior's grief and tears.
an-guish knelt is not for-sak-en by his God.
are the strains that gen-tly soothe the Sav-ior's woe.

WORDS: William B. Tappan, 1822
MUSIC: William B. Bradbury, 1853

OLIVE'S BROW
LM

When I Survey the Wondrous Cross 195

1. When I sur - vey the won - drous cross on which the
2. For - bid it, Lord, that I should boast, save in the
3. See, from his head, his hands, his feet, sor - row and
4. Were the whole realm of na - ture mine, that were a

Prince of glo - ry died, my rich - est gain I
death of Christ, my God; all the vain things that
love flow min - gled down! Did e'er such love and
pres - ent far too small; love so a - maz - ing,

count but loss, and pour con - tempt on all my pride.
charm me most I sac - ri - fice them to his blood.
sor - row meet, or thorns com - pose so rich a crown?
so di - vine, de - mands my soul, my life, my all.

WORDS: Isaac Watts, 1707
MUSIC: Lowell Mason, 1824

HAMBURG
LM

Alt. tune: ROCKINGHAM

196 Go to Dark Gethsemane

1. Go to dark Geth - sem - a - ne, all who feel the
2. Fol - low to the judg - ment hall; view the Lord of
3. Cal - v'ry's mourn - ful moun - tain climb; there, a - dor - ing
4. Ear - ly hast - en to the tomb where they laid his

temp - ter's pow'r; your Re - deem - er's con - flict see,
life ar - raigned, O the worm - wood and the gall!
at his feet, mark that mir - a - cle of time,
breath - less clay; all is sol - i - tude and gloom.

watch with him one bit - ter hour: turn not from his
O the pangs his soul sus - tained! Shun not suf - f'ring,
God's own sac - ri - fice com - plete: "It is fin - ished!"
Who has tak - en him a - way? Christ is ris'n! He

griefs a - way; learn of Je - sus Christ to pray.
shame, or loss; learn of him to bear the cross.
hear the cry; learn of Je - sus Christ to die.
meets our eyes; Sav - ior, teach us so to rise.

WORDS: James Montgomery, 1825, alt.
MUSIC: Richard Redhead, 1853

REDHEAD 76
77.77.77

Beneath the Cross of Jesus

197

1. Be - neath the cross of Je - sus I fain would take my stand,
2. Up - on that cross of Je - sus mine eye at times can see
3. I take, O cross, thy shad - ow for my a - bid - ing place;

the shad - ow of a might - y rock with - in a wea - ry land;
the ver - y dy - ing form of one who suf - fered there for me;
I ask no oth - er sun - shine than the sun - shine of his face;

a home with - in the wil - der - ness, a rest up - on the way,
and from my strick - en heart with tears two won - ders I con - fess:
con - tent to let the world go by, to know no gain nor loss,

from the burn - ing of the noon - tide heat, and the bur - den of the day.
the won - ders of re - deem - ing love and my un - wor - thi - ness.
my sin - ful self my on - ly shame, my glo - ry all the cross.

WORDS: Elizabeth C. Clephane, 1872
MUSIC: Frederick C. Maker, 1881

ST. CHRISTOPHER
76.86.86.86

198 Were You There

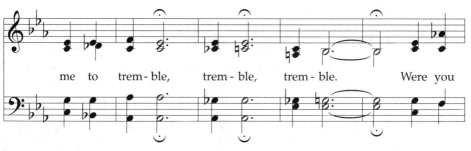

1. Were you there when they cru-ci-fied my Lord? (were you
2. Were you there when they nailed him to the tree? (were you
3. Were you there when they laid him in the tomb? (were you

there) Were you there when they cru-ci-fied my Lord? (were you
there) Were you there when they nailed him to the tree? (were you
there) Were you there when they laid him in the tomb? (were you

there) Oh! Some-times it caus-es

me to trem-ble, trem-ble, trem-ble. Were you

WORDS: African-American spiritual
MUSIC: African-American spiritual; adapt. and arr. William Farley Smith, 1986

WERE YOU THERE
Irr.

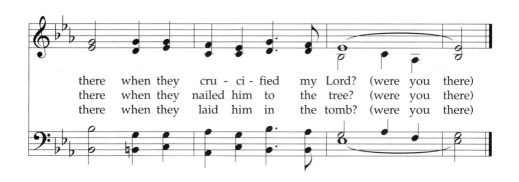

there   when they   cru - ci - fied   my Lord? (were you there)
there   when they   nailed him to   the tree? (were you there)
there   when they   laid him in   the tomb? (were you there)

When Jesus Wept

199

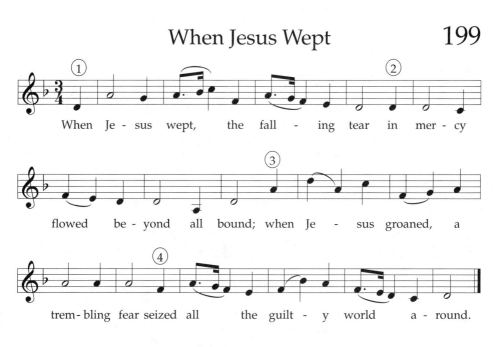

When Je - sus wept, the fall - ing tear in mer - cy

flowed be - yond all bound; when Je - sus groaned, a

trem - bling fear seized all the guilt - y world a - round.

May be sung as a round

WORDS and MUSIC: William Billings, 1770

WHEN JESUS WEPT
LM

♩=88-96

200 What Wondrous Love Is This

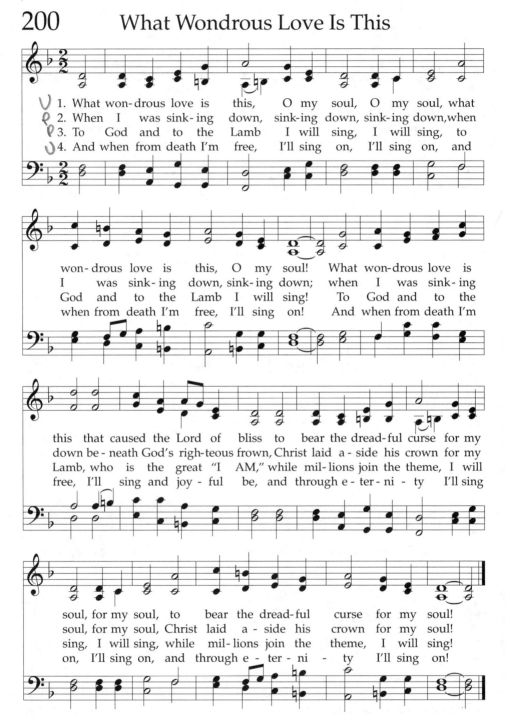

1. What won-drous love is this, O my soul, O my soul, what
2. When I was sink-ing down, sink-ing down, sink-ing down,when
3. To God and to the Lamb I will sing, I will sing, to
4. And when from death I'm free, I'll sing on, I'll sing on, and

won-drous love is this, O my soul! What won-drous love is
I was sink-ing down, sink-ing down; when I was sink-ing
God and to the Lamb I will sing! To God and to the
when from death I'm free, I'll sing on! And when from death I'm

this that caused the Lord of bliss to bear the dread-ful curse for my
down be - neath God's righ-teous frown, Christ laid a - side his crown for my
Lamb, who is the great "I AM," while mil-lions join the theme, I will
free, I'll sing and joy - ful be, and through e - ter - ni - ty I'll sing

soul, for my soul, to bear the dread-ful curse for my soul!
soul, for my soul, Christ laid a - side his crown for my soul!
sing, I will sing, while mil-lions join the theme, I will sing!
on, I'll sing on, and through e - ter - ni - ty I'll sing on!

WORDS and MUSIC: Appalachian folk hymn

WONDROUS LOVE
12 9.12 12 9

Litany of the Passion

The response is sung to the refrain of "Let Us Break Bread Together."

Christ Jesus, in agony in the garden of Olives,
        troubled by sadness and fear,
           comforted by an angel:
  O Lord, have mercy on me.

Christ Jesus, betrayed by Judas' kiss,
        abandoned by your apostles,
           delivered into the hands of sinners:
  O Lord, have mercy on me.

Christ Jesus, accused by false witnesses,
        condemned to die on the cross,
           struck by servants, covered with spittle:
  O Lord, have mercy on me.

Christ Jesus, disowned by Peter, your apostle,
        delivered to Pilate and Herod,
           counted among the likes of Barabbas:
  O Lord, have mercy on me.

Christ Jesus, carrying your cross to Calvary,
        consoled by the daughters of Jerusalem,
           helped by Simon of Cyrene:
  O Lord, have mercy on me.

Christ Jesus, stripped of your clothes,
        given vinegar to drink,
           crucified with thieves:
  O Lord, have mercy on me.

Christ Jesus, insulted on the cross,
        praying for your executioners,
           pardoning the good thief:
  O Lord, have mercy on me.

Christ Jesus, entrusting your mother to your beloved disciple,
        giving up your spirit into the hands of your Father,
           dying for all of us sinners:
  O Lord, have mercy on me.

By your sufferings, Lord, heal the wounds in our hearts.
Let your tears be the source of joy for us, and let your death give us life.
  O Lord, have mercy on me.

—*Lucien Deiss, 20th-century French Catholic liturgist*

202   O Sacred Head, Now Wounded

1. O sa - cred Head, now wound- ed, with grief and shame weighed down;
2. What thou, O Christ, hast suf - fered was all for sin - ners' gain:
3. What lan - guage shall I bor - row to thank thee, dear - est Friend,

now scorn - ful- ly sur - round - ed with thorns, thine on - ly crown;
mine, mine was the trans - gres - sion, but thine the dead - ly pain.
for this thy dy - ing sor - row, thy pit - y with - out end?

how pale thou art with an - guish, with sore a - buse and scorn!
Lo, here I fall, my Sav - ior! 'Tis I de - serve thy place;
O make me thine for - ev - er; and should I faint - ing be,

How does that vis - age lan - guish which once was bright as morn!
look on me with thy fa - vor, and keep me in thy grace.
O, let me nev - er, nev - er out - live my love to thee.

WORDS: Attr. Bernard of Clairvaux (12th century); tr. James W. Alexander, 1830   PASSION CHORALE
MUSIC: Hans L. Hassler, 1601; harm. Johann Sebastian Bach, 1729   76.76D

Here Hangs a Man Discarded   **203**

1. Here hangs a man discarded,
     a scarecrow hoisted high,
   a nonsense pointing nowhere
     to all who hurry by.

2. Can such a clown of sorrows
     still bring a useful word
   where faith and love seem phantoms
     and every hope absurd?

3. Yet here is help and comfort
     to lives by comfort bound
   when drums of dazzling progress
     give strangely hollow sound:

4. Life emptied of all meaning,
     drained out in bleak distress,
   can share in broken silence
     our deepest emptiness;

5. And love that freely entered
     the pit of life's despair
   can name our hidden darkness
     and suffer with us there.

6. Lord, if you now are risen,
     help all who long for light
   to hold the hand of promise
     till faith receives its sight.

WORDS: Brian Wren, 1973, rev. 1995

© 1973, 1995 Hope Publishing Co.

Recommended tune:
PASSION CHORALE
(76.76D)

204 Alas! And Did My Savior Bleed?

1. A - las! And did my Sav - ior bleed? And
2. Was it for crimes that I have done he
3. Well might the sun in dark - ness hide and
4. But drops of grief can ne'er re - pay the

did my Sov - 'reign die? Would he de - vote that
groaned up - on the tree? A - maz - ing pit - y!
shut his glo - ries in, when Christ, the might - y
debt of love I owe: here, Lord, I give my -

sa - cred head for sin - ners such as I!
grace un - known! and love be - yond de - gree! p 195
Mak - er, died for mor - tal crea - tures' sin.
self a - way— 'tis all that I can do!

Refrain

At the cross, at the cross where I first saw the light and the

WORDS: Isaac Watts, 1707; refrain: Ralph E. Hudson, 1885
MUSIC: Attr. Ralph E. Hudson, c. 1885

HUDSON
CM w. refrain

bur-den of my heart rolled a - way— it was there by faith

I re - ceived my sight, and now I am hap-py all the day!

Behold the Love, the Grace of God   205

Behold the love, the grace of God,
displayed in Jesus' precious blood;
my soul's on fire, it yearns to prove
the fullness of redeeming love.

The cross I view—O wondrous love!
My sins expire, my fears remove;
my native enmity is slain
I'm reconciled—I'm born again.

Our God is love—O, leap, my soul!
Let warm hosannas gently roll!
Love gave a Son to save our race,
and Jesus died through sov'reign grace!

What love has done, sing earth around!
Angels prolong the eternal sound!
Lo, Jesus bleeding on the tree!
There, there, the love of God I see!

Barton W. Stone, 19th-century Disciples forebear

Recommended tune:
HAMBURG
(LM)

206 The Blood Will Never Lose Its Power

1. The blood that Je - sus shed for me,
2. It soothes my doubts and calms my fears,

'way back on Cal - va - ry; the
and it dries all my tears; the

blood that gives me strength from day to
blood that gives me strength from day to

day, it will nev - er lose its power.
day, it will nev - er lose its power.

It reach-es to the high - est moun- tain, it flows to the

WORDS and MUSIC: Andraé Crouch, 1962

THE BLOOD
Irr.

© 1966 Manna Music, Inc.

♩=96-100

low - est val - ley. The blood that gives me strength from

day to day, it will nev - er lose its power.

In the Cross of Christ I Glory 207

1. In the cross of Christ I glo - ry, tower-ing o'er the wrecks of time;
2. When the woes of life o'er- take me, hopes de-ceive, and fears an- noy,
3. When the sun of bliss is beam-ing light and love up - on my way,
4. Bane and bless-ing, pain and plea-sure, by the cross are sanc - ti- fied;

all the light of sa - cred sto - ry gath-ers round its head sub- lime.
nev - er shall the cross for - sake me; lo! it glows with peace and joy.
from the cross the ra - diance stream-ing adds new lus - ter to the day.
peace is there, that knows no mea- sure, joys that through all time a - bide.

WORDS: John Bowring, 1825
MUSIC: Ithamar Conkey, 1849

RATHBUN
87.87

208 He Never Said a Mumbalin' Word

1. He nev - er said a mum - ba - lin' word, he
2. I know it was the blood, I
3. He suf - fered, bled, and died, he
(O - yeh)

nev - er said a mum - ba - lin' word, he
know it was the blood, I
suf - fered, bled, and died, he
(O - yeh)

nev - er said a mum - ba - lin' word for me. (for me.) One
know it was the blood me. me. (shed for me.)
suf - fered, bled, and died for me. (died for me.)

day when I was lost Christ died up - on the cross; I
(O - yeh) (O - yeh)

WORDS: African-American spiritual
MUSIC: African-American spiritual; arr. Floyd Knight, Jr.

MUMBALIN' WORD
Irr.

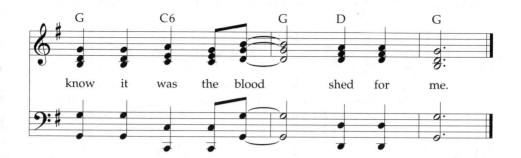

know it was the blood shed for me.

The Wondrous Cross: a Litany 209

Cantor: "When I survey the wondrous cross
on which the Prince of glory died,
my richest gain I count but loss,
and pour contempt on all my pride."

Leader: God be praised for the wondrous cross, the tree of life,

Left: **which bears upon itself the scars and wounds of the world,**

Right: **yet heals the sick, brings hope to the desperate,
and comforts the oppressed.**

Left: **God be praised for the cross, which guides the lost,
feeds the hungry, and shelters the poor;**

Right: **inspires the anxious, illumines the wise,
and challenges the fearless;**

Unison: **saves the condemned, and meets the need
of every age and every land.**

Leader: God forbid that we should glory,
except in the cross of Jesus Christ our Lord.

Unison: **"When I survey the wondrous cross
on which the Prince of glory died,
my richest gain I count but loss,
and pour contempt on all my pride."**

—Inspired by a sermon of John Mbiti, Uganda, 1972

210 Ah, Holy Jesus, How Hast Thou Offended

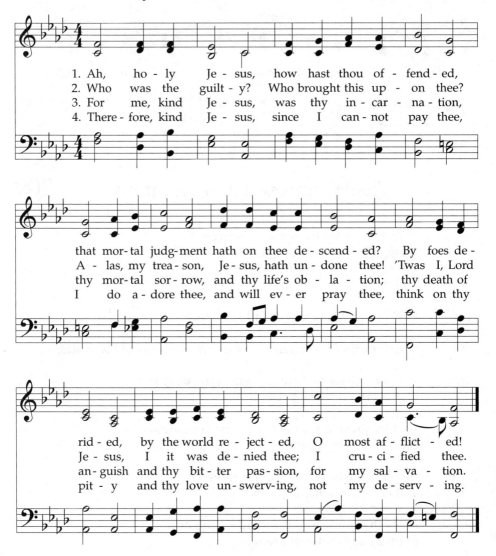

1. Ah, ho-ly Je-sus, how hast thou of-fend-ed,
2. Who was the guilt-y? Who brought this up-on thee?
3. For me, kind Je-sus, was thy in-car-na-tion,
4. There-fore, kind Je-sus, since I can-not pay thee,

that mor-tal judg-ment hath on thee de-scend-ed? By foes de-
A-las, my trea-son, Je-sus, hath un-done thee! 'Twas I, Lord
thy mor-tal sor-row, and thy life's ob-la-tion; thy death of
I do a-dore thee, and will ev-er pray thee, think on thy

rid-ed, by the world re-ject-ed, O most af-flict-ed!
Je-sus, I it was de-nied thee; I cru-ci-fied thee.
an-guish and thy bit-ter pas-sion, for my sal-va-tion.
pit-y and thy love un-swerv-ing, not my de-serv-ing.

WORDS: Johann Heerman, 1630; tr. Robert S. Bridges, 1899, alt.
MUSIC: Johann Crüger, 1640

HERZLIEBSTER JESU
11 11 11.5

Jesus Walked This Lonesome Valley 211

1. Je - sus walked this lone-some val - ley, he had to walk it by him - self; O, no-bod-y else could walk it for him, he had to walk it by him - self.
2. We must walk this lone-some val - ley, we have to walk it by our-selves; O, no-bod-y else can walk it for us, we have to walk it by our - selves.
3. You must go and stand your tri - al, you have to stand it by your-self, O, no-bod-y else can stand it for you, you have to stand it by your - self.

WORDS: American spiritual
MUSIC: American spiritual; arr. Bill Thomas, 1994

LONESOME VALLEY
88.10 8

212

In Suff'ring Love

1. In suff - 'ring love the thread of life is
2. There is a rock, a place se - cure with -
3. In love's deep womb our fears are held; there
4. Christ, to our hearts your joy com - mit, in -
5. In suff - 'ring love our God comes now, hope's

1. wov - en through our care, for God is with us:
2. in the storm's cold blast; con - cealed with - in the
3. God's rich tears are sown and bring to birth, in
4. to our hands your pain; so send us out to
5. vi - sion born in gloom; with tears and laugh - ter

1. not a - lone our pain and toil we bear.
2. suff - 'ring night God's cov - e - nant stands fast.
3. hope new - born, the strength to jour - ney on.
4. touch the world with bless - ings in your name.
5. shared and blessed the des - ert yet will bloom.

WORDS: Robert M. Johns, 1983
MUSIC: William Gardiner's *Sacred Melodies*, 1815

BELMONT
CM

Who Would Ever Have Believed It? 213

1. Who would ev - er have be - lieved it? Who could
2. We de - spised him, we dis - owned him, though he
3. Though our sins let him be wound - ed, though our
4. We, like sheep de - spite our wis - dom, all had
5. Who would ev - er have be - lieved it? Who could

1. ev - er have con - ceived it? Who dared trace God's hand be -
2. clear - ly hurt and suf - fered: we, be - liev - ing he was
3. cruel - ty left him beat - en, yet, through how and why he
4. wan - dered from God's pur - pose; and our due in pain and
5. ev - er have con - ceived it? Who dared trace God's hand be -

1. hind it when a ser - vant came a - mong us?
2. worth - less, nev - er looked on him with fa - vor.
3. suf - fered, God re - vealed our hope of heal - ing.
4. an - ger God let fall on one a - mong us.
5. hind it when a ser - vant came a - mong us?

WORDS: Iona Community, 1988
MUSIC: Swedish melody

TRYGGARE KAN INGEN VARA
LM

Words © 1988 Iona Community; used by permission of GIA Publications, Inc.

♩=76-80

214   Rock of Ages, Cleft for Me

1. Rock of A - ges, cleft for me, let me hide my-self in thee; let the wa - ter and the blood, from thy wound - ed side which flowed, be of sin the dou - ble cure; save from wrath and make me pure.

2. Not the la - bors of my hands can ful - fill thy law's de-mands; could my zeal no res - pite know, could my tears for - ev - er flow, all for sin could not a - tone; thou must save, and thou a - lone.

3. Noth - ing in my hand I bring, sim - ply to the cross I cling; na - ked, come to thee for dress; help - less, look to thee for grace; foul, I to the foun - tain fly; wash me, Sav - ior, or I die.

4. While I draw this fleet - ing breath, when mine eyes shall close in death, when I soar to worlds un - known, see thee on thy judg-ment throne, Rock of A - ges, cleft for me, let me hide my - self in thee.

WORDS: Augustus M. Toplady, 1776
MUSIC: Thomas Hastings, 1830

TOPLADY
77.77.77

Come, Ye Faithful, Raise the Strain 215

1. Come, ye faith-ful, raise the strain of tri-um-phant glad-ness;
2. 'Tis the spring of souls to-day; Christ hath burst his pris-on,
3. Now the bright-est sea-son dawns with the day of splen-dor,

God hath brought forth Is - ra - el in - to joy from sad-ness;
and from three days' sleep in death as a sun hath ris-en;
now the roy - al feast of feasts comes its joy to ren-der;

loosed from Phar-aoh's bit-ter yoke Ja - cob's sons and daugh-ters,
all the win - ter of our sins, long and bleak, is fly - ing
comes to glad Je - ru - sa - lem, who with true af - fec - tion

led them with un - moist-ened foot through the Red Sea wa - ters.
from his light, to whom we give laud and praise un - dy - ing.
wel-comes in un - wea-ried strains Je - sus' res - ur - rec - tion.

WORDS: John of Damascus (8th century); tr. John Mason Neale, 1859
MUSIC: Arthur S. Sullivan, 1872

ST. KEVIN
76.76D

216 Christ the Lord Is Risen Today

Descant

4. Soar we now where Christ has led, A - le - lu - ia!

1. Christ the Lord is risen to - day,
2. Lives a - gain our glo - rious King,
3. Love's re - deem - ing work is done,
4. Soar we now where Christ has led,

Al - le - lu - ia!

Fol - low - ing our Head, A - le - lu - ia!

All cre - a - tion, join to say,
Where, O death, is now your sting?
Fought the fight, the bat - tle won,
Fol - lowing our ex - alt - ed Head,

Al - le - lu - ia!

A - le - lu - ia! A-le-lu - ia! A-le - lu - ia!

Raise your joys and tri - umphs high,
Je - sus died, our souls to save,
Death in vain for - bids him rise,
Made like him, like him we rise,

Al - le - lu - ia!

WORDS: Charles Wesley, 1739, alt.
MUSIC: *Lyra Davidica*, 1708; desc. Charles H. Webb

EASTER HYMN
77.77 w. alleluias

Ours the cross, the grave, the skies, A - le - lu - ia!

Sing, O heavens, and earth re - ply,
Where your vic - to - ry, O grave?
Christ has op - ened par - a - dise.
Ours the cross, the grave, the skies,

Al - le - lu - ia!

The Easter Affirmations 217

RESPONSE

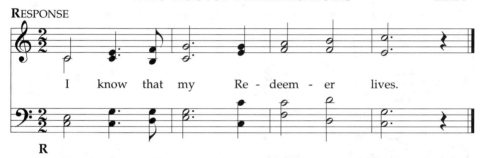

I know that my Re - deem - er lives.

R

Clean out the old yeast so that you may be a new batch,
    as you really are unleavened.
For our paschal lamb, Christ, has been sacrificed.
Therefore, let us celebrate the festival,
        not with the old yeast, the yeast of malice and evil,
        but with the unleavened bread of sincerity and truth.   R

We know that Christ, being raised from the dead,
    will never die again;
    death no longer has dominion over him.
The death he died, he died to sin, once for all;
    but the life he lives, he lives to God.
So you also must consider yourselves dead to sin
        and alive to God in Christ Jesus.   R

But in fact Christ has been raised from the dead,
    the first fruits of those who have died.
For since death came through a human being,
        the resurrection of the dead
        has also come through a human being;
    for as all die in Adam,
        so all will be made alive in Christ.   R

WORDS: 1 Cor. 5:7–8; Romans 6:9–11; 1 Cor. 15:20–22; Response, Job 19:25a
MUSIC: *Psalmodia Evangelica*, 1789

218 Thine Is the Glory

1. Thine is the glo - ry, ris - en, con - quering Son,
2. Lo! Je - sus meets us, ris - en from the tomb;
3. No more we doubt thee, glo - rious Prince of life!

end - less is the vic - tory thou o'er death hast won.
lov - ing - ly he greets us, scat - ters fear and gloom;
Life is nought with - out thee; aid us in our strife;

An - gels in bright rai - ment rolled the stone a - way,
let the church with glad - ness hymns of tri - umph sing,
make us more than con - querors, through thy death - less love.

kept the fold - ed grave-clothes where thy bod - y lay.
for our Lord now liv - eth; death hath lost its sting.
Bring us safe through Jor - dan to thy home a - bove.

WORDS: Edmond L. Budry, 1904; tr. R. Birch Hoyle, 1923
MUSIC: George Frederick Handel, 1746

MACCABEUS
55.65.65.65 w. refrain

Tr. and harm. © The World Student Christian Federation

Thine is the glo - ry, ris - en, con-quering Son,

end - less is the vic - tory thou o'er death hast won.

Christ Present in Worship 219

"Where two or three are gathered in my name," declared Jesus,
    "there am I in the midst of them."
Whenever baptismal waters cover a sincere believer
    who emerges to the risen life,
    the risen Lord is present.
Whenever preaching faithfully proclaims the word,
    the living Word is there.
Whenever prayer rises from a trusting heart,
    the Hearer of prayer is at hand.
Whenever a devoted offering is made to God,
    the true Offering of God is present.
Whenever the bread is broken in faith,
    the living Bread, come down from heaven, is there.

—G. Edwin Osborn, 20th-century Disciples scholar

220 O Sons and Daughters, Sing Your Praise

1,7. O sons and daugh - ters, sing your praise
2. When Mag - da - lene and Sa - lo - me
3. An an - gel greet - ed them and said,
4. A - mong dis - ci - ples Christ ap - peared.
5. "Come, Thom - as, see my hands and side.
6. "How blest are those who do not see

1,7. on this most ho - ly day of days.
2. and Mar - y went where Je - sus lay
3. "The Christ is ris - en from the dead.
4. "My peace be with you," was his word,
5. I am the one they cru - ci - fied."
6. yet place their faith and trust in me.

1,7. For Christ from death to life is raised.
2. they found the stone was rolled a - way.
3. To Gal - i - lee he goes a - head."
4. but Thom - as doubt - ed when he heard.
5. "My God, my Sav - ior!" Thom - as cried.
6. They shall have life e - ter - nal - ly."

WORDS: Jean Tisserand (15th century); tr. Ruth Duck, 1993
MUSIC: French carol (15th century)

O FILII ET FILIAE
888 w. alleluias

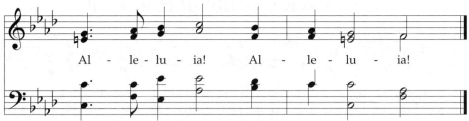

1 Corinthians 15:53–57

The Strife Is O'er

221

1. The strife is o'er, the bat - tle done,
2. The powers of death have done their worst,
3. The three sad days are quick - ly sped,
4. Lord, by your wounds on Cal - va - ry

the vic - to - ry of life is won; the song of
but Christ their le - gions has dis - persed: let shouts of
Christ ris - es glo - rious from the dead: all glo - ry
from death's dread sting your ser - vants free, that we may

tri - umph has be - gun. Al - le - lu - ia!
ho - ly joy out - burst. Al - le - lu - ia!
to our ris - en Head! Al - le - lu - ia!
live e - ter - nal - ly. Al - le - lu - ia!

WORDS: Latin, 1695; tr. Francis Pott, 1861
MUSIC: Giovanni P. da Palestrina, 1591; adapt. William Henry Monk, 1861

VICTORY
888 w. alleluia

222 Christ Is Risen! Shout Hosanna!

1. Christ is ris - en! Shout ho - san - na! Cel - e - brate this day of days.
2. Christ is ris - en! Raise your spir - its from the cav - erns of des - pair.
3. Christ is ris - en! Earth and heav - en nev - er - more shall be the same.

Christ is ris - en! Hush in won - der; all cre - a - tion is a - mazed.
Walk with glad - ness in the morn - ing. See what love can do and dare.
Break the bread of new cre - a - tion where the world is still in pain.

In the des - ert all - sur - round - ing, see, a spread - ing tree has grown.
Drink the wine of res - ur - rec - tion, not a ser - vant, but a friend;
Tell its grim, de - mon - ic cho - rus: "Christ is ris - en! Get you gone!"

Heal - ing leaves of grace a - bound - ing bring a taste of love un - known.
Je - sus is our strong com - pan - ion. Joy and peace shall nev - er end.
God the first and last is with us. Sing Ho - san - na ev - ery - one!

WORDS: Brian Wren, 1984
MUSIC: Polish carol; arr. Edith M. G. Reed, 1926; harm. Austin C. Lovelace, 1964

W ZLOBIE LEZY
447.447D

♩=88-96

Woman, Weeping in the Garden   223

1. Wom - an, weep - ing in the gar - den, who has pushed the stone a - side? Who has tak - en Je - sus' bod - y; Je - sus Christ, the cru - ci - fied?
2. Wom - an, wait - ing in the gar - den, af - ter men have come and gone; af - ter an - gels give their wit - ness, si - lent - ly you watch the dawn.
3. Wom - an, walk - ing in the gar - den, Je - sus takes you by sur - prise; when the gar - dener calls you, "Ma - ry!" faith and joy meet in your eyes.
4. Wom - an, weep - ing in the gar - den, weep for joy, for you have seen Je - sus, the Mes - si - ah, ris - en; Christ, of whom the proph - ets dream.
5. Wom - an, danc - ing from the gar - den, find the oth - ers and pro - claim Christ is ris - en as he prom - ised; tell the world he knew your name!

WORDS and MUSIC: Dan Damon, 1991

KAKIS
87.87

♩=88-96

224 Christ Arose!

1. Low   in the grave he lay, Je-sus my Sav-ior, wait-ing the com-ing day,
2. Vain - ly they watch his bed, Je-sus my Sav-ior; vain- ly they seal the dead,
3. Death can-not keep its prey, Je-sus my Sav-ior;   he tore the bars a - way,

Refrain

Je- sus my Lord!   Up from the grave he a - rose,   with a
                                                      (he a-rose)

might- y tri-umph o'er his foes;   he a-rose a vic-tor from the
                    (o'er his foes)

dark do-main, and he lives for - ev - er, with his saints to reign. He a-

rose!   He a - rose!   Hal - le - lu - jah! Christ a - rose!
(he a-rose)   (he a-rose)

WORDS and MUSIC: Robert Lowry, 1874

CHRIST AROSE
65.64 w. refrain

I Know That My Redeemer Liveth   225

1. I know that my Re-deem-er liv - eth, and on the earth   a-gain shall
2. I know his prom-ise nev-er fail - eth, the word he speaks,   it can-not
3. I know my man-sion he pre-par - eth, that where he is   there I may

stand; I know   e - ter - nal life he giv - eth, that grace and
die; tho' cru - el death my flesh as-sail - eth, yet I shall
be; O won - drous tho't, for me he car - eth, and he at

pow'r   are in his hand.   I know, I know   that Je-sus liv-eth,
see   him by and by.   I know, I know
last   will come for me.

and on the earth   a-gain shall stand;   I know, I know
and on the earth   I know, I know

that life he giv - eth, that grace and pow'r   are in his hand.
                      that grace and pow'r

WORDS: Jessie Brown Pounds, 1893   HANNAH
MUSIC: James H. Fillmore, 1893   98.98 w. refrain

226 He Lives!

1. I serve a ris-en Sav-ior, he's in the world to-day;
2. In all the world a-round me I see his lov-ing care,
3. Re-joice, re-joice, O Chris-tian, lift up your voice and sing

I know that he is liv-ing, what-ev-er oth-ers say.
and though my heart grows wea-ry, I nev-er will de-spair.
e-ter-nal hal-le-lu-jahs to Je-sus Christ the King!

I see his hand of mer-cy, I hear his voice of cheer,
I know that he is lead-ing through all the storm-y blast;
The hope of all who seek him, the help of all who find;

and just the time I need him, he's al-ways near.
the day of his ap-pear-ing will come at last.
none oth-er is so lov-ing, so good and kind.

WORDS and MUSIC: Alfred H. Ackley, 1933

ACKLEY
76.76.76.74 w. refrain

227   In the Garden

1. I come to the gar-den a-lone, while the dew is
2. He speaks, and the sound of his voice is so sweet the
3. I'd stay in the gar-den with him though the night a-

still on the ros-es; and the voice I hear, fall-ing on my ear,
birds hush their sing-ing, and the mel-o-dy that he gave to me
round me be fall-ing, but he bids me go; through the voice of woe

Refrain

the Son of God dis-clos - es.
with - in my heart is ring - ing.   And he walks with me, and he
his voice to me is call - ing.

talks with me, and he tells me I am his own, and the

WORDS and MUSIC: C. Austin Miles, 1913

GARDEN
89.557 w. refrain

joy we share, as we tar-ry there, none oth-er has ev-er known.

The Day of Resurrection!   228

1. The day of resurrection! Earth, tell it out abroad;
   the Passover of gladness, the Passover of God.
   From death to life eternal, from sin's dominion free,
   our Christ has brought us over with hymns of victory.

2. Our hearts be pure from evil, that we may see aright
   the Lord in rays eternal of resurrection light;
   and, listening to his accents, may hear so calm and plain
   the voice of Christ, and hearing, may raise the victor strain.

3. Now let the heavens be joyful! Let earth its song begin!
   The world resound in triumph, and all that is therein;
   let all things seen and unseen their notes of gladness blend;
   for Christ the Lord has risen, our joy that has no end.

WORDS: John of Damascus (8th century); tr. John Mason Neale, 1862, alt.

Recommended tune:
LANCASHIRE
(76.76D)

229 That Easter Day with Joy Was Bright

1. That Eas - ter day with joy was bright,
2. His ris - en flesh with ra - diance glowed;
3. O Je - sus, strong in gen - tle - ness,
4. Come, ris - en Christ, with us a - bide

the sun shone out with fair - er light,
his wound - ed hands and feet he showed
come now your - self our hearts pos - sess,
in this our joy - ful Eas - ter - tide;

when, to their long - ing eyes re - stored,
those scars their sol - emn wit - ness gave
that we may give you all our days
your own re - deemed for ev - er shield

the glad a - pos - tles saw their Lord.
that Christ was ris - en from the grave.
the trib - ute of our grate - ful praise.
from ev - 'ry weap - on death can wield.

WORDS: Latin hymn (5th century); tr. John Mason Neale, 1852, alt.
MUSIC: Trier manuscript (15th century); adapt. Michael Praetorius, 1609;
  harm. George R. Woodward, 1904

PUER NOBIS NASCITUR
LM

Now the Green Blade Rises

230

1. Now the green blade ris - es from the bur - ied grain,
2. In the grave they laid the love by ha - tred slain,
3. Christ came forth at Eas - ter, like the ris - en grain,
4. When our hearts are win - try, griev - ing, or in pain,

wheat that in dark earth man - y days has lain;
think - ing that Je - sus would not wake a - gain,
who that for three days in the grave had lain;
your touch can call us back to life a - gain,

love lives a - gain, that with the dead has been;
laid in the earth like grain that sleeps un - seen;
raised from the dead, the ris - en Christ is seen;
fields of our hearts that dead and bare have been;

Love is come a - gain like wheat a - ris - ing green.

WORDS: John M. C. Crum, 1928
MUSIC: French carol

Words © 1928 Oxford University Press

NOËL NOUVELET
11 10.10 11

♩=72-80

231 Sing of One Who Walks Beside Us

1. Sing of one who walks beside us and this day is
living still, one who now is clos-er to us
than the thoughts our hearts dis-till, Christ who once up-
on a hill-top, raised a-gainst the power of sin,

2. We have walked with him as strang-ers through the jour-ney
of the day, and have told him of the vi-o-lence
that has swept our hope a-way. He has of-fered
words of com-fort, words of en-er-gy and light.

3. Ris-en one, stay with us, raise us, once a-gain the
night is near. Dine with us and share your wis-dom,
free our hearts from ev-'ry fear. In the calm of
each new eve-ning, in the fresh-ness of each dawn,

WORDS: Ralph Wright, 1989, alt.
MUSIC: Attr. William Moore, 1825; harm. Charles Anders, 1969, alt.

HOLY MANNA
87.87D

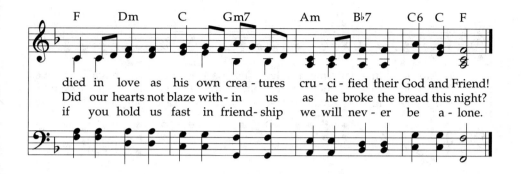

died in love as his own crea - tures   cru - ci - fied their God and Friend!
Did our hearts not blaze with- in   us   as he broke the bread this night?
if   you hold us fast in friend- ship   we will nev - er   be   a - lone.

In the Great Quiet of God   232

In the great quiet of God,
    my troubles are but pebbles on the road,
My joys are like the everlasting hills.
So it is when I step through the gate of prayer
    from time into eternity.
When I am in the consciousness of God,
    my brothers and sisters are not far-off and forgotten,
    but close and strangely dear.
They shine, as if a light were glowing within them.
Even those who frown on me
    and love me not
    seem part of the great scheme of God.

—Walter Rauschenbusch, 20th-century pioneer of Social Gospel movement

233   Alleluia! Sing to Jesus

1. Al - le - lu - ia! Sing to Je - sus, ris - en now to reign in love.
2. Al - le - lu - ia! not as or - phans we are left in sor - row now.
3. Al - le - lu - ia! Bread of Heav - en, be on earth our food and stay.

Al - le - lu - ia! Praise the Sav - ior; with the mul - ti - tudes a - bove.
Al - le - lu - ia! Christ is near us, faith be - lieves, nor ques - tions how.
Al - le - lu - ia! here the sin - ful flee to you from day to day.

There the songs of saints and mar - tyrs thun - der like a might - y flood,
Though the cloud from sight re - ceived him when the for - ty days were o'er,
In - ter - ces - sor, friend of sin - ners, earth's re - deem - er, plead for me,

"Je - sus out of ev - ery na - tion has re - deemed us by his blood."
shall our hearts for - get the prom - ise, "I am with you ev - er - more"?
where the songs of all the sin - less sweep a - cross the crys - tal sea.

WORDS: William C. Dix, 1866, alt.   HYFRYDOL
MUSIC: Rowland H. Prichard, 1830   87.87D

Crown Him with Many Crowns 234

1. Crown him with man - y crowns, the Lamb up - on his throne.
2. Crown him the Lord of life, who tri-umphed o'er the grave,
3. Crown him the Lord of peace, whose power a scep - ter sways
4. Crown him the Lord of love; be - hold his hands and side,

Hark! how the heaven-ly an - them drowns all mu - sic but its own.
and rose vic - to - rious in the strife for those he came to save;
from pole to pole, that wars may cease, and all be prayer and praise.
those wounds, yet vis - i - ble a - bove, in beau - ty glo - ri - fied.

A - wake, my soul, and sing of him who died for thee,
his glo - ries now we sing who died, and rose on high,
His reign shall know no end, and round his pierc - ed feet
All hail, Re - deem - er, hail! For thou hast died for me;

and hail him as thy match-less King through all e - ter - ni - ty.
who died, e - ter-nal life to bring, and lives that death may die.
fair flowers of par - a - dise ex - tend their fra-grance ev - er sweet.
thy praise and glo-ry shall not fail through-out e - ter - ni - ty.

WORDS: Matthew Bridges, 1851, and Godfrey Thring, 1874
MUSIC: George J. Elvey, 1868

DIADEMATA
SMD

GOD Present in the Holy Spirit

235   Spirit Praise

Holy Spirit,
    making life alive,
        moving in all things,
            root of all created being,
        cleansing the cosmos of every impurity,
    effacing guilt,
anointing wounds.
    You are lustrous and praiseworthy life,
        you waken and re-awaken everything that is.

—Hildegard of Bingen, 12th-century Benedictine abbess

Wind Who Makes All Winds That Blow 236

1. Wind who makes all winds that blow—gusts that bend the sap-lings low,
2. Fire who fuels all fires that burn— suns a-round which plan-ets turn,
3. Ho - ly Spir- it, Wind and Flame, move with-in our mor - tal frame.

gales that heave the sea in waves, stir-rings in the mind's deep caves—
bea - cons mark-ing reefs and shoals, shin-ing truth to guide our souls—
Make our hearts an al - tar pyre, kin-dle them with your own fire.

aim your breath with stead- y power on your church this day, this hour.
come to us as once you came: burst in tongues of sa - cred flame!
Breathe and blow up - on that blaze till our lives, our deeds and ways,

Raise, re - new the life we've lost, Spir - it God of Pen - te - cost.
Light and Pow- er, Might and Strength, fill your church, its breadth and length.
speak that tongue which ev- ery land by your grace shall un - der - stand.

WORDS: Thomas H. Troeger, 1983   ABERYSTWYTH
MUSIC: Joseph Parry, 1879   77.77D

237 On Pentecost They Gathered

Descant

4. O Spir - it, sent from heav-en on that day long a - go,

1. On Pen - te - cost they gath - ered quite ear-ly in the day,
2. The peo - ple all a - round them were star-tled and a - mazed
3. God pours the Ho - ly Spir - it on all who would be-lieve,
4. O Spir-it, sent from heav - en on that day long a - go,

re - kin - dle faith a - mong us in all life's ebb and flow.

a band of Christ's dis - ci - ples, to wor - ship, sing, and pray.
to un - der-stand their lan - guage, as Christ the Lord they praised.
on wom-en, men, and chil - dren who would God's grace re - ceive.
re - kin - dle faith a - mong us in all life's ebb and flow.

Give ears to lis - ten and tongues a - flame with praise,

A might-y wind came blow-ing, filled all the swirl-ing air,
What u - ni - ver- sal mes-sage, what great good news was here?
That Spir-it knows no lim - it, be - stow-ing life and power.
O give us ears to lis - ten and tongues a - flame with praise,

WORDS: Jane Parker Huber, 1981
MUSIC: *Gesangbuch*, Meiningen, 1693; harm. Felix Mendelssohn, 1847;
desc. O. I. Cricket Harrison, 1994

MUNICH
76.76D

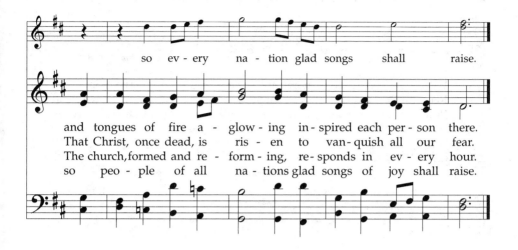

so ev - ery na - tion glad songs shall raise.

and tongues of fire a - glow - ing in - spired each per - son there.
That Christ, once dead, is ris - en to van - quish all our fear.
The church, formed and re - form - ing, re - sponds in ev - ery hour.
so peo - ple of all na - tions glad songs of joy shall raise.

I Want to Be Counted in the Upper Room 238

I want to be counted among those
who are in the upper room waiting,
contrite of heart, singing together
and unanimous in prayer.

I want to be counted among those
who are ardently desiring
that on this day of Pentecost
(friends, I hope that you are also yearning),
that the Burning Flame of the Spirit of God
descend upon you, upon me...that both our hearts
be entirely burned and thus purified:

Free from anger, hatred and passion;
free from ill will, jealousy and envy;
free from transgression, criticism and gossip;
free from malice, animosity and grudges...

Lord, here are my knees, my heart and my tears.
So, here I will wait that with your Holy Spirit
you may light my life.

—*Julian Ibarra Zapata, 20th-century Mexican Disciples pastor*

239 Wake, the Dawn Is Now Full Rising

Unison

1. Wake, the dawn is now full ris - ing, by the Spir - it
2. Rise and stand in noon's high glo - ry, Christ is here in
3. Rest while eve - ning shad - ows length - en; God's own church is

we are roused; see - ing, touch - ing, hear - ing feel - ing,
new ar - ray, crowns of fire our count'-nance bright - en;
now full born. Know the peace by Spir - it giv - en,

Christ's new life in us is housed. Al - le - lu - ia!
winds of hope re - fresh our way. Al - le - lu - ia!
share the hush of pil - grims worn. Al - le - lu - ia!

Praise the Spir - it who for earth a church de - signs.
Raise the sing - ing, now one tongue God's love em - ploys.
God, we won - der at your great - ness still un - told.

WORDS: Jim Miller, 1992
MUSIC: William Walker's *Southern Harmony*, 1835;
   harm. *Lutheran Book of Worship*, 1978

JEFFERSON
87.87D

Alt. tune: HYMN TO JOY

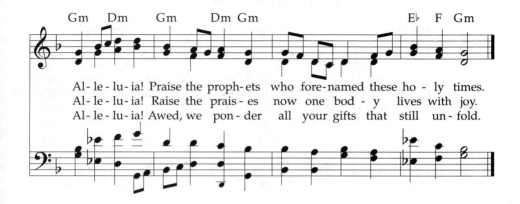

Al- le - lu- ia! Praise the proph- ets who fore-named these ho - ly times.
Al- le - lu- ia! Raise the prais- es now one bod - y lives with joy.
Al- le - lu- ia! Awed, we pon- der all your gifts that still un - fold.

Pentecost Prayer 240

Spirit of God, we have gathered together in this place, to pray,
  and to make ourselves ready for your coming.

Give us faith,
  that when you come like the wind,
  though we do not see you,
  yet we may hear what you are saying to us
  and discern your movement.

Give us courage, that we may not fear the tongues of flame:
  let all that is unworthy, impure, and sinful be burned from our lives.
  May we know that it is love that burns so brightly
  and love that strips away our sin.

Give us an open mind, Lord,
that the truth you bring may make its home with us:
  truth to set us free
  truth to guide us and inform us
  truth to lead us in the way of your will.

Give us an open heart, Lord
  that we may seek all people for your realm,
  and set no limits to the proclaiming of your word.

Holy Spirit, with the whole church we wait for you
in every place and in every generation.
  Come, wind.
  Come, fire.
  Come, truth.
  Come, love.
  In Jesus' name. Amen.

—Michael J. Walker, 20th-century English Baptist minister

241 Holy Spirit, Truth Divine

1. Ho - ly Spir - it, Truth di - vine, dawn up-
2. Ho - ly Spir - it, Love di - vine, glow with-
3. Ho - ly Spir - it, Pow'r di - vine, fill and
4. Ho - ly Spir - it, Peace di - vine, still this
5. Ho - ly Spir - it, Joy di - vine, glad - den

1. on this soul of mine. Voice of God, and
2. in this heart of mine. Kin - dle ev - 'ry
3. nerve this will of mine. Bold - ly may I
4. rest - less heart of mine. Speak to calm this
5. now this heart of mine. In the de - sert

1. in - ward Light, wake my spir - it, clear my sight.
2. high de - sire, pur - i - fy me with your fire.
3. al - ways live, brave - ly serve and glad - ly give.
4. toss - ing sea, grant me your tran - quil - i - ty.
5. ways I sing, spring, O liv - ing Wa - ter, spring!

WORDS: Samuel Longfellow, 1864
MUSIC: Louis M. Gottschalk, 1854; arr. Edwin P. Parker, c. 1888

MERCY
77.77

Shaping Spirit, Move Among Us   242

Descant for last verse

Ah_____   Ah,__ ah_____

Unison

1. Shap-ing spir-it, move a-mong us, liv-ing lead-er, be our friend;
2. En-er-gy of new cre-a-tion, work like yeast with-in the soul;
3. Man-y are the ways you seek us, great the joy when each is found.

Ah_____ is ho-ly ground.

source of our mys-te-rious be-ing, greet us at our jour-ney's end.
hu-man sav-ior, heav'n-ly ar-tist, in your ser-vice make us whole.
Once your gift of faith ig-nites it all the world is ho-ly ground.

WORDS: Elizabeth Cosnett, 1992
MUSIC: Ian Sharp, 1992

MEADWAY
87.87

Words © 1992 Elizabeth Cosnett; music © 1992 Ian Sharp

♩=100-108

Holy Spirit, Come   243

O God, the Holy Spirit, come to us, and among us:
    come as the wind, and cleanse us;
    come as the fire, and burn;
    come as the dew, and refresh.
Convict, convert, and consecrate many hearts and lives
    to our great good and your greater glory.

—Anonymous

244 Loving Spirit

1,5. Lov - ing Spir - it, lov - ing Spir - it, you have cho - sen me to be—
2. Like a moth - er you en - fold me, hold my life with - in your own,
3. Like a fa - ther you pro - tect me, teach me the dis - cern - ing eye,
4. Friend and lov - er, in your close - ness I am known and held and blessed:

you have drawn me to your won - der, you have set your sign on me.
feed me with your ver - y bod - y, form me of your flesh and bone.
hoist me up up - on your shoul - der, let me see the world from high.
in your prom - ise is my com - fort, in your pres - ence I may rest.

WORDS: Shirley Erena Murray, 1987
MUSIC: David Gregof Corner, 1631; arr. William Smith Rockstro (19th century)

OMNI DIE
87.87

Words © 1987 The Hymn Society, used by permission of Hope Publishing Co.

♩=64-68

245 Like the Murmur of the Dove's Song

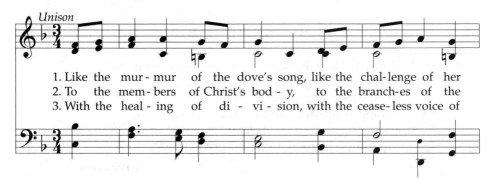

Unison

1. Like the mur - mur of the dove's song, like the chal - lenge of her
2. To the mem - bers of Christ's bod - y, to the branch - es of the
3. With the heal - ing of di - vi - sion, with the cease - less voice of

WORDS: Carl P. Daw, Jr., 1981
MUSIC: Peter Cutts, 1968

BRIDEGROOM
87.87.6

Words © 1982, music © 1969, Hope Publishing Co.

♩=86-90

flight, like the vig - or of the wind's rush, like the
Vine, to the church in faith as - sem - bled, to our
prayer, with the power to love and wit - ness, with the

new flame's ea- ger might: come, Ho - ly Spir - it, come.
midst as gift and sign: come, Ho - ly Spir - it, come.
peace be- yond com - pare: come, Ho - ly Spir - it, come.

Litany of the Spirit 246

(As a response, sing the last phrase of "Like the Murmur of the Dove's Song")

From out of our silent depths into visible corporate acts,
Come, Holy Spirit, come!

Gathering the fragments of our church into a living icon
of the redeeming, reconciling, prophetic Christ,
Come, Holy Spirit, come!

Bonding together the dissenter, the affirmer and the questor,
Come, Holy Spirit, come!

Radiating the power and the light of our rainbow-hued people,
Come, Holy Spirit, come!

Revealing your presence in and among each perceived
or self-defined minority, wounded, lonely or angry,
Come, Holy Spirit, come!

Gathering the fragments of our church into dynamic communities of faith
engaged in prophetic, redemptive and reconciling ministries of love,
Come, Holy Spirit, come!

—Harold Johnson, 20th-century Disciples church executive

247 Wind upon the Waters

1. Wind up-on the wa - ters, voice up-on the deep, rouse your sons and daugh - ters, wake us from our sleep, breath-ing life in - to all
2. Show - ers from the hea - vens, wa - ter from the earth, gift so whol - ly giv - en, source of ev - 'ry birth; joy of ev - 'ry liv - ing
3. Rock and hill and gar - den, wood and des - ert sand, prai - rie, field and mead - ow, shaped by Love's own hand, love that fills the world a -
4. Blaz - ing light of won - der, flame that pierc - es night, burst the dark a - sun - der, fill our souls with light. Lord of glo - ry, fill the
5. Wind up - on the wa - ters, rains up - on the sand, grace your sons and daugh - ters, new - born by your hand. Come, O Spir - it, and re -

Cue notes = optional 2nd part

WORDS and MUSIC: Marty Haugen, 1986

© 1986 GIA Publications, Inc.

WIND UPON THE WATERS
65.65.77.11

♩=96-104

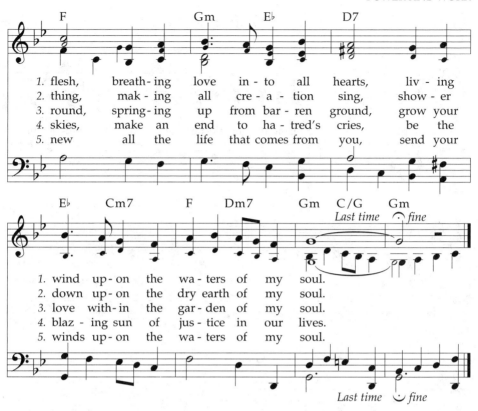

1. flesh, breath-ing love in-to all hearts, liv-ing
2. thing, mak-ing all cre-a-tion sing, show-er
3. round, spring-ing up from bar-ren ground, grow your
4. skies, make an end to ha-tred's cries, be the
5. new all the life that comes from you, send your

Last time ⌢ *fine*

1. wind up-on the wa-ters of my soul.
2. down up-on the dry earth of my soul.
3. love with-in the gar-den of my soul.
4. blaz-ing sun of jus-tice in our lives.
5. winds up-on the wa-ters of my soul.

Last time ⌣ *fine*

Come, Holy Spirit, Heavenly Dove 248

1. Come, Ho-ly Spir-it, heaven-ly dove, with all your quick-ening powers;
2. Ho-san-nas lan-guish on our tongues, and our de-vo-tion dies.
3. Come, Ho-ly Spir-it, heaven-ly dove, with your en-liv-ening ways;

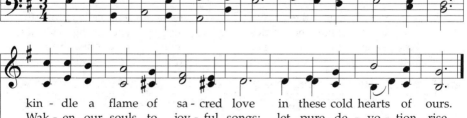

kin-dle a flame of sa-cred love in these cold hearts of ours.
Wak-en our souls to joy-ful songs; let pure de-vo-tion rise.
come, shed a-broad the Sav-ior's love, and teach our hearts to praise.

WORDS: Isaac Watts, 1707, alt.
MUSIC: John B. Dykes, 1866

ST. AGNES
CM

249 Spirit

Spir - it, Spir-it of gen-tle-ness, blow through the wil-der-ness,
call-ing and free, Spir - it, Spir-it of rest-less-ness,
stir me from plac-id-ness, wind, wind on the sea.

1. You moved on the wa - ters, you called to the
2. You swept through the des - ert, you stung with the
3. You sang in a sta - ble, you cried from a
4. You call from to-mor - row, you break an - cient

WORDS and MUSIC: James K. Manley, 1975

© 1978 James K. Manley

SPIRIT
Irr.

♩=132-140

deep,
sand,
hill,
schemes,

then you coaxed up the moun - tains from the
and you gift - ed your peo - ple with a
then you whis-pered in si - lence when the
from the bond-age of sor - row the

val - leys of sleep,
law and a land,
whole world was still,
cap - tives dream dreams;

and o - ver the e - ons you
when they were con - found - ed with
and down in the cit - y you
our wom - en see vi - sions, our

called to each thing,
i - dols and lies,
called once a - gain
men clear their eyes.

"A - wake from your slum -
then you spoke through your proph -
when you blew through your peo -
With bold new de - ci -

D.C. al Fine

bers and rise on your wings."
ets to o - pen their eyes.
ple on the rush of the wind.
sions your peo - ple a - rise.

250 O Breath of Life

1. O Breath of Life, come sweeping through us,
2. O Wind of God, come, bend us, break us,
3. O Breath of Love, come, breathe within us,

re - vive your church with life and power.
till hum - bly we con - fess our need.
re - new - ing thought and will and heart.

O Breath of Life, come, cleanse, re - new us,
Then in your ten - der - ness re - make us;
Come, love of Christ, a - fresh to win us;

and fit your church to meet this hour.
re - vive, re - store, for this we plead.
re - vive your church in ev - ery part.

WORDS: Bessie Porter Head, 1920
MUSIC: Clement C. Scholefield, 1874

ST. CLEMENT
98.98

O Holy Spirit, Root of Life 251

1. O Ho-ly Spir-it, Root of life, Cre-a-tor,
2. E-ter-nal Vig-or, Sav-ing One, you free us
3. O Ho-ly Wis-dom, Soar-ing Power, en-com-pass

cleans-er of all things, a-noint our wounds, a-
by your liv-ing Word, be-com-ing flesh to
us with wings un-furled, and car-ry us, en-

wak-en us with lus-trous move-ment of your wings.
wear our pain, and all cre-a-tion is re-stored.
cir-cling all, a-bove, be-low, and through the world.

WORDS: Jean Janzen, 1991, based on the writings of Hildegard of Bingen (12th century)
MUSIC: Trier manuscript (15th century); adapt. Michael Praetorius, 1609; harm. George R. Woodward, 1904

PUER NOBIS NASCITUR
LM

Breathe Deeply in Faith 252

Teach us, O God, not to torture ourselves,
not to make martyrs of ourselves through stifling reflection;
but rather teach us to breathe deeply in faith,
through Jesus, our Lord. Amen.

—*Søren Kierkegaard, 19th-century Danish theologian*

253   Spirit, Come, Dispel Our Sadness

1. Spir-it, come, dis-pel our sad-ness; pierce the clouds of
2. Let your fire heal our dis-sen-sions, let your flame re-
3. Au-thor of the new cre-a-tion, come, a-noint us

na-ture's night; come, O Source of joy and glad-ness,
fine our goals, let your peace re-solve our ten-sions,
with your power. Make our hearts your hab-i-ta-tion;

breathe your life and spread your light. From the height that
send your dove to soothe our souls. Let your wind flow
with your grace our spir-its shower. Hear, O hear our

knows no mea-sure, as a gra-cious shower de-scend,
fresh with-in us, sweep-ing clean all hate and strife
sup-pli-ca-tion, bless-ed Spir-it, God of peace!

WORDS: St. 1, 3, Paul Gerhardt, 1648; tr. John Christian Jacobi, c. 1725, alt.;
     st. 2, Jane Marshall, 1975
MUSIC: Joshua Leavitt's *Christian Lyre*, 1830; harm. Richard Proulx, 1986

PLEADING SAVIOR
87.87D

♩=52-56

St. 2 © 1975 Hinshaw Music, Inc.; harm. © 1986 GIA Publications, Inc.

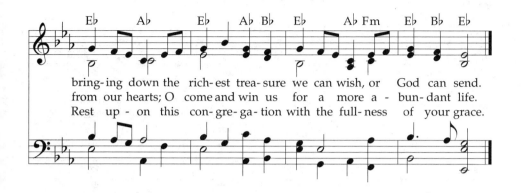

bring-ing down the rich-est trea-sure we can wish, or God can send.
from our hearts; O come and win us for a more a - bun-dant life.
Rest up - on this con-gre-ga-tion with the full-ness of your grace.

Breathe on Me, Breath of God 254

1. Breathe on me, Breath of God, fill me with life a - new,
2. Breathe on me, Breath of God, un - til my heart is pure,
3. Breathe on me, Breath of God, till I am whol - ly thine,
4. Breathe on me, Breath of God, so shall I nev - er die,

that I may love what thou dost love, and do what thou wouldst do.
un - til with thee I will one will to do and to en - dure.
un - til this earth - ly part of me glows with thy fire di - vine.
but live with thee the per - fect life of thine e - ter - ni - ty.

WORDS: Edwin Hatch, 1878, alt.   TRENTHAM
MUSIC: Robert Jackson, 1888   SM

255   She Is the Spirit

1. She sits like a bird,
(2. She) wings o - ver earth,
(3. She) danc - es in fire,
(4. For) she is the Spir-it,

brood-ing on the wa - ters. Hov-'ring on the cha - os of the
rest - ing where she wish - es, light-ing close at hand or soar-ing
start - ling those who see her, wak-ing tongues of ec - sta - sy where
one with God in es - sence, gift - ed by the Sav - ior in e -

world's first day; she sighs and she sings,
through the skies; she nests in the womb,
dull - ness reigned; she weans and in - spires
ter - nal love; she is the key

In Hebrew, the word used for the Spirit is ruach, *a feminine noun.*

WORDS and MUSIC: John Bell, 1988

THAINAKY
11 11.11 11

♩=84-92

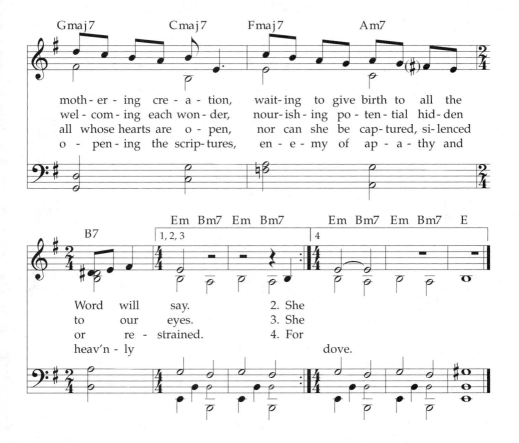

moth-er-ing cre-a-tion, wait-ing to give birth to all the
wel-com-ing each won-der, nour-ish-ing po-ten-tial hid-den
all whose hearts are o-pen, nor can she be cap-tured, si-lenced
o-pen-ing the scrip-tures, en-e-my of ap-a-thy and

Word will say. 2. She
to our eyes. 3. She
or re-strained. 4. For
heav'n-ly dove.

She Who Makes All Things New   256

May holy wisdom,
   kind to humanity,
      steadfast, sure and free,
   the breath of the power of God;
may she who makes all things new, in every age,
   enter our souls,
      and make us friends of God,
through Jesus Christ. Amen.

—Janet Morley, 20th-century British churchwoman

257   There's a Spirit in the Air

Unison

1. There's a spir - it in the air, tell - ing Chris - tians
2. Lose your shy - ness, find your tongue, tell the world what
3. When be - liev - ers break the bread, when a hun - gry
4. Still the Spir - it gives us light, see - ing wrong and
5. When a stran - ger's not a - lone, where the home - less
6. May the Spir - it fill our praise, guide our thoughts and
7. There's a Spir - it in the air, call - ing peo - ple

1. ev - ery-where: "Praise the love that Christ re - vealed,
2. God has done: God in Christ has come to stay.
3. child is fed, praise the love that Christ re - vealed,
4. set - ting right: God in Christ has come to stay.
5. find a home, praise the love that Christ re - vealed,
6. change our ways. God in Christ has come to stay.
7. ev - ery-where: praise the love that Christ re - vealed,

1. liv - ing, work - ing, in our world."
2. Live to - mor - row's life to - day.
3. liv - ing, work - ing, in our world.
4. Live to - mor - row's life to - day.
5. liv - ing, work - ing, in our world.
6. Live to - mor - row's life to - day.
7. liv - ing, work - ing, in our world.

Small notes: organ only

WORDS: Brian Wren, 1969, rev. 1990
MUSIC: John Wilson, 1969

LAUDS
77.77

♩.=54-60

Holy Wisdom

Unison

1. Who comes from God, as Word and Breath? Ho-ly Wis-dom. Who
2. Who lifts her voice for all to hear? Joy-ful Wis-dom. Who
3. Whom should we seek with all our heart? Lov-ing Wis-dom. Who,

holds the keys of life and death? Might-y Wis-dom. Craft-er
shapes a thought and makes it clear? Truth-ful Wis-dom. Teach-er,
once re-vealed, will not de-part? Faith-ful Wis-dom. Part-ner,

and Cre-a-tor too, El-dest, she makes all things new; Wis-dom guides what
draw-ing out our best, mag-ni-fies what we in-vest, names our truth, di-
Coun-se-lor, Com-for-ter, love has found none love-li-er, life is glad-ness

God will do, Wis-est One, Ra-diant One, wel-come, Ho-ly Wis-dom.
rects our quest, Wis-est One, Ra-diant One, wel-come, Ho-ly Wis-dom.
lived with her, Wis-est One, Ra-diant One, wel-come, Ho-ly Wis-dom.

WORDS: Patrick Michaels, 1989
MUSIC: *Choralemelodien zum heiligen Gesange*, 1808;
arr. Hal H. Hopson, 1991

SALVE REGINA COELITUM
84.84.777.66

♩=100-108

259 Spirit of the Living God

Spir - it of the liv - ing God, fall a-fresh on me.

Spir - it of the liv - ing God, fall a-fresh on me.

Melt me, mold me, fill me, use me.

Spir - it of the liv - ing God, fall a-fresh on me.

WORDS and MUSIC: Daniel Iverson, 1926

LIVING GOD
75.75.875

Let It Breathe on Me

Let it breathe on me, let it breathe on me,

let the breath of the Lord, now, breathe on me,

let it breathe on me, let it breathe on me,

let the breath of the Lord, now, breathe on me.

WORDS: Magnolia Lewis-Butts, 1941
MUSIC: Magnolia Lewis-Butts, 1941; harm. W. O. Hoyle

LET IT BREATHE ON ME
Irr.

261 Sweet, Sweet Spirit

There's a sweet, sweet Spir-it in this place, and I
know that it's the Spir-it of the Lord; there are
sweet ex-pres-sions on each face, and I
know they feel the pres-ence of the Lord.

Refrain

Sweet Ho-ly Spir-it, sweet heav-en-ly Dove, stay right here

WORDS and MUSIC: Doris Akers, 1962

SWEET, SWEET SPIRIT
Irr. w. refrain

with us, fill-ing us with your love; and for these bless-ings

we lift our hearts in praise; with-out a doubt we'll know

that we have been re-vived when we shall leave this place.

You Are the Work of God 262

It is not you who shape God;
    it is God that shapes you.
If then you are the work of God,
    await the hand of the Artist
    who does all things in due season.
Offer the Potter your heart,
    soft and tractable,
    and keep the form in which
    the Artist has fashioned you.
Let your clay be moist,
    lest you grow hard and lose
    the imprint of the Potter's fingers.

Irenaeus, 2nd-century theologian

263 Surely the Presence of the Lord

WORDS and MUSIC: Lanny Wolfe, 1977

WOLFE
11 11.9 7 12

♩=92-100

Where the Spirit of the Lord Is 264

Where the Spir-it of the Lord is, there is peace. Where the

Spir-it of the Lord is, there is love. There is com-fort in life's

dark-est hour, there is light and life, there is help and

pow-er in the Spir-it, in the Spir-it of the Lord.

WORDS and MUSIC: Stephen R. Adams, 1973

ADAMS
Irr.

♩=104-112

265 Spirit of God, Descend upon My Heart

1. Spir - it of God, de - scend up - on my heart;
2. I ask no dream, no proph - et ec - sta - sies,
3. Teach me to feel that thou art al - ways nigh;
4. Teach me to love thee as thine an - gels love,

wean it from earth, through all its puls - es move;
no sud - den rend - ing of the veil of clay,
teach me the strug - gles of the soul to bear:
one ho - ly pas - sion fill - ing all my frame;

stoop to my weak - ness, might - y as thou art,
no an - gel vis - it - ant, no o - pening skies,
to check the ris - ing doubt, the reb - el sigh;
the bap - tism of the heaven - de - scend - ed Dove.

and make me love thee as I ought to love.
but take the dim - ness of my soul a - way.
teach me the pa - tience of un - an - swered prayer.
My heart an al - tar, and thy love the flame.

WORDS: George Croly, 1867
MUSIC: Frederick C. Atkinson, 1870

MORECAMBE
10 10.10 10

Gracious Spirit, Dwell with Me 266

1. Gra - cious Spir - it, dwell with me: I my - self would
2. Truth - ful Spir - it, dwell with me: I my - self would
3. Si - lent Spir - it, dwell with me: I my - self would
4. Might - y Spir - it, dwell with me: I my - self would
5. Ho - ly Spir - it, dwell with me: I my - self would

1. gra - cious be, and, with words that help and heal,
2. truth - ful be, and, with wis - dom kind and clear,
3. si - lent be, qui - et as the grow - ing blade,
4. might - y be, might - y so as to pre - vail
5. ho - ly be, break from sin and choose the good,

1. would thy life in mine re - veal, and, with ac - tions
2. let thy life in mine ap - pear, and, with ac - tions
3. which through earth its way has made, si - lent - ly, like
4. where un - aid - ed I would fail, ev - er, by a
5. cher - ish what my Sav - ior would, and what - ev - er

1. bold and meek, would for Christ my Sav - ior speak.
2. lov - ing - ly, mir - ror Christ's sin - cer - i - ty.
3. morn - ing light, put - ting mists and chills to flight.
4. might - y hope, press - ing on and bear - ing up.
5. I can be, give to God who gave me thee.

WORDS: Thomas T. Lynch, 1855, alt.
MUSIC: Charles F. Gounod, 1872; harm. A. Eugene Ellsworth, 1994

LUX PRIMA
77.77.77

Harm. © 1995 Chalice Press

267

Blessed Quietness

1. Joys are flow-ing like a riv-er, since the Com-fort-er has come; Christ a-bides with us for-ev-er, makes the trust-ing heart a home.

2. Bring-ing life and health and glad-ness all a-round, this heaven-ly Guest ban-ished un-be-lief and sad-ness, changed our wea-ri-ness to rest.

3. Like the rain that falls from heav-en, like the sun-light from the sky, so the Spir-it too is giv-en, com-ing on us from on high.

4. See, a fruit-ful field is grow-ing, bless-ed fruit of righ-teous-ness; and the streams of life are flow-ing in the lone-ly wil-der-ness.

5. What a won-der-ful sal-va-tion, when we al-ways see Christ's face, what a per-fect hab-i-ta-tion, what a qui-et rest-ing place.

WORDS: Manie P. Ferguson, c. 1897

MUSIC: W. S. Marshall, c. 1897; arr. J. Jefferson Cleveland and Verolga Nix, 1981, alt.

BLESSED QUIETNESS
87.87 w. refrain

♩=76-84

Refrain

Bless-ed qui-et-ness, ho-ly qui-et-ness, what as-
sur-ance in my soul. On the storm-y sea, Je-sus
speaks to me, and the bil-lows cease to roll.

God Be in Me

268

God be in my head and in my understanding;
God be in my eyes and in my looking;
God be in my mouth and in my speaking;
God be in my heart and in my thinking;
God be at my end and at my departing.

—*Sarum Primer, 16th century*

269   Come, Holy Spirit, Fill This Place

1. Come, Ho - ly Spir - it, fill this place, a- noint these ser - vants
2. Come Ho - ly Spir - it, Com - for - ter, the Gift of God, En -
3. Your sev'n- fold gifts we seek this hour; your wis- dom, know - ledge,
4. Come, Ho - ly Spir - it, come re - new this church com- mis - sioned

with your grace. In - spire and guard them with your might
ligh - te - ner; a liv - ing well from which to draw
truth and power. May coun - sel, love and peace pre - vail.
to pur - sue the Pen - te - cos - tal wind and flame

and be, Cre - a - tor, their de - light.
the trea - sures of God's love and law.
Such gifts from you will ne - ver fail.
pro - claimed to - day in Je - sus' name. A - men.

WORDS: Daniel B. Merrick, 1986
MUSIC: Sarum plainsong, Mode VIII (4th century);
   harm. C. Winfred Douglas

VENI CREATOR SPIRITUS
LM

Alt. tune: TALLIS' CANON

Of All the Spirit's Gifts to Me

270

1. Of all the Spir - it's gifts to me,
2. The Spir - it shows me love's the root
3. The Spir - it shows if I pos - sess
4. Though what's a - head is mys - ter - y,
5. We go in peace, but made a - ware

1. I pray that I may nev - er cease to take and
2. of ev - ery gift sent from a - bove, of ev - ery
3. a love no e - vil can de - stroy; how - ev - er
4. and life it - self is ours on lease, each day the
5. that, in a need - y world like this, our clear - est

1. trea - sure most these three: love, joy, and peace.
2. flower, of ev - ery fruit, that God is love.
3. great is my dis - tress, then this is joy.
4. Spir - it says to me, "Go forth in peace!"
5. pur - pose is to share love, joy, and peace.

WORDS: Fred Pratt Green, 1979
MUSIC: John B. Dykes, 1865

ALMSGIVING
88.84

♩=96-100

GOD'S Church

271 The Church

Within the whole family of God on earth, the church appears wherever believers in Jesus Christ are gathered in his name. Transcending all barriers within the human family such as race and culture, the church manifests itself in ordered communities of disciples bound together for worship, for fellowship and for service, and in varied structures for mission, witness and mutual discipline, and for the nurture and renewal of its members. All dominion in the church belongs to Jesus Christ, its Lord and head, and any exercise of authority in the church on earth stands under his judgment.

—The Design of the Christian Church (Disciples of Christ)

272 The Church's One Foundation

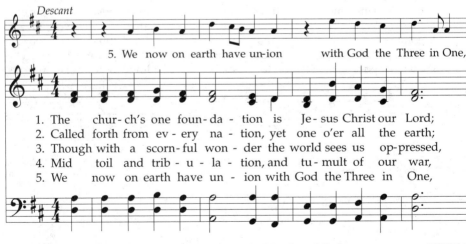

Descant

5. We now on earth have un-ion with God the Three in One,

1. The chur-ch's one foun-da - tion is Je- sus Christ our Lord;
2. Called forth from ev - ery na - tion, yet one o'er all the earth;
3. Though with a scorn-ful won - der the world sees us op-pressed,
4. Mid toil and trib - u - la - tion, and tu - mult of our war,
5. We now on earth have un - ion with God the Three in One,

WORDS: Samuel J. Stone, 1866, alt.; st. 2 adapt. Laurence Hull Stookey, 1983, alt.
MUSIC: Samuel S. Wesley, 1864; desc. Charles H. Webb, 1980

AURELIA
76.76D

and mys-tic sweet com-mu-nion with those whose rest is won.

1. we are his new cre - a - tion by wa - ter and the Word;
2. our char-ter of sal - va - tion: one Lord, one faith, one birth.
3. by schis-ms rent a - sun - der, by her - e - sies dis-tressed,
4. we wait the con-sum-ma - tion of peace for - ev - er - more;
5. and mys-tic sweet com-mu - nion with those whose rest is won.

Oh, hap-py ones, Lord, give us grace that we

1. from heaven he came and sought us to be his ho - ly bride;
2. One ho - ly name pro-fess - ing and at one ta - ble fed,
3. yet saints their watch are keep - ing; their cry goes up, "How long?"
4. till with the vi - sion glo - rious our long-ing eyes are blest,
5. Oh, hap - py ones, and ho - ly! Lord, give us grace that we

like them, the meek, on high may dwell with thee.

1. with his own blood he bought us, and for our life he died.
2. to one hope al - ways press - ing, by Christ's own Spir - it led.
3. And soon the night of weep - ing shall be the morn of song.
4. and the great church vic - to - rious shall be the church at rest.
5. like them, the meek and low - ly, on high may dwell with thee.

273   Built on the Rock

1. Built on the rock the church does stand, e - ven when stee- ples are fall - ing. Christ builds the church in ev - ery land; bells still are chim- ing and call - ing; call - ing the young and old to rest, call - ing the souls of

2. Not just in tem - ples made with hands, God, the Most Ho - ly, is dwell - ing. Hid - den from sight God's tem - ple stands, all earth- ly tem- ples ex - cel - ling. The one whom heavens can- not con- tain chose here a - mong us

3. We are a house of liv - ing stones built for God's own hab - i - ta - tion; God fills our hearts, these hum - ble thrones, grant- ing us life and sal - va - tion. Were two or three to pray for grace, Christ in their midst would

WORDS: Nicolai F. S. Grundtvig, 1837; tr. Carl Doving, 1909, alt.
MUSIC: Ludwig M. Lindeman, 1840

KIRKEN DEN ER ET
88.88.888

♩=120-132

I Love Your Church, O God 274

those dis-tressed, long-ing for life ev-er - last - ing.
to re - main, built in our bod-ies a tem - ple.
show his face, bless-ings up - on them be - stow - ing.

1. I love your church, O God, on earth your
2. I love your church, O God, whose walls be -
3. In love my tears shall fall, in love my
4. Be - yond my high - est joys, I prize your
5. Sure as your truth shall last, to Zi - on

1. blest a - bode, the peo - ple our re -
2. fore you stand, dear as the ap - ple
3. prayers as - cend, to serve your church, my
4. peo - ple's ways, the sweet com - mun - ion,
5. shall be given the bright - est glo - ries

1. deem - er saved with his own pre - cious blood.
2. of your eye, and grav - en on your hand.
3. toils be given, till toils and cares shall end.
4. sol - emn vows, the hymns of love and praise.
5. earth can yield, and bright - er bliss of heaven.

WORDS: Timothy Dwight, 1801, alt.
MUSIC: Aaron Williams, 1770

ST. THOMAS
SM

275   Christ Is Made the Sure Foundation

1. Christ is made the sure foun - da - tion, Christ the head and cor - ner - stone, cho - sen of the Lord and pre - cious, bind - ing all the church in one; ho - ly Zi - on's help for - ev - er, and our con - fi - dence a - lone.

2. To this tem - ple, where we call you, come, O Lord of Hosts, to - day; with your faith - ful lov - ing kind - ness hear your peo - ple as they pray, and your full - est ben - e - dic - tion shed with - in its walls al - way.

3. Here be - stow on all your ser - vants what they ask of you to gain, what they gain from you for - ev - er with the bless - ed to re - tain, and here - af - ter in your glo - ry ev - er - more with you to reign.

WORDS: Latin hymn (7th century); tr. John Mason Neale, 1851, alt.
MUSIC: Henry Purcell, c. 1680; adapt. Ernest Hawkins, 1842

WESTMINSTER ABBEY
87.87.87

Alt. tune: REGENT SQUARE

We Gather Together

276

1. We gath-er to-geth-er to ask for God's bless-ing,
2. Be - side us to guide us, O God, we per - ceive you
3. May all sing your prais - es, Re - deem - er tri - um-phant,

to turn to a wis - dom sur - pass - ing our own;
or - dain - ing, main - tain - ing the pow - er of life.
de - fend us, be - friend us, what - ev - er may be.

the pow'rs that op - press us now cease to dis - tress us.
Yes, yours be the glo - ry; let all tell the sto - ry.
May your con - gre - ga - tion es - cape trib - u - la - tion.

O God, be pres - ent with us, and make your will known.
Our God, be ev - er with us, in glad - ness and strife.
Your name be praised for - ev - er, O God, make us free!

WORDS: *Nederlandtsche Gedenckclanck*, 1626; tr. Theodore Baker, 1894;
 adapt. Ruth Duck, 1981
MUSIC: Dutch melody (16th century); arr. Edward Kremser, 1877

KREMSER
Irr.

277 Christians, We Have Met to Worship

1. Chris-tians, we have met to   wor-ship   and a-dore the liv-ing God;
2. Is   there here a trem-bling jail-er,   seek-ing grace and filled with fears?
3. Let   us   love our God su-preme-ly,   let us love each oth-er, too;

will you pray with all your pow-er,   while we   try   to preach the Word?
Is there here a weep-ing Mar-y   pour-ing forth a   flood of tears?
let us   pray for all earth's peo-ple   till our God makes all things new.

All   is vain un-less the Spir-it   of the Ho-ly One comes down;
Tell them all   a-bout the   Sav-ior, how in Christ the lost are   found.
Christ will call us   home to heav-en, at the ta-ble we'll sit   down;

Chris-tians, pray, and ho-ly   man-na   will be show-ered all a-round.
Pray, oh   pray, and ho-ly   man-na   will be scat-tered all a-round.
Christ will wel-come us and serve   us   liv-ing man-na   all a-round.

WORDS: Attr. George Atkins (19th century); alt.
MUSIC: *Columbian Harmony*, 1825

HOLY MANNA
87.87D

Here, O Lord, Your Servants Gather 278

Unison

1. Here, O Lord, your ser-vants gath-er, hand we link with hand;
2. Man - y are the tongues we speak, scat-tered are the lands,
3. Na - ture's se - crets o - pen wide, chang-es nev - er cease.
4. Grant, O God, an age re - newed, filled with death-less love;

look - ing toward our Sav-ior's cross, joined in love we stand.
yet our hearts are one in God, one in love's de - mands.
Where, oh where, can wea - ry souls find the source of peace?
help us as we work and pray, send us from a - bove

As we seek the realm of God, we u - nite to pray:
E'en in dark-ness hope ap - pears, call-ing age and youth:
Un - to all those sore dis-tressed, torn by end - less strife:
truth and cour-age, faith and power, need - ed in our strife:

Je - sus, Sav - ior, guide our steps, for you are the Way.
Je - sus, teach-er, dwell with us, for you are the Truth.
Je - sus, heal - er, bring your balm, for you are the Life.
Je - sus, Mas - ter, be our Way, be our Truth, our Life.

WORDS: Tokuo Yamaguchi, 1958; tr. Everett M. Stowe, 1958
MUSIC: Isao Koizumi, 1958

TOKYO
77.77

Tr. © 1958 The United Methodist Publishing House; music © 1958 JASRAC

♩=46-50

279 Reach Out and Worship

Sisters and brothers—Arise.
Lift your hearts
Lift your eyes
Lift your voices.

The living God,
the living, moving Spirit of God
has called us together—
in witness
in celebration
in struggle.

Reach out toward each other.
Our God reaches out toward us!
Let us worship God!

—Elizabeth Rice, 20th-century American churchwoman

280 God Is Here!

1. God is here! As we your peo-ple meet to of - fer
2. Here are sym-bols to re - mind us of our life - long
3. Here our chil-dren find a wel-come in the Shep - herd's
4. Lord of all, of church and king-dom, in an age of

praise and prayer, may we find in full - er mea-sure
need of grace; here are ta - ble, fount, and pul - pit;
flock and fold; here as bread and wine are tak - en,
change and doubt keep us faith - ful to the gos - pel;

WORDS: Fred Pratt Green, 1978
MUSIC: Cyril V. Taylor, 1941

ABBOT'S LEIGH
87.87D

♩=106-112

what   it   is   in Christ we share. Here, as   in   the   world   a -
here   the cross has cen - tral place. Here   in hon - es - ty   of
Christ sus-tains   us, as   of old. Here   the ser - vants of   the
help   us work   your pur - pose out. Here, in this day's ded -   i -

round us,   all   our var - ied skills and arts   wait   the
preach-ing,   here   in   si - lence, as   in speech, here,   in
Ser - vant   seek   in   wor - ship to   ex - plore what   it
ca - tion,   all   we   have   to   give, re - ceive; we,   who

com - ing   of   the Spir - it   in - to   o - pen minds and hearts.
new - ness and re - new - al, God the Spir - it comes to each.
means in   dai - ly liv - ing to   be - lieve and to   a - dore.
can - not   live with-out you,   we   a - dore you! We   be - lieve!

Creator, Spirit, Hear Us Sing   281

Creator, Spirit, hear us sing;
breathe fire into the praise we bring.
The mighty wind still lives in power;
the church renewed responds this hour.

WORDS: Ann Smith, 1989

Recommended tune:
TALLIS' CANON
(LM)

282   Light of Light Eternal

Leader: I will bless you, God! You fill the world with awe!
You dress yourself in light, rich, majestic light.

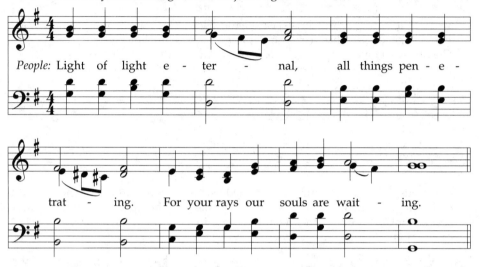

People: Light of light e - ter - nal, all things pen - e - trat - ing. For your rays our souls are wait - ing.

Leader: To you, O God, we lift up our souls.

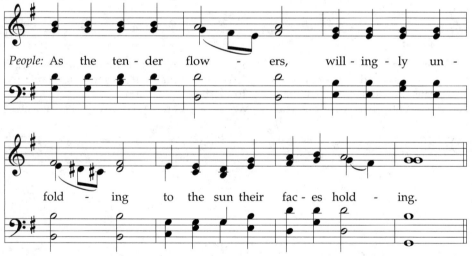

People: As the ten - der flow - ers, will - ing - ly un - fold - ing to the sun their fac - es hold - ing.

TEXT: Psalm 104:1–2; 86:4; 103:1   ARNSBERG
WORDS: Gerhard Tersteegen, 1729; tr. composite   668.668.666
MUSIC: Joachim Neander, 1680

Leader: My soul, bless God!
   All my being, bless God's holy name!

People: Ev - er so would we do, light from you ob -
tain - ing, strength to serve you gain - ing.

Jesus, Stand Among Us 283

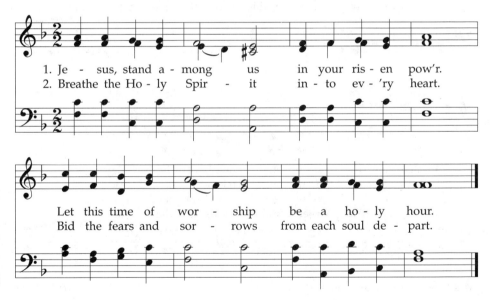

1. Je - sus, stand a - mong us in your ris - en pow'r.
2. Breathe the Ho - ly Spir - it in - to ev - 'ry heart.

Let this time of wor - ship be a ho - ly hour.
Bid the fears and sor - rows from each soul de - part.

WORDS: William Pennefather, 1873
MUSIC: Friedrich Filitz, 1847

WEM IN LEIDENSTAGEN
65.65

284   Gather Us In

1. Here in this place, the new light is stream-ing, sha-dows of doubt are
2. We are the young—our lives are a mys-tery; we are the old, who
3. Here we re-ceive new life in the wa-ters; here we re-ceive the
4. Not just in build-ings, small and con-fin-ing, not in some heav-en,

van-ished a-way. See in this space our fears and our dream-ings,
yearn for your face. We have been sung through-out all of his-tory,
bread of new birth; here you shall call your sons and your daugh-ters,
light years a-way, here in this place the new light is shin-ing;

brought here to you in the light of this day.
called to be light to the whole hu-man race.
call us a-new to be salt for the earth.
now is God pres-ent, and now is the day.

WORDS and MUSIC: Marty Haugen, 1981

GATHER US IN
Irr.

♩·=54-60

285 How Lovely, Lord, How Lovely

1. How love-ly, Lord, how love - ly is your a - bid - ing place;
2. In your blest courts to wor - ship, O God, a sin - gle day
3. A sun and shield for - ev - er are you, O God most high;

my soul is long-ing, faint - ing, to feast up - on your grace.
is bet - ter than a thou - sand if I from you should stray.
you show-er us with bless - ings no good will you de - ny.

The spar - row finds a shel - ter, a place to build her nest;
I'd rath - er keep the en - trance and claim you as my Lord
The saints, your grace re - ceiv - ing, from strength to strength shall go,

and so your tem - ple calls us with - in its walls to rest.
than rev - el in the rich - es the ways of sin af - ford.
and from their life shall riv - ers of bless-ing o - ver - flow.

WORDS: Arlo D. Duba, 1984
MUSIC: Hal H. Hopson, 1983

MERLE'S TUNE
76.76D

♩=108-116

This Is the Day

WORDS: Psalm 118:24, para. Les Garrett, 1967
MUSIC: Les Garrett, 1967

THE LORD'S DAY
Irr.

287 As a Chalice Cast of Gold

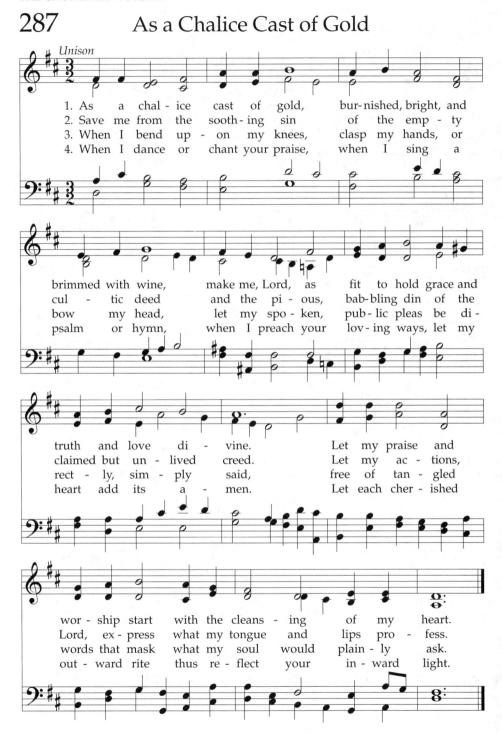

Unison

1. As a chal-ice cast of gold, bur-nished, bright, and
2. Save me from the sooth-ing sin of the emp-ty
3. When I bend up-on my knees, clasp my hands, or
4. When I dance or chant your praise, when I sing a

brimmed with wine, make me, Lord, as fit to hold grace and
cul-tic deed and the pi-ous, bab-bling din of the
bow my head, let my spo-ken, pub-lic pleas be di-
psalm or hymn, when I preach your lov-ing ways, let my

truth and love di-vine. Let my praise and
claimed but un-lived creed. Let my ac-tions,
rect-ly, sim-ply said, free of tan-gled
heart add its a-men. Let each cher-ished

wor-ship start with the cleans-ing of my heart.
Lord, ex-press what my tongue and lips pro-fess.
words that mask what my soul would plain-ly ask.
out-ward rite thus re-flect your in-ward light.

WORDS: Thomas H. Troeger, 1984
MUSIC: Carol Doran, 1984

INWARD LIGHT
77.77.77

© 1985 Oxford University Press

Alt. tune: LUX PRIMA

O God of Vision

1. O God of vi - sion far great - er than all hu - man schem -
2. Pour out your Spir - it on all now as - sem - bled be - fore
3. Grant to us in - sight, O God, for this time of de - ci -
4. Break the sun's rays in - to col - or, a rain - bow a - round
5. Grate - ful, we come now by Christ's in - vi - ta - tion clear - spo -

1. ing, gath - er us now in your pres - ence, re - fresh - ing, re -
2. you. May our di - ver - si - ty here be a means to a -
3. sion. May we dream chal - leng - ing dreams of both depth and pre -
4. us. Storm clouds, though real and near, are not e - nough to con -
5. ken. We seek the nour - ish - ment found in fruit crushed and bread

1. deem - ing. Show us a - new life in your breath - tak - ing
2. dore you. Wom - en and men, young, old, and youth - ful a -
3. ci - sion. Speak through the dark. Dis - pel by light - ning's bright
4. found us. Arched in the sky, beau - ty and pro - mise are
5. bro - ken. Christ for us all! Come, let us an - swer the

1. view, love - ly be - yond all our dream - ing.
2. gain, make us as one, we im - plore you.
3. spark what - ev - er clouds dim our vi - sion.
4. high, giv - ing us hope to as - tound us.
5. call, of - fering our lives as the to - ken.

WORDS: Jane Parker Huber, 1981
MUSIC: *Erneuerten Gesangbuch*, 1665

LOBE DEN HERREN
14 14.478

Descant: #25

289 What Is This Place

1. What is this place where we are meet-ing? On-ly a house, the
2. Words from a-far, stars that are fall-ing, sparks that are sown in
3. And we ac-cept bread at this ta-ble, bro-ken and shared, a

earth its floor, walls and a roof shel-ter-ing peo-ple, win-dows for
us like seed. Names for our God, dreams, signs, and won-ders sent from the
liv-ing sign. Here in this world, dy-ing and liv-ing, we are each

light, an o-pen door. Yet it be-comes a bod-y that lives when
past are what we need. We in this place re-mem-ber and speak a-
oth-er's bread and wine. This is the place where we can re-ceive what

we are gath-ered here, and know our God is near.
gain what we have heard: God's free re-deem-ing word.
we need to in-crease: God's jus-tice and God's peace.

WORDS: Huub Oosterhuis, 1967; tr. David Smith, 1970
MUSIC: *Nederlandtsche Gedenckclanck*, 1626; arr. B. Huijbers, 1967

KOMT NU MET ZANG
98.98.966

♩=100-108

I Cannot Dance, O Love

Unison

1. I can-not dance, O Love, un-less you lead me on.
2. Love is the mu-sic 'round us, we glide as birds in air,
3. O bless-ed Love, your cir-cling u-nites us, God and soul.

I can-not leap in glad-ness un-less you lift me up.
en-twin-ing, soul and bod-y, your wings hold us with care.
Your arms from the be-gin-ning, em-brace and make us whole.

Harmony

From love to love we cir-cle, be-yond all knowl-edge grow,
Your Spir-it is the harp-ist and all your chil-dren sing;
Hold us in steps of mer-cy from which you nev-er part,

Unison

for when you lead we fol-low, to new worlds you can show.
her hands the cur-rents 'round us, your love the gold-en strings.
that we may know more ful-ly the dan-ces of your heart.

WORDS: Jean Janzen, 1991, based on the writing of Mechthild of Magdeburg BRED DINA VIDA VINGAR
MUSIC: Swedish folk tune; harm. Lahrae Knatterud, 1983 76.76.D

♩=104-112

Psalm 24:3–4

291 Señor, Yo Quiero Entrar
(O God, I Want to Enter)

Se - ñor, yo quie-ro en - trar en tu san-
O God, I want to en - ter your

tua - rio para a - do - rar. rar.
tem - ple and wor-ship you. you.

Da - me ma-nos lim - pias y un cora-zon
Give me clean hands and a pure

pu - ro, y sin va-ni - da-des, que se-pa a-
heart, from van-i-ty save me, and teach me to

mar; da - des, que se-pa a - mar.
love. save me, and teach me to love.

WORDS: Anonymous, based on Psalm 24:3–4; tr. David L. Edwards, 1994
MUSIC: Latin American melody (20th century)

ADORACION
Irr.

Tr. © 1995 Chalice Press

♩=80-88

¡Miren Qué Bueno!
(O Look and Wonder)

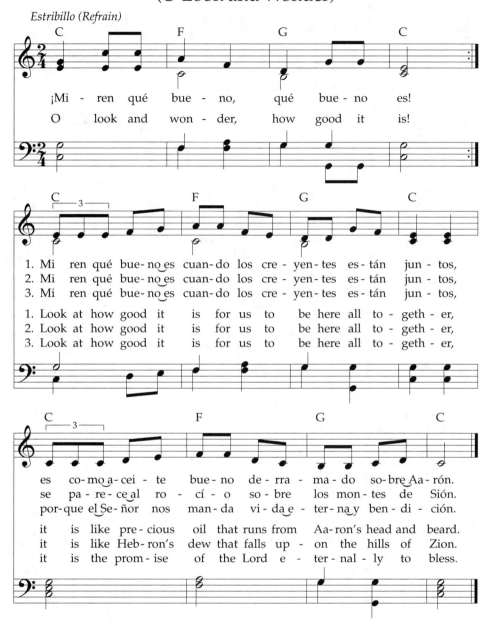

WORDS: Pablo Sosa, 1979; tr. George Lockwood
MUSIC: Pablo Sosa, 1979; arr. Alvin Schutmaat

MIREN QUÉ BUENO
Irr.

© 1979 Cancionero Abierto, Buenos Aires, Argentina; tr. © George Lockwood

♩=80-88

293   Out of Need and Out of Custom

1. Out of need and out of cus - tom, we have gath-ered here a-
2. Come we now our masks dis - play - ing, fear-ing that we shall be
3. We have heard the glow-ing sto - ries of the things that God has

gain; to the gath-ering we are bring - ing love and
known, fool-ish games for - ev - er play - ing, feel- ing
done, of the pow - er and the glo - ry, of God's

laugh - ter, grief and pain. Some be - liev - ing, some re -
mean-while so a - lone. Let pre - ten-sion's power be
love in Christ the Son. God of hu - man trans - for -

joic - ing, some a - fraid, and some in doubt, come we
bro - ken, to be hu - man let us dare; let the
ma - tion, for your pres-ence now we pray, lead us

WORDS and MUSIC: Ken Medema, 1972

GATHERING
87.87D

♩=88-96

now our ques-tions voic - ing, we would search these mat-ters out.
truth in love be spo - ken, let us now the quest-ing share.
ev - er on the jour - ney as we gath - er here to - day.

Here We Gather as God's People 294

Here we gath - er as God's peo - ple with our friends from far and near;

let our voic - es sound with prais - es know-ing Christ has called us here.

Now we seek and greet each oth - er, now in joy ap-proach our friends.

Here we min - gle, bound to - geth - er as to all our love ex-tends.

WORDS: Daniel B. Merrick, 1991
MUSIC: Wyeth's *Repository of Sacred Music, Part Second*, 1813

NETTLETON
87.87D

Words © 1995 Chalice Press

Harmonization: #16

295 In This Very Room

1. In this ver-y room there's quite e-nough love for one like me,
2. In this ver-y room there's quite e-nough love for all of us,
3. In this ver-y room there's quite e-nough love for all the world,

and in this ver-y room there's quite e-nough joy for one like me;
and in this ver-y room there's quite e-nough joy for all of us;
and in this ver-y room there's quite e-nough joy for all the world;

and there's quite e-nough hope, and

quite e-nough pow'r to chase a-way an-y gloom, for

Je-sus, Lord Je-sus, is in this ver-y room.

WORDS and MUSIC: Ron and Carol Harris, 1979

IN THIS VERY ROOM
Irr.

♩=80-88

Give to Us Your Peace 296

Ostinato

Do - na no - bis pa - cem Do - mi - ne.
Give to us your peace, O Je - sus Christ.

WORDS: Traditional Latin; tr. the Taizé Community
MUSIC: Jacques Berthier and the Taizé Community

DONA NOBIS PACEM DOMINE
Irr.

© 1982, 1983, 1984, Les Presses de Taizé (France); used by permission of GIA Publications, Inc.

Dona Nobis Pacem 297

Do - na no - bis pa - cem, pa - cem. Do - na

no - bis pa - cem. Do - na no - bis pa - cem.

Do - na no - bis pa - cem. Do - na

no - bis pa - cem. Do - na no - bis pa - cem.

May be sung as a canon

WORDS: Traditional Latin
MUSIC: Traditional

DONA NOBIS PACEM
Irr.

298 Kyrie Eleison

Ky - ri - e e - lei - son.* Ky - ri - e e - lei - son.

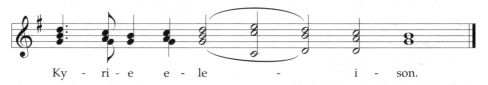

Ky - ri - e e - le - - i - son.

* Lord, have mercy

WORDS: Ancient Greek
MUSIC: Russian Orthodox liturgy

ORTHODOX KYRIE
Irr.

299 Lord, Have Mercy

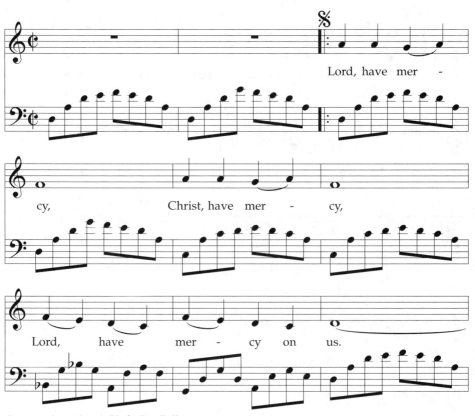

Lord, have mer - cy, Christ, have mer - cy, Lord, have mer - cy on us.

Accompaniment is suitable for handbells.

WORDS and MUSIC: Swee Hong Lim, Singapore (20th century)

SINGAPURA
Irr.

Used by permission of Asian Institute for Liturgy and Music

♩=54-60

Though red like crim-son is my sin, great-er yet is for-give-ness found in Christ.

Lord, Have Mercy upon Us 300

Lord, have mer-cy up-on us. Christ, have mer-cy up-on us. Lord, have mer-cy up-on us.

WORDS: *Kyrie eleison*
MUSIC: Healey Willan, 1928

WILLAN KYRIE
Irr.

♩=76-84

Psalm 19:14

301 Let the Words of My Mouth

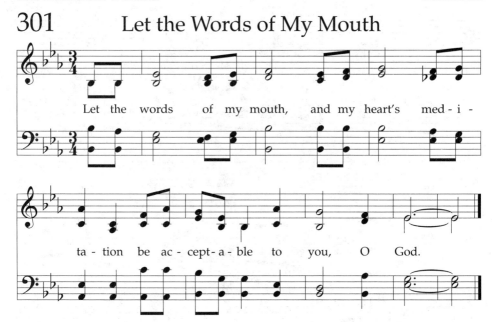

Let the words of my mouth, and my heart's med-i-ta-tion be ac-cept-a-ble to you, O God.

WORDS and MUSIC: Warren W. Wiersbe, 1989

WIERSBE
Irr.

© 1989 Hope Publishing Co.

Matthew 7:7

302 Ask Your God

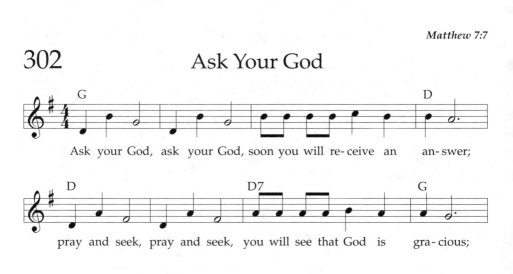

Ask your God, ask your God, soon you will re-ceive an an-swer;

pray and seek, pray and seek, you will see that God is gra-cious;

WORDS: Matthew 7:7, para. James Minchin (20th century)
MUSIC: Subronto K. Atmodjo, Indonesia (20th century)

MINTALAH
Irr.

Used by permission of Asian Institute for Liturgy and Music

♩=108-116

come and knock, come and knock, heav-en's door will o - pen to you,

heav-en's door will o - pen to you, to ev - 'ry one who knocks.

In This Time 303

With warmth

In this time of qui-et rev-'rence, God,

fill us now with ev-er-last-ing peace, and may each and ev-'ry

rit.

day we live bring true faith in your a-bid-ing love.

WORDS and MUSIC: Larry Sivis, 1985

SIVIS
99.99

♩=72-80

304 Into My Heart

In - to my heart, in - to my heart, come
in - to my heart, Lord Je - sus; come in to-day, come
in to stay, come in-to my heart, Lord Je - sus.

WORDS and MUSIC: Harry D. Clarke, 1924

INTO MY HEART
LM

© 1924, renewed 1952, Hope Publishing Co.

305 Lord, Listen to Your Children Praying

Lord, lis-ten to your chil-dren pray-ing, Lord, send your spir-it

WORDS and MUSIC: Ken Medema, 1973

CHILDREN PRAYING
Irr.

© 1973 Hope Publishing Co.

♩=66-72

in this place; Lord, lis-ten to your chil-dren pray-ing,

1 (optional) | Final

send us love, send us pow'r, send us grace. grace!

Psalm 143:1

Hear Our Prayer, O Lord 306

Hear our prayer, O Lord, hear our prayer, O Lord,

in-cline thine ear to us, and grant us thy peace. A-men.

WORDS: Psalm 143:1
MUSIC: George Whelpton, 1897

HEAR OUR PRAYER
Irr.

307 The Lord's Prayer

Unison

Our Fa - ther, which art in heav - en, hal - low - ed be thy name. Thy king-dom come, thy will be done on earth as it is in heav - en. Give us this day our dai - ly bread, and for-

WORDS: Matthew 6:9–13 (KJV)
MUSIC: Albert Hay Malotte, 1935; arr. Donald P. Hustad, 1984

MALOTTE
Irr.

give us our debts, as we for-give our debt-ors.

(may be omitted)

And lead us not in-to temp-ta-tion but de-liv-er us from

e-vil: for thine is the king-dom, and the pow - er,

and the glo - ry, for-ev - er,

A - men, A - men.

Matthew 6:9–13

308 The Lord's Prayer

Unison

1. Our Fa - ther, which art in heav-en,
2. Done on earth as it is in heav-en,
3. And for - give all our debts,
4. Lead us not in - to temp - ta - tion,
5. Thine is the king-dom, pow-er, and glo - ry,
6. A - men, a - men, a - men,

hal-low-ed-a be thy

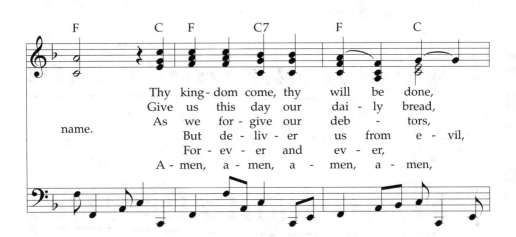

name.

Thy king - dom come, thy will be done,
Give us this day our dai - ly bread,
As we for - give our deb - tors,
But de - liv - er us from e - vil,
For - ev - er and ev - er,
A - men, a - men, a - men, a - men,

hal - low - ed - a be thy name.

Fine

WORDS: Matthew 6:9-13; adapt. J. Jefferson Cleveland and Verolga Nix, 1981
MUSIC: West Indian folk tune; arr. Carlton R. Young, 1988

WEST INDIAN
Irr.

The Lord's Prayer

309

Let the words   of my mouth, let the words   of my mouth and the

med-i-ta-tions of my heart   be ac-cept-a-ble in thy sight; wilt thou

teach   me how to   serve thee, wilt thou teach me   how   to   pray?

Our Father who art in heaven,   hallowed   be   thy   name.
Give us this day   our   dai - ly   bread:
Lead us not into temptation,   but deliver   us   from   evil:

thy kingdom come: thy will be done on   earth as it   is   in   heav-en.
forgive us our trespasses,   as we forgive   those who tres-pass a - gainst us.
for thine is the kingdom,   and the power,
         and the glory, for- ev-er and   ev-er a - men.

WORDS: Psalm 19:14; Matthew 6:9–13   LET THE WORDS
MUSIC: C. E. Leslie   Irr.

Matthew 6:9–13

310 The Lord's Prayer

Our Fa-ther in heav-en, hal-low-ed be your name, your king-dom come, your will be done on earth as in heav-en. Give us to-day our

WORDS: Matthew 6:9–13
MUSIC: David Haas, 1986, alt.

HAAS
Irr.

♩=100–104

Amens

311

A- men, a - men.

MUSIC: Dresden

312

A- men, a-men, a - men.

MUSIC: Danish

313

A - men. A - men.

A - men. A - men.

A - men.

MUSIC: John Stainer, c. 1870

314

A – men. A – men. A – men.

MUSIC: McNeil Robinson II, 1984

Amens

315

316

A - men, a-men, a - men.

A - men, a - men.

317

A - men. A - men. A - men. A - men. A - men.

MUSIC: African-American

Harm. © 1990 Westminster/John Knox Press

318

319

A - men.

A men. A - men.

MUSIC: Melvin West, 1984

© 1984 Melvin West

MUSIC: Larry Sivis, 1992

© 1995 Chalice Press

320

Al - le - lu - ia, a - men, a - men.

MUSIC: Carl Wiltse, 1982

© 1989 The United Methodist Publishing House

321 Break Thou the Bread of Life

1. Break thou the bread of life, dear Lord, to me,
as thou didst break the loaves beside the sea;
be - yond the sa - cred page I seek thee, Lord,
my spir - it pants for thee, O liv - ing Word.

2. Bless thou the truth, dear Lord, to me, to me,
as thou didst bless the bread by Gal - i - lee;
then shall all bond - age cease, all fet - ters fall;
and I shall find my peace, my all in all.

3. O send thy Spir - it, Lord, now un - to me;
touch thou my long - ing eyes that I may see;
give me to eat and live with thee a - bove;
teach me to love thy truth, for thou art love.

WORDS: St. 1, 2, Mary A. Lathbury, 1877; st. 3, Alexander Groves, 1913, alt.
MUSIC: William F. Sherwin, 1877

BREAD OF LIFE
64.64D

O Word of God Incarnate

1. O Word of God incarnate, O Wisdom from on high,
O Truth unchanged, unchanging, O Light of our dark sky:
we praise you for the radiance that from the hallowed page,
a lantern to our footsteps, shines on from age to age.

2. The church from you, our Savior, received the gift divine;
and still that light is lifted o'er all the earth to shine.
Your word is chart and compass that, all life's voyage through,
mid mists and rocks and quicksands still guides, O Christ, to you.

3. O make your church, dear Savior, a lamp of burnished gold
to bear before the nations your true light as of old.
O teach your wandering pilgrims by this our path to trace,
till, clouds and darkness ended, we see you face to face.

WORDS: William W. How, 1867, alt.
MUSIC: *Gesangbuch*, Meiningen, 1693

MUNICH
76.76D

323 Wonderful Words of Life

1. Sing them o-ver a-gain to me, won-der-ful words of life;
2. Christ, the bless-ed one, gives to all, won-der-ful words of life;
3. Sweet-ly ech-o the gos-pel call, won-der-ful words of life;

let me more of their beau-ty see, won-der-ful words of life.
sin-ner, list to the lov-ing call, won-der-ful words of life.
of-fer par-don and peace to all, won-der-ful words of life.

Words of life and beau-ty, teach me faith and du-ty;
All so free-ly giv-en, woo-ing us to heav-en;
Je-sus, on-ly Sav-ior, sanc-ti-fy for-ev-er;

Refrain

beau-ti-ful words, won-der-ful words, won-der-ful words of life,

WORDS and MUSIC: Philip P. Bliss, 1874

WORDS OF LIFE
86.86.66 w. refrain

beau - ti - ful words, won-der-ful words, won-der-ful words of life.

Your Words to Me Are Life and Health   324

1. Your words to me are life and health; pour strength in-to my soul;
2. Your words to me are light and truth; from day to day they show
3. Your words to me are full of joy, of beau-ty, peace, and grace;
4. Your words you have ful-filled on earth, your-self, the liv-ing Word;

en - a - ble, guide, and teach my heart to reach its per-fect goal!
their wis-dom, pass-ing earth-ly lore, as in their truth I grow.
from them I learn your bless-ed will, through them I see your face.
with - in my heart your im-age print in clear-est lines, O Lord.

WORDS: George Currie Martin, c. 1920, alt.
MUSIC: Thomas Este's *Whole Book of Psalms*, 1592

WINCHESTER OLD
CM

On Reading the Book of God   325

Every one who opens the Book of God, with one aim, with one ardent desire—intent only to know the will of God—to such a person the knowledge of God is easy; for the Bible is framed to illuminate such, and only such, with the salutary knowledge of things celestial and divine.

Humility of mind, or what is in effect the same, contempt for all earth-born pre-eminence, prepares the mind for the reception of this light; or, what is virtually the same, opens the ears to hear the voice of God.

—Alexander Campbell, 19th-century Disciples forebear

326 Thy Word

Thy word is a lamp un-to my feet and a light un-to my path.

WORDS: Amy Grant, 1984
MUSIC: Michael W. Smith, 1984; arr. Keith Phillips

THY WORD
Irr.

Jeremiah 31:33

327 Write These Words in Our Hearts

Write these words in our hearts, we be-seech you, O God.

WORDS: Based on Jeremiah 31:33
MUSIC: Ancient chant; adapt. John F. Wilson, 1988

328 God, You Will Show Us the Path of Life

God, you will show us the path of life.

WORDS and MUSIC: Anonymous, 1986

Come, Be Glad!

Unison

1. Come, be glad! Sing and praise! See what God has done!
2. Come, my soul, lift your eyes! See what God has done!
3. Come, re-joice! Praise God's name! See what God has done!
4. Come, with joy! Fill your hearts! See what God has done!
5. Come, give thanks! Sing God's praise! See what God has done!

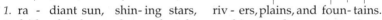

1. Formed the earth, spread the seas, set in place the moun-tains;
2. Led the slaves through the sea to a prom-ised bless-ing;
3. When full time came to be Christ ap-peared re-deem-ing;
4. Ho-ly Flame, Spir-it, Fire burns in each be-liev-er
5. Sends us out to o-bey "Go and make dis-ci-ples."

1-4   5.

1. ra-diant sun, shin-ing stars, riv-ers, plains, and foun-tains.
2. faith-ful love, day and night guard-ing and pro-tect-ing.
3. proph-ets, priests, mar-tyrs, saints, Je-sus' name con-fess-ing.
4. bring-ing life, love, and joy, bind-ing all to-geth-er.
5. Christ a-live! Christ a-lone reigns in glo-ry al-ways.

WORDS: Daniel B. Merrick, 1978
MUSIC: Caribbean folk melody; harm. Carlton R. Young, 1989

PORTOBELLO
65.66.66

♩=62-68

330 Alleluia! Hear God's Story

1. Al - le - lu - ia! Hear God's sto - ry, still un - fold - ing with each dawn.
2. Al - le - lu - ia! Sing the sto - ry; God's great faith - ful - ness pro - claim.
3. Al - le - lu - ia! Dance the sto - ry; ev - 'ry sin - ew now en - gage.

Taste the wine and bod - y bro - ken: God's cre - a - tive love lives on.
Tell of proph - ets and a - pos - tles; sing the pow'r of Je - sus' name.
Teth - ered close in truth - ful wor - ship, bold - ly face the com - ing age.

Who the neigh - bor? Who the hun - gry? Who is thirst - y for sha - lom?
Who the neigh - bor? Who the list - 'ner? Who has ears to hear our song?
Who the neigh - bor? Who the watch - ful? Who will wel - come life's em - brace?

God of jour - ney, in your sto - ry; lead us, with the neigh - bor, home.
God of his - t'ry, tune our voic - es, make our hope - ful wit - ness strong.
God of gos - pel, tell the sto - ry through our danc - ing of your grace.

WORDS: Mary Anne Parrott, 1986
MUSIC: Polish folk melody; adapt. A. E. Rusbridge

W ZLOBIE LEZY
87.87.88.77

Sing of a God in Majestic Divinity 331

1. Sing of a God in ma - jes - tic di - vin - i - ty,
2. Sing of a child who was cra - dled so ten - der- ly,
3. Sing of a Spir - it who dai - ly ad - dress- ing us,
4. Sing of this God who in glo - ry and mys - ter - y

seed - ing the heav - ens with num - ber - less stars,
sing of a boy - hood by Gal - i - lee's lake;
lives in our sci - en - ces, na - ture and arts;
choos - es to lie in hu - man - i - ty's womb,

form - ing our dust and our dreams of in - fin - i - ty,
sing of a cross and a Sav - ior who won - drous- ly
mov - ing through all of cre - a - tion and bless - ing us,
en - ters the pris - on and pain of our his - to - ry,

God of our lives and the judge of our wars.
suf - fered and died for hu - man - i - ty's sake.
guid - ing our minds and en - gag - ing our hearts.
ris - es tri - um - phant and o - pens the tomb.

WORDS: Herbert O'Driscoll, 1980
MUSIC: Johann H. Rheinhardt's *Choralbuch*, Üttingen, 1754

ÜTTINGEN
12 10.12 10

♩=100-104

332 God of Wondrous Darkness

O living God, you dwell in clouds and thick darkness.
We lift our eyes to the night sky
and sense depth and fullness beyond our grasp.
You freed your children from Egyptian bondage
under the security of nightfall.
When you were born, the star came in the night heavens.
A black man carried your cross.
You made your pure sacrifice of love in the midday darkness.

Rain falls from black clouds.
Babies grow in uterine shadows.
Prophets speak in ebony voices.
Treasures of darkness!
Help us receive them as riches from you. Amen.

—Ronald Allen, 20th-century Disciples scholar

333 Joyful Is the Dark

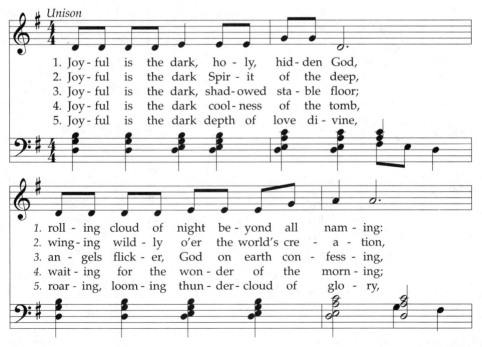

Unison

1. Joy-ful is the dark, ho-ly, hid-den God,
2. Joy-ful is the dark Spir-it of the deep,
3. Joy-ful is the dark, shad-owed sta-ble floor;
4. Joy-ful is the dark cool-ness of the tomb,
5. Joy-ful is the dark depth of love di-vine,

1. roll-ing cloud of night be-yond all nam-ing:
2. wing-ing wild-ly o'er the world's cre-a-tion,
3. an-gels flick-er, God on earth con-fess-ing,
4. wait-ing for the won-der of the morn-ing;
5. roar-ing, loom-ing thun-der-cloud of glo-ry,

WORDS: Brian Wren, 1989
MUSIC: Gayle Schoepf, 1994

ORANGETHORPE
10 10.11 10

Words © 1989 Hope Publishing Co.; music © 1995 Chalice Press

♩=72-80

334 Sing My Song Backwards

Unison

1. Sing my song back-wards from end to be-gin-ning,
2. Whis-per a hope through the shame and the ag-o-ny,
3. Gath-er the bones and the sin-ews of mem-o-ry—
4. Stretch out a rain-bow from cross to na-tiv-i-ty.

Fri-day to Mon-day, from dy-ing to birth.
hor-ror and emp-ti-ness, dark-er than night,
heal-ings and par-a-bles, laugh-ter and strife,
Deck out the sta-ble with shep-herds and kings,

Noth-ing is al-tered, but hope chang-es ev-ery-thing:
vis-it the wounds, and the fail-ure of Cal-va-ry:
joy with the out-casts and love for the en-e-my—
an-gels and mir-a-cles, glo-ry and po-et-ry:

sing "Re-sur-rec-tion!" and "Peace up-on Earth!"
sing "Re-sur-rec-tion!" and bathe them in light!
breathe "Re-sur-rec-tion!" and dance them to life!
sing my song back-wards till all the world sings!

WORDS: Brian Wren, 1974, rev. 1994
MUSIC: Ann Loomes, 1974

HILARY
Irr.

♩.=44-48

Creating God, Your Fingers Trace   335

1. Cre - at - ing God, your fin - gers trace the
2. Sus - tain - ing God, your hands up - hold earth's
3. Re - deem - ing God, your arms em - brace all
4. In - dwell - ing God, your gos - pel claims one

bold de - signs of far - thest space; let sun and moon and
mys - teries known or yet un - told; let wa - ter's fra - gile
now de - spised for creed or race; let peace, de - scend - ing
fam - ily with a bil - lion names; let ev - ery life be

stars and light and what lies hid - den praise your might.
blend with air, en - a - bling life, pro - claim your care.
like a dove, make known on earth your heal - ing love.
touched by grace un - til we praise you face to face.

May be sung as a canon

WORDS: Jeffery Rowthorn, 1974
MUSIC: Thomas Tallis, 1561

TALLIS' CANON
LM

Words © 1979 The Hymn Society, used by permission of Hope Publishing Co.

Prayer of Deliverance   336

From silly devotions
and from sour-faced saints,
good Lord, deliver us.

—*Teresa of Avila, 16th-century theologian*

Matthew 4:18–20

337 Jesus Calls Us O'er the Tumult

1. Je - sus calls us o'er the tu - mult of our
2. Long a - go a - pos - tles heard it by the
3. Je - sus calls us from the wor - ship of the
4. In our joys and in our sor - rows, days of
5. Je - sus calls us! By thy mer - cies, Sav - ior,

1. life's wild rest - less sea, day by day his sweet voice
2. Gal - i - le - an lake, turned from home, and toil, and
3. vain world's gold - en store, from each i - dol that would
4. toil and hours of ease, still he calls, in cares and
5. may we hear thy call, give our hearts to thine o -

1. sound - eth, say - ing, "Chris - tian, fol - low me";
2. kin - dred, leav - ing all for his dear sake.
3. keep us, say - ing, "Chris - tian, love me more."
4. plea - sures, "Chris - tian, love me more than these."
5. be - dience, serve and love thee best of all.

WORDS: Cecil F. Alexander, 1852
MUSIC: William H. Jude, 1874

GALILEE
87.87

Who Is a Christian? 338

But who is a Christian? I answer, Every one that believes in one's heart that Jesus of Nazareth is the Messiah, the Son of God; repents of one's sins, and obeys him in all things according to one's measure of knowledge of his will.

—Alexander Campbell, 19th-century Disciples forebear

Just as I Am, Without One Plea 339

1. Just as I am, with-out one plea, but that thy blood was shed for me, and that thou bid'st me come to thee, O Lamb of God, I come, I come!
2. Just as I am, though tossed a-bout with man-y a con-flict, man-y a doubt; fight-ings and fears with-in, with-out, O Lamb of God, I come, I come!
3. Just as I am, thou wilt re-ceive, wilt wel-come, par-don, cleanse, re-lieve; be-cause thy prom-ise I be-lieve, O Lamb of God, I come, I come!
4. Just as I am, thy love un-known, hast bro-ken ev-'ry bar-rier down; now, to be thine, yea, thine a-lone, O Lamb of God, I come, I come!

WORDS: Charlotte Elliott, 1835
MUSIC: William B. Bradbury, 1849

WOODWORTH
LM

Matthew 11:28–30

340 Softly and Tenderly

1. Soft - ly and ten - der - ly Je - sus is call - ing,
2. Why should we lin - ger when Je - sus is plead - ing,
3. O for the won - der - ful love he has prom - ised,

call - ing for you and for me; pa - tient and lov - ing, he's
plead - ing for you and for me? Why should we wait, then, and
prom - ised for you and for me; tho' we have sinned he has

wait - ing and watch - ing, watch - ing for you and for me.
heed not his mer - cies, mer - cies for you and for me?
mer - cy and par - don, par - don for you and for me.

Refrain

Come home, come home, ye who are
Come home, come home,

WORDS and MUSIC: Will L. Thompson, 1880

THOMPSON
11 7.11 7 w. refrain

wea - ry, come home; ear - nest - ly, ten - der - ly,

Je - sus is call - ing— call - ing, "O sin - ner, come home!"

Welcoming a New Member 341

Reaffirming our own faith in Jesus the Christ,
we gladly welcome you into this community of faith,
**   enfolding you with our love**
**   and committing ourselves to your care.**
In the power of God's Spirit
**   let us mutually encourage each other to trust God**
**   and strengthen one another to serve others,**
that Christ's church may in all things stand faithful.

342 Tú Has Venido a la Orilla
(Lord, You Have Come to the Lakeshore)

WORDS: Cesareo Gabaraín, 1979; tr. Gertrude C. Suppe, George
  Lockwood, and Raquel Gutiérrez-Achon, 1987
MUSIC: Cesareo Gabaraín, 1979; harm. Skinner Chávez-Melo, 1987

PESCADOR DE HOMBRES
Irr. w. refrain

♩.=70-76

y son-rien-do has di-cho mi nom - bre;

and while smil - ing have spo-ken my name;

en la a - re - na he de - ja - do mi bar - ca;

now my boat's left on the shore-line be-hind me;

jun - to a ti bus-ca-ré o-tro mar.

by your side I will seek oth-er seas.

3.

Tú necesitas mis manos,
mi cansancio que a otros descanse,
amor que quiera seguir amando.
Estribillo

4.

Tú, pescador de otros mares,
ansia eterna de almas que esperan,
amigo bueno, que así me llamas.
Estribillo

3.

You need my hands, full of caring
through my labors to give others rest,
and constant love that keeps on loving.
Refrain

4.

You, who have fished other oceans,
ever longed for by souls who are waiting,
my loving friend, as thus you call me.
Refrain

343 Jesus Is Tenderly Calling Thee Home

1. Je-sus is ten-der-ly call-ing thee home— call-ing to-day,
2. Je-sus is call-ing the wea-ry to rest— call-ing to-day,
3. Je-sus is wait-ing, O come to him now— wait-ing to-day,
4. Je-sus is plead-ing, O list to his voice— hear him to-day,

call-ing to-day; why from the sun-shine of love wilt thou roam,
call-ing to-day; bring him thy bur-den and thou shalt be blest;
wait-ing to-day; come with thy sins, at his feet low-ly bow,
hear him to-day; they who be-lieve on his name shall re-joice;

Refrain

far-ther and far-ther a-way?
he will not turn thee a-way.
come, and no long-er de-lay.
quick-ly a-rise and o-bey.

Call - ing to-day,
Call - ing, call-ing to-day, to-day,

call - ing to-day; Je - sus is
call - ing, call-ing to-day, to-day; Je - sus is ten-der-ly

WORDS: Fanny J. Crosby, 1883
MUSIC: George C. Stebbins, 1883

CALLING TODAY
10 8.10 7 w. refrain

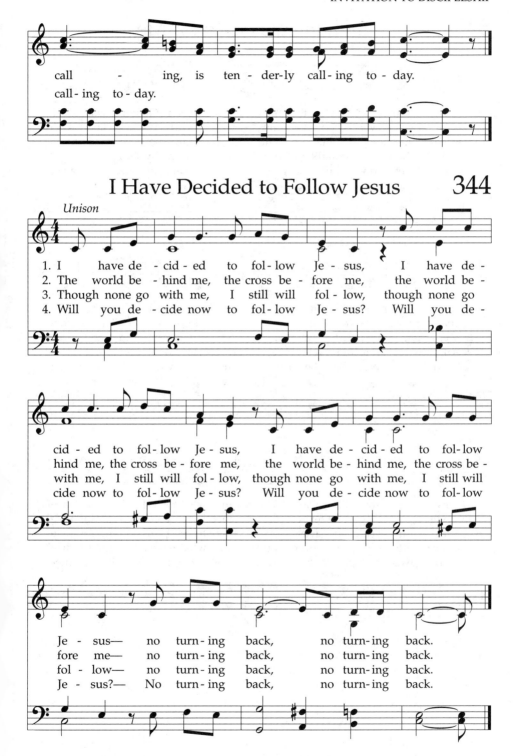

call - ing, is ten - der-ly call - ing to - day.
call - ing to - day.

I Have Decided to Follow Jesus 344

Unison

1. I have de - cid - ed to fol - low Je - sus, I have de -
2. The world be - hind me, the cross be - fore me, the world be -
3. Though none go with me, I still will fol - low, though none go
4. Will you de - cide now to fol - low Je - sus? Will you de -

cid - ed to fol - low Je - sus, I have de - cid - ed to fol - low
hind me, the cross be - fore me, the world be - hind me, the cross be -
with me, I still will fol - low, though none go with me, I still will
cide now to fol - low Je - sus? Will you de - cide now to fol - low

Je - sus— no turn - ing back, no turn - ing back.
fore me— no turn - ing back, no turn - ing back.
fol - low— no turn - ing back, no turn - ing back.
Je - sus?— No turn - ing back, no turn - ing back.

WORDS and MUSIC: Anonymous

ASSAM
10 10 10.8

345 Thy Life Was Giv'n for Me

1. Thy life was giv'n for me, thy blood, O Lord, was shed,
2. Long years were spent for me in wea - ri - ness and woe,
3. Thy Fa - ther's home of light, the rain - bow - cir - cled throne,
4. And thou hast brought to me, down from thy home a - bove,
5. O let my life be giv'n, my years for thee be spent;

1. that I might ran - somed be, and quick - ened from the dead;
2. that through e - ter - ni - ty thy glo - ry I might know;
3. were left for earth - ly night, for wan - d'rings sad and lone;
4. sal - va - tion full and free, thy par - don and thy love;
5. world - fet - ters all be riv'n, and joy with suf - f'ring blent;

1. thy life, thy life was giv'n for me; what have I giv'n for thee?
2. long years, long years were spent for me; have I spent one for thee?
3. yea! all, yea! all was left for me; have I left aught for thee?
4. great gifts, great gifts thou brought-est me; what have I brought to thee?
5. thou gav'st, thou gav'st thy - self for me, I give my - self to thee.

WORDS: Frances R. Havergal, 1859
MUSIC: Philip P. Bliss, 1873

KENOSIS
66.66.86.86

Where He Leads Me 346

1. I can hear my Sav-ior call-ing, I can hear my Sav-ior call-ing,
2. I'll go with him thru the judg-ment, I'll go with him thru the judg-ment,
3. He will give me grace and glo-ry, he will give me grace and glo-ry,

Refrain: Where he leads me I will fol-low, where he leads me I will fol-low,

I can hear my Sav-ior call-ing, "Take my cross and fol-low, fol-low me."
I'll go with him thru the judg-ment, I'll go with him, with him all the way.
he will give me grace and glo-ry, and go with me, with me all the way.

where he leads me I will fol-low— I'll go with him, with him all the way.

WORDS: E. W. Blandy, 1890
MUSIC: John S. Norris, 1890

NORRIS
888.9 w. refrain

The Great Commitment 347

What a sublime moment it is when we stand to confess with all our heart that Jesus is the Christ, the Son of the living God, and commit our all to him as Lord and personal Savior. In the light of God's infinite love as revealed in the life and death of our Lord, the confession becomes a love-binding commitment lasting to the end of our days. Surely, at such a moment heaven stoops to listen, the angels above break into singing, and God in Christ binds us to his heart with an everlasting love.

—Lin D. Cartwright, 20th-century Disciples editor

348 More About Jesus Would I Know

1. More a-bout Je-sus would I know, more of his grace to oth-ers show;
2. More a-bout Je-sus let me learn, more of his ho-ly will dis-cern;
3. More a-bout Je-sus; in his word, hold-ing com-mu-nion with my Lord;
4. More a-bout Je-sus on his throne, rich-es in glo-ry all his own;

more of his sav-ing full-ness see, more of his love who died for me.
Spir-it of God, my teach-er be, show-ing the things of Christ to me.
hear-ing his voice in ev-ery line, mak-ing each faith-ful say-ing mine.
more of his king-dom's sure in-crease; more of his com-ing, Prince of Peace.

Refrain

More, more a-bout Je-sus, more, more a-bout Je-sus;

more of his sav-ing full-ness see, more of his love who died for me.

WORDS: Eliza E. Hewitt, c. 1887
MUSIC: John R. Sweney, 1887

SWENEY
LM w. refrain

My Jesus, I Love Thee

349

1. My Je - sus, I love thee, I know thou art mine;
2. I love thee, be - cause thou hast first lov - ed me,
3. In man - sions of glo - ry and end - less de - light,

for thee all the fol - lies of sin I re - sign;
and pur - chased my par - don on Cal - va - ry's tree;
I'll ev - er a - dore thee in heav - en so bright;

my gra - cious Re - deem - er, my Sav - ior art thou;
I love thee for wear - ing the thorns on thy brow;
I'll sing with the glit - ter - ing crown on my brow,

if ev - er I loved thee, my Je - sus, 'tis now.

WORDS: William R. Featherstone, c. 1862
MUSIC: Adoniram J. Gordon, 1876

GORDON
11 11.11 11

350 I Bind My Heart This Tide

1. I bind my heart this tide to the Gal - i - le - an's side,
2. I bind my heart in thrall to the God, the Lord of all,

to the wounds of Cal - va - ry, to the Christ who died for me.
to the God, the poor ones' friend, and the Christ whom God did send.

I bind my soul this day to the broth - er far a - way,
I bind my - self to peace, to make strife and en - vy cease,

and the sis - ter near at hand, in this town, and in this land.
God, knit thou sure the cord of my thral - dom to my Lord.

WORDS: Lauchlan MacLean Watt, 1907, alt.
MUSIC: Grace Wilbur Conant, 1927

FEALTY
67.77D

Music used by permission of Fleming H. Revell Co.

Fill My Cup, Lord

351

1. Like the wom-an at the well I was seek-ing for things that
2. There are mil-lions in this world who are crav-ing the plea-sure
3. So, my friend, if all the things this world gave you leave hun-gers

could not sat-is-fy; and then I heard my Sav-ior speak-ing: "Draw
earth-ly things af-ford; but none can match the won-drous trea-sure
that won't pass a-way, my bless-ed Lord will come and save you,

from my well that nev-er shall run dry."
that I find in Je-sus Christ my Lord. Fill my cup, Lord, I lift it
if you kneel to him and hum-bly pray:

up, Lord! Come and quench this thirst-ing of my soul; Bread of Heav-en,

feed me 'til I want no more—fill my cup, fill it up and make me whole!

WORDS and MUSIC: Richard Blanchard, 1959

FILL MY CUP
Irr.

352 Spirit Song

1. O let the Son of God en-fold you with his
2. (O come and) sing this song with glad-ness as your

Spir - it and his love. Let him fill your heart and
hearts are filled with joy. Lift your hands in sweet sur-

sat - is-fy your soul. O let him have the things that
ren-der to his name. O give him all your tears and

hold you, and his Spir - it like a dove will de-
sad - ness; give him all your years of pain, and you'll

WORDS and MUSIC: John Wimber, 1979

SPIRIT SONG
97 11D

♩=108-116

353   Come to Me, O Weary Traveler

1. Come to me, O weary traveler; come to me with your distress; come to me, you heavy burdened; come to me and find your rest.
2. Do not fear, my yoke is easy; do not fear, my burden's light; do not fear the path before you; do not run from me in fright.
3. Take my yoke and leave your troubles; take my yoke and come with me. Take my yoke, I am beside you; take and learn humility.
4. Rest in me, O weary traveler; rest in me and do not fear. Rest in me, my heart is gentle; rest and cast away your care.

WORDS: Sylvia Dunstan, 1990
MUSIC: William P. Rowan, 1992

AUSTIN
87.87

𝅗𝅥=72-80

Seek Ye First

WORDS and MUSIC: Karen Lafferty, 1972

SEEK YE FIRST
Irr.

♩=72-80

355 A Disciples Affirmation

As members of the Christian Church,

We confess that Jesus is the Christ,
    the Son of the living God,
    and proclaim him Lord and Savior of the world.

In Christ's name and by his grace
    we accept our mission of witness
    and service to all people.

We rejoice in God,
    maker of heaven and earth,
    and in the covenant of love
    which binds us to God and one another.

Through baptism into Christ
    we enter into newness of life
    and are made one with the whole people of God.

In the communion of the Holy Spirit
    we are joined together in discipleship
    and in obedience to Christ.

At the table of the Lord
    we celebrate with thanksgiving
    the saving acts and presence of Christ.

Within the universal church,
    we receive the gift of ministry
    and the light of scripture.

In the bonds of Christian faith
    we yield ourselves to God
    that we may serve the One
    whose kingdom has no end.

Blessing, glory and honor
    be to God forever. Amen.

—Preamble to the Design for the Christian Church (Disciples of Christ)

We, Your People, God, Confessing 356

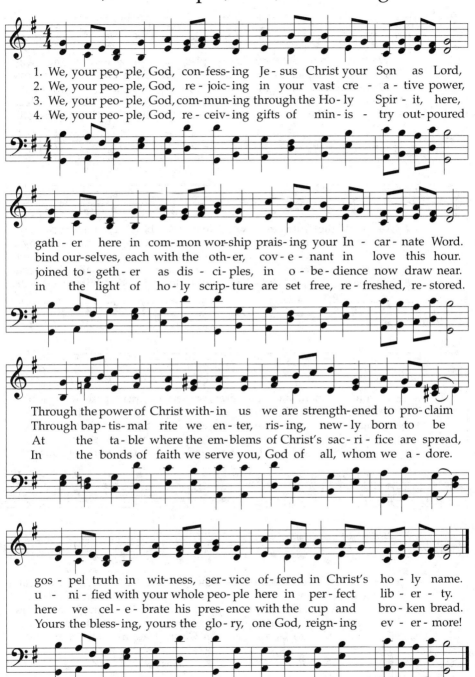

1. We, your peo-ple, God, con-fess-ing Je-sus Christ your Son as Lord,
2. We, your peo-ple, God, re-joic-ing in your vast cre-a-tive power,
3. We, your peo-ple, God, com-mun-ing through the Ho-ly Spir-it, here,
4. We, your peo-ple, God, re-ceiv-ing gifts of min-is-try out-poured

gath-er here in com-mon wor-ship prais-ing your In-car-nate Word.
bind our-selves, each with the oth-er, cov-e-nant in love this hour.
joined to-geth-er as dis-ci-ples, in o-be-dience now draw near.
in the light of ho-ly scrip-ture are set free, re-freshed, re-stored.

Through the power of Christ with-in us we are strength-ened to pro-claim
Through bap-tis-mal rite we en-ter, ris-ing, new-ly born to be
At the ta-ble where the em-blems of Christ's sac-ri-fice are spread,
In the bonds of faith we serve you, God of all, whom we a-dore.

gos-pel truth in wit-ness, ser-vice of-fered in Christ's ho-ly name.
u-ni-fied with your whole peo-ple here in per-fect lib-er-ty.
here we cel-e-brate his pres-ence with the cup and bro-ken bread.
Yours the bless-ing, yours the glo-ry, one God, reign-ing ev-er-more!

WORDS: From the Preamble to the Design of the Christian Church
    (Disciples of Christ), adapt. 1993
MUSIC: Traditional Dutch melody; arr. Julius Roentgen, 1906

IN BABILONE
87.87D

Adapt. © 1995 Chalice Press

357 We Call Ourselves Disciples

1. We call our-selves dis - ci - ples, as pil-grims on the way.
2. The cup and cross be - fore us, pro-claim our hope a - bove,
3. We're bap-tized in the Spir - it, in wa-ters God pro-vides.
4. We join with all dis - ci - ples to live the Word in deed,
5. So now the vi - sion bright-ens, the light of Christ burns still

1. We seek the truth in wis - dom, and beau-ty in each day.
2. the sign of our Re - deem - er, the ves - sel of his love.
3. In Christ we rise to new - ness, for in him we have died.
4. to share the cup of wa - ter and bread with all in need;
5. in hearts of all dis - ci - ples to be the church God wills.

1. As wom - en, men, and chil - dren, we serve, Christ's path to clear.
2. Once more the cross is lift - ed, the cup poured out for all.
3. Now dead to powers of e - vil, and free from hope-less fears,
4. to work till God's com-pass - ion and righ-teous-ness pre - vail,
5. From qui - et med - i - ta - tion, and joy - ous hymns of praise,

1. In joy - ful ex - pec - ta - tion we see God's reign draw near.
2. When gath-ered at the ta - ble we hear our com - mon call.
3. we live with faith and pur - pose, cre - a - tive through the years.
4. till all this plan - et's peo - ple know jus - tice with - out fail.
5. we go to do God's mis - sion! Christ, lead us all our days!

WORDS: Jim Miller, 1984
MUSIC: Henry T. Smart, 1836

LANCASHIRE
76.76D

Nicene Affirmation of Faith 358

We believe in one God,
> the Father, the Almighty,
> maker of heaven and earth,
> of all that is, seen and unseen.

We believe in one Lord, Jesus Christ,
> the only Son of God,
> eternally begotten of the Father,
> God from God, Light from Light,
> true God from true God,
> begotten, not made,
> of one Being with the Father;
> through him all things were made.
> For us and for our salvation
>> he came down from heaven,
>> was incarnate of the Holy Spirit and the Virgin Mary
>> and became truly human.
>> For our sake he was crucified under Pontius Pilate;
>> he suffered death and was buried.
>> On the third day he rose again
>> in accordance with the Scriptures;
>> he ascended into heaven
>> and is seated at the right hand of the Father.
>> He will come again in glory
>> to judge the living and the dead,
>> and his kingdom will have no end.

We believe in the Holy Spirit, the Lord, the giver of life,
> who proceeds from the Father and the Son,
> who with the Father and the Son
>> is worshiped and glorified,
> who has spoken through the prophets.
> We believe in the one holy catholic* and apostolic church.
> We acknowledge one baptism
>> for the forgiveness of sins.
> We look for the resurrection of the dead,
>> and the life of the world to come. Amen.

*universal

359   Apostolic Affirmation of Faith

I believe in God, the Father almighty,
    creator of heaven and earth.
I believe in Jesus Christ, his only Son, our Lord.
      He was conceived by the power of the Holy Spirit
        and born of the Virgin Mary.
      He suffered under Pontius Pilate,
        was crucified, died, and was buried.
      He descended to the dead.
      On the third day he rose again.
      He ascended into heaven,
        and is seated at the right hand of the Father.
      He will come again to judge the living and the dead.
I believe in the Holy Spirit,
    the holy catholic church,
    the communion of saints,
    the forgiveness of sins,
    the resurrection of the body,
    and the life everlasting. Amen.

360   United Church of Canada Statement of Faith

We are not alone, we live in God's world.
We believe in God:
    who has created and is creating,
    who has come in Jesus, the Word made flesh,
      to reconcile and make new,
    who works in us and others by the Spirit.
We trust in God.
We are called to be the church:
    to celebrate God's presence,
    to love and serve others,
    to seek justice and resist evil,
    to proclaim Jesus, crucified and risen,
      our judge and our hope.
In life, in death, in life beyond death,
    God is with us.
We are not alone.
Thanks be to God. Amen.

United Church of Christ Statement of Faith 361

We believe in you, O God, Eternal Spirit,
God of our Savior Jesus Christ and our God,
and to your deeds we testify.

> You call the worlds into being,
>> create persons in your own image
>> and set before each one the ways of life and death.

> You seek in holy love to save all people from aimlessness and sin.

> You judge people and nations by your righteous will
> declared through prophets and apostles.

> In Jesus Christ, the man of Nazareth, our crucified and risen Savior,
>> you have come to us
>> and shared our common lot,
>> conquering sin and death
>> and reconciling the world to yourself.

> You bestow upon us your Holy Spirit,
>> creating and renewing the church of Jesus Christ,
>> binding in covenant faithful people of all ages,
>> tongues and races.

> You call us into your Church
>> to accept the cost and joy of discipleship,
>> to be your servants in the service of others,
>> to proclaim the gospel to all the world,
>> to resist the powers of evil,
>> to share in Christ's baptism and eat at his table,
>> to join him in his passion and victory.

> You promise to all who trust you
>> forgiveness of sins and fullness of grace,
>> courage in the struggle for justice and peace,
>> your presence in trial and rejoicing,
>> and eternal life in your realm which has no end.

Blessing and honor, glory and power be unto you. Amen.

362 Filled with the Joy and Gladness

1. Filled with the joy and glad-ness of life's won - der,
2. Filled with the won - der, stand-ing in your pres - ence,
3. By all your work and love's di-vine in - ten - tion

we stand be - fore you, new life in our hands,
this new-born child be - fore your life we lay.
we have been born to new life in your name.

trem - bling with fear be - fore the un - known fu - ture,
You wait up - on the small and bear the ten - der,
Your liv - ing word sur - rounds this cel - e - bra - tion.

ear - nest but awed be - fore life's stern de - mands.
you who com - mand the plan - ets on their way.
Lord, let this child your love and faith pro - claim.

WORDS: Daniel B. Merrick, 1986
MUSIC: Joseph Barnby, 1889

O PERFECT LOVE
11 10.11 10

Here, Savior, We Would Come 363

1. Here, Sav-ior, we would come in your ap-point-ed way
2. O bless this sa-cred rite to make us whole and free.

o-be-dient to your high com-mand, our sol-emn vows to pay.
Now may we serve with faith-ful-ness and love e-ter-nal-ly.

WORDS: Anonymous, from Alexander Campbell's *The Christian Hymnbook*, 1865, alt. TRENTHAM
MUSIC: Robert Jackson, 1888 SM

Blessing of Children 364

O God, as a mother comforts her children,
    you strengthen, sustain, and provide for us.
We come before you with gratitude
    for the gift of this child,
    for the joy that has come into this family,
    and for the grace with which you surround them
    and all of us.
As a father cares for his children,
    so you continually look upon us
    with compassion and goodness.
Pour out your Spirit.
Enable your servants to abound in love,
    and establish our homes in holiness;
through Jesus Christ our Lord.
Amen.

365 Wash, O God, Your Sons and Daughters

Unison

1. Wash, O God, your sons and daugh-ters, new-born crea-tures of your womb. Num-ber them a-mong your peo - ple, raised like Christ from death and tomb. Weave them gar - ments bright and spark-ling; com-pass them with love and light. Fill, a-
2. Ev - 'ry day we need your nur - ture; by your milk may we be fed. Let us join your feast, par - tak - ing cup of bless - ing, liv - ing bread. God, re - new us; guide our foot - steps; free from sin and all its snares, one with
3. O how deep your ho - ly wis - dom! Un - i - mag - ined, all your ways! To your name be glo - ry, hon - or! With our lives we wor-ship, praise! We your peo - ple stand be - fore you, wa - ter-washed and Spir - it - born. By your

WORDS: Ruth Duck, 1987, rev. 1993
MUSIC: Attr. B. F. White, 1844; harm. James H. Wood, 1958

BEACH SPRING
87.87D

♩=74-78

noint them; send your Spir - it, ho - ly dove and heart's de - light.
Christ in liv - ing, dy - ing, by your Spir - it, chil - dren, heirs.
grace, our lives we of - fer. Re - cre - ate us; God, trans-form!

Water, River, Spirit, Grace   366

Unison

Wa - ter, Riv - er, Spir - it,

Grace, sweep o - ver me, sweep o - ver me! Re - carve the

depths your fin - gers traced in sculpt- ing me

1. in sculpt- ing me

2. sculpt- ing me.

WORDS: Thomas H. Troeger, 1987
MUSIC: O. I. Cricket Harrison, 1994

TRES RIOS
Irr.

Words © 1987, 1991, Oxford University Press; music © 1995 Chalice Press

♩=96-100

367 Take Me to the Water

1. Take me to the wa - ter, take me to the wa - ter, take me to the wa - ter to be bap - tized.
2. None but the righ - teous, none but the righ - teous, none but the righ - teous shall see God.
3. I love Je - sus, I love Je - sus, I love Je - sus, yes, I do.
4. He's my Sav - ior, he's my Sav - ior, he's my Sav - ior, yes, he is.

WORDS and MUSIC: African-American spiritual

TAKE ME TO THE WATER
Irr.

368 I Come to Be Baptized Today

Unison

1. I come to be bap - tized to - day to die with
2. I join with those who went be - fore the fam - i -
3. The wa - ters clear shall soon en - fold my bo - dy
4. I seek re - lease from for - mer ways and grace, for -

WORDS: Susan Adams, 1993
MUSIC: English folk melody; harm. John Weaver, 1988

O WALY WALY
LM

Words © 1995 Chalice Press; harm. © 1990 John Weaver

♩=56-60

Christ	and	rise	a -	gain.	I	choose	through	Christ	to
ly	of	God	on	earth.	I	stand	be -	fore	the
and	my	old	life,	too.	Through	Spir -	it's	gift	I
give -	ness	through	this	rite.	I	come	to	walk	my

walk	God's	way	and	seek	a	new	life	with -	out	end.
o -	pen	door.	Re -	ceive	me,	God,	and	give	new	birth.
will	be	bold	to	start	to	live	my	life	a -	new.
fu -	ture	days	with	Christ	a -	long	the	path	of	light.

Welcome After Baptism   369

Minister: *Name* and *Name have* risen from the waters of baptism
       to newness of life.
     They have become one with the witnesses of God
       from all times and places.
     Through baptism, God promises *them* the gift of the Holy Spirit
       to nurture *them* all the days of their lives.
     Let us add our blessing and pledge our love
       as we welcome *them* into this living community of faith.

People: **We rejoice in God's empowering love,**
       freely given to each and all.
     We welcome you, newly baptized,
       into the circle of love in Christ's church.
     We praise God for the gifts for ministry
       that you bring to this community.
     We promise to pray for you,
       to seek the depths of faith with you,
       to support you, and to love you.
     We covenant with you to love God
       with all our hearts, minds, souls and strength,
       and our neighbors as ourselves.

370   I Am Baptized

We must hold boldly and fearlessly to our baptism, and hold it up against all sins and terrors of conscience, and humbly say, "I know full well that I have not a single work which is pure, but I am baptized, and through my baptism God, who cannot lie, has bound himself in a covenant with me, not to count my sin against me, but to slay it and blot it out."

—Martin Luther, 16th-century German Protestant reformer

371   Wade in the Water

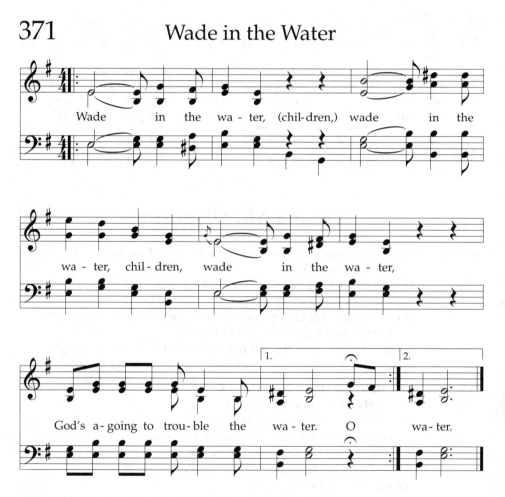

WORDS: African-American spiritual
MUSIC: African-American spiritual; harm. Willa A. Townsend

WADE IN THE WATER
Irr.

1. See that host all dressed in white,
2. See that band all dressed in red,
3. Look o - ver yon - der, what do I see?
4. If you don't be - lieve I've been re - deemed,

(Hum)

God's a-going to trou-ble the wa-ter; the lead - er looks like the
God's a-going to trou-ble the wa-ter; looks like the band that
God's a-going to trou-ble the wa-ter; the Ho - ly Ghost a -
God's a-going to trou-ble the wa-ter; just fol - low me down to

(Hum)

D.C.

Is - ra - el - ite, God's a - going to trou - ble the wa - ter.
Mo - ses led, God's a - going to trou - ble the wa - ter.
com - ing on me, God's a - going to trou - ble the wa - ter.
Jor - dan's stream, God's a - going to trou - ble the wa - ter.

Born from the Water of Baptism 372

We rose from the water to manifest the presence of Christ. We are the laos, the people of God born from the water of baptism into a sacramental ministry, manifesting the presence of Christ.

—*Peter Morgan, 20th-century Disciples church executive*

From *Mid-Stream*, 1985; used by permission of the Council on Christian Unity

373 Be in Our Midst, O Christ

Unison

1. Be in our midst, O Christ, for bless- ing
2. Held by your might - y arms en - fold-ing,
3. Coun-sel them, grant your Spir - it's guid-ing.
4. Shel - ter them with your ten - der car-ing.
5. Help them re - call their wa - ter's sign-ing.

1. your sons and daugh - ters loved by you.
2. wel - come them home by bound-less grace.
3. Lead them in paths of peace and love.
4. Here in God's house - hold be their host.
5. Bap - tized, their fear of death is gone.

1. They come, your glo - rious name con - fess-ing,
2. Safe-guard them al - ways in your hold-ing.
3. Keep them a - ware you are pro - vid - ing
4. Your gra - cious ban - quet ta - ble shar-ing,
5. Bap - tized, they break from sin's con - fin - ing.

WORDS: Colbert S. Cartwright, 1993
MUSIC: Carlton R. Young, 1984

BEGINNINGS
98.98

Words © 1995 Chalice Press; music © 1987 Hope Publishing Co.

♩·=50-54

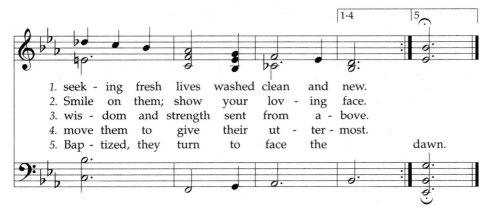

1. seek - ing fresh lives washed clean and new.
2. Smile on them; show your lov - ing face.
3. wis - dom and strength sent from a - bove.
4. move them to give their ut - ter - most.
5. Bap - tized, they turn to face the dawn.

Romans 6:4

If We Have Died to Ourselves 374

If we have died to our - selves in Je - sus,

then we shall a - rise to new life in him.

Al - le - lu - ia, al - le - lu - ia!

WORDS and MUSIC: Marty Haugen, 1984

IF WE HAVE DIED
10.10 w. alleluias

♩.=50-54

375   In Water We Grow

Unison

1. In wa-ter we grow, se-cure in the womb,
2. In wa-ter we wash: the dirt of each day,
3. In wa-ter we dive, and can-not draw breath,
4. In wa-ter we dwell, for by its deep flow

and speech-less-ly know love's safe-ty and room.
its trou-ble and rush are car-ried a-way.
then sur-face a-live, re-bound-ing from death.
through blood-stream and cell, we live, think, and grow.

Bap-tiz-ing and bless-ing, we pub-lish for good
In Christ re-cre-a-ted by love's cleans-ing art,
Our old self goes un-der, in Christ dead and drowned.
Praise God, love out-flow-ing, whose well of new birth

the free-ing, ca-ress-ing safe-keep-ing of God.
self-will and self-ha-tred dis-solve and de-part.
We rise, washed in won-der, by love clad and crowned.
bap-tiz-es our know-ing, and wa-ters the earth.

WORDS: Brian Wren, 1989
MUSIC: Carl F. Schalk, 1987

STANLEY BEACH
10 10.11 11

Words © 1993 Hope Publishing Co.; music © 1989 The United Methodist Publishing House

♩=100-104

We Know That Christ Is Raised 376

1. We know that Christ is raised and dies no more. Em-
braced by death, he broke its fear-ful hold, and
our de-spair he turned to blaz-ing joy. Al-le-lu - ia!

2. We share by wa-ter in his sav-ing death. Re-as
born, we share with him an Eas-ter life as
liv-ing mem-bers of our Sav-ior Christ. Al-le-lu - ia!

3. A new cre-a-tion comes to life and grows as
Christ's new bod-y takes on flesh and blood. The
un-i-verse re-stored and whole will sing: Al-le-lu - ia!

WORDS: John Brownlow Geyer, 1969
MUSIC: Lawrence P. Schreiber, 1965

NATIONAL CITY
10 10 10 w. alleluia

♩=100-108

Words © 1969 John Brownlow Geyer; music © 1967 Chalice Press

Baptism an Embodiment 377

Baptism is a sort of embodiment of the gospel, and a solemn expression of it all in a single act. In baptism we are passive in every thing but in giving our consent. We are buried and we are raised by another. Hence in no view of baptism can it be called a good work.

—*Alexander Campbell, 19th-century Disciples forebear*

378 Wonder of Wonders, Here Revealed

Unison

1. Won - der of won - ders, here re - vealed; God's cov - e -
2. This child of God, though young or old, we wel - come
3. Here in this sac - ra - ment we see God's grace un -
4. Our vows of faith we now re - new, stretch wide our

nant with us is sealed. And long be - fore we
now in - to Christ's fold, to know with us God's
bound, for all, for me! May we re - spond with
sights to glo - bal view, and claim with Chris - tians

know or pray, God's love en - folds us ev - ery day.
lov - ing care; here all our joys and sor - rows share.
joy - ful praise in lov - ing serv - ice all our days.
far and near a larg - er fam - i - ly held dear.

WORDS: Jane Parker Huber, 1980   CONDITOR ALME
MUSIC: Plainsong, Mode IV; harm. C. Winfred Douglas, 1943, alt.   LM

Accept, O God, the Gifts We Bring   379

Ac - cept, O   God, the gifts we bring of spir - it and of   clay,

trans-form them in - to   bless - ings on   those   we serve to - day.

Re - kin - dle deep with - in   us   all   a   pas-sion to ful - fill

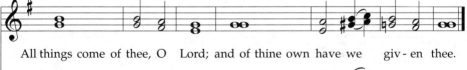

the   min - is - try dis - ci - ples have, em-power'd to do your will.

WORDS: Mary Anne Parrott, 1982   ELLACOMBE
MUSIC: *Gesangbuch der H. W. k. Hofkapelle*, 1784   CMD

Words © 1985 Chalice Press   Harmonization: #64

1 Chronicles 29:14b

All Things Come of Thee   380

All things come of thee, O   Lord; and of thine own have we   giv - en thee.

WORDS: 1 Chronicles 29:14b   OFFERING
MUSIC: Anonymous   Irr.

381   Take My Gifts

1. Take my gifts and let me love you, God who first of
all loved me, gave me light and food and shel - ter,
gave me life and set me free, now be - cause your
love has touched me, I have love to give a - way,

2. Take the fruit that I have gath - ered from the tree your
Spir - it sowed, har - vest of your own com - pas - sion,
juice that makes the wine of God, spiced with hu - mor,
laced with laugh - ter— fla - vor of the Je - sus life,

3. Take what - ev - er I can of - fer— gifts that I have
yet to find, skills that I am slow to sharp - en,
tal - ents of the hand and mind, things made beau - ti -
ful for oth - ers in the place where I must be:

WORDS: Shirley Erena Murray, 1988
MUSIC: Colin Gibson, 1988

TALAVERA TERRACE
87.87D

♩=112-120

now the bread of love is ris - ing, loaves of love to
tang of risk and new ad - ven - ture, taste and zest be -
take my gifts and let me love you, God who first of

1, 2

mul - ti - ply!
yond be - lief.

3

all loved me.

We Give Thee but Thine Own 382

1. We give thee but thine own, what - e'er the gift may be;
2. May we thy boun - ties thus as stew-ards true re - ceive,
3. To com - fort and to bless, to find a balm for woe,
4. The cap - tive to re - lease, to God the lost to bring,
5. And we be - lieve thy Word, though dim our faith may be;

1. all that we have is thine a - lone, a trust, O Lord, from thee.
2. and glad - ly, as thou bless-est us, to thee our first-fruits give.
3. to tend the lone - ly in dis - tress, is an - gels' work be - low.
4. to teach the way of life and peace— it is a Christ-like thing.
5. what- e'er for thine we do, O Lord, we do it un - to thee.

WORDS: William W. How, c. 1858
MUSIC: Mason and Webb's *Cantica Laudis*, 1850

SCHUMANN
SM

383   Savior, Thy Dying Love

1. Sav - ior, thy dy - ing love thou gav - est me,
2. Give me a faith - ful heart, guid - ed by thee,
3. All that I am and have, thy gifts so free,

nor should I aught with- hold, dear Lord, from thee;
that each de - part - ing day hence - forth may see
ev - er in joy or grief, my Lord, for thee;

in love my soul would bow, my heart ful - full its vow,
some work of love be - gun, some deed of kind - ness done,
and when thy face I see, my ran - somed soul shall be,

some of - fering bring thee now, some - thing for thee.
some wan - derer sought and won, some - thing for thee.
through all e - ter - ni - ty, of - fered to thee.

WORDS: Sylvanus Dryden Phelps, 1862, alt.   SOMETHING FOR JESUS
MUSIC: Robert Lowry, 1871   64.64.6664

Here at Thy Table, Lord   384

1. Here at thy ta - ble, Lord, this sa - cred hour,
2. Sit at the feast, dear Lord, break thou the bread;
3. Come then, O ho - ly Christ, feed us, we pray;

O let us feel thee near, in lov - ing power;
fill thou the cup that brings life to the dead;
touch with thy pierc - ed hand each com - mon day;

call - ing our thoughts a - way from self and sin.
that we may find in thee, par - don and peace;
mak - ing this earth - ly life full of thy grace,

As to thy ban - quet hall we en - ter in.
and from all bond - age win a full re - lease.
till in the home of heaven we find our place.

WORDS: May P. Hoyt (19th century)   BREAD OF LIFE
MUSIC: William F. Sherwin, 1877   64.64D

385 An Upper Room Did Our Lord Prepare

1. An up-per room did our Lord pre-pare for those he
2. A last-ing gift Je-sus gave his own: to share his
3. And af-ter sup-per he washed their feet, for ser-vice,
4. No end there is! We de-part in peace, he loves be-

loved un-til the end: and his dis-ci-ples still
bread, his lov-ing cup. What-ev-er bur-dens may
too, is sac-ra-ment. In Christ our joy shall be
yond the ut-ter-most: in ev-ery room in our

gath-er there to cel-e-brate their ris-en friend.
bow us down, he by his cross shall lift us up.
made com-plete: sent out to serve, as he was sent.
Fa-ther's house Christ will be there, as Lord and Host.

WORDS: Fred Pratt Green, 1973
MUSIC: English folk melody; harm. John Weaver, 1988

O WALY WALY
LM

♩=56-60

We Come as Guests Invited

386

1. We come as guests invited when Jesus bids us dine,
his friends on earth united to share the bread and wine;
the bread of life is broken, the wine is freely poured
for us, in solemn token of Christ our dying Lord.

2. We eat and drink, receiving from Christ the grace we need,
and in our hearts believing on him by faith we feed;
with wonder and thanksgiving for love that knows no end,
we find in Jesus living our ever-present friend.

3. One bread is ours for sharing, one single fruitful vine,
our fellowship declaring renewed in bread and wine:
renewed, sustained, and given by token, sign, and word,
the pledge and seal of heaven, the love of Christ our Lord.

WORDS: Timothy Dudley-Smith, 1975
MUSIC: Johann Steurlein, 1575

WIE LIEBLICH IST DER MAIEN
76.76D

♩=104-108

387 Bread of the World, in Mercy Broken

1. Bread of the world, in mer - cy bro - ken, wine of the
2. Look on the heart by sor - row bro - ken, look on the

soul, in mer - cy shed, by whom the words of life were
tears by sin - ners shed, and be thy feast to us the

spo - ken, and in whose death our sins are dead:
to - ken that by thy grace our souls are fed.

WORDS: Reginald Heber, 1827
MUSIC: John S. B. Hodges, 1868

EUCHARISTIC HYMN
98.98

388 Remember Me

Upon the loaf and upon the cup of the Lord, in letters which speak not to the eye, but to the heart of every disciple, is inscribed, "When this you see, remember me." Indeed, the Lord says to each disciple, when he receives the symbols into his hand, "This is my body broken for you." The loaf is thus constituted a representation of his body—first whole, then wounded for our sins. The cup is thus instituted a representation of his blood—once his life, but now poured out to cleanse us from our sins.

— Alexander Campbell, 19th-century Disciples forebear

Words of Institution

389

For I received from the Lord what I also handed on to you,
that the Lord Jesus on the night when he was betrayed
took a loaf of bread, and when he had given thanks,
he broke it and said,
"This is my body that is for you. Do this in remembrance of me."

In the same way he took the cup also, after supper, saying,
"This cup is the new covenant in my blood.
Do this, as often as you drink it, in remembrance of me."
For as often as you eat this bread and drink the cup,
you proclaim the Lord's death until he comes.

—1 Corinthians 11:23–26

Lord of Our Highest Love!

390

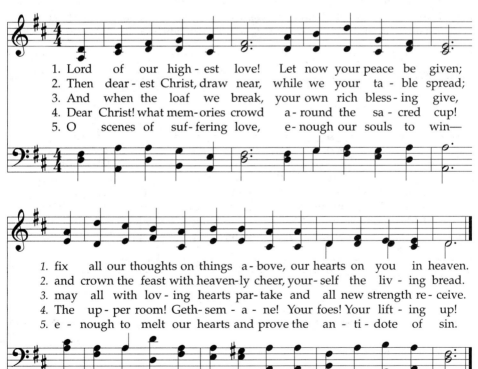

1. Lord of our high-est love! Let now your peace be given;
2. Then dear-est Christ, draw near, while we your ta-ble spread;
3. And when the loaf we break, your own rich bless-ing give,
4. Dear Christ! what mem-ories crowd a-round the sa-cred cup!
5. O scenes of suf-fering love, e-nough our souls to win—

1. fix all our thoughts on things a-bove, our hearts on you in heaven.
2. and crown the feast with heaven-ly cheer, your-self the liv-ing bread.
3. may all with lov-ing hearts par-take and all new strength re-ceive.
4. The up-per room! Geth-sem-a-ne! Your foes! Your lift-ing up!
5. e-nough to melt our hearts and prove the an-ti-dote of sin.

WORDS: G. Y. Tickle (19th century)
MUSIC: Johann B. Köenig, 1738; arr. W. H. Havergal, 1847

FRANCONIA
SM

391

These I Lay Down

1. Be - fore I take the bo - dy of my Lord, be -
2. The words of hope I of - ten failed to give, the
3. The nar - row - ness of vi - sion and of mind, the
4. Of those a - round in whom I meet my Lord, I
5. Lord Je - sus Christ, com - pan - ion at this feast, I

1. fore I share his life in bread and wine, I re - cog - nize the
2. prayers of kind - ness bur - ied by my pride, the signs of care I
3. need for oth - er folk to serve my will, and ev - ery word and
4. ask their par - don and I grant them mine that ev - ery con - tra -
5. emp - ty now my heart and stretch my hands, and ask to meet you

1. sor - ry things with - in: these I lay down.
2. ar - gued out of sight: these I lay down.
3. si - lence meant to hurt: these I lay down.
4. dic - tion to Christ's peace might be laid down.
5. here in bread and wine which you lay down.

WORDS and MUSIC: John Bell, 1989

LAYING DOWN
88.84

♩=96-100

Draw Us in the Spirit's Tether

392

WORDS: Percy Dearmer, 1931, alt.
MUSIC: Harold Friedell, 1957; adapt. Jet Turner, 1967

UNION SEMINARY
87.87.44.7

 1 Corinthians 10:16–17

393 One Bread, One Body

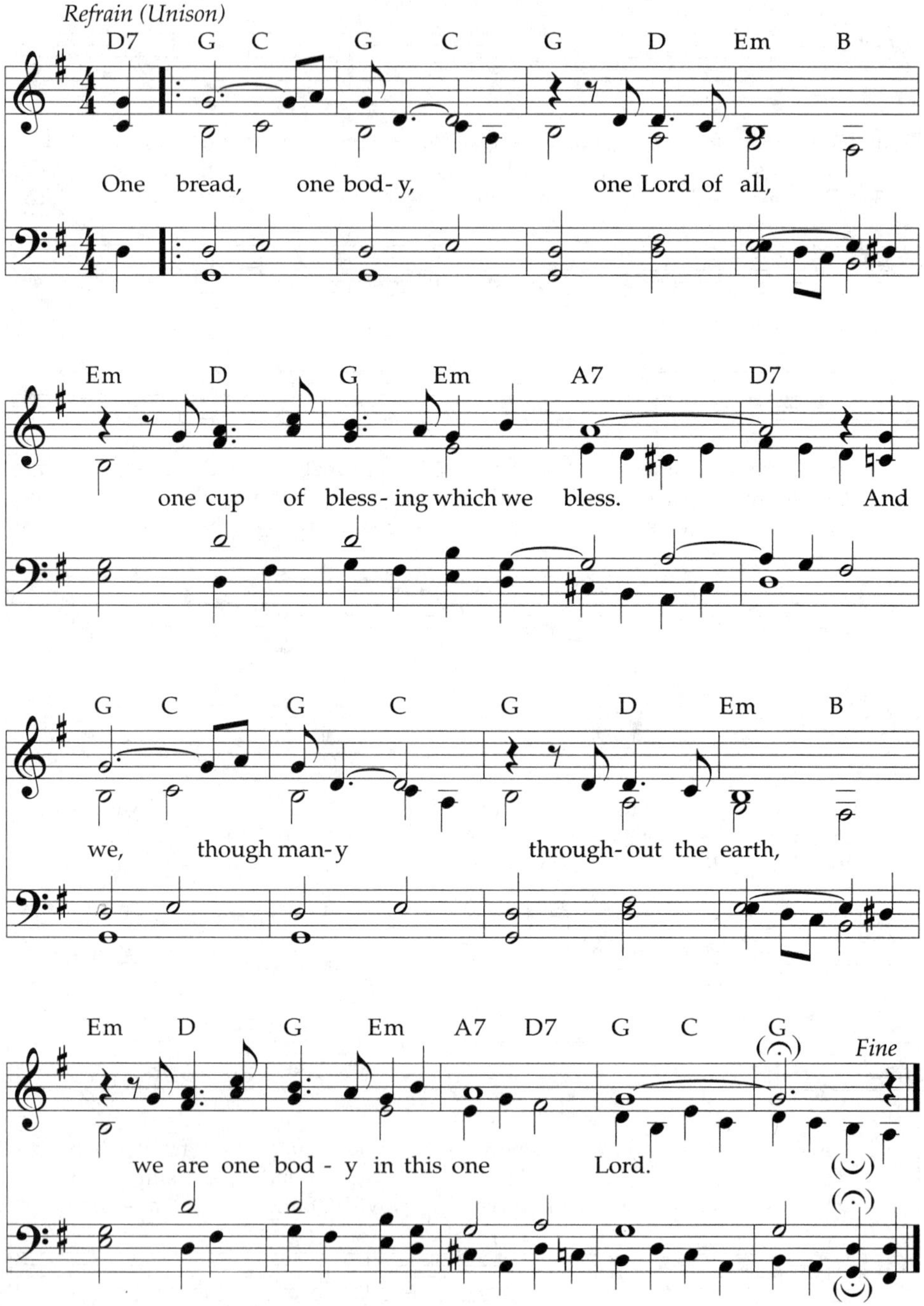
Refrain (Unison)
D7 G C G C G D Em B
One bread, one bod-y, one Lord of all,
Em D G Em A7 D7
one cup of bless-ing which we bless. And
G C G C G D Em B
we, though man-y through-out the earth,
Em D G Em A7 D7 G C G
Fine
we are one bod - y in this one Lord.

WORDS and MUSIC: John B. Foley, 1978

ONE BREAD, ONE BODY
44.6 w. refrain

♩=104-112

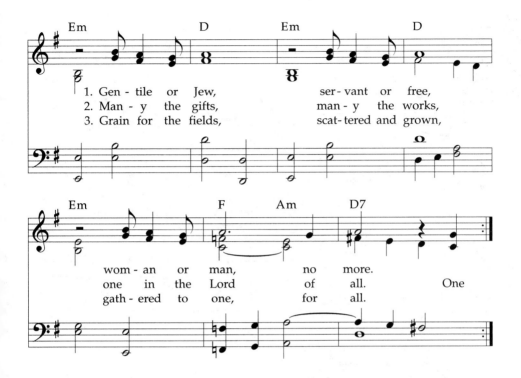

1. Gen - tile or Jew, ser - vant or free,
2. Man - y the gifts, man - y the works,
3. Grain for the fields, scat - tered and grown,

wom - an or man, no more.
one in the Lord of all. One
gath - ered to one, for all.

That the Church May Be One 394

As the bread which we break
was scattered over the mountains
and when brought together became one,
so let your church be brought together
from the ends of the earth into your eternal realm;
for yours is the glory and the power
through Jesus Christ for evermore.

—Didache, 2nd century, alt.

1 Corinthians 10:16–17

395 Seed, Scattered and Sown

Seed, scat-tered and sown, wheat, gath-ered and grown, bread, bro-ken and shared as one, the Liv-ing Bread of God. Vine, fruit of the land, wine, work of our hands, one cup that is shared by all; the Liv-ing Cup, the

WORDS: Dan Feiten, 1987

MUSIC: Dan Feiten, 1987; arr. Eric Gunnison and R. J. Miller, alt.

SEED SCATTERED

Irr.

♩=88-96

Liv - ing Bread of God. God.

1. Is not the bread we break a shar - ing in our
2. The seed which falls on rock will with - er and will
3. As wheat up - on the hills was gath - ered and was

Lord? Is not the cup we bless the
die. The seed with - in good ground will
grown, so may the church of God be

blood of Christ out - poured?
flow - er and have life.
gath - ered in - to one.

396

Una Espiga
(Sheaves of Summer)

Unísono (Unison)

1. U - na es - pi - ga do - ra - da por el sol,
2. Com - par - ti - mos la mis - ma co - mu - nión,
3. Co - mo gra - nos que han he - cho el mis - mo pan,
4. En la me - sa de Dios se sen - ta - rán,

1. Sheaves of sum - mer turned gold - en by the sun,
2. We are shar - ing the same com - mun - ion meal,
3. Like the grains which be - come one same whole loaf,
4. At God's ta - ble to - geth - er we shall sit.

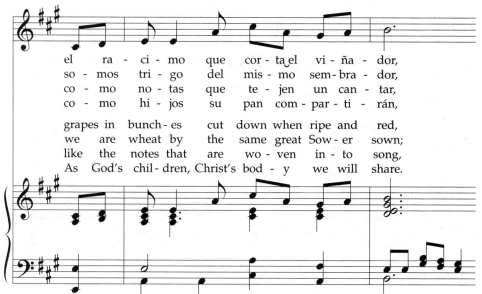

el ra - ci - mo que cor - ta el vi - ña - dor,
so - mos tri - go del mis - mo sem - bra - dor,
co - mo no - tas que te - jen un can - tar,
co - mo hi - jos su pan com - par - ti - rán,

grapes in bunch - es cut down when ripe and red,
we are wheat by the same great Sow - er sown;
like the notes that are wo - ven in - to song,
As God's chil - dren, Christ's bod - y we will share.

WORDS: Cesareo Gabaraín, 1973; tr. George Lockwood, 1989
MUSIC: Cesareo Gabaraín, 1973, alt.; harm. Skinner Chávez-Melo, 1973

UNA ESPIGA
Irr.

♩=88-96

se con - vier-ten   a - hor-ra‿en pan y   vi - no de‿a-mor,
un mo -li-no‿a   la vi - da nos tri - tu - ra con do - lor,
co - mo go-tas   de a - gua que se   fun-den en el mar,
u - na mis-ma‿es-pe - ran - za ca - mi - nan-do can-ta - rán,

are con - vert-ed   in - to   the bread and wine of   God's love
like a mill-stone life grinds us down with sor-row   and pain,
like the drop-lets   of wa - ter that are blend-ed in the sea,
One same hope we   will sing   to - geth - er   as we walk a - long.

en el cuer-po‿y   la san - gre del Se - ñor.
Dios nos ha - ce pue - blo nue - vo‿en el   a - mor.
los cris - tia - nos   un cuer - po for - ma - rán.
en la vi - da co - mo‿her - ma - nos se‿a - ma - rán.

in the bod - y   and blood of our dear Lord.
but God makes us   new peo - ple bound by love.
we, as Chris - tians one bod - y shall be - come.
Broth-ers, sis - ters,   in life,   in love, we'll be.

397   Come, Risen Lord

1. Come, ris-en Lord, and deign to be our guest;
no, let us your guest be— with you we dine.
Your-self at your own board be man-i-fest
in this your sac-ra-ment of bread and wine.

2. We meet, as in that up-per room they met;
here at the ta-ble, bless-ing, still you stand.
"This is my bod-y"— you are with us yet;
faith still re-ceives the cup as from your hand.

3. We are one bod-y, for we all par-take,
one church u-nit-ed in com-mun-ion blessed;
one name we bear, one bread of life we break,
with all your saints on earth and saints at rest.

4. One with each oth-er, Lord, so let us be;
one with our Sav-ior and our liv-ing Head.
Then op-en now our eyes, that we may see;
be known to us in break-ing of the bread.

WORDS: George W. Briggs, 1931, alt.
MUSIC: Eric H. Thiman, 1948

HOLBORN
10 10.10 10

Be Known to Us in Breaking Bread   398

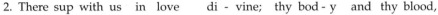

1. Be known to us in break - ing bread, but do not then de - part;
2. There sup with us in love di - vine; thy bod - y and thy blood,

Sav - ior, a - bide with us, and spread thy ta - ble in our heart.
that liv - ing bread, that heaven-ly wine, be our im - mor - tal food.

WORDS: James Montgomery, 1825   ST. AGNES
MUSIC: John B. Dykes, 1866   CM

O God, Unseen Yet Ever Near   399

1. O God, un - seen yet ev - er near, re - veal thy pres - ence now,
2. Here may thy faith - ful peo - ple know the bless-ings of thy love—
3. A - while be - side the fount we stay and eat this bread of thine;

while we, in love that hath no fear, be - fore thy glo - ry bow.
the streams that thro' the des - ert flow, the man - na from a - bove.
then go, re - joic- ing, on our way, re - newed with strength di - vine.

WORDS: Edward Osler, 1836; alt.   BELMONT
MUSIC: William Gardiner's *Sacred Melodies*, 1815   CM

400 When You Do This, Remember Me

1. You my friend, a stran-ger once, do now be-long to
2. Now my Lord is al-so yours, my peo-ple are your
3. All your sor-rows shall be mine, your joy shall be my
4. So let us re-new our faith, re-mem-ber-ing our

heaven. Once far a-way, you are brought home in-
own; em-braced to-geth-er in God's arms, I enjoy; in-debt-ed to God's love in Christ, we
Lord; to our strong hope we will hold fast, un-

to God's fam-i-ly. "When you do this, re-mem-ber me."
fold you now in mine. "When you do this, re-mem-ber me."
die and reign with him. "When you do this, re-mem-ber me."
shak-en to the end. "When you do this, re-mem-ber me."

WORDS: Alexander Campbell (19th century); adapt. David
  L. Edwards, 1988
MUSIC: David L. Edwards, 1988; arr. Jane Marshall, 1993

LORETTO
76.86.8

♩=102-106

Communion Affirmation 401

You, my beloved, once an alien, are now a citizen of heaven: once a stranger, are now brought home to the family of God. You have owned my Lord as your Lord, my people as your people.

Under Jesus the Messiah we are one. Mutually embraced in the everlasting arms, I embrace you in mine: your sorrows shall be my sorrows, and your joys my joys.

Joint debtors to the favor of God and the love of Jesus, we shall jointly suffer with him, that we may jointly reign with him.

Let us, then, renew our strength, remember our Sovereign, and hold fast our boasted hope unshaken to the end.

— Alexander Campbell, 19th-century Disciples forebear

1 Corinthians 11:23–26

According to Thy Gracious Word 402

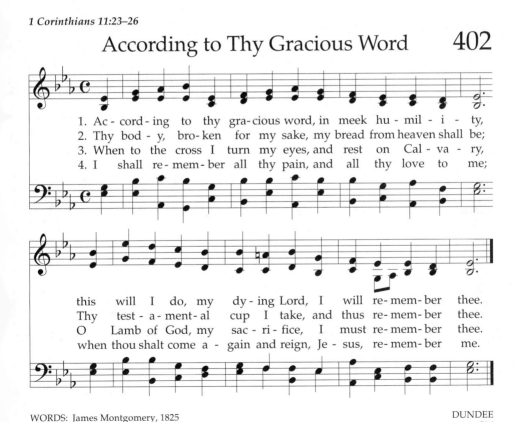

1. Ac - cord - ing to thy gra - cious word, in meek hu - mil - i - ty,
2. Thy bod - y, bro - ken for my sake, my bread from heaven shall be;
3. When to the cross I turn my eyes, and rest on Cal - va - ry,
4. I shall re - mem - ber all thy pain, and all thy love to me;

this will I do, my dy - ing Lord, I will re - mem - ber thee.
Thy test - a - ment - al cup I take, and thus re - mem - ber thee.
O Lamb of God, my sac - ri - fice, I must re - mem - ber thee.
when thou shalt come a - gain and reign, Je - sus, re - mem - ber me.

WORDS: James Montgomery, 1825
MUSIC: *Scottish Psalter*, 1615, alt.

DUNDEE
CM

1 Corinthians 11:23–25

403   In Remembrance of Me

1. In re - mem-brance of me, eat this bread. In re -
2. (In re -) mem-brance of me, heal the sick. In re -

mem-brance of me, drink this wine. In re-mem-brance of me,
mem-brance of me, feed the poor. In re-mem-brance of me,

pray for the time when God's own will is done. In re -
o - pen the door and let your neigh-bor

in, let them in. Take, eat, and be com-fort-ed;

WORDS: Ragan Courtney, 1972
MUSIC: Buryl Red, 1972; arr. Robert F. Douglas

RED
Irr.

♩=112-120

404 A Hymn of Joy We Sing

1. A hymn of joy we sing a - round your ta - ble, Lord;
2. Here do we see your face, and feel your pres - ence here;
3. In self - for - get - ting love be our com - mu - nion shown,

a - gain our grate - ful trib - ute bring, our sol - emn vows re - cord.
so may the sav - or of your grace in word and life ap - pear.
un - til we join the church a - bove, and know as we are known.

WORDS: Aaron R. Wolfe, 1858, alt.
MUSIC: Lowell Mason, 1832

BOYLSTON
SM

Luke 22:14–20

405 In Memory of the Savior's Love

1. In mem - ory of the Sav - ior's love, we keep the sa - cred feast,
2. By faith we take the bread of life by which our souls are fed,
3. In faith and mem - ory here we sing the won - ders of his love,

where ev - ery hum - ble, con - trite heart is made a wel - come guest.
the cup in to - ken of his blood that was for sin - ners shed.
and thus an - tic - i - pate by faith the heaven - ly feast a - bove.

WORDS: Thomas Cotterill, 1805
MUSIC: Johann Michael Haydn (18th century), adapt.

SALZBURG
CM

Beneath the Forms of Outward Rite 406

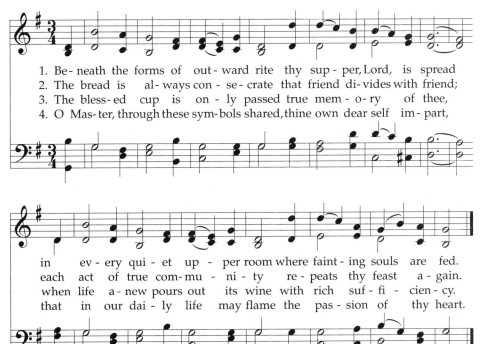

1. Be- neath the forms of out - ward rite thy sup - per, Lord, is spread
2. The bread is al- ways con - se - crate that friend di- vides with friend;
3. The bless- ed cup is on - ly passed true mem - o- ry of thee,
4. O Mas- ter, through these sym-bols shared, thine own dear self im- part,

in ev - ery qui - et up - per room where faint - ing souls are fed.
each act of true com- mu - ni - ty re - peats thy feast a - gain.
when life a - new pours out its wine with rich suf - fi - cien - cy.
that in our dai - ly life may flame the pas - sion of thy heart.

WORDS: James A. Blaisdell, 1837, alt.
MUSIC: William Gardiner's *Sacred Melodies*, 1815

BELMONT
CM

Call to Communion 407

Alexander Campbell, a founder of the Disciples of Christ, reports the following call to communion given by an elder in the early nineteenth century. With these words we gather with the saints of the ages at the table of our one Lord.

In memory of his death, this monumental table was instituted; and as the Lord ever lives in heaven, so he ever lives in the hearts of his people. As the first disciples, taught by the Apostles in person, came together into one place to eat the Lord's Supper, and as they selected the first day of the week, in honor of his resurrection for this purpose; so we, having the same Lord, the same faith, the same hope with them, have vowed to do as they did. We owe as much to the Lord as they; and ought to love, honor, and obey him as much as they.

—*Millennial Harbinger*, 1830

408   Come, Share the Lord

1. We gath - er here in Je - sus' name,
2. He joins us here, he breaks the bread,
3. We'll gath - er soon where an - gels sing;

his love is burn - ing in our hearts like liv - ing flame;
the Lord who pours the cup is ris - en from the dead;
we'll see the glo - ry of our Lord and com - ing King;

for through the lov - ing Son the Fa - ther makes us one:
the one we love the most is now our gra - cious host:
now we an - ti - ci - pate the feast for which we wait:

Come, take the bread, come, drink the wine, come, share the Lord.
Come, take the bread, come, drink the wine, come, share the Lord.
Come, take the bread, come, drink the wine, come, share the Lord.

WORDS and MUSIC: Bryan Jeffery Leech, 1984

DIVERNON
Irr.

♩=72-76

1. No one is a stranger here, everyone belongs;
   finding our forgiveness here, we in turn forgive all wrongs.
2. We are now a family of which the Lord is head;
   though unseen he meets us here in the breaking of the bread.

D. C.

I Hunger and I Thirst 409

1. I hunger and I thirst; Jesus, my manna be!
   O living waters, burst out of the rock for me!
2. O bruised and broken Bread, my life-long needs supply.
   As living souls are fed, so feed me, or I die.
3. O true life-giving Vine, let me your goodness prove.
   By your life sweeten mine, refresh my soul with love.
4. For still the desert lies behind me and before:
   O living waters, rise within me evermore!

WORDS: John S. B. Monsell, 1866, alt.
MUSIC: Maria Tiddeman, 1875, alt.

IBSTONE
66.66

410   Now We Come Before God's Presence

1. Now we come be-fore God's pres - ence, full of
2. Bread of life, so free - ly giv - en, keep-ing
3. Cup of sor - row, cup of joy, fill - ing
4. Love be-yond all com - pre - hen - sion, of-fered

joy with songs of praise for the cup and
hun - gry spir - its fed. We, in turn, with
souls that come in thirst, like-wise, we shall
through this feast di - vine, we can on - ly

bread life-giv - ing, heal - ing all our sin - ful ways.
great thanks-giv - ing, free - ly share our world-ly bread.
fill the cups of those who thirst through-out the earth.
go in joy to share with all our bread and wine.

WORDS and MUSIC: Peter Olejar, 1992

ST. PAUL'S
87.87

© 1995 Chalice Press

♩=102-108

For the Bread, Which You Have Broken 411

1. For the bread, which you have bro - ken, for the
2. By these pledg - es that you love us, by your
3. In your ser - vice, Lord, de - fend us; help us

wine, which you have poured, for the words, which you have
gift of peace re - stored, by your call to heaven a -
to o - bey your word; in the world to which you

spo - ken, now we give you thanks, O Lord.
bove us, con - se - crate our lives, O Lord.
send us let your will be done, O Lord.

WORDS: Louis F. Benson, 1924, alt.
MUSIC: Charles J. Dickinson, 1861

AGAPE
87.87

Alt. tune: KINGDOM

The Miracle of Communion 412

The miracle of Communion means the rich bowing down with the poor, the learned with the unlearned, the clean with the filthy, the master with the slave, the privileged with the deprived, the white with the black, and the black with the white.

—*Rosa Page Welch, 20th-century African-American Disciples singer*

413 Take Our Bread

Refrain (Unison)

1. Take our bread, we ask you; take our hearts, we love you.
Take our lives, O Fa-ther, we are yours, we are yours.

1. Yours as we stand at the ta-ble you set;
2. Your ho-ly peo-ple stand-ing washed in your blood,

yours as we eat the bread our hearts can't for-get.
Spir-it-filled yet hun-gry we a-wait your food. We are

We are the sign of your life with us yet,
poor, but we've brought our-selves the best that we could;

WORDS and MUSIC: Joe Wise, 1966

TAKE OUR BREAD
Irr. w. refrain

♩=76-80

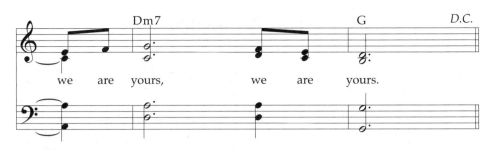

we are yours, we are yours.

John 6:35

Eat This Bread

414

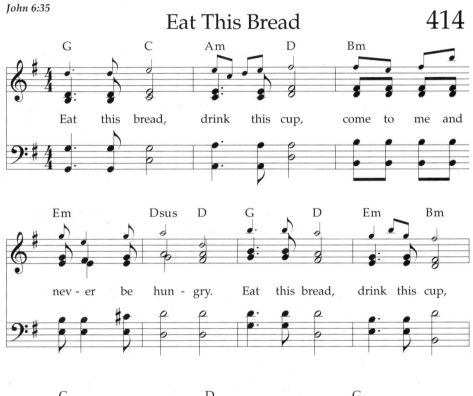

Eat this bread, drink this cup, come to me and

nev-er be hun-gry. Eat this bread, drink this cup,

trust in me and you will not thirst.

Descant for C instrument
May be sung throughout communion

WORDS: Robert Batastini and the Taizé Community, 1982
MUSIC: Jacques Berthier, 1982

BERTHIER
Irr.

♩=60-66

415 Now the Silence

Now the si-lence Now the peace Now the emp-ty hands up-
lift-ed Now the kneel-ing Now the plea Now the Fa-ther's
arms in wel-come Now the hear-ing Now the power
Now the ves-sel brimmed for pour-ing

WORDS: Jaroslav J. Vajda, 1968
MUSIC: Carl F. Schalk, 1969

NOW
Irr.

♩·=56-60

Now the bod - y Now the blood Now the joy - ful

cel - e - bra - tion Now the wed - ding Now the songs

Now the heart for - giv - en leap - ing Now the Spir - it's

vis - i - ta - tion Now the Son's e - piph - a - ny

Now the Fa - ther's bless - ing Now Now Now

416 Here, O My Lord, I See Thee Face to Face

1. Here, O my Lord, I see thee face to face;
   here would I touch and handle things unseen;
   here grasp with firmer hand eternal grace,
   and all my weariness upon thee lean.

2. Here would I feed upon the bread of God;
   here drink with thee the royal wine of heav'n;
   here would I lay aside each earthly load;
   here taste afresh the calm of sin forgiv'n.

3. Too soon we rise; the symbols disappear;
   the feast, tho' not the love, is past and gone;
   the bread and wine remove, but thou art here—
   nearer than ever— still my shield and sun.

4. Feast after feast thus comes and passes by;
   yet, passing, points to the glad feast above—
   giving sweet foretaste of the festal joy,
   the Lamb's great bridal feast of bliss and love.

WORDS: Horatius Bonar, 1855
MUSIC: Felix Mendelssohn (19th century)

CONSOLATION
10 10.10 10

We Place upon Your Table, Lord 417

1. We place up-on your ta-ble, Lord, the
2. With-in these sim-ple things there lie the
3. Ac-cept them, Lord, they come from you; we

food of life, the bread and wine, as sym-bols of our
height and depth of hu-man life: our pain and tears, our
take them hum-bly from your hand. These gifts of yours for

dai-ly work, ac-cord-ing to your grand de-sign.
thoughts and toils, our hopes and fears, our joy and strife.
high-er use we of-fer up as you com-mand.

WORDS: M. F. C. Wilson (20th century), alt.
MUSIC: Adapt. from *Musicalisches Handbuch*, Hamburg, 1690

WINCHESTER NEW
LM
Alt. tune: OLD HUNDREDTH

Behold These Emblems 418

With what heart-felt assurance should we make God's sheltering wings our refuge! With what reverential joy should we approach the sacred memorials of God's grace, here presented before us, and "banquet on his love's repast."

Behold these emblems! They speak to the heart.
They tell of God's love—the love of the One from whom all love proceeds.
They tell of sorrows borne for us; of humiliation, pain, and death.
Let us consider them. We come to Jesus, and he meets us here.

—Robert Richardson, 19th-century Disciples leader, alt.

419 All Who Hunger, Gather Gladly

1. All who hun-ger, gath-er glad-ly; ho-ly man-na is our bread.
2. All who hun-ger, nev-er strang-ers, seek-er, be a wel-come guest.
3. All who hun-ger, sing to-geth-er; Je-sus Christ is liv-ing bread.

Come from wil-der-ness and wan-d'ring. Here, in truth, we will be fed.
Come from rest-less-ness and roam-ing. Here, in joy, we keep the feast.
Come from lone-li-ness and long-ing. Here, in peace, we have been led.

You that yearn for days of full-ness, all a-round us is our food.
We that once were lost and scat-tered in com-mu-nion's love have stood.
Blest are those who from this ta-ble live their days in grat-i-tude.

Taste and see the grace e-ter-nal. Taste and see that God is good.
Taste and see the grace e-ter-nal. Taste and see that God is good.
Taste and see the grace e-ter-nal. Taste and see that God is good.

WORDS: Sylvia Dunstan, 1990
MUSIC: *Columbian Harmony*, 1825

HOLY MANNA
87.87D

♩=56-60

I Come with Joy

Unison

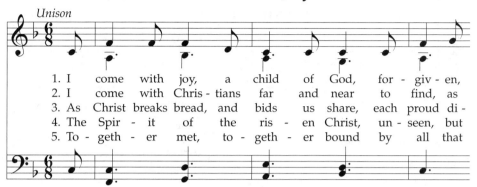

1. I come with joy, a child of God, for - giv - en,
2. I come with Chris - tians far and near to find, as
3. As Christ breaks bread, and bids us share, each proud di -
4. The Spir - it of the ris - en Christ, un - seen, but
5. To - geth - er met, to - geth - er bound by all that

1. loved and free, the life of Je - sus to re - call, in
2. all are fed, the new com - mun - i - ty of love in
3. vi - sion ends. The love that made us, makes us one, and
4. ev - er near, is in such friend - ship bet - ter known, a -
5. God has done, we'll go with joy, to give the world the

1. love laid down for me, in love laid down for me.
2. Christ's com - mun - ion bread, in Christ's com - mun - ion bread.
3. strang - ers now are friends, and strang - ers now are friends.
4. live a - mong us here, a - live a - mong us here.
5. love that makes us one, the love that makes us one.

WORDS: Brian Wren, 1969; rev. 1982, 1995
MUSIC: *Southern Harmony*, 1835; harm. Charles H.
Webb, 1987

DOVE OF PEACE
CM

♩.=66-72

421 Hasta Tu Altar
(Unto Your Table, Lord)

Unison

1. Has - ta tu al - tar ve - ni - mos hoy, Se -
2. Gra - cias Se - ñor por dar - nos es - te

1. Un - to your ta - ble, Lord, we come to -
2. We thank you, God, for giv - ing us the

ñor, con gus - to y a - le - gri - a; a pre - sen -
pan, por dar - nos es - te vi - no; gra - cias tam -

day with joy and with thanks - giv - ing. We bring the
bread; for giv - ing us the wine. We thank you

tar el vi - no y el pan y to - da nues - tra vi - da.
bién por to - da tu bon - dad, por to - do tu ca - ri - ño.

wine, we al - so bring the bread, and all our lives as of - f'ring.
too for all your love to us and all your gra - cious mer - cies.

Has - ta tu al - tar ve - ni - mos hoy, Se -
Gra - cias Se - ñor, por com - par - tir tu a -

Un - to your ta - ble, Lord, we come to -
We thank you, God, for giv - ing us your

WORDS: Carlos Rosas, 1991; tr. Luis Ferrer, 1994
MUSIC: Carlos Rosas, 1991; arr. Felicia Fina, 1995

HASTA TU ALTAR
Irr.

© 1991 Carlos Rosas; tr. © 1995 Chalice Press; arr. © 1995 The United Methodist Publishing House

♩=120-132

422   Let Us Talents and Tongues Employ

1. Let us tal-ents and tongues em-ploy. Reach-ing out with a
2. Christ is a-ble to make us one. At the ta-ble he
3. Je-sus calls us in, sends us out bear-ing fruit in a

shout of joy: bread is bro-ken, the wine is poured,
sets the tone, teach-ing peo-ple to live to bless,
world of doubt, gives us love to tell, bread to share:

Christ is spo-ken and seen and heard.
love in word and in deed ex-press. Je-sus lives a-gain,
God (Im-man-u-el) ev-ery-where!

Maracas, tambourine, and other rhythm instruments may also be used.

WORDS: Fred Kaan, 1975
MUSIC: Jamaican folk melody, adapt. Doreen Potter, 1975

LINSTEAD
LM w. refrain

♩=128-136

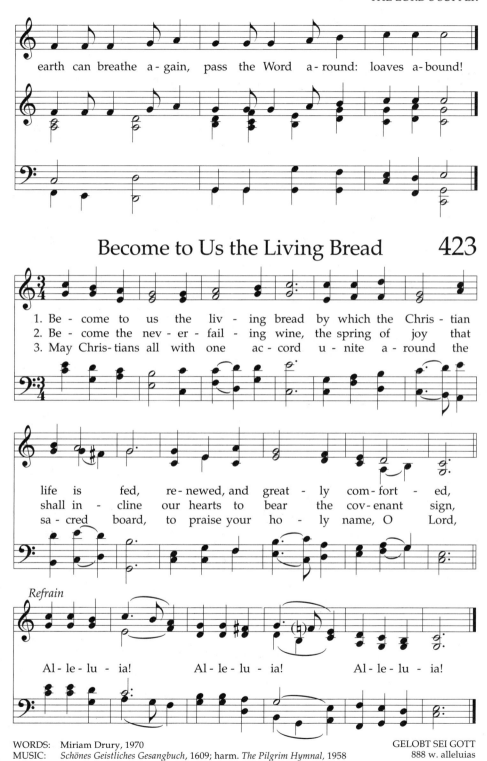

earth can breathe a-gain, pass the Word a-round: loaves a-bound!

Become to Us the Living Bread 423

1. Be - come to us the liv - ing bread by which the Chris - tian
2. Be - come the nev - er - fail - ing wine, the spring of joy that
3. May Chris - tians all with one ac - cord u - nite a - round the

life is fed, re - newed, and great - ly com - fort - ed,
shall in - cline our hearts to bear the cov - enant sign,
sa - cred board, to praise your ho - ly name, O Lord,

Refrain

Al - le - lu - ia! Al - le - lu - ia! Al - le - lu - ia!

WORDS: Miriam Drury, 1970
MUSIC: *Schönes Geistliches Gesangbuch*, 1609; harm. *The Pilgrim Hymnal*, 1958

GELOBT SEI GOTT
888 w. alleluias

Words © 1972 Westminster/John Knox Press

Alt. tune: O FILII ET FILIAE

424 I'm Gonna Eat at the Welcome Table

1. I'm gon-na eat at the wel-come ta - ble,
2. I'm gon-na eat and drink with my Je - sus,
3. I'm gon-na join with sis - ters, broth - ers,

I'm gon-na eat at the wel-come ta - ble, Al - le - lu.
I'm gon-na eat and drink with my Je - sus, Al - le - lu.
I'm gon-na join with sis - ters, broth-ers, Al - le - lu.

I'm gon-na eat at the wel-come ta - ble, I'm gon-na
I'm gon-na eat and drink with my Je - sus, I'm gon-na
I'm gon-na join with sis - ters, broth - ers, I'm gon-na

eat at the wel - come ta - ble, Al - le - lu.
eat and drink with my Je - sus, Al - le - lu.
join with sis - ters, broth - ers, Al - le - lu.

4. Here all the world will find a welcome.
5. We're gonna feast on milk and honey.

WORDS: African-American spiritual, alt.
MUSIC: African-American spiritual; arr. Carl Ditson, alt.

WELCOME TABLE
Irr.

Arr. © 1980 G. Shirmer, Inc.

♩=124-132

Let Us Break Bread Together

1. Let us break bread to-geth-er on our knees; (on our knees)
2. Let us drink wine to-geth-er on our knees; (on our knees)
3. Let us praise God to-geth-er on our knees; (on our knees)

let us break bread to-geth-er on our knees. (on our knees)
let us drink wine to-geth-er on our knees. (on our knees)
let us praise God to-geth-er on our knees. (on our knees)

Refrain

When I fall on my knees, with my face to the ris-ing sun,

O Lord, have mer-cy on me. (on me)

WORDS: African-American spiritual
MUSIC: African-American spiritual; arr. Carlton R. Young, 1964, alt.

LET US BREAK BREAD
Irr.

426 The Voice of Jesus Calls His People

Unison

1. The voice of Je - sus calls his peo - ple, "Come to my ta - ble and be fed!" For those who come to him be - liev - ing, he is the Wine, he is the Bread. All who are lost, or bear great bur - dens, all who need com - fort or re - lease, come where the

2. Chil - dren and eld - ers, men and wom - en, what - ev - er col - or, race or tongue, in Je - sus find them - selves u - nit - ed, in him a home where they be - long. We hear your lov - ing voice, O Je - sus, we long, we hun - ger to be fed; in joy we

WORDS and MUSIC: Joy F. Patterson, 1993

THE VOICE OF JESUS
98.98D

♩=76

pres - ence of Christ Je - sus will nour - ish us with rest and peace.
gath - er at the ta - ble where you are Wine, and you are Bread.

Loving Lord, as Now We Gather   427

1. Lov - ing Lord, as now we gath - er, of that love un - wor - thy still,
2. Ho - ly Lord, as here you give us bread and wine, as means of grace,

give us cour - age to sur - ren - der reb - el heart and stub - born will,
grant to all who call you Sav - ior, now to meet you face to face,

and in us, in faith ma - tur - ing, all your prom - is - es ful - fill.
and to own, in si - lent won - der, Lord, how ho - ly is this place.

WORDS: Fred Pratt Green, 1977
MUSIC: Welsh melody

RHUDDLAN
87.87.87

Words © 1982 Hope Publishing Co.

♩=88-96

428 An Upper Room with Evening Lamps Ashine

1. An up-per room with eve-ning lamps a-shine,
2. We see by faith up - on the cross dis-played
3. Dead for our sins, yet reign-ing now a - bove:
4. So send us out, to love and serve and praise,

the twelve dis - ci - ples, and the ta - ble spread;
his bod - y bro - ken and his blood out - poured;
still to our hearts we find his pres-ence given;
filled with his Spir - it, as the Mas - ter said:

now in our turn Christ bids us pour the wine,
in that dread robe of maj - es - ty ar - rayed
take for our - selves the pledg - es of his love,
love, joy and peace the wine of all our days,

and in re - mem-brance bless and break the bread.
we gaze in wor - ship on the dy - ing Lord.
fore - taste and to - ken of that feast in heaven.
Christ and his life our true and liv - ing bread.

WORDS: Timothy Dudley-Smith, 1987
MUSIC: William Henry Monk, 1861

EVENTIDE
10 10.10 10

You Satisfy the Hungry Heart

429

Refrain

You sat-is-fy the hun-gry heart with gift of fin-est wheat;

Fine

come give to us, O sav-ing Lord, the bread of life to eat.

1. With joy-ful lips we sing to you our praise and grat-i-tude
2. Is not the cup we bless and share the blood of Christ out-poured?
3. The mys-tery of your pres-ence, Lord, no mor-tal tongue can tell:
4. You give your-self to us, O Lord; then self-less let us be,

D.C.

that you should count us wor-thy, Lord, to share this heaven-ly food.
Do not one cup, one loaf, de-clare our one-ness in the Lord?
whom all the world can-not con-tain comes in our hearts to dwell.
to serve each oth-er in your name in truth and char-i-ty.

WORDS: Omer Westendorf, 1976
MUSIC: Robert E. Kreutz, 1976

FINEST WHEAT
CM w. refrain

♩=80-88

Matthew 28:20

430   Lo, I Am with You

Unison

1. Lo, I am with you to the end of the world.
2. Lo, I am with you in the break - ing of bread.
3. Lo, I am with you in the drink - ing of wine.

Lo, I am with you to the end of the world.
Lo, I am with you in the break - ing of bread.
Lo, I am with you in the drink - ing of wine.

Lo, I am with you,   Lo, I am with you,
Lo, I am with you,   Lo I am with you,
Lo, I am with you,   Lo, I am with you,

Lo, I am with you to the end of the world.
Lo, I am with you in the break - ing of bread.
Lo, I am with you in the drink - ing of wine.

4. Lo, I am with you in the struggle for peace.   6. Lo, I am with you in the shadow of death.
5. Lo, I am with you in the way of the cross.   7. Lo, I am with you to the end of the world.

WORDS: St. 1, 4, 5, 6, 7 Iona Community, 1988; st. 2, 3 Guy Aydelott, 1991
MUSIC: John Bell, 1988

PRESENCE
11 11.10 11

Go, My Children, with My Blessing 431

1. Go, my chil-dren, with my bless-ing, nev - er a - lone;
2. Go, my chil-dren, sins for-giv-en, at peace and pure,
3. Go, my chil-dren, fed and nour-ished, clos - er to me;

wak - ing, sleep-ing, I am with you, you are my own;
here you learned how much I love you, what I can cure;
grow in love and love by serv-ing, joy - ful and free.

in my love's bap - tis - mal riv - er I have made you mine for
here you heard my Son's dear sto - ry, here you touched him, saw his
Here my Spir - it's pow - er filled you, here his ten - der com - fort

ev - er, go, my chil-dren, with my bless-ing you are my own.
glo - ry, go, my chil-dren, sins for-giv - en at peace and pure.
stilled you; go, my chil-dren, fed and nour-ished, joy - ful and free.

WORDS: Jaroslav J. Vajda, 1983
MUSIC: Traditional Welsh melody; harm. Ralph Vaughan Williams

AR HYD Y NOS
84.84.888.4

432   O Christ, the Way, the Truth, the Life

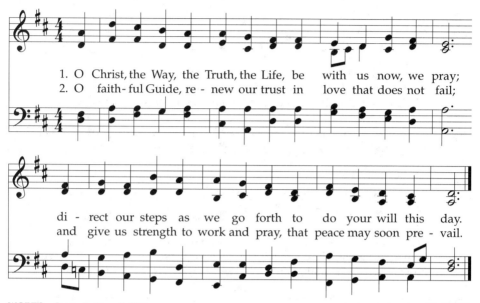

1. O Christ, the Way, the Truth, the Life, be with us now, we pray;
2. O faith-ful Guide, re-new our trust in love that does not fail;

di-rect our steps as we go forth to do your will this day.
and give us strength to work and pray, that peace may soon pre-vail.

WORDS: James L. Merrell, 1991
MUSIC: Alexander R. Reinagle, 1836
Words © 1995 Chalice Press

ST. PETER
CM

433   Blest Be the Tie That Binds

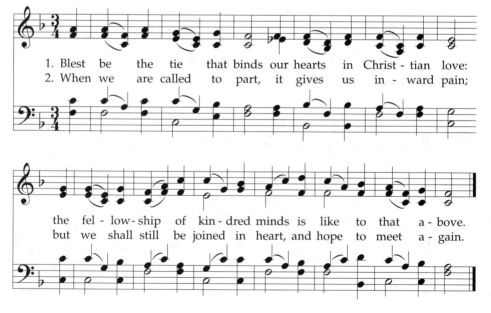

1. Blest be the tie that binds our hearts in Christ-tian love:
2. When we are called to part, it gives us in-ward pain;

the fel-low-ship of kin-dred minds is like to that a-bove.
but we shall still be joined in heart, and hope to meet a-gain.

WORDS: John Fawcett, 1872
MUSIC: Johann G. Nägeli, 1828; arr. Lowell Mason, 1845

DENNIS
SM

God Be with You Till We Meet Again 434

1-4. God be with you till we meet a - gain;

lov - ing coun - sels guide, up - hold you, with a shep - herd's
un - seen wings, pro - tect - ing, hide you, dai - ly man - na
when life's per - ils thick con - found you, put un - fail - ing
keep love's ban - ner float - ing o'er you, smite death's threat - ening

care en - fold you: God be with you till we meet a - gain.
still pro - vide you: God be with you till we meet a - gain.
arms a - round you: God be with you till we meet a - gain.
wave be - fore you: God be with you till we meet a - gain.

Refrain

Till we meet till we meet, till we meet at Je - sus' feet;
Till we meet, till we meet, till we meet;

till we meet, till we meet, God be with you till we meet a - gain.
till we meet, till we meet,

WORDS: Jeremiah E. Rankin, 1880, alt.
MUSIC: William G. Tomer, 1880

GOD BE WITH YOU
98.89 w. refrain

435 God Be with You

God be with you, God be with you, God be with you till we meet a-gain, O God be with you, God be with you, God be with you till we meet a-gain.

Till we meet (till we meet), till we meet (till we meet), till we meet our spir-its keep, till we meet (till we meet), till we

WORDS and MUSIC: Thomas A. Dorsey and Artelia W. Hutchins, 1940

DORSEY
Irr.

♩=60

436 Shalom to You Now

Sha-lom to you now, sha-lom, my friends.

May God's full mer-cies bless you, my friends.

In all your liv-ing and through your lov-ing,

Christ be your sha-lom, Christ be your sha-lom.

WORDS: Elise S. Eslinger, 1980
MUSIC: Traditional Spanish melody; harm. Carlton R. Young, 1989

Words © 1983, harm. © 1989, The United Methodist Publishing House

SOMOS DEL SEÑOR
Irr.

♩=112-120

Alt. setting: #536

Go Now in Peace

437

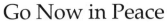

Go now in peace, go now in peace, may the love of

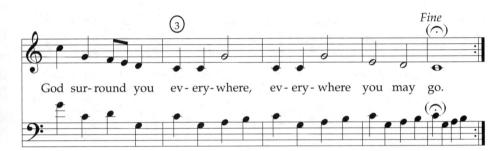

God sur-round you ev-ery-where, ev-ery-where you may go.

May be sung as a round

WORDS and MUSIC: Natalie Sleeth, 1976

GO IN PEACE
Irr.

© 1976 Hinshaw Music, Inc.

Shalom Chaverim

438

Sha - lom cha-ve-rim sha - lom cha-ve-rim. Sha - lom, sha - lom.
Fare - well, dear friends, stay safe, dear friends, have peace, have peace.

Le - hit - ra - ot, le - hit - ra - ot, sha - lom, sha - lom.
We'll see you a-gain, we'll see you a-gain, have peace, have peace.

May be sung as a round

WORDS: Traditional Hebrew blessing; tr. Roger N. Deschner, 1982
MUSIC: Israeli melody

SHALOM
Irr.

Tr. © 1982 The United Methodist Publishing House

439 God, Dismiss Us with Your Blessing

1. God, dis-miss us with your bless-ing; fill our hearts with
2. Thanks we give and ad-o-ra-tion for your gos-pel's

joy and peace; let us each, your love pos-sess-ing,
joy-ful sound. May the fruits of your sal-va-tion

tri-umph in re-deem-ing grace. O re-fresh us,
in our hearts and lives a-bound; ev-er faith-ful,

O re-fresh us, trav-eling through this wil-der-ness.
ev-er faith-ful to the truth may we be found.

WORDS: Attr. John Fawcett, 1773, alt.
MUSIC: *The European Magazine and Review*, 1792; harm. *The Methodist Hymn and Tune Book*, 1889, alt.

SICILIAN MARINERS
87.87.87

May Our God Watch Between Us   440
(Mizpah Benediction)

May our God watch be - tween us un -

til we meet one an - oth - er a - gain.

WORDS: Adapt. from Genesis 31:49   ASHOKAN FAREWELL
MUSIC: Jay Ungar, 1983; adapt. O. I. Cricket Harrison, 1994   Irr.

Music © 1983, 1990, Swinging Door Music

♩=112-120

Peace Be upon You   441

Peace be up - on you and guard you for - ev - er.

Go in the knowl - edge that God is with you.

WORDS and MUSIC: Daniel S. Wilshire, 1993   PEACE
                                                               Irr.

442

We Are Walking
(Siyahamba/Caminando)

We are walk ing* in the light of God, we are
Si - ya - hamb' e - ku-kha-nyen' kwen-khos', si - ya -
Ca - mi - nan - do en la luz de Dios, ca - mi -

1.
walk - ing in the light of God. We are
hamb' e - ku - kha-nyen' kwen - khos. Si - ya -
nan - do en la luz de Dios. Ca - mi -

of God we are
kwen - khos' si - ya
de Dios ca - mi

2.
walk - ing in the light of the light of God. We are
hamb' e - ku - kha-nyen' kwen kha - nyen' kwen-khos'. Si - ya
nan - do en la luz de la luz de Dios. Ca - mi -

of God
kwen - khos'
de Dios

marching/singing/dancing/praying

WORDS and MUSIC: South Africa (20th century)

SIYAHAMBA
Irr.

© 1984 Utryck; used by permission of Walton Music Corp.

Joy Through Involvement   443

O Lord Jesus Christ, help the church be able to see and describe itself as the source of freedom and power, so that it can communicate with the world and participate in the revolutionary changes that are taking place. And help it to find the joy that comes through involvement, with your help, in making all persons free.

—Rosa Page Welch, 20th-century African-American Disciples singer

444 Let Us Now Depart in Thy Peace

Let us now de-part in thy peace, bless-ed Je - sus.

Send us to our homes with God's love in our hearts.

Let not the bus-y world claim all our loy-al-ties.

Keep us ev-er mind-ful, dear Lord, of thee. A - men.

WORDS and MUSIC: New Mexican folk song;
adapt. Lee Hastings Bristol, 1961

A LA PUERTA
12 11.12 10

♩=88-96

Go in Peace

WORDS: Barber L. Waters, 1982
MUSIC: Kenneth E. White, 1982

© 1982 Barber L. Waters and Kenneth E. White

OCEAN PARK
Irr.

446 The Lord Bless You and Keep You

The Lord bless you and keep you. The Lord lift his coun-te-nance up-

on you, and give you peace,

on you, and give you peace and give you

and give you peace. The Lord make his face to shine up-

The Lord make his face to shine up-

peace.

on you and be gra - cious un-to you, be gra-cious;

on you and be gra-cious, and be gra-cious;

WORDS: Numbers 6:24–26 (KJV)
MUSIC: Peter C. Lutkin, 1900

BENEDICTION
Irr.

447

Thuma Mina
(Send Me, Jesus)

WORDS: South African text
MUSIC: South African melody

THUMA MINA
Irr.

♩=100-104

May the Blessing of God

448

Sing unaccompanied or with simple accompaniment

May the bless - ing of God go be -

fore you. May her grace and peace a - bound. May her

Spir - it live with - in you. May her love wrap you

'round. May her bless - ing re - main with you

al - ways. May you walk on ho - ly ground.

WORDS and MUSIC: Miriam Therese Winter, 1987

BLESSING SONG
Irr.

♩=80

May God Embrace Us

449

May the God who dances in creation,
who embraces us with human love,
who shakes our lives like thunder,
bless us and drive us out with power
to fill the world with her justice.
Amen.

—Janet Morley, 20th-century British churchwoman

450 God the Spirit, Guide and Guardian

1. God the Spir - it, guide and guard - ian, wind - sped flame and
2. Christ our Sav - ior, sov - ereign, shep - herd, word made flesh, love
3. Great Cre - a - tor, life - be - stow - er, truth be - yond all
4. Tri - une God, mys - te - rious be - ing, un - di - vid - ed

hov - ering dove, breath of life and voice of proph - ets, sign of
cru - ci - fied, teach - er, heal - er, suf - fering ser - vant, friend of
thought's re - call, fount of wis - dom, womb of mer - cy, giv - ing
and di - verse, deep - er than our minds can fath - om, great - er

bless - ing, power of love: give to those who lead your
sin - ners, foe of pride: in your tend - ing may all
and for - giv - ing all: as you know our strength and
than our creeds re - hearse: help us in our var - ied

peo - ple, fresh a - noint - ing of your grace; send them forth as
pas - tors* learn and live a shep - herd's care; grant them cour - age
weak - ness, so may those the church ex - alts o - ver - see its
call - ings your full im - age to pro - claim, that our min - is -

*When appropriate, minsters, leaders, elders, teachers, or deacons may be substituted for pastors.

WORDS: Carl P. Daw, Jr., 1987, alt.   HYFRYDOL
MUSIC: Rowland H. Prichard, 1844; harm. from *The English Hymnal*, 1906   87.87D

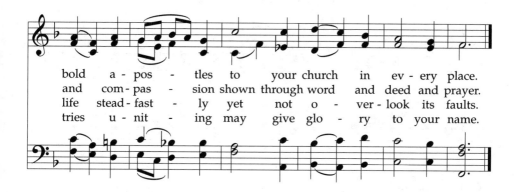

bold   a - pos - tles to   your church in   ev - ery place.
and   com - pas - sion shown through word and deed and prayer.
life   stead - fast - ly   yet   not o -   ver - look its faults.
tries   u - nit - ing may   give glo - ry   to your name.

Litany of Ministry   451

O God, who sent Jesus into the world
not to be ministered unto, but to minister,
and to give his life to set others free,
shape us for your ministry.

Claim us, O God, for your service, and direct us toward your will.

You have graced all members of Christ's body, one by one,
with gifts of the Spirit to fulfill their vocation:
> to lead lives worthy of your calling,
> to be workers who have no reason to be ashamed,
> to shine as lights to your glory.

**You have granted each of us the manifestation of the Spirit
for the common good.**

You give grace according to the measure of Christ's gift,
> and some are called to be apostles,
> some prophets,
> some evangelists,
> some pastors and teachers,
> to equip the saints for the work of ministry,
> for building up the body of Christ.

**Grant that together we may all come to the unity of the faith
and of the knowledge of your Son, to the full stature of Christ.**

Through your grace, O God, may we lead a life
worthy of the vocation to which you call us.

Claim us, O God, for your service, and direct us toward your will.

Adapted from New Testament texts by Colbert S. Cartwright

Isaiah 6:8

452 Here I Am, Lord

1. I, the Lord of sea and sky, I have heard my peo-ple cry.
2. I, the Lord of snow and rain, I have borne my peo-ple's pain.
3. I, the Lord of wind and flame, I will tend the poor and lame.

All who dwell in deep-est sin my hand will save.
I have wept for love of them, they turn a-way.
I will set a feast for them, my hand will save.

I who made the stars of night, I will make their dark-ness bright.
I will break their hearts of stone, give them hearts for love a-lone.
Fin-est bread I will pro-vide till their hearts be sat-is-fied.

WORDS: Daniel L. Schutte, 1981
MUSIC: Daniel L. Schutte, 1981; harm. James Snyder, 1994

HERE I AM, LORD
77.74 w. refrain

♩=110

Who will bear my light to them? Whom shall I send?
I will speak my word to them. Whom shall I send?
I will give my life to them. Whom shall I send?

Harmony

Here I am, Lord. Is it I, Lord? I have heard you call-ing in the

night. I will go, Lord, if you lead me. I will

hold your peo-ple in my heart.

heart.
heart, in my heart.

heart, in my heart.

453 Called as Partners in Christ's Service

1. Called as part-ners in Christ's ser-vice, called to min-is-tries of grace,
2. Christ's ex-am-ple, Christ's in-spir-ing, Christ's clear call to work and worth,
3. Thus new pat-terns for Christ's mis-sion, in a small or glob-al sense,
4. So God grant us for to-mor-row ways to or-der hu-man life

we re-spond with deep com-mit-ment fresh new lines of faith to trace.
let us fol-low, nev-er fal-tering, rec-on-cil-ing folk on earth.
help us bear each oth-er's bur-dens, break-ing down each wall or fence.
that sur-round each per-son's sor-row with a calm that con-quers strife.

May we learn the art of shar-ing, side by side and friend with friend,
Men and wom-en, rich-er, poor-er, all God's peo-ple, young and old,
Words of com-fort, words of vi-sion, words of chal-lenge, said with care,
Make us part-ners in our liv-ing, our com-pas-sion to in-crease,

e - qual part-ners in our car-ing to ful-fill God's cho-sen end.
blend-ing hu-man skills to-geth-er gra-cious gifts from God un-fold.
bring new power and strength for ac-tion, make us col-leagues, free and fair.
mes-sen-gers of faith, thus giv-ing hope and con-fi-dence and peace.

WORDS: Jane Parker Huber, 1981
MUSIC: John Zundel, 1870

BEECHER
87.87D

Come, Celebrate the Call of God 454

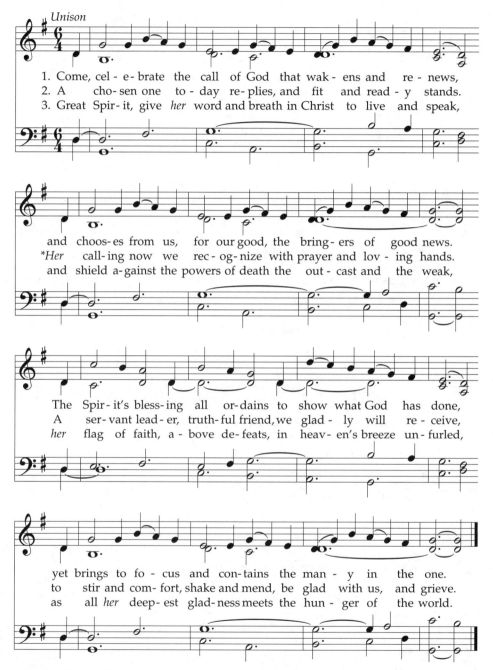

1. Come, cel-e-brate the call of God that wak-ens and re-news,
and choos-es from us, for our good, the bring-ers of good news.
The Spir-it's bless-ing all or-dains to show what God has done,
yet brings to fo-cus and con-tains the man-y in the one.

2. A cho-sen one to-day re-plies, and fit and read-y stands.
*Her call-ing now we rec-og-nize with prayer and lov-ing hands.
A ser-vant lead-er, truth-ful friend, we glad-ly will re-ceive,
to stir and com-fort, shake and mend, be glad with us, and grieve.

3. Great Spir-it, give *her* word and breath in Christ to live and speak,
and shield a-gainst the powers of death the out-cast and the weak,
her flag of faith, a-bove de-feats, in heav-en's breeze un-furled,
as all *her* deep-est glad-ness meets the hun-ger of the world.

* For *her,* sing *his* when appropriate.

WORDS: Brian Wren, 1989
MUSIC: Hal H. Hopson, 1993

ALIDA'S TUNE
CMD

♩.=44-46

455 You Have Called Me

1. You have called me from my hid-ing place and giv-en me a name; from this mo-ment on my life can nev-er be the same. I have seen the beck-on-ing vi-sion, though I want-ed to re-main, here I am, send me, here I am.

2. You have called me from my wil-der-ness and giv-en me a way. The man-y paths I've trav-eled have but brought me to this day. And the jour-ney that is call-ing me no long-er will de-lay. Here I am, send me, here I am.

3. You have called me from my si-lence and have giv-en me a word. I was dy-ing in my cold-ness till a fire with-in me stirred. Now I can keep still no long-er, I must speak what I have heard. Here I am, send me, here I am.

WORDS: David L. Edwards, 1983
MUSIC: David L. Edwards, 1983; arr. Darrell R. Faires, Sr., 1994

KAYE'S SONG
Irr.

© David L. Edwards, 1983; arr. © 1995 Shalom Publications

♩=124-132

Refrain

"Who will go in-to the dark-ness where my peo-ple live in fear? Who will speak of truth and char-i-ty so all of them can hear? If you go where I am send-ing you, I al-ways will be near. Here I am, go for me, here I am."

Prayer from the Heart 456

When you pray,
    rather let your heart be without words
        than your words without heart.

—*John Bunyan, 17th-century English author*

457 Colorful Creator

Unison

1. Col - or - ful Cre - a - tor, God of mys - ter - y,
2. Har - mo - ny of ag - es, God of list - 'ning ear,
3. Au - thor of our jour - ney, God of near and far,
4. God of truth and beau - ty, Po - et of the Word,

thank you for the art - ist teach-ing us to see
thank you for com - po - sers tun - ing us to hear
praise for tale and dra - ma tell-ing who we are,
may we be cre - a - tors by the Spir - it stirred,

glimp-ses of the mean - ing of the com - mon - place,
ech - oes of the Gos - pel in the songs we sing,
strip-ping to the es - sence strug-gles of our day,
o - pen to your pres - ence in our joy and strife,

vi - sions of the ho - ly in each hu - man face.
sounds of love and long - ing from the deep - est spring.
times of change and con - flict when we choose our way.
ves - sels of the ho - ly cours-ing through our life.

WORDS: Ruth Duck, 1992
MUSIC: Carlton R. Young, 1992

HOUGHTON
11 11.11 11

© 1993 Hope Publishing Co.

♩=100-104

Ours the Journey

Unison

1. In the midst of new di-men-sions, in the face of chang-ing ways,
2. Through the flood of starv-ing peo-ples, war-ring fac-tions and de-spair,
3. Though we reach the high-est heav-ens, hold-ing worlds at our com-mand,
4. Should the threats of dire pre-dic-tions cause us to with-draw in pain,

who will lead the pil-grim peo-ples wan-der-ing their sep-'rate ways?
who will lift the ol-ive branch-es? Who will light the flame of care?
we are yet a des-ert peo-ple search-ing for the prom-ised land.
may your blaz-ing phoe-nix spir-it res-ur-rect the church a-gain.

Refrain

God of rain-bow, fier-y pil-lar, lead-ing where the ea-gles soar,

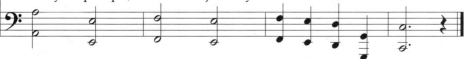

we your peo-ple, ours the jour-ney now and ev-er-more.

WORDS and MUSIC: Julian B. Rush, 1979

OURS THE JOURNEY
87.87 w. refrain

♩=108-112

459 Lord, You Give the Great Commission

1. Lord, you give the great com-mis-sion: "Heal the sick and
2. Lord, you call us to your ser-vice: "In my name bap-
3. Lord, you make the com-mon ho-ly: "This my bod - y,
4. Lord, you show us love's true mea-sure: "Fa - ther, what they
5. Lord, you bless with words as - sur-ing: "I am with you

1. preach the word." Lest the church ne - glect its mis - sion,
2. tize and teach." That the world may trust your prom - ise,
3. this my blood." Let us all, for earth's true glo - ry,
4. do, for - give." Yet we hoard as pri - vate trea - sure
5. to the end." Faith and hope and love re - stor - ing,

1. and the gos - pel go un - heard, help us wit - ness
2. life a - bun - dant meant for each, give us all new
3. dai - ly lift life heav - en - ward, ask - ing that the
4. all that you so free - ly give. May your care and
5. may we serve as you in - tend and, a - mid the

1. to your pur - pose with re - newed in - teg - ri - ty.
2. fer - vor, draw us clos - er in com - mu - ni - ty.
3. world a - round us share your chil - dren's lib - er - ty.
4. mer - cy lead us to a just so - ci - e - ty.
5. cares that claim us, hold in mind e - ter - ni - ty.

WORDS: Jeffery Rowthorn, 1978
MUSIC: Cyril V. Taylor, 1941

ABBOT'S LEIGH
87.87D

♩=106-112

Refrain

With the Spir-it's gifts em-power us for the work of min - is - try.

The Church in Mission 460

Gracious God,
    we celebrate with thanksgiving your acts of creation,
    your making all humanity in your own image,
    and your presence throughout the world in all of life.

We thank you for the gift of redemption in Jesus of Nazareth
    in whom "the Word became flesh and dwelt among us,
    full of grace and truth."

We rejoice that you have never, in any time or place, been without witness.
We take joy in making known your deeds throughout the earth
    and your transforming power in Jesus Christ.

Be with your church in every time and place as we seek
    to be faithful in witness to your power and love.
Give us strength to challenge all attempts
    to deprive persons of their humanity.
Encourage us to support all who suffer on behalf of justice and freedom.
May your church always witness to the gospel's declaration
    of the uniqueness and value of all persons as your children.

We bless you for your everlasting love that impels us
    to share the good news of Jesus Christ,
    to witness to the ultimate hope for the world
        in the fulfillment of your will on earth, and
    to prepare the way for Christ
        to be known deeply in each individual life.

We pray in Christ Jesus that the church may forever bring praise to you.
Work your power in us to do far more than we dare ask or think. Amen.

—"General Principles and Policies," Division of Overseas Ministries, adapt.

461 Lord, Whose Love Through Humble Service

1. Lord, whose love through hum-ble ser - vice bore the weight of
2. Still your chil - dren wan-der home - less; still the hun-gry
3. As we wor - ship, grant us vi - sion, till your love's re -
4. Called by wor - ship to your ser - vice, forth in your dear

hu - man need, who up - on the cross, for - sak - en,
cry for bread; still the cap - tives long for free - dom;
veal - ing light in its height and depth and great - ness
name we go to the child, the youth, the a - ged,

of - fered mer - cy's per - fect deed: we, your ser - vants, bring the
still in grief we mourn our dead. As, O Lord, your deep com -
dawns up - on our quick-ened sight, mak- ing known the needs and
love in liv - ing deeds to show; hope and health, good will and

wor - ship not of voice a - lone, but heart, con - se - crat - ing
pas - sion healed the sick and freed the soul, use the love your
bur - dens your com-pas-sion bids us bear, stir-ring us to
com - fort, coun-sel, aid, and peace we give, that your ser - vants,

WORDS: Albert F. Bayly, 1961, alt.
MUSIC: Attr. B. F. White, 1844; harm. Ronald A. Nelson, 1978

BEACH SPRING
87.87D

♩=64-70

to your pur - pose ev - ery gift that you im - part.
Spir - it kin - dles still to save and make us whole.
tire - less striv - ing your a - bun - dant life to share.
Lord, in free - dom may your mer - cy know, and live.

God's Covenant 462

RESPONSE
Unison

The peo- ple who walked in dark-ness have seen a great light.

R

Here is my servant, whom I uphold,
 my chosen, in whom my soul delights;
I have put my spirit upon him;
 he will bring forth justice to the nations.
He will not cry or lift up his voice,
 or make it heard in the street;
a bruised reed he will not break,
 and a dimly burning wick he will not quench;
 he will faithfully bring forth justice.
He will not grow faint or be crushed
 until he has established justice in the earth;
 and the coastlands wait for his teaching. **R**

Thus says God, the LORD,
 who created the heavens and stretched them out,
 who spread out the earth and what comes from it,
who gives breath to the people upon it
 and spirit to those who walk in it:
I am the LORD, I have called you in righteousness,
 I have taken you by the hand and kept you;
I have given you as a covenant to the people,
 a light to the nations,
 to open the eyes that are blind,
to bring out the prisoners from the dungeon,
 from the prison those who sit in darkness. **R**

WORDS: Isaiah 42:1–7; Response, Isaiah 9:2, adapt.
MUSIC: Carlton R. Young, 1989

Adapt., music © 1989 The United Methodist Publishing House

463 Renew Your Church

1. Re - new your church, our min - is - tries re - store: both to serve and a - dore.
2. Teach us your word, re - veal its truth di - vine, on our path let it shine.
3. Teach us to pray, for you are ev - er near, your still voice let us hear.
4. Teach us to love, with strength of heart and mind, each and all— hu - man - kind!

Make us a - gain as salt through-out the land, and as light from a stand.
Tell of your works, your might - y acts of grace, from each page show your face.
Our souls are rest - less 'til they rest in you: Love's de - sign, ev - er new.
Break down old walls of pre - ju - dice and hate, leave us not to our fate.

'Mid som - ber shad - ows of the night, where greed and ha - tred spread their blight,
As you have sent your Christ to save, in love to tri - umph o'er the grave,
Be - fore your pres - ence keep us still that we may find for us your will
As you have loved and giv'n your life to end hos - til - i - ty and strife,

O send us forth with power en - dued. Help us, God, be re - newed.
O let our hearts with love be stirred, help us, God, know your word.
and seek your guid - ance ev - ery day. Teach us, God, how to pray.
O share your grace from heav'n a - bove, teach us, God, how to love.

WORDS: Kenneth L. Cober, 1960, alt.
MUSIC: American folk melody, c. 1840

ALL IS WELL
10 6.10 6.88.86

God of Grace and God of Glory 464

1. God of grace and God of glo-ry, on thy peo-ple
2. Lo! the hosts of e-vil round us scorn thy Christ, as-
3. Cure thy chil-dren's war-ring mad-ness; bend our pride to
4. Set our feet on loft-y pla-ces; fill our lives that
5. Save us from weak res-ig-na-tion to the e-vils

1. pour thy power; crown thine an-cient church-'s sto-ry;
2. sail thy ways! From the fears that long have bound us,
3. thy con-trol; shame our wan-ton, self-ish glad-ness,
4. we may be strength-ened with all Christ-like gra-ces
5. we de-plore; let the search for thy sal-va-tion

1. bring its bud to glo-rious flower. Grant us wis-dom, grant us cour-age,
2. free our hearts to faith and praise. Grant us wis-dom, grant us cour-age,
3. rich in things and poor in soul. Grant us wis-dom, grant us cour-age,
4. pledged to set all cap-tives free. Grant us wis-dom, grant us cour-age,
5. be our glo-ry ev-er-more. Grant us wis-dom, grant us cour-age,

1. for the fac-ing of this hour, for the fac-ing of this hour.
2. for the liv-ing of these days, for the liv-ing of these days.
3. lest we miss thy righ-teous goal, lest we miss thy righ-teous goal.
4. lest we fail our call from thee, lest we fail our call from thee.
5. serv-ing thee whom we a-dore, serv-ing thee whom we a-dore.

WORDS: Harry Emerson Fosdick, 1930
MUSIC: John Hughes, 1907

CWM RHONDDA
87.87.877

Alt. tune: REGENT SQUARE

465 We Are Called to Follow Jesus

Guitar capo: 1; play Em

1. When pain of the world sur-rounds us and fills us with des - pair,
2. We see with fear and trem - bling our ach-ing world in need,
3. The church is a ho - ly ves - sel the liv-ing wa - ters fill
4. We praise you for our jour - ney and your a - bun-dant grace,

when search-ing just con-founds us with false hopes ev - 'ry - where,
con - fess-ing to each oth - er our waste-ful - ness and greed.
to nour-ish all its peo - ple God's pur-pose to ful - fill.
your sav - ing word that guid - ed a strug-gling hu - man race.

when lives are starved for mean - ing and des - ti - ny is bare,
May we with stead-fast car - ing the hun-gry chil-dren feed.
May we with hum - ble cour - age be o - pen to God's will.
O God with all cre - a - tion, your fu - ture we em - brace.

WORDS and MUSIC: Jim Strathdee, 1978

WE ARE CALLED
86.76.76.88

♩=108-116

we are called to fol-low Je - sus and let God's heal-ing
We are called to fol-low Je - sus and let God's jus-tice
We are called to fol-low Je - sus and let God's Spir - it
We are called to fol-low Je - sus and let God's chang-es

flow through us.
flow through us.
flow through us.
flow through us. We are called to fol-low

Je - sus and let God's chang-es flow through us.

A Disciples Identity Statement 466

The Christian Church (Disciples of Christ) proclaims Jesus as Lord, draws its inspiration from Scripture and the Holy Spirit, witnesses and serves among the whole human family, acknowledges that Christian unity and Christian mission are inseparable, and claims as its particular mission the quest for the reunion of the Body of Christ, celebrating weekly around the Lord's Table the life, death, resurrection and continuing presence of its Lord.

—*Kenneth L. Teegarden, 20th-century Disciples General Minister and President*

467 Fill the World with Love

1. With the vi-sion in our minds of how the world could be, and the
2. All the peo-ple in this world liv-ing lives of pain and fear, cry-ing
3. We whose spir-its long to share, long to com-fort and to heal, know that
4. Let us hes-i-tate no long-er in our doubt and our dis-may; there's a

full-ness of our hearts from the suf-fer-ing we see; when we
out in-to the night, won-d'ring when some-one will hear; while there
when we act a-lone, hope is dif-fi-cult to feel; but to-
pow'r at work with-in us that has pro-mised a new day. And the

make all that we are and have part of God's des-ti-ny, we can
are so man-y others hav-ing so much they can share, can we
geth-er as we la-bor God's com-pas-sion to re-veal we will
time will sure-ly come, it will not be long de-layed when God

WORDS: David L. Edwards, 1992
MUSIC: David L. Edwards, 1992; arr. Susan Adams, 1994

COMPASSION
Irr.

© 1992 David L. Edwards; arr. © 1995 Chalice Press

♩=84-88

fill the world with love, we can fill the world with love.
fill the world with love, can we fill the world with love.
fill the world with love, we will fill the world with love.
fills the world with love, when God

fills the world with love.

Prayer of St. Francis   468

Lord, make me an instrument of your peace;
where there is hatred, let me sow love;
where there is injury, pardon;
where there is doubt, faith;
where there is despair, hope;
where there is darkness, light;
and where there is sadness, joy.

O Divine Master,
grant that I may not so much seek
to be consoled as to console;
to be understood, as to understand;
to be loved, as to love;
for it is in giving that we receive,
it is in pardoning that we are pardoned,
and it is in dying that we are born to eternal life.

—attributed to Francis of Assisi, Italy, 13th century

469 I Am the Light of the World!

"I am the light of the world!
You peo - ple come and fol - low me!" If you
fol - low and love you'll learn the mys - ter - y of
what you were meant to do and be.

WORDS: Jim Strathdee, 1969, in response to a Christmas poem
  by Howard Thurman
MUSIC: Jim Strathdee, 1969

LIGHT OF THE WORLD
Irr.

♩=92-100

1. When the song of the an-gels is stilled, when the
2. To find the lost and lone-ly one, to
3. To free the pris-'ner from all chains, to
4. To bring hope to ev-'ry task you do, to

star in the sky is gone, when the
heal the bro-ken soul with love, to
make the pow-er-ful care, to
dance at a ba - by's new birth, to

ma - gi and the shep-herds have found their way home, the
feed the hun-gry chil-dren with warmth and good food, to
re - build the na-tions with strength of good will, to
make mu-sic in an old per-son's heart, and

work of Christ-mas is be - gun:
feel the earth be-low, the sky a - bove!
see God's chil-dren ev - 'ry-where!
sing to the col - ors of the earth!

470 When the Church of Jesus

Unison

1. When the church of Je - sus shuts its out - er door,
2. If our hearts are lift - ed where de - vo - tion soars
3. Lest the gifts we of - fer, mon - ey, tal - ents, time,

lest the roar of traf - fic drown the voice of prayer,
high a - bove this hun - gry, suf - fering world of ours,
serve to salve our con - science, to our se - cret shame,

may our prayers, Lord, make us ten times more a - ware
lest our hymns should drug us to for - get its needs,
Lord, re - prove, in - spire us by the way you give;

that the world we ban - ish is our Chris - tian care.
forge our Chris - tian wor - ship in - to Chris - tian deeds.
teach us, dy - ing Sav - ior, how true Chris - tians live.

WORDS: Fred Pratt Green, 1968
MUSIC: Ralph Vaughan Williams, 1925

KING'S WESTON
65.65D

♩=100-108

Now It Is Evening

471

WORDS: Fred Pratt Green, 1973
MUSIC: David Haas, 1985

EVENING HYMN
55.54D

♩=84-92

Alt. tune: BUNESSAN

472 We Are Living, We Are Dwelling

1. We are liv-ing, we are dwell-ing in a grand and
2. Will you play, for-ev-er stall-ing? Will you dal-ly
3. Sworn to yield, to wa-ver, nev-er; con-se-crat-ed,

aw-ful time, in an age on ag-es tell-ing,
far be-hind? Up! To work! For God is call-ing!
born a-new; sworn to be Christ's peo-ple ev-er,

to be liv-ing is sub-lime.
Give your strength, your heart, your mind!
O to Christ be ev-er true.

See the wak-ing of the na-tions to a wid-er
See the plan of God un-fold-ing. Seek for good with
O let all the soul with-in you spread the word of

WORDS: Arthur C. Coxe, 1840, alt.; st. 2 adapt. Ruth Duck, 1995
MUSIC: Thomas J. Williams, 1890

EBENEZER
87.87D

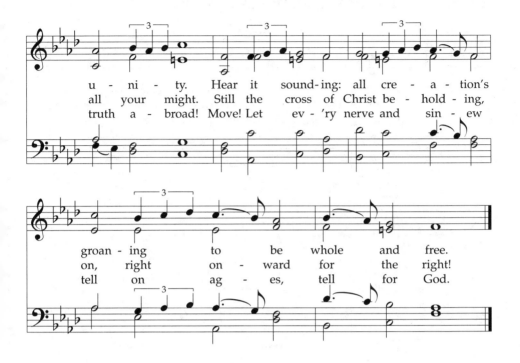

u - ni - ty. Hear it sound-ing: all cre - a - tion's
all your might. Still the cross of Christ be - hold - ing,
truth a - broad! Move! Let ev - 'ry nerve and sin - ew

groan - ing to be whole and free.
on, right on - ward for the right!
tell on ag - es, tell for God.

Be God's Kindness 473

Be the living expression of God's kindness:
    kindness in your face,
    kindness in your eyes,
    kindness in your smile,
    kindness in your warm greeting.
In the slums we are the light of God's kindness to the poor.
To children, to the poor, to all who suffer and are lonely,
    give always a happy smile—
Give them not only your care,
    but also your heart.

    —Mother Teresa of Calcutta, 20th-century missionary to the poor

474 I Will Go Wherever God Calls

1. I will go wher-ev-er God calls; God has called, and
2. I will bring God's love to the world, fac-ing e-vil,
3. All the glo-ry, hon-or and praise be to Christ who

I will go. I will on-ly fol-low Je-sus,
sin and greed. I will glad-ly bring the gos-pel
bore the cross, and the cross of per-se-cu-tion,

wheth-er joy or sor-row I know. Who can stop me?
where the hun-gry cry in their need. Ev-'ry-thing I
I will bear, what-ev-er the loss. I will serve with

Will death stop me? Christ will lead me down life's path-way.
am or will be I will give to God who calls me.
glad thanks-giv-ing, trust-ing God with all my liv-ing.

WORDS: Houn Lee, Korea (20th century); tr. Sandra Bonnette-Kim and Ruth Duck, 1994
MUSIC: Yoo Sun Lee, Korea (20th century)

I WILL GO
87.88.88.87

♩=66-72

From the *Korean-English Hymnbook*, published by the Korean-English Hymnbook Publication Commission; used by pemission; tr. © 1995 Chalice Press

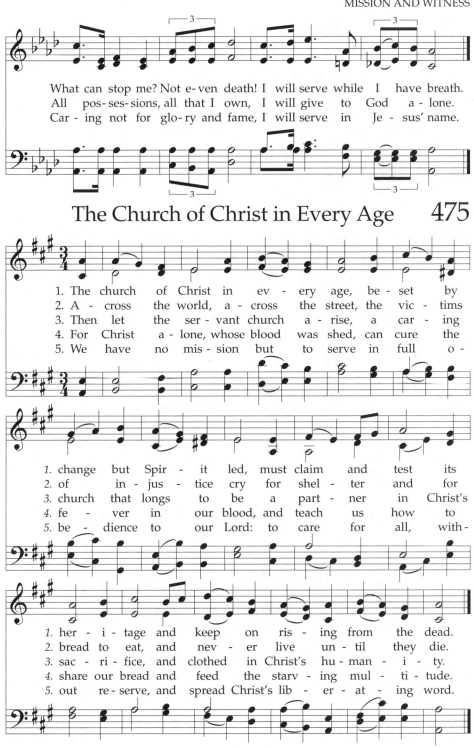

What can stop me? Not e-ven death! I will serve while I have breath.
All pos-ses-sions, all that I own, I will give to God a-lone.
Car-ing not for glo-ry and fame, I will serve in Je-sus' name.

The Church of Christ in Every Age 475

1. The church of Christ in ev-ery age, be-set by
2. A-cross the world, a-cross the street, the vic-tims
3. Then let the ser-vant church a-rise, a car-ing
4. For Christ a-lone, whose blood was shed, can cure the
5. We have no mis-sion but to serve in full o-

1. change but Spir-it led, must claim and test its
2. of in-jus-tice cry for shel-ter and for
3. church that longs to be a part-ner in Christ's
4. fe-ver in our blood, and teach us how to
5. be-dience to our Lord: to care for all, with-

1. her-i-tage and keep on ris-ing from the dead.
2. bread to eat, and nev-er live un-til they die.
3. sac-ri-fice, and clothed in Christ's hu-man-i-ty.
4. share our bread and feed the starv-ing mul-ti-tude.
5. out re-serve, and spread Christ's lib-er-at-ing word.

WORDS: Fred Pratt Green, 1969
MUSIC: William Knapp, 1738

WAREHAM
LM

476 Rejoice in God's Saints

1. Re - joice in God's saints, to - day and all days;
2. Some march with e - vents to turn them God's way;
3. Re - joice in those saints, un - praised and un - known,
4. Re - joice in God's saints, to - day and all days;

a world with - out saints for - gets how to praise.
some need to with - draw, the bet - ter to pray.
who bear some - one's cross or shoul - der their own.
a world with - out saints for - gets how to praise.

Their faith in ac - quir - ing the hab - it of prayer,
Some car - ry the gos - pel through fire and through flood;
They shame our com - plain - ing, our com - forts, our cares;
In lov - ing, in liv - ing, they prove it is true:

their depth of a - dor - ing, God, help us to share.
our world is their par - ish; their pur - pose is God.
what pa - tience in car - ing, what cour - age, is theirs!
the way of self - giv - ing, God, leads us to you.

WORDS: Fred Pratt Green, 1977
MUSIC: Attr. William Croft, 1708

HANOVER
10 10.11 11

Pass It On

1. It only takes a spark to get a fire go - ing,
2. What a won- drous time is spring when all the trees are bud - ding,
3. I wish for you, my friend, this hap - pi- ness that I've found—

and soon all those a - round can warm up in its glow - ing;
the birds be - gin to sing, the flow- ers start their bloom - ing;
on God you can de - pend, it mat - ters not where you're bound;

that's how it is with God's love, once you've ex - per- i- enced it:
that's how it is with God's love, once you've ex - per- i- enced it:
I'll shout it from the moun- tain top, I want my world to know:

you spread God's love to ev - ery - one, you want to pass it on.
you want to sing, it's fresh like spring, you want to pass it on.
the Lord of love has come to me, I want to pass it on.

WORDS and MUSIC: Kurt Kaiser, 1969

PASS IT ON
Irr.

478

Sois la Semilla
(You Are the Seed)

WORDS: Cesareo Gabaraín, 1979; tr. Raquel Gutiérrez-Achon and Skinner Chávez-Melo
MUSIC: Cesareo Gabaraín, 1979; harm. Skinner Chávez-Melo, 1987

ID Y ENSEÑAD
10 9.10 8 w. refrain

♩=100-108

cian- do_el a - mor, men - sa - je - ros de la vi - da,
re - su- rrec- ción. Id lle- van- do mi pre - sen - cia;

love to all, mes - sen- gers of my for - giv - ing peace,
dead I a - rose; "Lo, I'll be with you for - ev - er,

de la paz y_el per- dón.

e - ter - nal love.

con vo- so- tros es - toy.

till the end of the world."

2.
Sois una llama que ha de_encender
resplandores de fe_y caridad.
Sois los pastores que han de llevar
al mundo por sendas de paz.
Sois los amigos que quise_escoger,
sois palabra que_intento esparcir.
Sois reino nuevo que_empieza_a_engendrar
justicia, amor y verdad.
Estribillo

2.
You are the flame that will lighten the dark,
sending sparkles of hope, faith, and love;
you are the shepherds to lead the whole world
through valleys and pastures of peace.
You are the friends that I chose for myself,
the word that I want to proclaim.
You are the new kingdom built on a rock
where justice and truth always reign.
Refrain

3.
Sois fuego_y sabia que vine_a traer,
sois la ola que_agita la mar.
La levadura pequeña de_ayer
fermenta la masa del pan.
Una ciudad no se puede_esconder,
ni los montes se han de_ocultar,
en vuestras obras que buscan el bien
el mundo al Padre verá.
Estribillo

3.
You are the life that will nurture the plant;
you're the waves in a turbulent sea;
yesterday's yeast is beginning to rise,
a new loaf of bread it will yield.
There is no place for a city to hide,
nor a mountain can cover its might;
may your good deeds show a world in despair
a path that will lead all to God.
Refrain

479 We Have Heard a Joyful Sound

1. We have heard a joy-ful sound, Je-sus saves, Je-sus saves;
2. Waft it on the roll-ing tide, Je-sus saves, Je-sus saves;
3. Sing a-bove the bat-tle's strife, Je-sus saves, Je-sus saves;
4. Give the winds a might-y voice, Je-sus saves, Je-sus saves;

spread the glad-ness all a-round, Je-sus saves, Je-sus saves;
tell to sin-ners, far and wide, Je-sus saves, Je-sus saves;
by his death and end-less life, Je-sus saves, Je-sus saves;
let the na-tions now re-joice, Je-sus saves, Je-sus saves;

bear the news to ev-'ry land, climb the steeps, and cross the waves,
sing, ye is-lands of the sea, ech-o back, ye o-cean caves,
sing it soft-ly thro' the gloom, when the heart for mer-cy craves,
shout sal-va-tion, full and free, high-est hills and deep-est caves,

on-ward, 'tis our Lord's com-mand, Je-sus saves, Je-sus saves.
earth shall keep the ju-bi-lee, Je-sus saves, Je-sus saves.
sing in tri-umph o'er the tomb, Je-sus saves, Je-sus saves.
this our song of vic-to-ry, Je-sus saves, Je-sus saves.

WORDS: Priscilla J. Owens, 1868
MUSIC: William J. Kirkpatrick, 1882

JESUS SAVES
76.76.77.76

I Love to Tell the Story

1. I love to tell the story of un-seen things a-bove, of
2. I love to tell the story; 'tis pleas-ant to re-peat what
3. I love to tell the story, for those who know it best seem

Je - sus and his glo-ry, of Je - sus and his love. I love to
seems, each time I tell it, more won-der-ful-ly sweet. I love to
hun - ger-ing and thirst-ing to hear it like the rest. And when, in

tell the story, be-cause I know 'tis true; it sat-is-fies my
tell the story, for some have nev-er heard the mes-sage of sal-
scenes of glo-ry, I sing the new, new song, 'twill be the old, old

long-ings as noth-ing else can do.
va - tion from God's own ho-ly word. I love to tell the sto-ry, 'twill
sto - ry that I have loved so long.

be my theme in glo-ry, to tell the old, old sto-ry of Je-sus and his love.

WORDS: Katherine Hankey, c. 1868
MUSIC: William G. Fischer, 1869

HANKEY
76.76D w. refrain

481   The Church Is One

We submit that the Church of Christ upon earth is essentially, intentionally, and constitutionally one, consisting of all those in every place that profess their faith in Christ and obedience to him in all things according to the scriptures, and manifest the same by their tempers and conduct, and of none else, as none else can be truly and properly called Christians.

—Thomas Campbell, "Declaration and Address," 1809

482   O Christians, Haste

1. O Chris-tians, haste, your mis-sion high ful - fill - ing,
to tell the world that God is one who cares,
that God who made all na - tions is not will - ing

2. Pro - claim to ev - ery peo - ple, tongue, and na - tion,
that God in whom we live and move, is love.
Tell how God stooped to save a lost cre - a - tion,

3. Give of your sons to bear the mes - sage glo - rious;
give of your daugh - ters, speed them on their way.
Pour out your soul for them in prayer vic - to - rious,

WORDS: Mary A. Thomson, 1894, alt.
MUSIC: James Walch, 1875

TIDINGS
11 10.11 10 w. refrain

one   life should   per - ish,   lost   in   deep   de - spair.
and   died on   earth   that   we might live   a - bove.
till   God shall   bring   a   new and   joy - ful   day.

Refrain

Pub - lish glad tid - ings,   tid - ings of   peace,

tid - ings of   Je - sus, re - demp - tion and   re - lease.

For a Renewed Sense of Compassion   483

All-merciful tender God
you have given birth to our world,
conceiving and bearing all that lives and breathes.
We come to you as your daughters and sons,
aware of our aggression and anger,
our drive to dominate and manipulate others.
We ask you to forgive us,
and by the gentle touch of your Spirit
help us to find a renewed sense of compassion
that we may truly live as your people
in service to all humanity.

—*Janet Berry, 20th-century English churchwoman*

484 We've a Story to Tell to the Nations

1. We've a sto - ry to tell to the na - tions that shall turn their
2. We've a song to be sung to the na - tions that shall lift their
3. We've a mes - sage to give to the na - tions, that the Lord who
4. We've a Sav - ior to show to the na - tions, who the path of

hearts to the right, a sto - ry of truth and mer - cy, a
hearts to the Lord; a song that shall con - quer e - vil and
reign - eth a - bove hath sent us the Son to save us, and
sor - row has trod, that all of the world's great peo - ples might

sto - ry of peace and light, a sto - ry of peace and light.
shat - ter the spear and sword, and shat - ter the spear and sword.
show us that God is love, and show us that God is love.
come to the truth of God, might come to the truth of God.

Refrain

For the dark-ness shall turn to dawn-ing, and the dawn-ing to noon-day bright,

WORDS and MUSIC: H. Ernest Nichol, 1896

MESSAGE
10 8.877 w. refrain

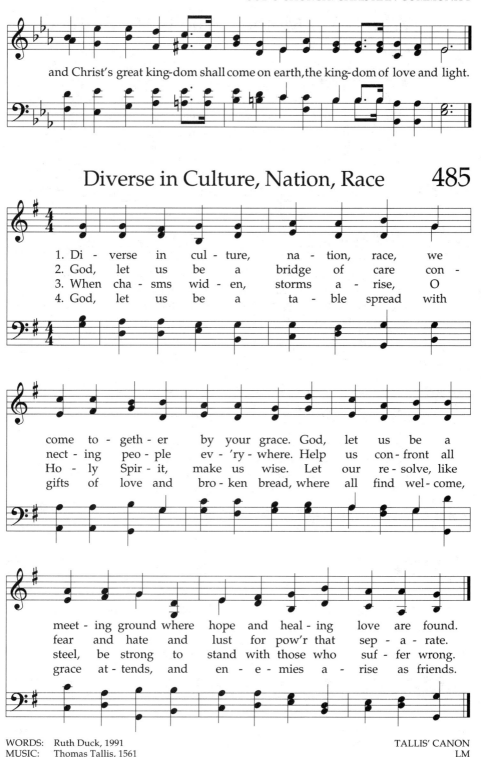

and Christ's great king-dom shall come on earth, the king-dom of love and light.

Diverse in Culture, Nation, Race   485

1. Di - verse in cul - ture, na - tion, race, we
2. God, let us be a bridge of care con -
3. When cha - sms wid - en, storms a - rise, O
4. God, let us be a ta - ble spread with

come to - geth - er by your grace. God, let us be a
nect - ing peo - ple ev - 'ry - where. Help us con - front all
Ho - ly Spir - it, make us wise. Let our re - solve, like
gifts of love and bro - ken bread, where all find wel - come,

meet - ing ground where hope and heal - ing love are found.
fear and hate and lust for pow'r that sep - a - rate.
steel, be strong to stand with those who suf - fer wrong.
grace at - tends, and en - e - mies a - rise as friends.

WORDS: Ruth Duck, 1991
MUSIC: Thomas Tallis, 1561

TALLIS' CANON
LM

486 Who Is My Mother, Who Is My Brother?

Unison

1. Who is my moth-er, who is my broth-er?
2. Dif-ferent-ly a-bled, dif-ferent-ly la-beled
3. Love will re-late us— col-or or sta-tus
4. Bound by one vi-sion, met for one mis-sion

all those who gath-er round Je-sus Christ:
wid-en the cir-cle round Je-sus Christ:
can't seg-re-gate us, round Je-sus Christ:
we claim each oth-er, round Je-sus Christ:

Spir-it-blown peo-ple, born from the Gos-pel
crutch-es and stig-mas, cul-tures' en-ig-mas
fam-i-ly fail-ings, hu-man de-rail-ings—
here is my moth-er, here is my broth-er,

sit at the ta-ble, round Je-sus Christ.
all come to-geth-er round Je-sus Christ.
all are ac-cept-ed, round Je-sus Christ.
kin-dred in Spir-it, through Je-sus Christ.

WORDS: Shirley Erena Murray, 1991
MUSIC: Jack Schrader, 1991

KINDRED
55.54D

♩=120-126

Help Us Accept Each Other

487

1. Help us ac-cept each oth-er as Christ ac-cept-ed us;
2. Teach us, O Lord, your les-sons, as in our dai-ly life
3. Let your ac-cep-tance change us, so that we may be moved
4. Lord, for to-day's en-coun-ters with all who are in need,

teach us as sis-ter, broth-er, each per-son to em-brace.
we strug-gle to be hu-man and search for hope and faith.
in liv-ing sit-u-a-tions to do the truth in love;
who hun-ger for ac-cep-tance, for righ-teous-ness and bread,

Be pres-ent, Lord, a-mong us and bring us to be-lieve
Teach us to care for peo-ple, for all, not just for some,
to prac-tice your ac-cep-tance, un-til we know by heart
we need new eyes for see-ing, new hands for hold-ing on;

we are our-selves ac-cept-ed and meant to love and live.
to love them as we find them or as they may be-come.
the ta-ble of for-give-ness and laugh-ter's heal-ing art.
re-new us with your Spir-it; Lord, free us, make us one!

WORDS: Fred Kaan, 1974
MUSIC: John Ness Beck, 1977

ACCEPTANCE
76.76D

♩=64-72

488 A Litany of the Saints

Leader: Gracious God, you are to be praised
for the women and men whose faithful witness to your love
inspires the generations of your people:

All: Abraham and Sarah, who believed your promise
even though they were old and barren;

Women: Ruth, whose loyalty to Naomi became a model
for people of every time and place;

Men: Isaiah of Jerusalem, who in time marked by terror,
proclaimed that the lion would lie down with the lamb;

All: Mary Magdalene, who ran from the tomb crying out
that Jesus was alive;

Women: Paul of Tarsus, who was beaten and shipwrecked
while carrying the gospel to us, the Gentiles;

All: Augustine, who when the cities of the world were falling,
saw the city of God;

Men: Martin Luther, who spoke afresh of salvation by grace alone
through faith;

Women: Sojourner Truth, who dreamed of women and men,
black and white, all of them free;

Men: Thomas Campbell, Barton Stone, and Alexander Campbell,
who yearned for a church with the vitality
of the New Testament church;

Women: Mae Yoho Ward and other Disciples of our own time
who prayed and worked for the life of the world
to be shaped by the power of the Spirit;

Men: Martin Luther King, Jr., who prophesied of the day
when we all will be judged by the content of character
and not by the color of skin;

Women: Mother Teresa, who made her bed among the homeless,
fed the hungry, and clothed the naked.

[The litany can be expanded to include saints known in the congregation.]

All: As we recall the names of these witnesses,
we pray that you will embolden us with the spirit of faithfulness
that made them live for you.

Bless Now, O God, the Journey

489

Unison

1. Bless now, O God, the jour-ney that all your peo-ple make,
2. Bless so-journ-ers and pil-grims who share this wind-ing way,
3. Di - vine E-ter-nal Lov-er, you meet us on the road.

the path through noise and si-lence, the way of give and take.
whose hope burns through the ter-rors, whose love sus-tains the day.
We wait for lands of prom-ise where milk and hon-ey flow.

Harmony

The trail is found in des-ert and winds the moun-tain round,
We yearn for ho-ly free-dom while of-ten we are bound.
But wait-ing not for plac-es, you meet us all a - round.

Unison

then leads be-side still wa-ters, the road where faith is found.
To - geth-er we are seek-ing the road where faith is found.
Our cov-e-nant is writ-ten on roads, as faith is found.

WORDS: Sylvia Dunstan, 1989
MUSIC: Swedish folk tune; harm. Lahrae Knatterud, 1983

BRED DINA VIDA VINGAR
76.76D

♩=104-112

490 Sister, Let Me Be Your Servant

1. Sis - ter, let me be your ser - vant, bro - ther,
2. We are pil - grims on a jour - ney, fel - low
3. I will weep when you are weep - ing, when you
4. When we sing to God in heav - en, we shall
5. Broth - er, let me be your ser - vant, sis - ter,

1. let me walk with you; pray that I may
2. trav - 'lers on the road. We are here to
3. laugh I'll laugh with you. I will share your
4. find such har - mo - ny, born of all we've
5. let me walk with you; pray that I may

1. have the grace to let you be my ser - vant too.
2. help each oth - er walk the mile and bear the load.
3. joy and sor - row till we've seen this jour - ney thro'.
4. known to - geth - er of great love and ag - o - ny.
5. have the grace to let you be my ser - vant too.

WORDS: Richard Gillard, 1977, alt.
MUSIC: Richard Gillard, 1977; arr. A. Eugene Ellsworth, 1994

THE SERVANT SONG
87.87

♩=100-104

As Grain on Scattered Hillsides 491

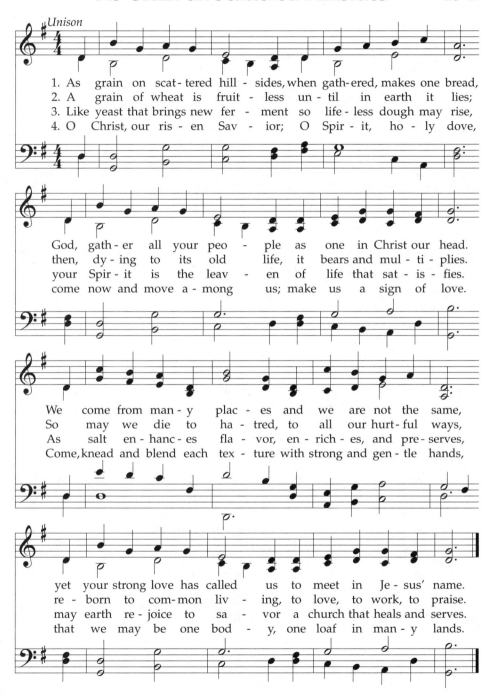

Unison

1. As grain on scat-tered hill - sides, when gath-ered, makes one bread,
2. A grain of wheat is fruit - less un - til in earth it lies;
3. Like yeast that brings new fer - ment so life-less dough may rise,
4. O Christ, our ris - en Sav - ior; O Spir - it, ho - ly dove,

God, gath - er all your peo - ple as one in Christ our head.
then, dy - ing to its old life, it bears and mul - ti - plies.
your Spir - it is the leav - en of life that sat - is - fies.
come now and move a - mong us; make us a sign of love.

We come from man - y plac - es and we are not the same,
So may we die to ha - tred, to all our hurt-ful ways,
As salt en - hanc - es fla - vor, en - rich - es, and pre - serves,
Come, knead and blend each tex - ture with strong and gen - tle hands,

yet your strong love has called us to meet in Je - sus' name.
re - born to com-mon liv - ing, to love, to work, to praise.
may earth re - joice to sa - vor a church that heals and serves.
that we may be one bod - y, one loaf in man - y lands.

WORDS: Ruth Duck, 1986, 1990
MUSIC: Hal H. Hopson, 1983

MERLE'S TUNE
76.76D

♩=56-60

492   Many Are the Lightbeams

1. Man - y are the light-beams from the one light.
2. Man - y are the bran - ches of the one tree.
3. Man - y are the gifts giv'n, love is all one.
4. Man - y ways to serve God, the Spir - it is one;
5. Man - y are the mem - bers, the bod - y is one;

1. Our one light is Je - sus. Man - y are the
2. Our one tree is Je - sus. Man - y are the
3. Love's the gift of Je - sus. Man - y are the
4. ser - vant spir - it of Je - sus. Man - y ways to
5. mem - bers all of Je - sus. Man - y are the

1. light-beams from the one light; we are one in Christ.
2. bran - ches of the one tree; we are one in Christ.
3. gifts giv'n, love is all one; we are one in Christ.
4. serve God, the Spir - it is one; we are one in Christ.
5. mem - bers, the bod - y is one; we are one in Christ.

WORDS: *De unitate ecclesiae*, Cyprian of Carthage, 252;
    tr. Anders Frostenson, 1972, 1986
MUSIC: Olle Widestrand, 1974; harm. A. Eugene Ellsworth, 1994

MANY ARE THE LIGHTBEAMS
10 6.10 5

♩=104-112

Somos Uno en Cristo
(We're United in Jesus)

So-mos u-no en Cris-to, so-mos u-no, so-mos u-no,
We're u-nit-ed in Je-sus we're u-nit-ed. Like a fam-i-ly,

u-no so-lo. so-lo. Un so-lo Dios, un so-lo Se-ñor,
we're u-nit-ed. nit-ed. We have one God, one Ho-ly Lord.

u-na so-la fe, un so-lo a-mor, un so-lo bau-tis-mo, un
We have one faith, on-ly one Love. Just one bap-ti-sm, one

so-lo Es-pí-ri-tu, y e-se es el Con-so-la-dor.
Ho-ly Spir-it, one Com-fort-er sent from God a-bove.

WORDS: Latin America (20th century); tr. Frank Colon, 1994　　　　SOMOS UNO
MUSIC: Latin America (20th century)　　　　　　　　　　　　　　Irr.

♩=104-112

494   They'll Know We Are Christians

Guitar capo: 1; play Em

Unison   Em

1. We are one in the Spir-it, we are one in the Lord,
2. We will walk with each oth-er, we will walk hand in hand,
3. We will work with each oth-er, we will work side by side,
4. All praise to the Fa-ther, from whom all things come,

Am   Em

we are one in the Spir-it, we are one in the Lord,
we will walk with each oth-er, we will walk hand in hand,
we will work with each oth-er, we will work side by side,
and all praise to Christ Je-sus, God's on-ly Son,

Am   Em

and we pray that all u-ni-ty may one day be re-stored:
and to-geth-er we'll spread the news that God is in our land:
and we'll guard each one's dig-ni-ty and save each one's pride:
and all praise to the Spir-it, who makes us one:

Refrain   C   G   C   G   Em   Am

And they'll know we are Chris-tians by our love, by our love,

WORDS and MUSIC: Peter Scholtes, 1966

ST. BRENDAN'S
76.76.86 w. refrain

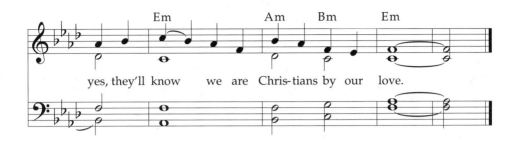

yes, they'll know we are Chris-tians by our love.

Weave

495

Weave, weave, weave us to-geth-er. Weave us to-geth-er in

u-ni-ty and love. Weave, weave, weave us to-geth-er.

Weave us to-geth-er, to-geth-er in love.

WORDS and MUSIC: Rosemary Crow, 1979

WEAVE
Irr.

♩.=48-52

496

Unidos
(Together)

WORDS: Benjamín Villanueva, 1982; tr. George Lockwood, 1983
MUSIC: Benjamín Villanueva, 1982; arr. Esther Frances, 1983, alt.

UNIDOS
Irr.

♩·=76-80

dre - mos. U - ni - dos, siem - pre u - ni - dos, to - mán - do - nos las
round us. To - geth - er we're u - nit - ed; we hold hands as we

ma - nos i - re - mos por el mun - do can - tan - do al a - mor.
strug - gle; we walk in-to the world sing-ing God's song of love.

La glo - ria de Je - sus, al fin res - plan - de - ce - rá Y el
The glo - ry of Je - sus will ev - er shine in splen - dor. The

mun - do lle - na - rá de a - mor y de paz.
whole world will be joy - ful with love and peace.

paz, de a - mor y de paz, de a - mor y de paz.
peace with love and peace, with love and peace.

497 In Loving Partnership

1. In lov - ing part - ner - ship we come
2. We are the hands and feet of Christ
3. Lov - ing com - mu - ni - ty we seek;
4. In lov - ing part - ner - ship, O God,

seek - ing, O God, your will to do.
serv - ing, by grace, each oth - er's need.
your hope and strength with - in us move.
help us your fu - ture to pro - claim.

Our prayers and ac - tions now re - ceive,
We dare to risk and sac - ri - fice
The poor and rich, the strong and weak
Jus - tice and peace be our de - sire

we free - ly of - fer them to you.
with truth - ful word and faith - ful deed.
are brought to - geth - er in your love.
we hum - bly pray in Je - sus' name.

WORDS and MUSIC: Jim Strathdee, 1983

PARTNERSHIP
LM

$\downarrow \cdot = 40\text{-}44$

O God, Who Gave Humanity Its Name 498

Unison

1. O God, who gave humanity its name,
2. May through their union other lives be blessed,
3. From stage to stage on life's unfolding way
4. God bless us all to whom this day brings joy,

in whom we live and move, from whom we came:
their door be wide to stranger and to guest;
bring to their mind the vows they make this day;
let no events our unity destroy,

be with these two who now before you wait;
give them the understanding that is kind;
your Spirit be their guide in every move,
and help us, till all sense of time is lost,

en - large the love they come to con - se - crate.
grant them the bless - ing of an o - pen mind.
their faith in Christ the touch-stone of their love.
to live and love and not to count the cost.

WORDS: Fred Kaan, 1968, rev.
MUSIC: Alfred Morton Smith, 1941

SURSUM CORDA
10 10.10 10

Words © 1968 Hope Publishing Co.

♩=104-112

499

When Love Is Found

WORDS: Brian Wren, 1978, rev. 1992
MUSIC: Traditional English melody; harm. Martin West

O WALY WALY
44.44D

Words and harm. © 1983 Hope Publishing Co.

♩=56-60

God Made from One Blood

500

1. God made from one blood all the fam-ilies of earth,
   the cir-cles of nur-ture that raised us from birth,
   com-pan-ions who join us to walk through each stage
   of child-hood and youth and a-dult-hood and age.

2. We turn to you, God, with our thanks and our tears
   for all of the fam-ilies we've known through the years,
   the in-ti-mate net-works on whom we de-pend
   of par-ent and part-ner and room-mate and friend.

3. We learn through our fam-ilies how close-ness and trust
   in-crease when our ac-tions are lov-ing and just.
   Yet fam-ilies have al-so dis-tort-ed their roles,
   mis-treat-ing their mem-bers and bruis-ing their souls.

4. Give, Lord, to each fam-ily in con-flict and storm
   a sense of your wis-dom and grace that trans-form
   sharp an-ger to in-sight which strength-ens the heart
   and makes clear the place where re-build-ing can start.

5. Then wid-en that wis-dom and grace to in-clude
   the rac-es and view-points our fam-ilies ex-clude
   till peace in each home bears and nur-tures the bud
   of peace shared by all you have made from one blood.

WORDS: Thomas H. Troeger, 1989, rev. 1995
MUSIC: Welsh folk melody

ST. DENIO
11 11.11 11

501 There Is a Balm in Gilead

WORDS: African-American spiritual
MUSIC: African-American spiritual; arr. Harold Moyer

BALM IN GILEAD
Irr.

Come, You Disconsolate

502

1. Come, you dis-con-so-late, wher-e'er you lan-guish,
2. Joy of the des-o-late, light of the stray-ing,
3. Here see the bread of life; see wa-ters flow-ing

come to the mer-cy seat, fer-vent-ly kneel!
hope of the pen-i-tent, fade-less and pure!
forth from the throne of God, pure from a-bove:

Here bring your wound-ed hearts, here tell your an-guish:
Here speaks the Com-fort-er, ten-der-ly say-ing,
Come to the feast of love; come, ev-er know-ing

Earth has no sor-row that heaven can-not heal.
"Earth has no sor-row that heaven can-not cure."
Earth has no sor-row but heaven can re-move.

WORDS: Thomas Moore, 1816; adapt. Thomas Hastings, 1831
MUSIC: Samuel Webbe, Sr., 1792

CONSOLATOR
11 10.11 10

503   O Christ, the Healer

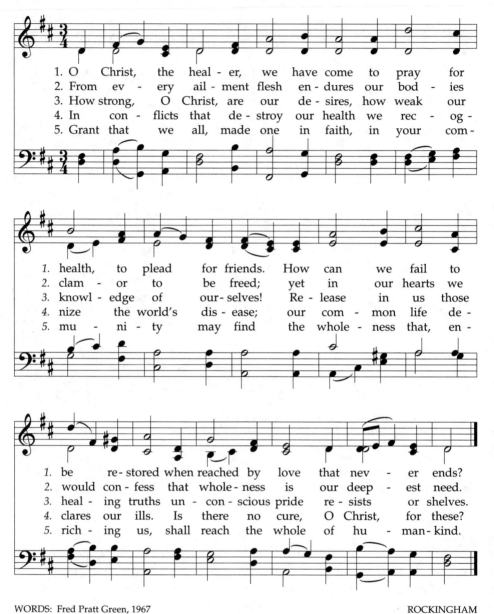

1. O Christ, the heal - er, we have come to pray for
2. From ev - ery ail - ment flesh en - dures our bod - ies
3. How strong, O Christ, are our de - sires, how weak our
4. In con - flicts that de - stroy our health we rec - og -
5. Grant that we all, made one in faith, in your com -

1. health, to plead for friends. How can we fail to
2. clam - or to be freed; yet in our hearts we
3. knowl - edge of our - selves! Re - lease in us those
4. nize the world's dis - ease; our com - mon life de -
5. mu - ni - ty may find the whole - ness that, en -

1. be re - stored when reached by love that nev - er ends?
2. would con - fess that whole - ness is our deep - est need.
3. heal - ing truths un - con - scious pride re - sists or shelves.
4. clares our ills. Is there no cure, O Christ, for these?
5. rich - ing us, shall reach the whole of hu - man - kind.

WORDS: Fred Pratt Green, 1967   ROCKINGHAM
MUSIC: Anonymous; harm. Edward Miller, 1790   LM

     ♩=100-104

Heal Me, Hands of Jesus 504

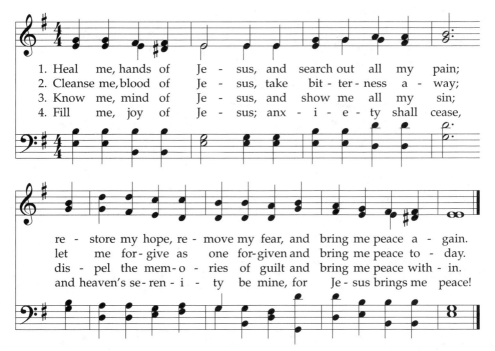

1. Heal me, hands of Je - sus, and search out all my pain;
2. Cleanse me, blood of Je - sus, take bit - ter - ness a - way;
3. Know me, mind of Je - sus, and show me all my sin;
4. Fill me, joy of Je - sus; anx - i - e - ty shall cease,

re - store my hope, re - move my fear, and bring me peace a - gain.
let me for - give as one for - given and bring me peace to - day.
dis - pel the mem - o - ries of guilt and bring me peace with - in.
and heaven's se - ren - i - ty be mine, for Je - sus brings me peace!

WORDS: Michael Perry, 1982
MUSIC: Herbert S. Irons, 1861, alt.

Words © 1982 Hope Publishing Co.

SOUTHWELL
SM

♩=56-60

Prayer for Healing 505

By your power, great God, our Lord Jesus healed the sick
    and gave new hope to the hopeless.
Though we cannot command or possess your power,
    we pray for those who want to be healed
    (especially for _____).
Mind their wounds, soothe fevered brows,
    and make broken people whole again.
Help us to welcome every healing as a sign that,
    though death is against us, you are for us,
    and have promised renewed and risen life
    in Jesus Christ the Lord. Amen.

506　Healer of Our Ev'ry Ill

Refrain

Heal-er of our ev-'ry ill, light of each to-mor-row,
give us peace be-yond our fear, and hope be-yond our sor-row.

Stanzas

1. You who know our fears and sad-ness, grace us with your
   peace and glad-ness, Spir-it of all com-fort: fill our hearts.
2. In the pain and joy be-hold-ing, how your grace is
   still un-fold-ing, give us all your vi-sion: God of love.
3. Give us strength to love each oth-er, ev-'ry sis-ter,
   ev-'ry broth-er, Spir-it of all kind-ness: be our guide.
4. You who know each thought and feel-ing, teach us all your
   way of heal-ing, Spir-it of com-pas-sion: fill each heart.

WORDS and MUSIC: Marty Haugen, 1987

© 1991 GIA Publications, Inc.

HEALER
88.63 w. refrain

♩=96-104

Sometimes God Begins a Project 507

Unison

1. Some-times God be - gins a proj - ect that will nev - er come to be. While we wait, ex - pect-ant, hope - ful, there's a change in des - ti - ny.

2. Does this mean that God's un - car - ing, tak - ing back a par - ent's role? No, our God, is lov - ing, heal - ing, holds us, lifts us, makes us whole.

3. In our times of dis - ap - point - ment, we will ques - tion, grieve, and cry, search-ing for our suf-fering's rea - son, ask - ing God to tell us why.

4. Time will ease the depth of sor - row, though the mem - o - ry will stay. Faith - ful life will see our ques - tions an - swered in some fu - ture day.

WORDS: Mary R. Bittner, 1993
MUSIC: Latvian melody; harm. Geoffrey Laycock, 1971

KAS DZIEDAJA
87.87

♩=82-86

For One Who Suffers 508

I know I cannot enter all you feel
Nor bear with you the burden of your pain
I can but offer what my love does give—
The strength of caring
The warmth of one who seeks to understand
This I do in quiet ways—
That on your lonely path you may not walk alone.

—*Howard Thurman, 20th-century African-American church leader*

509 Holy and Good Is the Gift of Desire

1,4. Ho - ly and good is the gift of de - sire.
2. God weeps for peo - ple a - ban-doned, a - bused.
3. God calls to wom - en and God calls to men:

God made our bod - ies for pas - sion and fire, in -
God weeps for peo - ple whose bod - ies are bruised. God
"Don't hide from ter - ror, or ter - ror will win. I

tend - ing that love would draw from the flame
weeps when the flame that God has in - fused is
made you for love, but love must be - gin by

lives that would shine with God's im - age and name.
turned from its pur - pose and bru - tal - ly used.
fac - ing the vio - lence with - out and with - in."

WORDS: Thomas H. Troeger, 1988
MUSIC: Floyd Knight, Jr., 1980

ANGELIQUE
10 10.10 10

Words © 1988, 1991, Oxford University Press; music © 1980 Floyd Knight, Jr.

♩=96-104

Out of the Depths

510

Unison

1. Out of the depths, O God, we call to you.
2. Out of the depths of fear, O God, we speak.
3. God of the lov - ing heart, we praise your name.

* Wounds of the past re - main, af - fect - ing all we do.
Break - ing the si - lenc - es, the sear - ing truth we seek.
Dance through our lives and loves; a - noint with Spir - it flame.

Fac - ing our lives, we need your love so
Safe a - mong friends, our grief and rage we
Your light il - lu - mines each fa - mil - iar

much. Here in this com - mu - ni - ty, heal us by your touch.
share. Here in this com - mu - ni - ty, hold us in your care.
face. Here in this com - mu - ni - ty, meet us with your grace.

Alt. 2nd line, st. 1, for AIDS healing services: Free us from fear of death, our faith and hope renew.
Alt. 2nd line, st. 1, for services dealing with those abused as children: Wounds of abuse remain...

511 Strong, Gentle Children

Unison
G C/G G C/G
1. Strong, gen - tle chil - dren, God made you beau - ti - ful,
2. Strong, hurt - ing chil - dren, an - gry and ter - ri - fied,
3. Strong, know - ing chil - dren, ut - ter your cry a - loud,
Bm Em7 Am7 D
gave you the wis - dom and pow - er you need;
op - en the se - crets your life has con - cealed;
hon - or the wis - dom God gave you at birth;
G C/G G C/G
speak in the still - ness all you are long - ing for;
though you are wound - ed, know you are not to blame;
speak to your el - ders till they have heard your voice;
Bm7 Em7 Am7 D7 G
live out your call - ing to love and to lead.
cry out your sto - ry till truth is re - vealed.
sing out your vi - sion of heal - ing on earth.

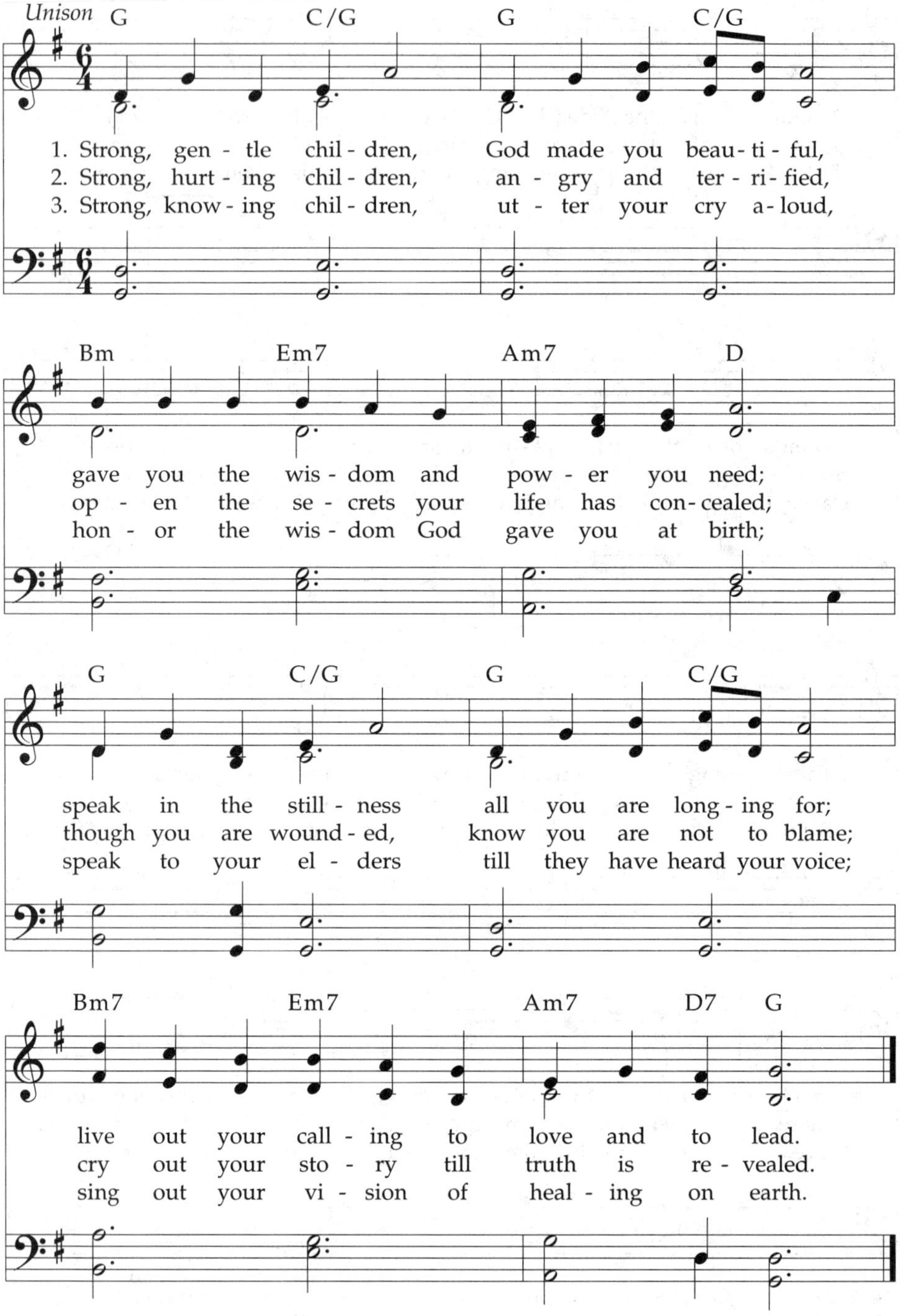

WORDS and MUSIC: Dan Damon, 1991

TWILIGHT
56.10D

𝅗𝅥. = 44-46

When Aimless Violence Takes Those We Love 512

Unison

1. When aim-less vi-o-lence takes those we love,
2. When pass-ing years rob sight and strength and mind
3. Our faith may flick-er low, and hope grow dim,
4. Be-cause your Child knew ag-o-ny and loss,

when ran-dom death strikes child-hood's prom-ise down,
yet fail to still a strong-ly beat-ing heart,
yet you, O God, are with us in our pain;
felt des-o-la-tion, grief and scorn and shame,

when wrench-ing loss be-comes our dai-ly bread,
and grief be-comes the fab-ric of our days,
you grieve with us and for us day by day,
we know you will be with us, come what may,

we know, O God, you leave us not a-lone.
dear God, you do not stand from us a-part.
and with us, shar-ing sor-row, will re-main.
your lov-ing pres-ence near, al-ways the same.

WORDS: Joy F. Patterson, 1992
MUSIC: Alfred Morton Smith, 1941

SURSUM CORDA
10 10.10 10

♩=104-112

513 Now I Have New Life in Christ

1. Now I have new life in Christ who has set me free.
2. Now that my own life is hid in the heart of Christ,
3. Moun-tains and riv - ers and trees are made new in Christ.
4. Rough is the road, and the jour - ney is long and hard,

I'm a new crea - ture; the old things have passed a - way.
all that I loved be - fore no long - er holds its sway.
Sin - ners change, en - e - mies come to em - brace as friends.
yet I will fol - low Christ, wor - ship - ing God with song.

New life is flow - ing, a riv - er that fills my heart,
Now I have tast - ed the grace and the peace of heaven;
Heav - en greets all who have Christ liv - ing in their hearts,
All of my life I will serve God with heart and mind.

shin - ing with love, like the sun - light of a new day.
prais - ing and pray - ing, with Christ I will live each day.
for they have tast - ed of new life that nev - er ends.
Liv - ing in Christ, I will sing praise the whole day long.

WORDS: Houn Lee, Korea (20th century); tr. Sandra Bonnette-Kim
and Ruth Duck, 1994
MUSIC: Taijoon Park, Korea (20th century)

NEW LIFE IN CHRIST
12 12.12 12 w. refrain

♩=108-112

From the *Korean-English Hymnbook*, published by the Korean-English Hymnbook
Publication Commission; used by permission; tr. © 1995 Chalice Press

Refrain

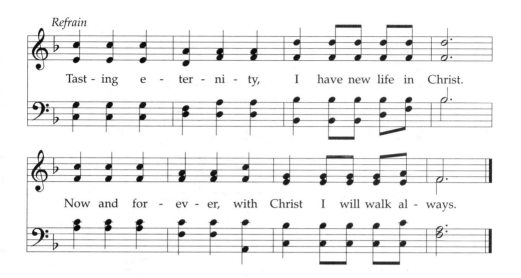

Tast - ing e - ter - ni - ty, I have new life in Christ.

Now and for - ev - er, with Christ I will walk al - ways.

God, Who Touches Earth with Beauty 514

1. God, who touch - es earth with beau - ty, make my heart a - new.
2. Like your springs and run - ning wa - ters, make me crys - tal pure.
3. Like your danc - ing waves in sun - light, make me glad and free.
4. Like the arch - ing of the heav - ens, lift my thoughts a - bove.
5. God, who touch - es earth with beau - ty, make my heart a - new.

1. With your Spir - it re - cre - ate me pure and strong and true.
2. Like your rocks of tower - ing gran - deur, make me strong and sure.
3. Like the straight - ness of the pine trees let me up - right be.
4. Turn my dreams to no - ble ac - tion, min - is - tries of love.
5. Keep me ev - er, by your Spir - it, pure and strong and true.

WORDS: Mary S. Edgar, 1925, alt.
MUSIC: C. Harold Lowden (20th century)

GENEVA
85.85

515 Give Me a Clean Heart

Give me a clean heart so I may serve thee. Lord, fix my heart so that I may be used by

thee. For I'm not wor - thy of all these bless -

WORDS: Margaret J. Douroux
MUSIC: Margaret J. Douroux; harm. Albert Denis Tessier

DOUROUX
Irr.

♩.=56-60

ings. Give me a clean heart and I'll fol-low thee.

Song of Ezekiel 516

 RESPONSE

Let us see your kind-ness, God, grant us your sal - va - tion.

R
I will take you from the nations,
    and gather you from all the countries,
    and bring you into your own land.
I will sprinkle clean water upon you,
    and you shall be clean from all your uncleannesses,
    and from all your idols I will cleanse you.
A new heart I will give you,
    and a new spirit I will put within you;
and I will remove from your body the heart of stone
    and give you a heart of flesh.
I will put my spirit within you,
    and make you follow my statutes
    and be careful to observe my ordinances.
Then you shall live in the land that I gave to your ancestors;
    and you shall be my people,
    and I will be your God.   **R**

WORDS: Ezekiel 36:24–28; Response, Psalm 85:7
MUSIC: Adapt. from Leisentritt's *Gesangbuch*, 1567

517 Love Divine, All Loves Excelling

1. Love di-vine, all loves ex-cel-ling, joy of heaven, to earth come down;
2. Breathe, O breathe thy lov-ing Spir-it in-to ev-ery trou-bled breast;
3. Come, al-might-y to de-liv-er, let us all thy life re-ceive;
4. Fin-ish, then, thy new cre-a-tion; pure and spot-less let us be,

fix in us thy hum-ble dwell-ing, all thy faith-ful mer-cies crown;
let us all in thee in-her-it, let us find thy prom-ised rest;
sud-den-ly re-turn and nev-er, nev-er-more thy tem-ples leave.
let us see thy great sal-va-tion per-fect-ly re-stored in thee;

Je - sus, thou art all com-pas-sion, pure, un-bound-ed love thou art;
take a-way our love of sin-ning; al-pha and o-me-ga be;
Thee we would be al-ways bless-ing, serve thee as thy hosts a-bove,
changed from glo-ry in-to glo-ry, till in heaven we take our place,

vis - it us with thy sal - va-tion, en-ter ev-ery trem-bling heart.
end of faith, as its be - gin-ning, set our hearts at lib-er-ty.
pray, and praise thee with-out ceas-ing, glo-ry in thy per-fect love.
till we cast our crowns be-fore thee, lost in won-der, love, and praise.

WORDS: Charles Wesley, 1743
MUSIC: John Zundel, 1870

BEECHER
87.87D

This Is a Day of New Beginnings 518

Unison

1. This is a day of new be - gin - nings,
2. For by the life and death of Je - sus,
3. Then let us, with the Spir - it's dar - ing,
4. In faith we gath - er round the ta - ble

time to re - mem - ber and move on,
God's might - y Spir - it, now as then,
step from the past and leave be - hind
to taste and share what love can do.

time to be - lieve what love is bring - ing,
can make for us a world of dif - ference,
our dis - ap - point - ment, guilt, and griev - ing,
This is a day of new be - gin - nings;

[1-3]
lay - ing to rest the pain that's gone.
as faith and hope are born a - gain.
seek - ing new paths, and sure to find.
our God is mak - ing all things

[4]
new.

WORDS: Brian Wren, 1978, rev. 1987
MUSIC: Carlton R. Young, 1984

BEGINNINGS
98.98

♩·=50-5

Psalm 51:10–13

519

Create in Me

Unison

Cre - ate in

me   a new heart,   so that I'll give you more than part of this, the

life you've giv-en me, cre - ate in me   a new   heart, then will I

teach,   and oth-ers know, and I will learn, my faith will grow. With you I

can cre-ate new dreams, with you I can change less-er schemes, O God, new

WORDS and MUSIC: Gayle Schoepf, 1988

MILLAR
Irr.

♩=72-80

Isaiah 64:8

Yo Quiero Ser
(I Want to Be)

520

Guitar capo: 1; play D

Yo quie-ro ser, Se-ñor a-man-te, co-mo el
I want to be, my lov-ing Sav-ior, like the

ba-rro en ma-nos del al fa-re-ro, to-ma mi
clay in the pot-ter's hands, take my

vi-da y haz-la de nue-vo, yo quie-ro
life and re-mold me, I want to

ser, yo quie-ro ser un va-so nue-vo.
be, I want to be a brand new ves-sel.

WORDS and MUSIC: Latin America (20th century)

VASO NUEVO
Irr.

521   In All Things, Charity

In essentials, unity;
in nonessentials, liberty;
in all things, charity.

—early Disciples motto, attributed to Rupertus Meldenius

522   Amarte Sólo a Ti, Señor
(Loving Only You, O Christ)

1. A‑mar‑te só‑lo a ti, Se‑ñor, a‑mar‑te só‑lo a ti, Se‑ñor.
2. A‑mar‑te só‑lo a ti, Se‑ñor, siem‑pre lle‑var tu cruz, Se‑ñor.

1. Lov‑ing on‑ly you, O Christ, lov‑ing on‑ly you, O Christ,
2. Lov‑ing on‑ly you, O Christ, car‑ry‑ing your cross, O Christ,

A‑mar‑te só‑lo a ti, Se‑ñor, y no mi‑rar a trás.
A‑mar‑te só‑lo a ti, Se‑ñor, y ha cer tu vo‑lun tad.

lov‑ing on‑ly you, O Christ, and nev‑er look‑ing back,
lov‑ing on‑ly you, O Christ, I seek to do your will.

Se‑guir tu ca‑mi‑nar, Se‑ñor, se‑guir sin des‑ma‑yar, Se‑ñor.
Al dé‑bil pro‑te‑ger, Se‑ñor, al po‑bre de‑fen‑der, Se‑ñor.

I fol‑low in your steps, my Lord, while nev‑er giv‑ing up, my Lord.
I will pro‑tect the weak, my Lord, I will de‑fend the poor, my Lord.

WORDS: Latin America (20th century); tr. Luis Ferrer, 1994
MUSIC: Latin America (20th century)

AMARTE SÓLO
Irr.

♩=100-112

Pos- tra- do an- te tu al- tar, Se- ñor,   y no mi- rar a - trás.
Tu rei- no pro- cla - mar, Se- ñor,   y no vol- ver a - trás.

I   fall be- fore your al - tar, Lord,   while nev- er look-ing back.
I   will pro- claim your reign, my Lord,   while nev- er turn-ing back.

Live in Charity 523

Live in char - i - ty   and stead - fast   love,

live in char - i - ty;   God will dwell with you.

WORDS: Latin (9th century); tr. Taizé Community   UBI CARITAS
MUSIC: Jacques Berthier (20th century)   Irr.

© Les Presses de Taizé (France); used by permission of GIA Publications, Inc.

Prayer of the Restless Heart 524

O Omnipotent God, who cares for each of us as if no one else existed and for all of us as if we were all but one! Blessed is the person who loves You. To You I entrust my whole being and all I have received from You. You made me for Yourself, and my heart is restless until it rests in You.

—*Augustine of Hippo, 5th-century bishop and theologian*

525   Song of Love

RESPONSE

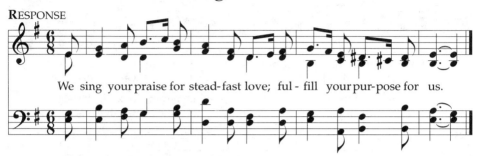

We sing your praise for stead-fast love; ful - fill your pur-pose for us.

R

Beloved, let us love one another,
    because love is from God;
everyone who loves is born of God
    and knows God.
Whoever does not love does not know God,
    for God is love.   **R**

Love is patient; love is kind;
    love is not envious or boastful or arrogant or rude.
Love does not insist on its own way;
    it is not irritable or resentful;
love does not rejoice in wrongdoing,
    but rejoices in the truth.
Love bears all things, believes all things,
    hopes all things, endures all things.
Love never ends.
But as for prophecies, they will come to an end;
    as for tongues, they will cease;
    as for knowledge, it will come to an end.
For we know only in part, and we prophesy only in part;
    but when the complete comes,
    the partial will come to an end.   **R**

For now we see in a mirror, dimly,
    but then we will see face to face.
Now I know only in part;
    then I will know fully,
    even as I have been fully known.
And now faith, hope, and love abide, these three;
    and the greatest of these is love.   **R**

WORDS: 1 John 4:7–8; 1 Corinthians 13:4–10, 12–13; Response, William C. Dix, c. 1865
MUSIC: English melody (16th century)

The Gift of Love

526

1. Though I may speak with brav-est fire,
   and have the gift to all in-spire,
   and have not love, my words are vain,
   as sound-ing brass, and hope-less gain.

2. Though I may give all I pos-sess,
   and striv-ing so my love pro-fess,
   but not be given by love with-in,
   the prof-it soon turns strange-ly thin.

3. Come, Spir-it, come, our hearts con-trol,
   our spir-its long to be made whole.
   Let in-ward love guide ev-ery deed;
   by this we wor-ship, and are freed.

WORDS: Hal H. Hopson, 1972
MUSIC: Traditional English melody; adapt. Hal H. Hopson, 1972

© 1972 Hope Publishing Co.

GIFT OF LOVE
LM

Alt. tune: O WALY WALY

527 More Love to Thee, O Christ

1. More love to thee, O Christ, more love to thee!
2. Once earth-ly joy I craved, sought peace and rest;
3. Let sor-row do its work, send grief and pain;
4. Then shall my lat-est breath whis-per thy praise;

Hear thou the pray'r I make, on bend-ed knee;
now thee a-lone I seek, give what is best;
sweet are thy mes-sen-gers, sweet their re-frain,
this be the part-ing cry my heart shall raise,

this is my ear-nest plea, more love, O Christ, to thee,
this all my pray'r shall be, more love, O Christ, to thee,
when they can sing with me, more love, O Christ, to thee,
this still its pray'r shall be, more love, O Christ, to thee,

more love to thee, more love to thee.
more love to thee, more love to thee.
more love to thee, more love to thee.
more love to thee, more love to thee.

WORDS: Elizabeth P. Prentiss, 1869
MUSIC: William H. Doane, 1870

MORE LOVE TO THEE
64.64.66.44

Give Thanks

528

Give thanks with a grate-ful heart, give thanks to the Ho-ly One, give thanks be-cause he's giv-en Je-sus Christ his Son. Give Son. And now let the weak say "I am strong"; let the poor say "I am rich" be-cause of what the Lord has done for us And us. Give us. Give thanks!

WORDS and MUSIC: Henry Smith, 1978

GIVE THANKS
Irr.

♩=60-68

529 I'm So Glad, Jesus Lifted Me

1. I'm so glad,
2. Sa - tan had me bound,
3. When I was in trou - ble,

Je - sus lift - ed me,

I'm so glad,
Sa - tan had me bound,
When I was in trou - ble,

Je - sus lift - ed me,

I'm so glad,
Sa - tan had me bound,
When I was in trou - ble,

Je - sus lift - ed me, sing - ing

WORDS: African-American spiritual
MUSIC: African-American spiritual; harm. Richard Smallwood

I'M SO GLAD
Irr.

Harm. © 1977 Richwood Music

♩=100

glo - ry, hal - le - lu - jah! Je - sus lift - ed me.

I've Got Peace Like a River 530

1. I've got peace like a riv - er, I've got peace like a
2. I've got joy like a foun - tain, I've got joy like a
3. I've got love like an o - cean, I've got love like an

riv - er, I've got peace like a riv - er in my
foun - tain, I've got joy like a foun - tain in my
o - cean, I've got love like an o - cean in my

soul. I've got riv - er in my soul.
soul. I've got foun - tain in my soul.
soul. I've got o - cean in my soul.

WORDS: African-American spiritual
MUSIC: African-American spiritual

PEACE LIKE A RIVER
77.10

531   Thank You, Lord

1. Thank you, Lord, thank you, Lord, thank you, Lord, I just want to thank you, Lord.
2. Been so good, been so good, been so good, I just want to thank you, Lord.
3. Been my friend, been my friend, been my friend, I just want to thank you, Lord.

WORDS: Traditional African-American song
MUSIC: Traditional African-American melody; harm. J. Jefferson Cleveland and
    Verolga Nix, alt.

THANK YOU, LORD
333.7

Harm. © 1981 The United Methodist Publishing House

532   Grace and Gratitude

Grace always demands the answer of gratitude.
Grace and gratitude belong together like heaven and earth.
Grace evokes gratitude like the voice of an echo.
Gratitude follows grace like thunder follows lightning.

—Karl Barth, 20th-century Swiss theologian

We've Come This Far by Faith 533

WORDS: Albert A. Goodson, 1965
MUSIC: Albert A. Goodson, 1965; harm. Richard Smallwood

FAITH
Irr.

534 When Our Confidence Is Shaken

1. When our con-fi-dence is shak - en in be-
2. So - lar sys-tems, void of mean - ing, freeze the
3. In the dis-ci-pline of pray - ing, when it's
4. God is love, and thus re-deems us in the

liefs we thought se - cure, when the spir - it in its
spir - it in - to stone; al - ways our re-search-es
hard - est to be - lieve; in the drudg-er - y of
Christ we cru - ci - fy; this is God's e - ter - nal

sick - ness seeks but can - not find a cure, God is
lead us to the ul - ti - mate un - known. Faith must
car - ing, when it's not e - nough to grieve; faith, ma -
an - swer to the world's e - ter - nal why. May we

ac - tive in the ten - sions of a faith not yet ma - ture.
die, or come full cir - cle to its source in God a - lone.
tur-ing, learns ac - cep - tance of the in - sights we re - ceive.
in this faith ma - tur - ing be con - tent to live and die!

WORDS: Fred Pratt Green, 1971
MUSIC: John Goss, 1869

LAUDA ANIMA
87.87.87

Faith, While Trees Are Still in Blossom 535

1. Faith, while trees are still in blos - som, plans the
2. Long be - fore the dawn is break - ing, faith an -
3. Faith, up - lift - ed, tamed the wa - ter of the
4. Faith be - lieves that God is faith - ful: God will

pick - ing of the fruit; faith can feel the thrill of
ti - ci - pates the sun. Faith is ea - ger for the
un - di - vid - ed sea, and the peo - ple of the
be what God will be! Faith ac - cepts the call, re -

har - vest when the buds be - gin to sprout.
day - light, for the work that must be done.
He - brews found the path that made them free.
spond - ing, "I am will - ing, Lord, send me."

WORDS: Anders Frostenson, 1960; tr. Fred Kaan, 1972
MUSIC: V. Earle Copes, 1960

KINGDOM
87.87

536

Pues Si Vivimos
(When We Are Living)

Unísono (Unison)

D   **Em**   **A7**   **D**

1. Pues   si vi - vi - mos,   pa- ra Él vi - vi - mos
2. En   es - ta vi - da,   fru- tos he- mos de   dar.

1. When   we are   liv - ing,   it is in Christ Je - sus,
2. Through all our   liv - ing,   we our fruits must give.

Bm   **Em**   **A7**   **D**

y   si mo - ri - mos   pa- ra Él mo - ri - mos.
Las   o - bras bue - nas   son pa- ra o - fren- dar.

and when we're dy - ing,   it is in   the Lord.
Good works of ser - vice   are for of - fer- ing.

G   **Em**   **A**   **F♯m**

Sea   que vi - va - mos   o   que mu - ra - mos,
Ya   sea que de - mos   o que re - ci - ba - mos,

Both   in our   liv - ing   and   in our   dy - ing,
When   we are   giv - ing,   or   when re - ceiv - ing,

WORDS: St. 1 anonymous, tr. Elise S. Eslinger, 1983;
    st. 2, 3, 4 Roberto Escamilla, 1983, tr. George Lockwood, 1987
MUSIC: Traditional Spanish melody; harm. *Celebremos*, 1983, alt.

SOMOS DEL SEÑOR
Irr.

♩=112-120

Tr. © 1989 The United Methodist Publishing House

3. En la tristeza y en el dolor,
   en la belleza y en el amor,
   sea que suframos o que gocemos,
   Estribillo

4. En este mundo, hemos de encontrar
   gente que llora y sin consolar.
   Sea que ayudemos o que alimentemos,
   Estribillo

3. 'Mid times of sorrow and in times of pain,
   when sensing beauty or in love's embrace,
   whether we suffer, or sing rejoicing,
   Refrain

4. Across this wide world, we shall always find
   those who are crying with no peace of mind,
   but when we help them, or when we feed them,
   Refrain

537 My Hope Is Built

1. My hope is built on noth-ing less than
2. When dark-ness veils his love-ly face, I
3. His oath, his cov-e-nant, his blood sup-
4. When he shall come with trum-pet sound, O

Je-sus' blood and righ-teous-ness. I dare not trust the
rest on his un-chang-ing grace. In ev-ery high and
port me in the whelm-ing flood. When all a-round my
may I then in him be found! Dressed in his righ-teous-

sweet-est frame, but whol-ly lean on Je-sus' name.
storm-y gale, my an-chor holds with-in the veil.
soul gives way, he then is all my hope and stay.
ness a-lone, fault-less to stand be-fore the throne!

Refrain

On Christ the sol-id rock I stand, all oth-er ground is

sink-ing sand; all oth-er ground is sink-ing sand.

WORDS: Edward Mote, 1834
MUSIC: William B. Bradbury, 1863

THE SOLID ROCK
LM w. refrain

Hope of the World

1. Hope of the world, O Christ of great com-pas-sion:
2. Hope of the world, God's gift from high-est heav-en,
3. Hope of the world, a-foot on dust-y high-ways,
4. Hope of the world, who by your cross did save us
5. Hope of the world, O Christ, o'er death vic-to-rious,

1. speak to our fear-ful hearts by con-flict rent;
2. bring-ing to hun-gry souls the bread of life:
3. show-ing to wan-dering souls the path of light:
4. from death and dark de-spair, from sin and guilt:
5. who by this sign did con-quer grief and pain:

1. save us, your peo-ple, from con-sum-ing pas-sion,
2. still let your Spir-it un-to us be giv-en
3. walk now be-side us, lest the tempt-ing by-ways
4. we ren-der back the love your mer-cy gave us;
5. we would be faith-ful to your gos-pel glo-rious;

1. who by our own false hopes and aims are spent.
2. to heal earth's wounds and end its bit-ter strife.
3. lure us a-way from you to end-less night.
4. take now our lives and use them as you will.
5. you are our Christ and you for-ev-er reign!

WORDS: Georgia Harkness, 1954, alt.
MUSIC: V. Earle Copes, 1963

VICAR
11 10.11 10

♩=52-54

539 Old Ship of Zion

1. I was lost in sin and sor-row on an isle in life's dark
2. I got up but hes-i-tat-ed won-d'ring who this friend could
3. Then I stepp'd a-board the ves-sel thro' the straights and thro' the

sea, when I saw far in the dis-tance there a
be, tho' the waves were wild and dash-ing seem-ing
gorge, man-y years it sail'd the wa-ters man-y

ship it seemed to be, then I saw the cap-tain
they would swal-low me, then he raised his hand
souls have made the voyage, then I rec - og-nized the

beck-on then he called out loud and free "I have
toward me calm'd the wild and rag-ing sea with a
cap-tain, it was Je - sus in com-mand 'tis the

WORDS and MUSIC: Thomas A. Dorsey, 1950

OLD SHIP OF ZION
Irr.

540   O Love That Wilt Not Let Me Go

1. O Love that wilt not let me go,
2. O Light that fol-lowest all my way,
3. O Joy that seek-est me through pain,
4. O Cross that lift-est up my head,

I rest my
I yield my
I can-not
I dare not

wea-ry soul in thee;   I give thee back the life I owe, that
flick-ering torch to thee;   my heart re-stores its bor-rowed ray, that
close my heart to thee;   I trace the rain-bow through the rain, and
ask to fly from thee;   I lay in dust life's glo-ry dead, and

in thine o-cean depths its flow may rich-er, full-er be.
in thy sun-shine's blaze its day may bright-er, fair-er be.
feel the prom-ise is not vain that morn shall tear-less be.
from the ground there blos-soms red life that shall end-less be.

WORDS: George Matheson, 1882
MUSIC: Albert L. Peace, 1884

ST. MARGARET
88.886

541   Draw Compassion from Us

Creator God, draw compassion from us.
Christ, draw compassion from us.
Spirit God, draw compassion from us.

—Hildegard of Bingen, 12th-century Benedictine abbess

Jesus, Lover of My Soul

542

1. Je - sus, lov - er of my soul, let me to thy bos - om fly,
2. Oth - er ref - uge have I none; hangs my help-less soul on thee;
3. Plen - teous grace with thee is found, grace to cov - er all my sin;

while the near- er wa - ters roll, while the tem-pest still is high;
leave, ah! leave me not a - lone, still sup - port and com - fort me.
let the heal- ing streams a - bound, make and keep me pure with - in.

hide me, O my Sav - ior, hide, till the storm of life is past;
All my trust on thee is stayed, all my help from thee I bring;
Thou of life the foun - tain art, free - ly let me take of thee;

safe in - to the ha - ven guide, O re - ceive my soul at last!
cov - er my de - fense- less head with the shad - ow of thy wing.
spring thou up with- in my heart, rise to all e - ter - ni - ty.

WORDS: Charles Wesley, 1740
MUSIC: Joseph Parry, 1879

ABERYSTWYTH
77.77D

543   Blessed Assurance

1. Bless-ed as-sur-ance, Je-sus is mine! O what a fore-taste of glo-ry di-
2. Per-fect sub-mis-sion, per-fect de-light, vi-sions of rap-ture now burst on my
3. Per-fect sub-mis-sion, all is at rest; I in my Sav-ior am hap-py and

vine! Heir of sal-va-tion, pur-chase of God, born of his
sight; an-gels de-scend-ing bring from a-bove ech-oes of
blest, watch-ing and wait-ing, look-ing a-bove, filled with his

Refrain

Spir-it, washed in his blood.
mer-cy, whis-pers of love. This is my sto-ry, this is my
good-ness, lost in his love.

song, prais-ing my Sav-ior all the day long; this is my

sto-ry, this is my song, prais-ing my Sav-ior all the day long.

WORDS: Fanny J. Crosby, 1873
MUSIC: Phoebe P. Knapp, 1873

ASSURANCE
9 10.99 w. refrain

No, Not One!

1. There's not   a friend like the low - ly   Je - sus— no, not one!
2. No   friend like him is   so high and   ho - ly— no, not one!
3. There's not   an hour that he   is   not near us— no, not one!
4. Was   e'er   a gift like the Sav - ior   giv - en?   No, not one!

no, not one!   None else could heal all   our soul's dis - eas - es—
no, not one!   And   yet   no friend is   so meek and   low - ly—
no, not one!   No   night so dark but   his love can cheer us—
no, not one!   Will   he   re - fuse us   a home in   heav - en?

Refrain

no,   not one!   no,   not one!   Je - sus knows all a -

bout our strug-gles,   he will guide   till   the   day   is   done;

there's not a friend like the low-ly Jesus— no, not one!   no, not one!

WORDS: Johnson Oatman, Jr., 1895
MUSIC: George C. Hugg, 1895

HARPER MEMORIAL
10 6.10 6 w. refrain

545 He Leadeth Me: O Blessed Thought!

1. He lead - eth me: O bless - ed thought! O
2. Lord, I would place my hand in thine, nor
3. And when my task on earth is done, when,

words with heaven - ly com - fort fraught! What - e'er I do, wher -
ev - er mur - mur nor re - pine; by wa - ters still, o'er
by thy grace, the vic - tory's won, e'en death's cold wave I

e'er I be, still 'tis God's hand that lead - eth me.
trou - bled sea, still 'tis thy hand that lead - eth me.
will not flee, since God thro' Jor - dan lead - eth me.

Refrain

He lead-eth me, he lead-eth me, by his own hand he lead-eth me:

his faith-ful fol-lower I would be, for by his hand he lead-eth me.

WORDS: Joseph H. Gilmore, 1862
MUSIC: William B. Bradbury, 1864

HE LEADETH ME
LM w. refrain

Amazing Grace!   546

1. A - maz - ing grace! How sweet the sound that saved a wretch like me! I once was lost, but now am found; was blind, but now I see.
2. 'Twas grace that taught my heart to fear, and grace my fears re - lieved; how pre - cious did that grace ap - pear the hour I first be - lieved.
3. Through man - y dan - gers, toils, and snares, I have al - read - y come; 'tis grace hath brought me safe thus far, and grace will lead me home.
4. When we've been there ten thou - sand years, bright shin - ing as the sun, we've no less days to sing God's praise than when we'd first be - gun.

WORDS: John Newton, 1779; st. 4 anonymous
MUSIC: *Virginia Harmony*, 1831; harm. Edwin O. Excell, 1900

NEW BRITAIN
CM

The Serenity Prayer   547

God, give us grace to accept with serenity the things that cannot be changed,
courage to change the things that should be changed,
and wisdom to distinguish the one from the other.

—*Reinhold Niebuhr, 20th-century American theologian*

548 The Old Rugged Cross

1. On a hill far a-way stood an old rug-ged cross,
2. O that old rug-ged cross, so de-spised by the world,
3. In that old rug-ged cross, stained with blood so di-vine,
4. To the old rug-ged cross I will ev-er be true,

the em-blem of suf-fering and shame;
has a won-drous at-trac-tion for me;
a won-drous beau-ty I see,
its shame and re-proach glad-ly bear;

and I love that old cross where the dear-est and best
for the dear Lamb of God left his glo-ry a-bove
for 'twas on that old cross Je-sus suf-fered and died,
then he'll call me some day to my home far a-way,

for a world of lost sin-ners was slain.
to bear it to dark Cal-va-ry.
to par-don and sanc-ti-fy me.
where his glo-ry for-ev-er I'll share.

WORDS and MUSIC: George Bennard, 1913

THE OLD RUGGED CROSS
Irr. w. refrain

Refrain

So I'll cher - ish the old rug - ged cross,
cross, the old rug - ged cross,
till my tro - phies at last I lay down;
I will cling to the old rug - ged cross,
cross, the old rug - ged cross,
and ex - change it some day for a crown.

Thoughtful Silence 549

O Jesus, Son of God, who was silent before Pilate,
do not let us wag our tongues without thinking
of what we are to say and how to say it.

—*A Gaelic prayer*

550 There's Within My Heart a Melody

1. There's with - in my heart a mel - o - dy—
2. All my life was wrecked by sin and strife,
3. Feast - ing on the rich - es of his grace,
4. Though some - times he leads through wa - ters deep,
5. Soon he's com - ing back to wel - come me

1. Je - sus whis - pers sweet and low,
2. dis - cord filled my heart with pain;
3. rest - ing 'neath his shel - t'ring wing,
4. tri - als fall a - cross the way,
5. far be - yond the star - ry sky;

1. "Fear not, I am with thee— peace, be still,"
2. Je - sus swept a - cross the bro - ken strings,
3. al - ways look - ing on his smil - ing face—
4. though some - times the path seems rough and steep,
5. I shall wing my flight to worlds un - known,

WORDS and MUSIC: Luther B. Bridgers, 1910

SWEETEST NAME
97.97 w. refrain

1. in all of life's ebb and flow.
2. stirred the slum - b'ring chords a - gain.
3. that is why I shout and sing.
4. see his foot - prints all the way.
5. I shall reign with him on high.

Refrain

Je - sus, Je - sus, Je - sus— sweet - est name I know,

fills my ev - ery long - ing, keeps me sing - ing as I go.

Outwitted 551

He drew a circle that shut me out—
Heretic, rebel, a thing to flout.
But Love and I had the wit to win
And we drew a circle that took him in!

—Edwin Markham, 19th- and 20th-century Disciples poet

552　Standing on the Promises

1. Stand - ing on　the prom - is - es　of Christ my　king,
2. Stand - ing on　the prom - is - es　that can - not　fail,
3. Stand - ing on　the prom - is - es　of Christ the　Lord,
4. Stand - ing on　the prom - is - es　I　can - not　fall,

through e - ter - nal a - ges let　his prais - es　ring;
when　the howl - ing storms of doubt　and fear　as - sail,
bound　to him　e - ter - nal - ly　by love's strong cord,
lis - t'ning ev - ery mo - ment to　the Spir - it's　call,

glo - ry　in　the high - est, I　will shout　and　sing,
by　the liv - ing Word　of God　I　shall　pre - vail,
o - ver-com - ing dai - ly with　the Spir - it's　sword,
rest - ing　in　my Sav - ior as　my　all　in　all,

stand - ing on　the prom - is - es　of　God.

WORDS and MUSIC: R. Kelso Carter, 1891

PROMISES
11 11.11 9 w. refrain

Refrain

Stand-ing, stand - ing, stand-ing on the prom-is-es of
stand-ing on the prom-is-es,

God my Sav-ior; stand - ing, stand - ing,
stand-ing on the prom-is-es,

I'm stand-ing on the prom-is-es of God.

The Disciples Mind 553

What do we mean by the Disciples mind? It is a way of approaching the Scriptures with a reverent intelligence. This style of professing Christian faith has accepted the reproach of advocating a "head religion" hurled by those who profess a "heart religion." Emphasizing faith with understanding, the Disciples mind puts the highest premium on rationality and faithfulness in action.

—*Ronald E. Osborn, 20th-century Disciples theologian*

554 You Are My Hiding Place

Unison

You are my hid - ing place, you al - ways fill my heart with

songs of de - liv - er - ance. When-ev- er I am a - fraid, I will trust in

Fine (last time)

you. I will trust in you; let the weak say,

D.C.

"I am strong in the strength of my God."

WORDS and MUSIC: Michael Ledner, 1981

HIDING PLACE
Irr.

♩=120-128

Through It All

Through it all, through it all,

I've learned to trust in Je-sus, I've learned to trust in God;

through it all, through it all,

I've learned to de-pend up-on God's word.

WORDS and MUSIC: Andraé Crouch, 1971

© 1971 Manna Music, Inc.

THROUGH IT ALL
Irr.

𝅗𝅥=56-64

556 Trust and Obey

1. When we walk with the Lord in the light of his word,
2. Not a bur-den we bear, not a sor-row we share,
3. But we nev-er can prove the de-lights of his love
4. Then in fel-low-ship sweet we will sit at his feet,

what a glo-ry he sheds on our way!
but our toil he will rich-ly re-pay;
un-til all on the al-tar we lay;
or we'll walk by his side in the way;

While we do his good will, he a-bides with us still,
not a grief or a loss, not a frown or a cross,
for the fa-vor he shows, for the joy he be-stows,
what he says we will do, where he sends we will go;

and with all who will trust and o-bey.
but is blest if we trust and o-bey.
are for them who will trust and o-bey.
nev-er fear, on-ly trust and o-bey.

WORDS: John H. Sammis, 1887
MUSIC: Daniel B. Towner, 1887

TRUST AND OBEY
669D w. refrain

Refrain

Trust and o - bey, for there's no oth - er way to be hap - py in Je - sus, but to trust and o - bey.

Just a Closer Walk with Thee 557

1. I am weak, but thou art strong; Je - sus, keep me from all wrong;
2. Through this world of toil and snares, if I fal - ter, Lord, who cares?
3. When my fee - ble life is o'er, time for me will be no more;
Refrain: Just a clos - er walk with thee, grant it, Je - sus, is my plea,

D. C. for Refrain

I'll be sat - is - fied as long as I walk, let me walk close to thee.
Who with me my bur - den shares? None but thee, dear Lord, none but thee.
guide me gent - ly, safe - ly o'er to thy shore, dear Lord, to thy shore.
dai - ly walk - ing close to thee: let it be, dear Lord, let it be.

WORDS and MUSIC: Anonymous

CLOSER WALK
Irr. w. refrain

558 Savior, Like a Shepherd Lead Us

1. Sav-ior, like a shep-herd lead us, much we need thy ten-der care;
2. We are thine; do thou be-friend us; be the guard-ian of our way;
3. Ear-ly let us seek thy fa-vor; ear-ly let us do thy will;

in thy pleas-ant pas-tures feed us, for our use thy folds pre-pare.
keep thy flock; from sin de-fend us; seek us when we go a-stray.
bless-ed Lord and on-ly Sav-ior, with thy love our spir-its fill.

Bless-ed Je-sus, bless-ed Je-sus, thou hast bought us, thine we are;
Bless-ed Je-sus, bless-ed Je-sus, hear thy chil-dren when we pray;
Bless-ed Je-sus, bless-ed Je-sus, thou hast loved us, love us still;

bless-ed Je-sus, bless-ed Je-sus, thou hast bought us, thine we are.
bless-ed Je-sus, bless-ed Je-sus, hear thy chil-dren when we pray.
bless-ed Je-sus, bless-ed Je-sus, thou hast loved us, love us still.

WORDS: Dorothy A. Thrupp, 1836
MUSIC: William B. Bradbury, 1859

BRADBURY
87.87D

All the Way My Savior Leads Me 559

1. All the way my Sav-ior leads me; what have I   to ask be-side?
2. All the way my Sav-ior leads me, cheers each wind-ing path I   tread,
3. All the way my Sav-ior leads me; oh, the full-ness of his love!

Can   I doubt his ten-der mer-cy, who through life has been my Guide?
gives me grace for ev-ery tri-al, feeds me   with the liv-ing bread.
Per-fect rest   to me is prom-ised in my   Fa-ther's house a-bove.

Heaven-ly peace, di-vin-est com-fort, here by faith in him to dwell!
Though my wea-ry steps may fal-ter, and my soul   a-thirst may be,
When my spir-it, clothed im-mor-tal, wings its flight to realms of day,

For   I know, what-e'er be-fall me, Je-sus do-eth all things well; well.
gush-ing from   the Rock be-fore me, Lo! a spring of joy I   see; see.
this my song through end-less a-ges: Je-sus led me all the way; way.

WORDS: Fanny J. Crosby, 1875
MUSIC: Robert Lowry, 1875

ALL THE WAY
87.87D w. repeat

560 Leaning on the Everlasting Arms

1. What a fel-low-ship, what a joy di-vine, lean-ing on the ev-er-
2. O how sweet to walk in this pil-grim way, lean-ing on the ev-er-
3. What have I to dread, what have I to fear, lean-ing on the ev-er-

last-ing arms; what a bless-ed-ness, what a peace is mine,
last-ing arms; O how bright the path grows from day to day,
last-ing arms? I have bless-ed peace with my Lord so near,

Refrain

lean-ing on the ev-er-last-ing arms. Lean - ing,
Lean-ing on Je - sus

lean - ing, safe and se-cure from all a-larms; lean -
lean-ing on Je-sus, lean-ing on

ing, lean - ing, lean-ing on the ev-er-last-ing arms.
Je-sus, lean-ing on Je-sus,

WORDS: Elisha A. Hoffman, 1887
MUSIC: Anthony J. Showalter, 1887

SHOWALTER
10 9.10 9 w. refrain

It Is Well with My Soul

561

1. When peace, like a riv - er, at - tend - eth my way,
2. Though Sa - tan should buf - fet, though tri - als should come,
3. My sin, oh, the bliss of this glo - ri - ous thought!
4. May God haste the day when my faith shall be sight,

when sor - rows like sea bil - lows roll; what - ev - er my
let this blest as - sur - ance con - trol, that Christ has re -
My sin, not in part but the whole, is nailed to the
the clouds be rolled back as a scroll; the trump shall re -

lot, thou hast taught me to say, it is well, it is
gard - ed my help - less es - tate, and hath shed his own
cross, and I bear it no more, praise the Lord, praise the
sound, and the Lord shall de - scend, e - ven so, it is

Refrain

well with my soul.
blood for my soul.   It is well   with my soul,
Lord, O my soul!
well with my soul.   It is well   with my soul,

it is well, it is well with my soul.

WORDS: Horatio G. Spafford, 1873
MUSIC: Philip P. Bliss, 1876

VILLE DU HAVRE
11 8.11 9 w. refrain

562 Because He Lives

1. God sent his Son, they called him Je - sus;
he came to love, heal, and for - give;
he lived and died to buy my par - don,
an emp - ty grave is there to prove my Sav - ior lives.

2. How sweet to hold a new-born ba - by,
and feel the pride and joy that gives;
but great - er still the calm as - sur - ance,
this child can face un - cer - tain days be-cause he lives.

3. And then one day I'll cross the riv - er;
I'll fight life's fi - nal war with pain;
and then as death gives way to vic - tory,
I'll see the lights of glo - ry and I'll know he reigns.

WORDS: Gloria and William J. Gaither, 1971
MUSIC: William J. Gaither, 1971

RESURRECTION
98.9 12 w. refrain

♩=66-72

Be-cause he lives, I can face to-mor-row;
be-cause he lives, all fear is gone;
be-cause I know he holds the fu-ture,
and life is worth the liv-ing just be-cause he lives.

Driven to My Knees 563

I have been driven many times to my knees by the overwhelming conviction that
I had nowhere else to go.

—Abraham Lincoln, 19th-century U.S. president

564   He Touched Me

1. Shack-led by a heav-y bur-den, 'neath a load of guilt and shame, then the hand of Je-sus touched me, and now I am no long-er the same.
2. Since I met this bless-ed Sav-ior, since he cleansed and made me whole, I will nev-er cease to praise him; I'll shout it while e-ter-ni-ty rolls.

Refrain

He touched me, O he touched me, and O the joy that floods my soul! Some-thing hap-pened, and now I know, he touched me and made me whole.

WORDS and MUSIC: William J. Gaither, 1963

HE TOUCHED ME
Irr. w. refrain

♩=108-116

If You Will Trust in God to Guide You 565

1. If you will trust in God to guide you, and hope in God through all your ways, God will give strength, what-e'er be-tide you, and bear you through the e-vil days. Who trusts in God's un-chang-ing love builds on the rock that will not move.

2. God will em-brace your pain and weep-ing, your help-less an-ger and dis-tress. If you are in God's care and keep-ing, in sor-row will God love you less? For Christ, who took for you a cross, will bring you safe through ev-ery loss.

3. Sing, pray, and keep God's ways un-swerv-ing; so do your own part faith-ful-ly, and trust God's word; though un-de-serv-ing, you'll find God's pro-mise true to be. God nev-er will for-sake in need the soul that trusts in God in-deed.

WORDS: Georg Neumark, 1657; tr. st. 1, 3, Catherine Winkworth, 1863, alt.;   WER NUR DEN LIEBEN GOTT
st. 2 tr. Jaroslav Vajda, alt.   98.98.88
MUSIC: Georg Neumark, 1657

St. 2 © 1978 *Lutheran Book of Worship*, used by permission of Augsburg Fortress

♩=108

566

Be Still, My Soul

1. Be still, my soul: for God is on your side;
2. Be still, my soul: for God will un - der - take
3. Be still, my soul: the hour is has - tening on

bear pa - tient - ly the cross of grief or pain.
to guide the fu - ture sure - ly as the past.
when we shall dwell with God for - ev - er more,

Trust in your God, your sav - ior and your guide,
Your hope, your con - fi - dence let noth - ing shake;
when dis - ap - point - ment, grief, and fear are gone,

who through all chang - es faith - ful will re - main.
all now mys - te - rious shall be bright at last.
sor - row for - got, love's pur - est joys re - stored.

WORDS: Katharina von Schlegel, 1752; tr. Jane Borthwick, 1855, alt.
MUSIC: Jean Sibelius, 1899; arr. *The Hymnal*, 1933

FINLANDIA
11 10.11 10.11 10

Be still, my soul: your best, your heaven - ly friend
Be still, my soul: the waves and winds still know
Be still, my soul: when change and tears are past,

through thorn - y ways leads to a peace - ful end.
the voice that calmed them in this world be - low.
all safe and bless - ed we shall meet at last.

Waiting and Wrestling with God 567

O God of patience and pardon, save us from the impoverishment and danger of hurry in our devotions, lest the bloom of our spiritual life be permanently blighted. Revive us from our leanness of soul and coldness of heart by awakening in us the sense of waiting and wrestling with thee. Hush within us the first rise of murmurings against the taxing necessities of prayer. May there be no counting of the cost of time and labor, lest our foundations be imperiled. O Lord, pardon us of all slovenliness in our devotions and set us to redeeming the time with gladness.

—Peter Ainslie, 20th-century Disciples ecumenist

568 'Tis the Gift to Be Simple

*Optional chord D.

WORDS: Shaker song (18th century)
MUSIC: Shaker melody; arr. Margaret W. Mealy, 1984

SIMPLE GIFTS
Irr. w. refrain

♩=60

bow and to bend we shan't be a-shamed, to turn, turn, will be our de-light till by turn-ing, turn-ing we come round right.

Luke 23:42

Jesus, Remember Me 569

Je-sus, re-mem-ber me when you come in-to your king-dom.

Je-sus, re-mem-ber me when you come in-to your king-dom.

WORDS: Luke 23:42
MUSIC: Jacques Berthier and the Community of Taizé, 1981

REMEMBER ME
Irr.

Music © 1981Les Presses de Taizé; used by permission of GIA Publications, Inc.

♩=84-92

570 Sweet Hour of Prayer!

1. Sweet hour of prayer! sweet hour of prayer! that calls me
2. Sweet hour of prayer! sweet hour of prayer! the joys I
3. Sweet hour of prayer! sweet hour of prayer! thy wings shall

from a world of care, and bids me at my
feel, the bliss I share of those whose anx - ious
my pe - ti - tion bear to him whose truth and

Fa - ther's throne make all my wants and wish - es known.
spir - its burn with strong de - sires for thy re - turn!
faith - ful - ness en - gage the wait - ing soul to bless.

In sea - sons of dis - tress and grief, my soul has
With such I has - ten to the place where God my
And since he bids me seek his face, be - lieve his

WORDS: William Walford, 1845
MUSIC: William B. Bradbury, 1861

SWEET HOUR
LMD

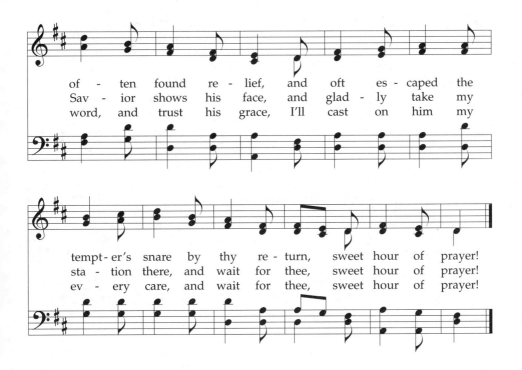

of - ten found re - lief, and oft es - caped the
Sav - ior shows his face, and glad - ly take my
word, and trust his grace, I'll cast on him my

tempt - er's snare by thy re - turn, sweet hour of prayer!
sta - tion there, and wait for thee, sweet hour of prayer!
ev - ery care, and wait for thee, sweet hour of prayer!

A Prayer of Confession 571

Most merciful God,
we confess that we have sinned against you in thought, word, and deed,
by what we have done, and by what we have left undone.
We have not loved you with our whole heart;
we have not loved our neighbors as ourselves.
We are truly sorry and we humbly repent.
For the sake of your son Jesus Christ, have mercy on us and forgive us;
that we may delight in your will, and walk in your ways,
to the glory of your name. Amen.

—The Book of Common Prayer, 1979

572 Take Time to Be Holy

1. Take time to be ho - ly, speak oft with thy Lord;
2. Take time to be ho - ly, the world rush-es on;
3. Take time to be ho - ly, let him be thy guide,
4. Take time to be ho - ly, be calm in thy soul;

a - bide in him al - ways, and feed on his word.
spend much time in se - cret with Je - sus a - lone.
and run not be - fore him, what - ev - er be - tide;
each thought and each mo - tive be - neath his con - trol;

Make friends of God's chil - dren; help those who are weak;
By look-ing to Je - sus, like him thou shalt be;
in joy or in sor - row, still fol - low thy Lord.
thus led by his spir - it to foun-tains of love,

for - get-ting in noth - ing God's bless-ing to seek.
thy friends in thy con - duct his like-ness shall see.
And, look-ing to Je - sus, still trust in his word.
thou soon shalt be fit - ted for ser - vice a - bove.

WORDS: W. D. Longstaff, 1882
MUSIC: George C. Stebbins, 1890

HOLINESS
65.65D

Purer in Heart, O God   573

1. Pur - er in heart, O God, help me to be; may I de-
vote my life whol - ly to thee. Watch thou my way - ward feet,
guide me with coun - sel sweet; pur - er in heart, help me to be.

2. Pur - er in heart, O God, help me to be; teach me to
do thy will most lov - ing - ly. Be thou my friend and guide,
let me with thee a - bide; pur - er in heart, help me to be.

3. Pur - er in heart, O God, help me to be; that I thy
ho - ly face one day may see. Keep me from se - cret sin,
reign thou my soul with - in; pur - er in heart, help me to be.

WORDS: Fannie Estelle Davison, 1877
MUSIC: James H. Fillmore, 1877

PURER IN HEART
64.64.66.44

Cleanse the Thoughts of Our Hearts   574

Almighty God,
    unto whom all hearts are open,
    all desires known,
    and from whom no secrets are hid,
cleanse the thoughts of our hearts
    by the inspiration of your Holy Spirit,
that we may perfectly love you,
    and worthily magnify your holy Name.

—*Gregorian Sacramentary (6th century), alt.*

575   Come and Find the Quiet Center

1. Come and find the qui-et center in the crowd-ed life we
2. Si-lence is a friend who claims us, cools the heat and slows the
3. In the Spir-it let us trav-el, o-pen to each oth-er's

lead, find the room for hope to en - ter, find the
pace, God it is who speaks and names us, knows our
pain, let our loves and fears un - rav - el, cel - e -

frame where we are freed: clear the cha - os and the
be - ing, touch-es base, mak - ing space with - in our
brate the space we gain: there's a place for deep-est

clut - ter, clear our eyes, that we can see all the
think - ing, lift - ing shades to show the sun, rais-ing
dream-ing, there's a time for heart to care, in the

WORDS: Shirley Erena Murray, 1989
MUSIC: Traditional American melody; arr. Jack Schrader

BEACH SPRING
87.87D

Words and arr. © 1992 Hope Publishing Co.

♩=70-74

things that real - ly   mat - ter, be at peace, and sim - ply be.
cour - age when we're shrink - ing, find - ing scope for faith be - gun.
Spir - it's live - ly   schem - ing there is al - ways room to spare!

My Faith Looks Up to Thee   576

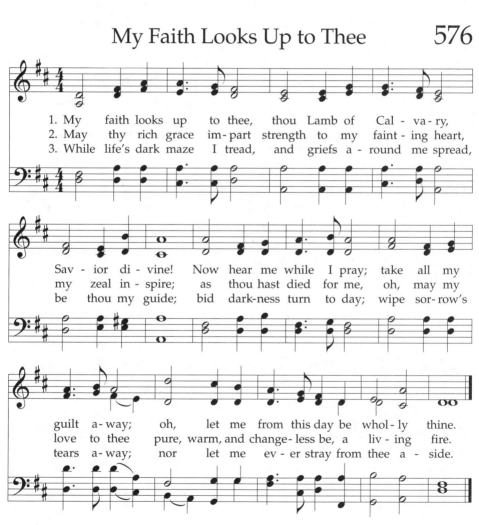

1. My   faith looks up   to thee,   thou Lamb of   Cal - va - ry,
2. May   thy rich grace im - part strength to my   faint - ing heart,
3. While life's dark maze I tread, and griefs a - round me spread,

Sav - ior di - vine! Now hear me while I pray; take all my
my zeal in - spire; as   thou hast died for me, oh, may my
be thou my guide; bid dark-ness turn to day; wipe sor - row's

guilt a - way;   oh,   let me from this day be whol - ly thine.
love to thee   pure, warm, and change - less be, a liv - ing fire.
tears a - way;   nor   let me ev - er stray from thee a - side.

WORDS: Ray Palmer, 1831, alt.   OLIVET
MUSIC: Lowell Mason, 1832   664.6664

577 Nearer, My God, to Thee

1. Near - er, my God, to thee, near - er to thee!
2. When like the wan - der - er, the sun gone down,
3. There let the way ap - pear, steps un - to heaven;
4. Then, with my wak - ing thoughts bright with thy praise,
5. Or if, on joy - ful wing cleav - ing the sky,

1. E'en though it be a cross that rais - eth me,
2. dark - ness be o - ver me, my rest a stone;
3. all that thou send - est me, in mer - cy given;
4. out of my ston - y griefs Beth - el I'll raise;
5. sun, moon, and stars for - got, up - ward I fly,

1. still all my song shall be, near - er, my God, to thee;
2. then in my dreams I'd be near - er, my God, to thee;
3. an - gels to beck - on me near - er, my God, to thee;
4. so by my woes to be near - er, my God, to thee;
5. still all my song shall be, near - er, my God, to thee;

near - er, my God, to thee, near - er to thee!

WORDS: Sarah F. Adams, 1841
MUSIC: Lowell Mason, 1856

BETHANY
64.64.6664

I Need Thee Every Hour

578

1. I need thee ev-ery hour, most gra - cious Lord;
2. I need thee ev-ery hour; stay thou near by;
3. I need thee ev-ery hour in joy or pain;
4. I need thee ev-ery hour; teach me thy will,

no ten - der voice like thine can peace af - ford.
temp - ta - tions lose their power when thou art nigh.
come quick - ly, and a - bide or life is vain.
and thy rich prom-is - es in me ful - fill.

Refrain

I need thee, oh, I need thee; ev - ery hour I need thee;

O bless me now, my Sav - ior, I come to thee.

WORDS: Annie S. Hawks, 1872; refrain, Robert Lowry, 1872
MUSIC: Robert Lowry, 1872

NEED
64.64 w. refrain

579 Standing in the Need of Prayer

Refrain

It's me (it's me), it's me, O Lord, stand-ing in the need of prayer. It's me (it's me), it's me, O Lord, stand-ing in the need of prayer.

Fine

1. Not my broth - er, not my sis - ter, but it's
2. Not the preach - er, not the teach - er, but it's
3. Not my fa - ther, not my moth - er, but it's
4. Not the strang - er, not my neigh - bor, but it's

WORDS: African-American spiritual
MUSIC: African-American spiritual; arr. William Farley Smith, 1986

PENITENT
Irr.

me, O Lord, stand-ing in the need of prayer.
me, O Lord, stand-ing in the need of prayer.
me, O Lord, stand-ing in the need of prayer.
me, O Lord, stand-ing in the need of prayer.

Not my broth - er, not my sis - ter, but it's
Not the preach - er, not the teach - er, but it's
Not my fa - ther, not my moth - er, but it's
Not the strang - er, not my neigh - bor, but it's

D. C.

me, O Lord, stand-ing in the need of prayer.
me, O Lord, stand-ing in the need of prayer.
me, O Lord, stand-ing in the need of prayer.
me, O Lord, stand-ing in the need of prayer.

For Health and Strength 580

4 Part Canon

① ② ③ ④

For health and strength, and dai-ly food, we praise your name, O God.

WORDS and MUSIC: Traditional Dutch folk song

GRACE
Irr.

581 Near to the Heart of God

1. There is a place of qui - et rest, near to the heart of God;
2. There is a place of com - fort sweet, near to the heart of God;
3. There is a place of full re - lease, near to the heart of God;

a place where sin can - not mo - lest, near to the heart of God.
a place where we our Sav - ior meet, near to the heart of God.
a place where all is joy and peace, near to the heart of God.

Refrain

O Je - sus, blest Re - deem - er, sent from the heart of God,

hold us who wait be - fore you near to the heart of God.

WORDS and MUSIC: Cleland B. McAfee, 1903

McAFEE
CM w. refrain

Come Down, O Love Divine

582

1. Come down, O Love di - vine, seek now this soul of mine,
2. O let it free - ly burn, till earth - ly pas - sions turn
3. And so the yearn - ing strong, with which the soul will long,

and vis - it it with your own ar - dor glow - ing;
to dust and ash - es in its heat con - sum - ing;
shall far out - pass the power of hu - man tell - ing;

O Com - fort - er, draw near, with - in my heart ap - pear,
and let your glo - rious light shine ev - er on my sight,
for none can guess its grace, till love cre - ates the place

and kin - dle it, your ho - ly flame be - stow - ing.
and clothe me round, the while my path il - lum - ing.
where - in the Ho - ly Spir - it makes its dwell - ing.

WORDS: Bianco of Siena (15th century); tr. Richard F. Littledale, 1867, alt.
MUSIC: Ralph Vaughan Williams, 1906

DOWN AMPNEY
66 11D

♩=56-62

583   Lead Me, Guide Me

Lead me, guide me, a - long the way,

for if you lead me, I can - not stray.

Lord, let me walk each day with thee.

WORDS: Doris Akers, 1953
MUSIC: Doris Akers, 1953; harm. Richard Smallwood

LEAD ME GUIDE ME
Irr.

Lead me, oh Lord, lead me.

Father, I Stretch My Hands to Thee 584

G   C/G   G/B   G/D D7   G

1. Fa - ther, I stretch my hands to thee, no
2. What did thine on - ly Son en - dure, be -
3. Sure - ly thou canst not let me die! O
4. Au - thor of faith! to thee I lift my

B7   Em   A7   D7   G   B7 ⌐3¬ Em   G7

oth - er help I know. If thou with - draw thy -
fore I drew my breath! What pain, what la - bor
speak and I shall live, and here I will un -
wea - ry, long - ing eyes. O let me now re -

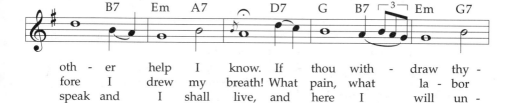

C   G ⌐3¬   D7   G   G/B C G/B Am/C G/D   D7   G
                                        ⌐3¬

self from me, ah! whith - er shall I go?
to se - cure my soul from end - less death!
wea - ried lie, till thou thy Spir - it give.
ceive that gift! My soul with - out it dies.

WORDS: Charles Wesley, 1741
MUSIC: Hugh Wilson, c. 1800; lined by J. Jefferson Cleveland and Verolga Nix, 1979

MARTYRDOM
CM

Arr. used by permission of J. Jefferson Cleveland Estate

585 What a Friend We Have in Jesus

1. What a friend we have in Je - sus, all our sins and griefs to bear!
2. Have we tri - als and temp - ta - tions? Is there trou-ble an - y-where?
3. Are we weak and heav-y lad - en, cum-bered with a load of care?

What a priv - i - lege to car - ry ev - ery-thing to God in prayer!
We should nev-er be dis - cour-aged; take it to the Lord in prayer!
Pre - cious Sav-ior, still our ref - uge, take it to the Lord in prayer!

Oh, what peace we of - ten for - feit, oh, what need-less pain we bear,
Can we find a friend so faith - ful, who will all our sor-rows share?
Do your friends de-spise, for-sake you? Take it to the Lord in prayer!

all be-cause we do not car - ry ev - ery-thing to God in prayer.
Je - sus knows our ev - ery weak-ness; take it to the Lord in prayer!
In his arms he'll take and shield you; you will find a sol-ace there.

WORDS: Joseph Scriven, 1855
MUSIC: Charles C. Converse, 1868

CONVERSE
87.87D

Open My Eyes, That I May See

586

1. O - pen my eyes, that I may see glimps-es of truth thou
2. O - pen my ears, that I may hear voic-es of truth thou
3. O - pen my mouth, and let me bear glad-ly the warm truth

hast for me; place in my hands the won-der-ful key
send - est clear; and while the wave - notes fall on my ear,
ev - ery-where; o - pen my heart and let me pre-pare

Refrain

that shall un - clasp and set me free.
ev - ery-thing false will dis - ap-pear. Si - lent-ly now I
love with thy chil - dren thus to share.

wait for thee, read - y, my God, thy will to see.

O - pen my eyes,
O - pen my ears, il - lu - mine me, Spir - it di - vine!
O - pen my heart,

WORDS and MUSIC: Clara H. Scott, 1895

OPEN MY EYES
88.98 w. refrain

587 Jesus, Keep Me Near the Cross

1. Je - sus, keep me near the cross: there a pre - cious foun - tain,
2. Near the cross, a trem - bling soul, love and mer - cy found me;
3. Near the cross! O Lamb of God, bring its scenes be - fore me;

free to all, a heal - ing stream, flows from Cal - v'ry's moun - tain.
there the bright and morn - ing star sheds its beams a - round me.
help me walk from day to day, with its shad - ow o'er me.

Refrain

In the cross, in the cross, be my glo - ry ev - er,

till my rap - tured soul shall find rest be - yond the riv - er.

WORDS: Fanny J. Crosby, 1869
MUSIC: William H. Doane, 1869

NEAR THE CROSS
76.76 w. refrain

Have Thine Own Way, Lord! 588

1. Have thine own way, Lord! Have thine own way!
Thou art the pot - ter; I am the clay.
Mold me and make me af - ter thy will,
while I am wait - ing, yield - ed and still.

2. Have thine own way, Lord! Have thine own way!
Search me and try me, Sav - ior to - day!
Wash me just now, Lord, wash me just now,
as in thy pres - ence hum - bly I bow.

3. Have thine own way, Lord! Have thine own way!
Wound - ed and wea - ry, help me I pray!
Pow - er, all pow - er, sure - ly is thine!
Touch me and heal me, Sav - ior di - vine!

4. Have thine own way, Lord! Have thine own way!
Hold o'er my be - ing ab - so - lute sway.
Fill with thy Spir - it till all shall see
Christ on - ly, al - ways, liv - ing in me!

WORDS: Adelaide A. Pollard, 1902
MUSIC: George C. Stebbins, 1907

ADELAIDE
54.54D

589   Lord, I Want to Be a Christian

1. Lord, I want to be a Chris-tian in-a my heart, in-a my heart,
2. Lord, I want to be more lov-ing in-a my heart, in-a my heart,
3. Lord, I want to be like Je - sus in-a my heart, in-a my heart,

Lord, I want to be a Chris-tian in-a my heart.
Lord, I want to be more lov - ing in-a my heart.
Lord, I want to be like Je - sus in-a my heart.

In-a my heart,   in-a my heart,
in-a my heart,   in-a my heart,

Lord, I want to be a Chris-tian in-a my heart. (in-a my heart.)
Lord, I want to be more lov - ing in-a my heart. (in-a my heart.)
Lord, I want to be like Je - sus in-a my heart. (in-a my heart.)

WORDS: African-American spiritual
MUSIC: African-American spiritual; harm. Larry Sivis, 1993

I WANT TO BE A CHRISTIAN
Irr.

Kum ba Yah

1. *Kum ba yah, my Lord, kum ba yah! Kum ba yah, my Lord, kum ba
2. Some-one's cry-ing, Lord, kum ba yah! Some-one's cry-ing, Lord, kum ba
3. Some-one's sing-ing, Lord, kum ba yah! Some-one's sing-ing, Lord, kum ba
4. Some-one's pray-ing, Lord, kum ba yah! Some-one's pray-ing, Lord, kum ba

yah! Kum ba yah, my Lord, kum ba yah! O Lord, kum ba yah!
yah! Some-one's cry-ing, Lord, kum ba yah! O Lord, kum ba yah!
yah! Some-one's sing-ing, Lord, kum ba yah! O Lord, kum ba yah!
yah! Some-one's pray-ing, Lord, kum ba yah! O Lord, kum ba yah!

*Come by here
WORDS: African-American spiritual
MUSIC: African melody

DESMOND
88.85

For God's Gifts

To be used responsively with the singing of "Kum ba Yah"

O Holy God, open unto me,
light for my darkness, courage for my fear, hope for my despair.

Kum ba yah, my Lord, kum ba yah! *(first musical phrase)*

O loving God, open unto me
wisdom for my confusion, forgiveness for my sins, love for my hate.

Kum ba yah, my Lord, kum ba yah! *(second musical phrase)*

O God of peace, open unto me
peace for my turmoil, joy for my sorrow, strength for my weakness.

Kum ba yah, my Lord, kum ba yah! *(third musical phrase)*

O Generous God, open my heart to receive all your gifts.

O, Lord, kum ba yah!

—*Howard Thurman, 20th-century African-American church leader*

592 Every Time I Feel the Spirit

WORDS: African-American spiritual
MUSIC: African-American spiritual; adapt. and arr. William Farley Smith, 1986

PENTECOST
Irr.

Adapt. and arr. © 1989 The United Methodist Publishing House

♩=100-108

D.C.

round me looks so fine, ask my Lord if all was mine.
one train on this track, runs to heav - en and right back.
leads me I'll not fear, I am shel - tered by God's care.

Psalm 5:8

Lead Me, Lord

593

Lead me, Lord, lead me in thy righ-teous-ness, make thy way plain be - fore my face. For it is thou, Lord, thou, Lord, on - ly, that mak - est me dwell in safe - ty.

WORDS: Based on Psalms 5:8; 4:8
MUSIC: Samuel S. Wesley, 1861

LEAD ME LORD
Irr.

594 Dear Lord, and Father of Mankind
(Dear God, Embracing Humankind)

1. Dear Lord, and Fa-ther of man-kind,* for-give our fool-ish ways! Re-clothe us in our right-ful mind, in pur-er lives thy ser-vice find, in deep-er rev-erence, praise.

2. In sim-ple trust like theirs who heard, be-side the Syr-ian sea, the gra-cious call-ing of the Lord, let us, like them, with-out a word, rise up and fol-low thee.

3. O Sab-bath rest by Gal-i-lee! O calm of hills a-bove, where Je-sus knelt to share with thee the si-lence of e-ter-ni-ty, in-ter-pret-ed by love!

4. Drop thy still dews of qui-et-ness, till all our striv-ings cease; take from our souls the strain and stress, and let our or-dered lives con-fess the beau-ty of thy peace.

5. Breathe through the heats of our de-sire thy cool-ness and thy balm; let sense be dumb, let flesh re-tire; speak through the earth-quake, wind, and fire, O still, small voice of calm.

* Dear God, embracing humankind

WORDS: John Greenleaf Whittier, 1872
MUSIC: Frederick C. Maker, 1887

REST
86.886

Be Thou My Vision

Unison

1. Be thou my vi - sion, O Lord of my heart;
2. Be thou my wis - dom, and thou my true word;
3. Rich - es I heed not, nor vain, emp - ty praise,
4. Great God of heav - en, my vic - to - ry won,

naught be all else to me, save that thou art
I ev - er with thee and thou with me, Lord;
thou mine in - her - i - tance, now and al - ways:
may I reach heav - en's joys, O bright heaven's Sun!

thou my best thought by day or by night,
thou my re - deem - er, my love thou hast won,
thou and thou on - ly, first in my heart,
Heart of my own heart, what - ev - er be - fall,

wak - ing or sleep - ing, thy pres - ence my light.
thou in me dwell - ing, and I with thee one.
Great God of heav - en, my trea - sure thou art.
still be my vi - sion, O Ru - ler of all.

WORDS: Irish song (8th century); tr. Mary E. Byrne, 1905; versed by Eleanor H. Hull, 1912, alt.
MUSIC: Traditional Irish melody; harm. Carlton R. Young, 1963

SLANE
10 10.9 10

596 Wellspring of Wisdom

1. Well - spring of Wis - dom, hear our cry.
2. Dawn of a New Day, put to flight
3. Gar - den of Grace, your gifts a - bound,
4. Call to Com - pas - sion, help us bring

The way a - head is parched and dry.
the ter - rors of a nu - clear night.
the sa - cred signs are all a - round,
our burn - ing need for nur - tur - ing,

We seek a source to sat - is - fy
As bear - ers of your lov - ing light,
the whole of earth is ho - ly ground.
the emp - ti - ness of ev - ery - thing

WORDS: Miriam Therese Winter, 1987
MUSIC: Miriam Therese Winter, 1987; harm. Don McKeever, 1987

WELLSPRING
888.9 10

♩=88-96

our thirst for sanc - ti - fy - ing wa - ters,
we hud - dle clos - er to your fire,
We learn, from all of life ex - press - ing,
to your em - brace, as we en - deav - or

wis - dom for your faith - filled sons and daugh- ters.
lift the lamp of hope a lit - tle high - er.
how to grow in sow - ing seeds of bless - ing.
to pro - claim your ho - ly name for - ev - er.

A Prayer for Shedding Pretenses 597

O God of a Thousand Faces,
    who sees through all our pretenses
    to that silent, secret space within
    where our true spirit sojourns,
prune away the duplicities that mask our best intentions
    and all those quick defenses that disguise who we really are.
Open us up to you and to all who would touch the truth of our being,
    so all may see the integrity of lives given over to you,
    now and forever. Amen.

    —*Miriam Therese Winter, 20th-century American Catholic missionary and liturgist*

598   I Love the Lord

Leader:

1. I	know I	am	a	child of God.
	wait un - til		the	vic - t'ry comes
2. I	love the	Lord:	who	heard my cry.
	as I	live		while trou - ble rise,

Congregation:

I	know	I	am
I'll	wait	un	- til
I	love	the	Lord:
Long	as	I	live

a	child	of
the	vic	- t'ry
who	heard	my
while	trou	- ble

Leader:

God.	al - though	I	move so slow.
comes	and	move at	God's com - mand.
cry.	And	pit - ied	ev - ery moan.
rise,	I'll	has - ten	to God's throne.

WORDS: Traditional African-American chant
MUSIC: Traditional African-American chant; transcribed by Floyd Knight, Jr., 1993

I LOVE THE LORD
CM

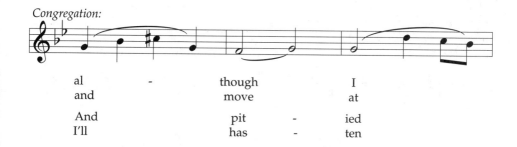

Congregation:

al	-	though	I
and		move	at
And		pit	-	ied
I'll		has	-	ten

Leader:

move	so	slow.	I'll
God's	com	-	mand.
ev	-	ery	moan.	Long
to	God's	throne.

3.
Leader: I love the Lord, who bowed an ear.
Congregation: I love the Lord, who bowed an ear.

Leader: And chased my grief away.
Congregation: And chased my grief away.

Leader: Oh, let my heart no more despair,
Congregation: Oh, let my heart no more despair,

Leader: while I have breath to pray.
Congregation: while I have breath to pray.

4.
Leader: The Lord beheld me sore distressed,
Congregation: The Lord beheld me sore distressed,

Leader: and bade my pains remove.
Congregation: and bade my pains remove.

Leader: Return, my soul, to God, thy rest,
Congregation: Return, my soul, to God, thy rest,

Leader: for thou hast known God's love.
Congregation: for thou hast known God's love.

599 Day by Day

Day by day, day by day,

O, dear Lord, three things I pray:

to see thee more clear - ly, love thee more dear - ly,

fol- low thee more near - ly, day by day.

day by day, by day, by day, by day, by day.

Small notes only on repeat

WORDS: Attr. Richard of Chichester (13th century), alt.
MUSIC: Stephen Schwartz, 1971

GODSPELL
Irr.

Music © 1971 Range Road Music Inc., Quartet Music, Inc., and New Cadenza Music Corp.

Jesu, Jesu

Refrain (Unison)

Je - su, Je - su, fill us with your love, show us how to serve the neigh-bors we have from you. *Fine*

1. Kneels at the feet of his friends, si - lent - ly wash-es their
2. Neigh-bors are rich and poor, var - ied in col - or and
3. These are the ones we should serve, these are the ones we should
4. Lov - ing puts us on our knees, serv - ing as though we are
5. Kneel at the feet of our friends, si - lent - ly wash-ing their

D.C.

1. feet, Mas - ter who acts as a slave to them.
2. race, neigh-bors are near and far a - way.
3. love; all these are neigh-bors to us and you.
4. slaves, this is the way we should live with you.
5. feet, this is the way we should live with you.

WORDS: Tom Colvin, 1969
MUSIC: Ghana folk song; arr. Tom Colvin, 1969; harm. Charles H. Webb, 1988

CHEREPONI
Irr. w. refrain

♩.=60-66

601 I Am Thine, O Lord

1. I am thine, O Lord, I have heard thy voice, and it told thy love to
2. Con - se - crate me now to thy serv - ice, Lord, by the pow'r of grace di -
3. O the pure de - light of a sin - gle hour that be - fore thy throne I
4. There are depths of love that I can - not know till I cross the nar - row

me; but I long to rise in the arms of faith, and be
vine; let my soul look up with a stead-fast hope, and my
spend, when I kneel in prayer, and with thee, my God, I com -
sea; there are heights of joy that I may not reach till I

Refrain

clos - er drawn to thee.
will be lost in thine. Draw me near - er, near-er, bless-ed Lord,
mune as friend with friend!
rest in peace with thee. near-er, near-er,

to the cross where thou hast died; draw me near-er, near-er,

near-er, bless-ed Lord, to thy pre - cious, bleed - ing side.

WORDS: Fanny J. Crosby, 1875
MUSIC: William H. Doane, 1875

I AM THINE
10 7.10 7 w. refrain

O Master, Let Me Walk with Thee 602

1. O Master, let me walk with thee in low-ly
   paths of ser - vice free; tell me thy se - cret;
   help me bear the strain of toil, the fret of care.

2. Help me the slow of heart to move by some clear,
   win - ning word of love; teach me the way - ward
   feet to stay, and guide them in the home - ward way.

3. Teach me thy pa - tience; still with thee in clos - er,
   dear - er com - pa - ny, in work that keeps faith
   sweet and strong, in trust that tri - umphs o - ver wrong.

4. In hope that sends a shin - ing ray far down the
   fu - ture's broad - ening way; in peace that on - ly
   thou canst give, with thee, O Mas - ter, let me live.

WORDS: Washington Gladden, 1879
MUSIC: Henry Percy Smith, 1874

MARYTON
LM

A Counsel on Prayer 603

To pray for anything for which we will not take counsel together, for which we will not jointly labor, for which we will not contribute with all our energies and means, is only mocking God and disappointing ourselves.

—Alexander Campbell, 19th-century Disciples forebear

604 That Cause Can Never Be Lost or Stayed

1. That cause can nev-er be lost or stayed which takes the
2. Each no-ble ser-vice that we have wrought was first con-
3. There-by it-self like a tree it shows; that high it
4. Be then no more by a storm dis-mayed, for by it

course of what God has made, and is not trust-ing in
ceived as a fruit-ful thought; each wor-thy cause with a
reach-es as deep it grows; and, when the storms are its
the full-grown seeds are laid; and though the tree by its

walls and tow-ers but slow-ly grow-ing from seeds to flow-ers.
fu-ture glo-rious by qui-et grow-ing be-comes vic-to-rious.
branch-es shak-ing, it deep-er root in the soil is tak-ing.
might it shat-ters, what then, if thou-sands of seeds it scat-ters!

WORDS: Kristian Ostergaard, 1892; tr. J. C. Aaberg, 1928, alt.* OSTERGAARD
MUSIC: Jorgen Nellemann (20th century); harm. Ellwood S. Wolf, 1966 99.10 10

* Original version with six stanzas has been altered: st. 1, 2, and 3 are from the original;
  st. 4 and 5 were eliminated; st. 6 is printed here as st. 4, alt.

For Each Day of Life We Thank You   605

Unison

1. For each day of life we thank you, God, the
2. As in days of youth-ful vig - or, may we
3. Give us dreams and in - ner vi - sion of a
4. May the in - sights gained from liv - ing be a

giv - er of all days; and with hearts filled
in all lat - er years know the joys of
new world to be gained, where all peo - ple
light up - on the way, guid - ing us, and

with thanks-giv - ing, we would serve you, now, al - ways.
use - ful pur-pose. Free us from our anx - ious fears.
live to - geth - er, by each oth - er's love sus - tained.
those to fol - low, to a bright - er, bet - ter day.

WORDS: H. Glen Lanier, 1976, alt.
MUSIC: Amos Pilsbury, 1799; arr. Carlton R. Young, 1964

CHARLESTOWN
87.87

♩=116-126

606 God, Whose Giving Knows No Ending

1. God, whose giv-ing knows no end-ing, from your rich and end-less store,
2. Skills and time are ours for press-ing toward the goals of Christ, your Son:
3. Trea - sure too you have en-trust-ed, gain thru powers your grace con-ferred;

na-ture's won-der, Je - sus' wis-dom, cost-ly cross, grave's shat-tered door:
all at peace in health and free-dom, rac-es joined, the church made one.
ours to use for home and kin-dred, and to spread the gos - pel Word.

gift - ed by you, we turn to you, of-fering up our-selves in praise;
Now di - rect our dai-ly la - bor, lest we strive for self a - lone;
O - pen wide our hands, in shar - ing, as we heed Christ's age-less call,

thank-ful song shall rise for - ev - er, gra-cious do - nor of our days.
born with tal - ents, make us ser-vants fit to an-swer at your throne.
heal - ing, teach-ing, and re-claim-ing, serv-ing you by lov-ing all.

WORDS: Robert L. Edwards, 1961
MUSIC: Wyeth's *Repository of Sacred Music, Part Second*, 1813

NETTLETON
87.87D

In All the Seasons Seeking God   607

Unison

1. Bril - liant spring paints beau - teous land - scapes;
2. Soft, south breez - es, warm, calm sum - mers,
3. Au - tumn's clear days glow with vig - or;
4. Snow - flakes bring cold win - ter weath - er;

flow'rs a - bound and grass is green:
green leaves spread in lush ar - ray:
fruit and grain, earth's yield is made:
earth is sil - very, chaste and bright.

when we're young we search and nur - ture
one's best years of strength soon van - ish;
we pre - sent our hearts as of - f'ring,
God for - gives our sins; this cleans us:

earn - est minds, hearts pure and clean.
seek to do God's work to - day.
these ex - cel gold, pearls and jade.
pure we rise to heav - en's height.

WORDS: Chen-Chang Yang, China; para. Mildred Wiant and Teng-Kiat Chiu, alt.
MUSIC: Chia-Jen Yang, China; harm. L. G. McKinney, alt.

SI-SHI
87.87

♩=92-100

608 I Would Be True

1. I would be true, for there are those who trust me;
2. I would be friend of all— the foe, the friend-less;

I would be pure, for there are those who care;
I would be giv - ing, and for - get the gift;

I would be strong, for there is much to suf - fer;
I would be hum - ble, for I know my weak - ness;

I would be brave, for there is much to dare,
I would look up, and laugh, and love, and lift,

I would be brave, for there is much to dare.
I would look up, and laugh, and love, and lift.

WORDS: Howard Arnold Walter, 1906
MUSIC: Joseph Yates Peek, 1909

PEEK
11 10.11 10 10

Take My Life

609

1. Take my life, and let it be con-se-crat-ed, Lord, to thee.
2. Take my hands, and let them move at the im-pulse of thy love.
3. Take my voice, and let me sing; un-to God my praise I bring.
4. Take my sil-ver and my gold, not a mite would I with-hold;
5. Take my will, and make it thine; it shall be no lon-ger mine.
6. Take my love; my Lord, I pour at thy feet its trea-sure store.

1. Take my mo-ments and my days; let them flow in
2. Take my feet, and let them be swift and beau-ti-
3. Take my lips and let them be filled with mes-sa-
4. Take my in-tel-lect, and use ev-ery power as
5. Take my heart, it is thine own; it shall be thy
6. Take my-self, and I will be ev-er, on-ly,

1. cease-less praise, let them flow in cease-less praise.
2. ful for thee, swift and beau-ti- ful for thee.
3. ges from thee, filled with mes-sa- ges from thee.
4. thou shalt choose, ev-ery power as thou shalt choose.
5. roy-al throne, it shall be thy roy-al throne.
6. all for thee, ev-er, on-ly, all for thee.

WORDS: Frances R. Havergal, 1874
MUSIC: H. A. César Malan, 1827

HENDON
77.77.7

610　Living for Jesus

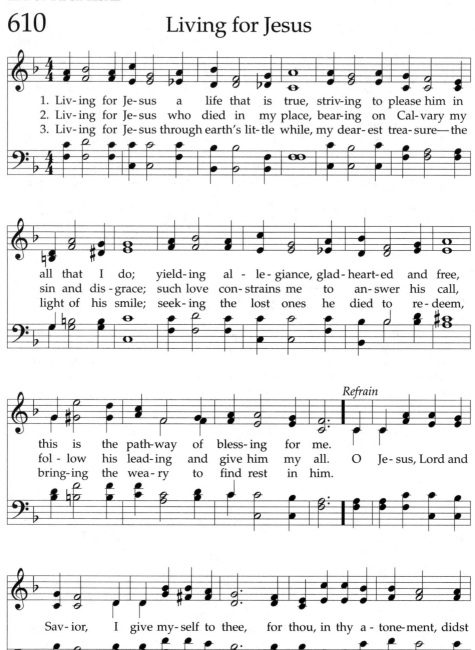

1. Liv-ing for Je-sus　a　life that is　true, striv-ing to please him in
2. Liv-ing for Je-sus　who　died in　my place, bear-ing on Cal-vary my
3. Liv-ing for Je-sus through earth's lit-tle while, my dear-est trea-sure—the

all that　I　do;　yield-ing　al - le-giance, glad-heart-ed and free,
sin and dis-grace;　such love con-strains me　to　an-swer his　call,
light of　his smile;　seek-ing　the　lost ones　he　died to　re-deem,

Refrain

this　is　the path-way　of　bless-ing　for　me.
fol - low　his lead-ing　and　give him　my　all.　O　Je-sus, Lord and
bring-ing　the wea-ry　to　find rest　in　him.

Sav-ior,　I　give my-self to thee,　for thou, in thy a - tone-ment, didst

WORDS: Thomas O. Chisholm, 1917
MUSIC: C. Harold Lowden, 1915

LIVING FOR JESUS
10 10.10 10 w. refrain

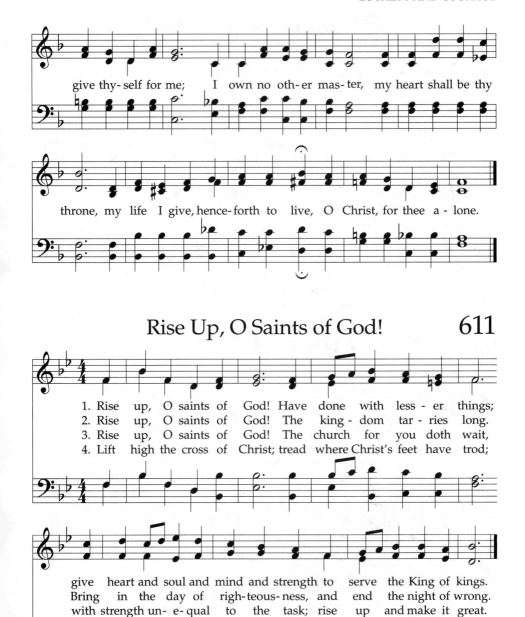

give thy-self for me; I own no oth-er mas-ter, my heart shall be thy

throne, my life I give, hence-forth to live, O Christ, for thee a - lone.

Rise Up, O Saints of God! 611

1. Rise up, O saints of God! Have done with less - er things;
2. Rise up, O saints of God! The king - dom tar - ries long.
3. Rise up, O saints of God! The church for you doth wait,
4. Lift high the cross of Christ; tread where Christ's feet have trod;

give heart and soul and mind and strength to serve the King of kings.
Bring in the day of righ-teous-ness, and end the night of wrong.
with strength un- e- qual to the task; rise up and make it great.
come sis-ters, broth-ers in the faith, rise up, O saints of God.

WORDS: William P. Merrill, 1911, alt.
MUSIC: William H. Walter, 1894

FESTAL SONG
SM

612 O Jesus, I Have Promised

1. O Je - sus, I have prom - ised to serve thee to the end;
2. O let me feel thee near me! The world is ev - er near;
3. O let me hear thee speak - ing, in ac - cents clear and still,
4. O Je - sus, thou hast prom - ised to all who fol - low thee

be thou for ev - er near me, my mas - ter and my friend;
I see the sights that daz - zle, the tempt - ing sounds I hear;
a - bove the storms of pas - sion, the mur - murs of self - will;
that where thou art in glo - ry there shall thy ser - vant be;

I shall not fear the bat - tle if thou art by my side,
my foes are ev - er near me, a - round me and with - in;
O speak to re - as - sure me, to has - ten or con - trol;
and, Je - sus, I have prom - ised to serve thee to the end;

nor wan - der from the path - way if thou wilt be my guide.
but, Je - sus, draw thou near - er, and shield my soul from sin.
O speak, and make me lis - ten, thou guard - ian of my soul.
O give me grace to fol - low, my mas - ter and my friend.

WORDS: John E. Bode, c. 1868
MUSIC: Arthur H. Mann, 1881

ANGEL'S STORY
76.76D

Stand Up, Stand Up for Jesus 613

1. Stand up, stand up for Je - sus, ye sol - diers of the cross;
2. Stand up, stand up for Je - sus, the trum - pet call o - bey;
3. Stand up, stand up for Je - sus, stand in his strength a - lone;
4. Stand up, stand up for Je - sus, the strife will not be long;

lift high his roy - al ban - ner, it must not suf - fer loss:
forth to the might - y con - flict, in this his glo - rious day:
the arm of flesh will fail you; ye dare not trust your own:
this day the noise of bat - tle, the next the vic - tor's song:

from vic - t'ry un - to vic - t'ry his ar - my shall he lead,
"ye that are brave, now serve him," a - gainst un - num-bered foes;
put on the gos - pel ar - mor, and, watch-ing un - to pray'r,
to those who o - ver - com - eth, a crown of life shall be;

till ev - 'ry foe is van-quished, and Christ is Lord in - deed.
let cour-age rise with dan - ger, and strength to strength op - pose.
where du - ty calls, or dan - ger, be nev - er want - ing there.
they with the King of glo - ry shall reign e - ter - nal - ly.

WORDS: George Duffield, 1858
MUSIC: George J. Webb, 1837

WEBB
76.76D

614   I'm Gonna Live So God Can Use Me

2. I'm gonna work...   3. I'm gonna pray...   4. I'm gonna sing...

WORDS: African-American spiritual
MUSIC: African-American spiritual; arr. Bill Thomas, 1994

I'M GONNA LIVE
Irr.

I Shall Not Be Moved

615

WORDS and MUSIC: African-American spiritual

I SHALL NOT BE MOVED
Irr.

616

Today I Live

Unison

1. To - day I live, but once shall come my death:
2. How I shall die, or when, I do not know,
3. When earth-ly life shall close, as close it must,
4. Mean - while I live and move and I am glad,

one day shall still my laugh-ter and my cry - ing,
nor where, for end - less is the world's ho - ri - zon;
let Je - sus be my broth - er and my mer - it.
en - joy this life and all its in - ter-weav - ing:

bring to a halt my heart - beat and my breath; God,
but save me, God, from thoughts that lay me low, from
Let me with-out re - gret re - call the past, then,
each giv - en day, as I take up the thread, let

give me faith for liv - ing and for dy - ing.
mor - bid fears that freeze my power of rea - son.
God, in - to your hands com-mit my spir - it.
love sug - gest my mode, my mood of liv - ing.

WORDS: Fred Kaan, 1975
MUSIC: James Snyder, 1994

IDA
10 11.10 11

♩=64

Yo Vivo, Señor, Porque Tú Vives 617
(I Am Living, Lord, Because You Live)

1. Yo vi-vo, Se-ñor, por-que tú vi-ves; por-que tú vi-ves,
2. Soy sal-vo, Se-ñor, pues me sal-vas-te, pues me sal-vas-te,

1. I am liv-ing, Lord, be-cause you live; be-cause you live,
2. Sal-va-tion, O Lord, is what you gave me, what you gave me,

Se-ñor, es que yo vi-vo. Me das con-sue-lo, me das a-
Se-ñor, e-ter-na-men-te. Yo voy al cie-lo; voy a la

O Lord, I am liv-ing. You give me com-fort, you give me
O Lord, is your sal-va-tion. I'm going to heav-en; I'm going to

bri-go, y en la a-flic-ción mi Se-ñor es-tás con-mi-go.
glo-ria, por-que Se-ñor, tú me dis-te la vic-to-ria.

shel-ter, and in af-flic-tions, O Lord, you are with me.
glo-ry, be-cause, O Lord, you have giv-en me the vic-tory.

WORDS: Adan Calderon, 1954; tr. Luis Ferrer and David L. Edwards, 1994
MUSIC: Adan Calderon, 1954; arr. Roberto C. Savage

YO VIVO SEÑOR
Irr.

♩=84-92

618   How Firm a Foundation

1. How firm a foundation, ye saints of the Lord,
2. "Fear not, I am with thee, oh, be not dis-mayed,
3. "When through the deep wa-ters I call thee to go,
4. "When through fi-ery tri-als thy path-way shall lie,
5. "The soul that on Je-sus still leans for re-pose,

1. is laid for your faith in God's ex-cel-lent word!
2. for I am thy God, and will still give thee aid.
3. the riv-ers of woe shall not thee o-ver-flow;
4. my grace, all suf-fi-cient, shall be thy sup-ply.
5. I will not, I will not de-sert to its foes;

1. What more can be said than to you God has said,
2. I'll strength-en thee, help thee, and cause thee to stand,
3. for I will be near thee, thy trou-bles to bless,
4. The flame shall not hurt thee; I on-ly de-sign
5. that soul, though all hell should en-deav-or to shake,

1. to you who for ref-uge to Je-sus have fled?
2. up-held by my righ-teous, om-nip-o-tent hand.
3. and sanc-ti-fy to thee thy deep-est dis-tress.
4. thy dross to con-sume, and thy gold to re-fine.
5. I'll nev-er, no nev-er, no nev-er for-sake!"

WORDS: John Rippon's *Selection of Hymns*, 1787, alt.
MUSIC: Traditional American melody

FOUNDATION
11 11.11 11

My Life Flows On

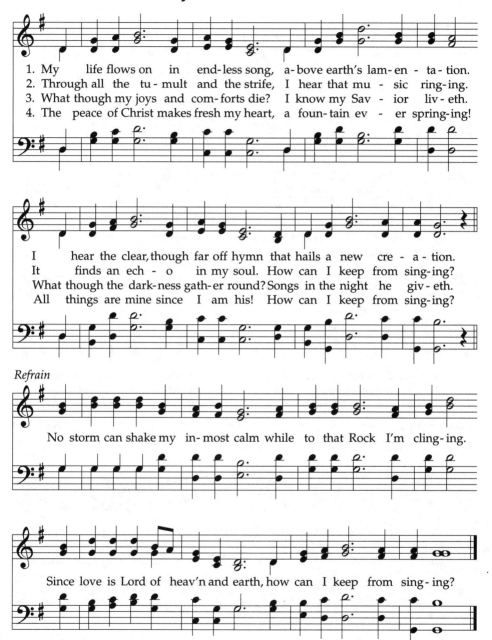

1. My life flows on in end-less song, a-bove earth's lam-en - ta - tion.
2. Through all the tu - mult and the strife, I hear that mu - sic ring-ing.
3. What though my joys and com-forts die? I know my Sav - ior liv - eth.
4. The peace of Christ makes fresh my heart, a foun-tain ev - er spring-ing!

I hear the clear, though far off hymn that hails a new cre - a - tion.
It finds an ech - o in my soul. How can I keep from sing-ing?
What though the dark-ness gath-er round? Songs in the night he giv - eth.
All things are mine since I am his! How can I keep from sing-ing?

Refrain

No storm can shake my in-most calm while to that Rock I'm cling-ing.

Since love is Lord of heav'n and earth, how can I keep from sing-ing?

WORDS and MUSIC: Robert Lowry, 1869, alt.

HOW CAN I KEEP FROM SINGING
87.87 w. refrain

620   The Lord Will Make a Way Somehow

1. Like a ship that's toss'd and driv-en, bat-tered by an an-gry sea,
2. Try to do my best in serv-ice, try to live the best I can,
3. Of-ten there's mis-un-der-stand-ing out of all the good I do,

when the storms of life are rag-ing and their fu-ry falls on me,
when I choose to do the right thing, e-vil's pre-sent on ev-'ry hand,
go to friends for con-so-la-tion and I find them com-plain-ing too,

I won-der what I have done that makes this race so hard to run,
I look up and won-der why that good for-tune pass me by,
so man-y nights I toss in pain, won-der-ing what the day will bring,

then I say to my soul, take cour-age, the Lord will make a way some-how.
then I say to my soul, be pa-tient, the Lord will make a way some-how.
but I say to my heart, don't wor-ry, the Lord will make a way some-how.

WORDS and MUSIC: Thomas A. Dorsey, 1943

SOMEHOW
Irr.

♩=92-100

621 "Are Ye Able," Said the Master

1. "Are ye a-ble," said the Mas-ter, "to be cru-ci-fied with me?"
2. "Are ye a-ble" to re-mem-ber, when a thief lifts up his eyes,
3. "Are ye a-ble" when the shad-ows close a-round you with the sod,
4. "Are ye a-ble?" Still the Mas-ter whis-pers down e-ter-ni-ty,

"Yea," the sturd-y dream-ers an-swered, "to the death we fol-low thee."
that his par-doned soul is wor-thy of a place in par-a-dise?
to be-lieve that spir-it tri-umphs, to com-mend your soul to God?
and he-ro-ic spir-its an-swer now, as then, in Gal-i-lee.

Refrain

"Lord, we are a-ble." Our spir-its are thine. Re-mold them,

make us, like thee, di-vine. Thy guid-ing ra-diance a-bove us shall

be a bea-con to God, to love and loy-al-ty.

WORDS: Earl Marlatt, 1926
MUSIC: Harry S. Mason, 1924

BEACON HILL
Irr.

Guide Me, O Thou Great Jehovah 622

1. Guide me, O thou great Je - ho - vah, pil - grim through this
2. O - pen now the crys - tal foun - tain, whence the heal - ing
3. When I tread the verge of Jor - dan, bid my anx - ious

bar - ren land; I am weak, but thou art might - y; hold me with thy
wa - ters flow; let the fire and cloud - y pil - lar lead me all my
fears sub - side; bear me through the swell - ing cur - rent; land me safe on

power - ful hand; bread of heav - en, bread of heav - en,
jour - ney through; strong De - liv - erer, strong De - liv - erer,
Ca - naan's side; songs of prais - es, songs of prais - es,

feed me till I want no more, feed me till I want no more.
be thou still my strength and shield, be thou still my strength and shield.
I will ev - er give to thee, I will ev - er give to thee.

WORDS: William Williams, 1745; tr. Peter Williams and the author, 1771
MUSIC: John Hughes, 1907

CWM RHONDDA
87.87.877

623 Woke Up This Morning

1. Oh, I woke up this morn - ing with my mind, (and it was)
2. Can't hate your neigh - bor in your mind, (if you keep it)
3. Makes you love ev - 'ry bod - y with your mind, (when you keep it)

stayed on Je - sus. Woke up this morn - ing with my
stayed on Je - sus. Can't hate your neigh - bor in your
stayed on Je - sus. Love ev - 'ry-bod - y with your

mind, (and it was) stayed on Je - sus,
mind, (if you keep it) stayed on Je - sus,
mind, (when you keep it) stayed on Je - sus,

woke up this morn - ing with my mind, (and it was)
can't hate your neigh - bor in your mind, (if you keep it)
love ev - 'ry-bod - y with your mind, (when you keep it)

WORDS and MUSIC: African-American spiritual

WOKE UP
Irr.

We Ask Not for Easy Lives 624

O God, come to us, we pray thee,
    with the resources of thy power,
    that we may be strong within.
We ask not for easy lives,
    but for adequacy.
We ask not to be freed from storms,
    but to build our houses on rock that will not fall.
We pray not for a smooth sea, but for a stout ship,
    a good compass, and a strong heart;
    in the name of him who faced enmity and death
    without flinching,
    thy Son Jesus Christ our Savior.

—Harry Emerson Fosdick, 20th-century American minister

Philippians 2:9–11

625 Precious Name

1. Take the name of Je - sus with you,
2. Take the name of Je - sus ev - er,
3. O the pre - cious name of Je - sus!
4. At the name of Je - sus bow - ing,

child of sor - row and of woe;
as a shield from ev - ery snare;
How it thrills our souls with joy,
fall - ing pros - trate at his feet,

it will joy and com - fort give you;
if temp - ta - tions round you gath - er,
when his lov - ing arms re - ceive us,
King of kings in heaven we'll crown him,

take it then, wher - e'er you go.
breathe that ho - ly name in prayer.
and his songs our tongues em - ploy!
when our jour - ney is com - plete.

WORDS: Lydia Baxter, 1870
MUSIC: William H. Doane, 1871

PRECIOUS NAME
87.87 w. refrain

Refrain

Pre - cious name, O how sweet!

Pre - cious name, O how sweet!

Hope of earth and joy of heaven. Pre - cious name,

Pre - cious name,

O how sweet! Hope of earth and joy of heaven.

O how sweet, how sweet!

A New Hebridean Prayer 626

O Jesus,
be the canoe that holds me in the sea of life;
be the steer that keeps me straight;
be the outrigger that supports me in times of great temptation.
Let your Spirit be my sail that carries me through each day.
Keep my body strong,
so that I can paddle steadfastly on,
in the long voyage of life.

—Anonymous

627 I Want Jesus to Walk with Me

Capo 3: Play Am

1. I want Je - sus to walk with me.
2. In my tri - als, Lord, walk with me.
3. When I'm trou - bled, Lord, walk with me.

I want Je - sus to walk with me.
In my tri - als, Lord, walk with me.
When I'm trou - bled, Lord, walk with me.

All a - long my pil - grim jour - ney,
When my heart is al - most break - ing,
When my head is bowed in sor - row,

O, I want Je - sus to walk with me.
O, I want Je - sus to walk with me.
O, I want Je - sus to walk with me.

WORDS: African-American spiritual
MUSIC: African-American spiritual; harm. J. Jefferson Cleveland and Verolga Nix, 1981

SOJOURNER
888.9

Precious Lord, Take My Hand

628

1. Pre - cious Lord, take my hand, lead me on, let me stand,
2. When my way grows drear, pre - cious Lord, lin - ger near,
3. When the dark - ness ap - pears and the night draws near,

I am tired, I am weak, I am worn;
when my life is al - most gone,
and the day is past and gone,

through the storm, through the night, lead me on to the light:
hear my cry, hear my call, hold my hand lest I fall:
at the riv - er I stand, guide my feet, hold my hand:

Refrain

Take my hand, pre - cious Lord, lead me home.

WORDS and MUSIC: Thomas A. Dorsey, 1932

PRECIOUS LORD
66.9D

© 1938 Unichappell Music Inc.

629

Stand By Me

1. When the storms of life are rag-ing, stand by me;
2. In the midst of trib - u - la - tion,
3. In the midst of faults and fail-ures, (stand by me);
4. In the midst of per - se - cu - tion,
5. When I'm grow - ing old and fee - ble,

1. when the storms of life are rag-ing, stand by me;
2. in the midst of trib - u - la - tion,
3. in the midst of faults and fail-ures, (stand by me)
4. in the midst of per - se - cu - tion,
5. when I'm grow - ing old and fee - ble,

1. when the world is toss-ing me, like a ship up-on the sea,
2. when the hosts of hell as-sail, and my strength be-gins to fail,
3. when I've done the best I can, and my friends mis-un-der-stand,
4. when my foes in war ar-ray un - der - take to stop my way,
5. when my life be-comes a bur-den, and I'm near - ing chil-ly Jor-dan,

WORDS: Charles Albert Tindley, c. 1906
MUSIC: Charles Albert Tindley, c. 1906; arr. Floyd Knight, Jr., 1993

STAND BY ME
83.83.77.83

1. thou who rul - est wind and wa - ter, stand by me.
2. thou who nev - er lost a bat - tle,
3. thou who know - est all a - bout me, (stand by me)
4. thou who saved Paul and Si - las,
5. O thou Lil - y of the Val - ley,

We Shall Overcome 630

1. We shall o - ver - come, we shall o - ver - come, we shall o - ver - come some - day! Oh, deep in my heart I do be - lieve we shall o - ver - come some - day!

2. The Lord will see us through.
3. We'll walk hand in hand.
4. We are not afraid (today).

5. The truth shall make us free.
6. We shall live in peace.

WORDS: African-American spiritual
MUSIC: African-American spiritual; adapt. William Farley Smith, 1986

MARTIN
Irr.

Adapt. © 1989 The United Methodist Publishing House

631   Lift Every Voice and Sing

1. Lift ev - ery voice and sing, till earth and heav - en ring,
2. Ston - y the road we trod, bit - ter the chas - ten - ing rod,
3. God of our wea - ry years, God of our si - lent tears,

ring with the har - mo - nies of lib - er - ty;
felt in the days when hope un - born had died;
thou who hast brought us thus far on the way;

let our re - joic - ing rise high as the lis - ten - ing skies,
yet with a stead - y beat, have not our wea - ry feet
thou who hast by thy might led us in - to the light,

let it re - sound loud as the roll - ing sea.
come to the place for which our peo - ple sighed?
keep us for - ev - er in the path, we pray.

WORDS: James Weldon Johnson, 1921
MUSIC: J. Rosamond Johnson, 1921

LIFT EVERY VOICE
Irr.

♩.=64-70

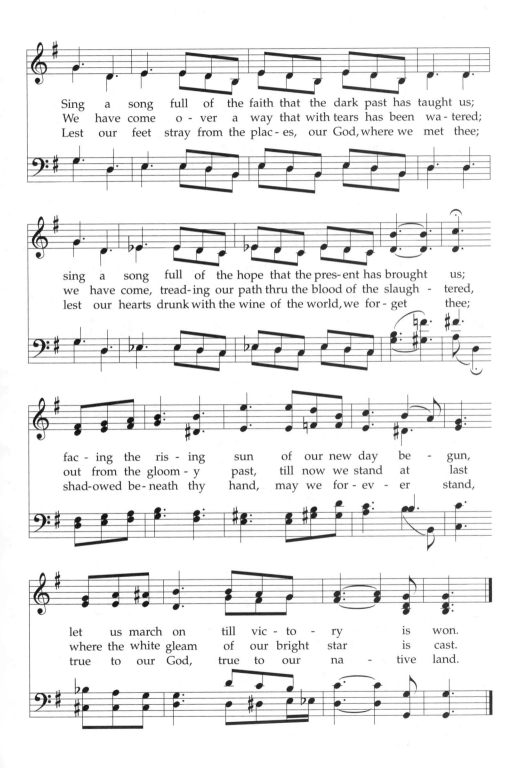

Sing a song full of the faith that the dark past has taught us;
We have come o - ver a way that with tears has been wa - tered;
Lest our feet stray from the plac - es, our God, where we met thee;

sing a song full of the hope that the pres - ent has brought us;
we have come, tread - ing our path thru the blood of the slaugh - tered,
lest our hearts drunk with the wine of the world, we for - get thee;

fac - ing the ris - ing sun of our new day be - gun,
out from the gloom - y past, till now we stand at last
shad - owed be - neath thy hand, may we for - ev - er stand,

let us march on till vic - to - ry is won.
where the white gleam of our bright star is cast.
true to our God, true to our na - tive land.

632 Lead On, O King Eternal

1. Lead on, O King e - ter - nal, the day of march has come;
2. Lead on, O King e - ter - nal, till sin's fierce war shall cease,
3. Lead on, O King e - ter - nal: we fol - low, not with fears,

hence-forth in fields of con - quest thy tents shall be our home;
and ho - li - ness shall whis - per the sweet a - men of peace;
for glad - ness breaks like morn - ing wher - e'er thy face ap - pears;

through days of prep - a - ra - tion thy grace has made us strong,
for not with swords loud clash - ing, nor roll of stir - ring drums;
thy cross is lift - ed o'er us; we jour - ney in its light;

and now, O King e - ter - nal, we lift our bat - tle song.
with deeds of love and mer - cy, the heaven - ly king - dom comes.
the crown a - waits the con - quest; lead on, O God of might.

WORDS: Ernest W. Shurtleff, 1887
MUSIC: Henry T. Smart, 1835

LANCASHIRE
76.76D

Lead On, O Cloud of Presence   633

1. Lead on, O cloud of pres-ence; the ex-o-dus is come;
2. Lead on, O fi-ery pil-lar; we fol-low yet with fears,
3. Lead on, O God of free-dom, and guide us on our way,

in wil-der-ness and des-ert our tribe shall make its home.
but we shall come re-joic-ing, though joy be born of tears.
and help us trust the prom-ise through strug-gle and de-lay.

Our bond-age left be-hind us, new hopes with-in us grow.
We are not lost, though wan-d'ring, for by your light we come,
We pray our sons and daugh-ters may jour-ney to that land

We seek the land of prom-ise where milk and hon-ey flow.
and we are still God's peo-ple. The jour-ney is our home.
where jus-tice dwells with mer-cy and love is law's de-mand.

WORDS: Ruth Duck, 1974, rev. 1989
MUSIC: Henry T. Smart, 1835
LANCASHIRE
76.76D

634   To Us All, to Every Nation

1. To us all, to ev - ery na - tion comes the mo - ment
2. By the light of burn - ing mar - tyrs, Je - sus' bleed - ing
3. Though the cause of e - vil pros - per, yet 'tis truth a -

to de - cide, in the strife of truth with false - hood,
feet I track, toil - ing up new Cal - varies ev - er
lone is strong, truth for - ev - er on the scaf - fold,

for the good or e - vil side;
with the cross that turns not back;
wrong for - ev - er on the throne.

WORDS: James Russell Lowell, 1845; adapt. W. Garrett Horder, alt.
MUSIC: Thomas J. Williams, 1890

EBENEZER
87.87D

some great cause, God's new en - dea - vor, of - fering each the
new oc - ca - sions teach new du - ties, time makes an - cient
Yet that scaf - fold sways the fu - ture, and, be - hind the

bloom or blight, and the choice goes by for - ev - er
good un - couth; they must up - ward still and on - ward,
dim un - known, God is stand - ing in the shad - ow

'twixt that dark - ness and that light.
who would keep a - breast of truth.
keep - ing watch be - side God's own.

635 Faith of Our Fathers

1. Faith of our fa - thers, liv - ing still in spite of dun - geon,
2. The mar - tyrs bound in pris - on chains were still in heart and
3. Faith of our moth - ers, we will love both friend and foe in

fire and sword, oh, how our hearts beat high with joy
con - science free, and bless'd would be their chil - dren's fate,
all our strife, and preach thee, too, as love knows how,

when-e'er we hear that glo - rious word! Faith of our fa - thers,
if they, like them, should live for thee! Faith of the mar - tyrs,
by sav - ing word and faith - ful life! Faith of our moth - ers,

ho - ly faith, we will be true to thee till death.
ho - ly faith, we will be true to thee till death.
ho - ly faith, we will be true to thee till death.

WORDS: Frederick W. Faber, 1849, alt.
MUSIC: Henri F. Hemy, 1864; adapt. James G. Walton, 1874

ST. CATHERINE
88.88.88

Abide with Me

636

1. A - bide with me; fast falls the e - ven - tide;
2. Swift to its close ebbs out life's lit - tle day;
3. I need thy pres - ence ev - ery pass - ing hour;
4. I fear no foe, with thee at hand to bless;
5. Hold thou thy cross be - fore my clos - ing eyes;

1. the dark - ness deep - ens, God, with me a - bide;
2. earth's joys grow dim; its glo - ries pass a - way;
3. what but thy grace can foil the temp - ter's power?
4. ills have no weight, and tears no bit - ter - ness;
5. shine through the gloom, and point me to the skies;

1. when oth - er help - ers fail, and com - forts flee,
2. change and de - cay in all a - round I see;
3. Who like thy - self my guide and stay can be?
4. where is death's sting? Where, grave, thy vic - to - ry?
5. heaven's morn - ing breaks, and earth's vain shad - ows flee;

1. Help of the help - less, O a - bide with me.
2. O thou who chang - est not, a - bide with me.
3. Through cloud and sun - shine, O a - bide with me.
4. I tri - umph still if thou a - bide with me.
5. in life, in death, O God, a - bide with me.

WORDS: Henry F. Lyte, 1847
MUSIC: William Henry Monk, 1861

EVENTIDE
10 10.10 10

637 For All the Saints

1. For all the saints, who from their la-bors rest, who
2. Thou wast their rock, their for-tress, and their might: their
3. O blest com-mun - ion, com-pa-ny di - vine!
4. And when the strife is fierce, the con-flict long,
5. From earth's wide bounds, from o-cean's far-thest coast, through

1. thee by faith be - fore the world con - fessed, thy
2. strength and sol - ace in the well-fought fight;
3. We live and strug - gle, they in glo - ry shine;
4. steals on the ear the dis - tant tri - umph song,
5. gates of pearl streams in the count-less host,

1. name, O Je - sus, be for - ev - er blest.
2. thou, in the dark - ness drear, the one true light.
3. yet all are one in thee, for all are thine.
4. and hearts are brave a - gain, and arms are strong.
5. sing - ing to Fa - ther, Son, and Ho - ly Ghost,

Al - le - lu - ia, al - le - lu - ia!

WORDS: William W. How, 1864, alt.
MUSIC: Ralph Vaughan Williams, 1906

SINE NOMINE
10 10 10 w. alleluias

In the Bulb There Is a Flower

638

1. In the bulb there is a flow - er; in the seed, an ap - ple tree;
2. There's a song in ev - ery si - lence, seek - ing word and mel - o - dy;
3. In our end is our be - gin - ning; in our time, in - fin - i - ty;

in co - coons, a hid - den prom - ise; but - ter - flies will soon be free!
there's a dawn in ev - ery dark - ness, bring - ing hope to you and me.
in our doubt there is be - liev - ing; in our life, e - ter - ni - ty.

In the cold and snow of win - ter there's a spring that waits to be,
From the past will come the fu - ture; what it holds, a mys - ter - y,
In our death, a res - ur - rec - tion; at the last, a vic - to - ry,

un - re - vealed un - til its sea - son, some - thing God a - lone can see.

WORDS and MUSIC: Natalie Sleeth, 1986

PROMISE
87.87D

♩=84-92

639 Let Hope and Sorrow Now Unite

1. Let hope and sor-row now u-nite to con-se-crate
2. With faith, or doubt, or o-pen mind we whis-per life's
3. Be glad for life, in age or youth; its worth is past

life's end - ing, and praise good friends now gone from sight,
great ques - tion. The ebb and flow of space and time
con - ceiv - ing. And stand by jus - tice, love, and truth

though grief and loss are rend - ing. The sto-ry in
sur - pass our small per - cep - tion. Yet knowl-edge grows
as pat-terns for be - liev - ing. Give thanks for all

a well-loved face, the years and days our thoughts re-trace,
with joy-ful gains and finds out won-ders far more strange
each per-son gives— as faith comes true, and Je - sus lives,

WORDS: Brian Wren, 1979, rev. 1983
MUSIC: Bohemian Brethren's *Kirchengesänge*, 1566

MIT FREUDEN ZART
87.87.887

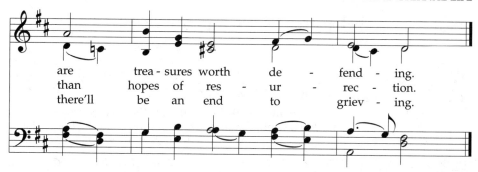

are   trea - sures worth   de - fend - ing.
than   hopes of res - ur - rec - tion.
there'll be   an   end   to   griev - ing.

God Is for Us

640

RESPONSE

Strong   is God's love   for us,   Al - le - lu - ia.

R

We know that all things work together for good
    for those who love God,
        who are called according to God's purpose.
What then are we to say about these things?
    If God is for us, who is against us?
God, who did not withhold God's own Son
    but gave him up for all of us—
        will God not also give us all things with him?
Who will separate us from the love of Christ?
Will hardship, or distress,
    or persecution, or famine,
    or nakedness, or peril, or sword?
No, in all these things we are more than conquerors
    through him who loved us.
For I am convinced that neither death, nor life,
    nor angels, nor rulers,
    nor things present, nor things to come,
nor powers, nor height, nor depth,
    nor anything else in all creation,
will be able to separate us from the love of God
    in Christ Jesus our Lord.   **R**

WORDS: Romans 8:28, 31–32, 35b, 37–39b; Response, Joseph Gelineau, 1963
MUSIC: David Clark Isele, 1979

641 I See the Morning Breakin'

WORDS: Appalachian folk hymn
MUSIC: Appalachian folk hymn; arr. Darrell R. Faires, Sr., 1989

MORNING BREAKIN'
Irr.

♩=112-120

Je-sus, bless my soul, bless my soul. I (4.) soul.
Je-sus, bless my soul, bless my soul. 2. I
Je-sus, bless my soul, bless my soul. 3. I

How Long, O God, How Long? 642

1. How long, O God, how long? The an-cient cry is ours.
2. And why, O God, and why? We ask with ev-ery age
3. The cross, O God, the cross! We think a-bout your Son:
4. Your hand, O God, your hand! We need your hand to hold,
5. We trust, O God, we trust in time our grief shall mend.

1. We wait in grief and ask how long be-fore we feel your powers.
2. and throw a-gainst your dis-tant sky the force of grief and rage.
3. you know the weight and edge of loss, your tears and ours are one.
4. to walk this dark un-chart-ed land where sol-id mean-ings fold.
5. Trans-formed by love that shaped our dust, your love that knows no end.

WORDS: Thomas H. Troeger, 1991
MUSIC: Brent Stratten, 1993

TAFT STREET
SM

Words © 1991 Oxford University Press; music © 1995 Chalice Press

♩=116

643 Swing Low, Sweet Chariot

WORDS: African-American spiritual
MUSIC: African-American spiritual; arr. Bill Thomas, 1994

SWING LOW
10 8.10 8 w. refrain

Steal Away to Jesus! 644

Refrain

Steal a-way, steal a-way, steal a-way to Je - sus!

Fine

Steal a-way, steal a-way home, I ain't got long to stay here.

1. My Lord, he calls me, he calls me by the thun-der;
2. Green trees are bend-ing, poor sin-ners stand a trem-bling;
3. My Lord, he calls me, he calls me by the light-ning;

the trum-pet sounds with-in my soul; I ain't got long to stay here.

WORDS and MUSIC: African-American spiritual

STEAL AWAY
57.87 w. refrain

645 I Cannot Think of Them as Dead

1. I can-not think of them as dead who walk with me no
2. And still their si-lent min-is-try with-in my heart has
3. Their lives are made for-ev-er mine; what they to me have
4. Mine are they by an own-er-ship nor time nor death can

more; a-long the path of life I tread they
place as when on earth they walked with me and
been has left hence-forth its seal and sign en-
free; for God has given to love to keep its

are but gone be-fore, they are but gone be-fore.
met me face to face, and met me face to face.
grav-en deep with-in, en-grav-en deep with-in.
own e-ter-nal-ly, its own e-ter-nal-ly.

WORDS: Frederick L. Hosmer, 1882
MUSIC: W. Frederick Wooden, 1992

DISTANT BELOVED
86.866

Music © 1992 Unitarian Universalist Association

♩=92-100

How Blest Are They Who Trust in Christ 646

1. How blest are they who trust in Christ when we and
2. In rip-ened age, their har-vest reaped, or gone from
3. In Christ, who tast-ed death for us, we rise a-

those we love must part; we yield them up, for
us in youth or prime, in Christ they have e-
bove our na-tural grief, and wit-ness to a

go they must, but do not lose them from our heart.
ter-nal life, re-leased from all the bonds of time.
strick-en world the strength and splen-dor of be-lief.

WORDS: Fred Pratt Green, 1972
MUSIC: Henry Percy Smith, 1874

MARYTON
LM

O Lord, Support Us 647

O Lord, support us all the day long,
until the shadows lengthen and the evening comes,
and the busy world is hushed, and the fever of life is over,
and our work is done.
Then, Lord, in your mercy grant us a safe lodging,
and a holy rest, and peace at the last;
through Jesus Christ our Lord.

—*attributed to John Henry Newman, England, 19th-century British churchman*

648 Some There Are Who by Their Living

1. Some there are who by their liv-ing lift us to a high-er plane,
2. Some there are who by their lov-ing lead us far be-yond our fears,
3. Some there are who by their dy-ing draw us clos-er to the Light,
4. Thanks to God for those in-vit-ing us to live more faith-ful-ly!

find-ing joy dis-closed in sor-row, heal-ing hid-den in their pain.
show-ing us by their com-pas-sion ha-tred washed a-way by tears.
find-ing death a bless-ed jour-ney in-to that most gra-cious night.
Thanks to God for those who show us rich-er lives of char-i-ty!

They are drawn by bright-er vi-sions, glad to give all they pos-sess
When con-tempts that we in-her-it fill us with hos-til-i-ty,
When we feel the sting of know-ing that our days are brief and swift,
Thanks for those we see no long-er, but whose mem'ries in us lie!

for a great-er good, dis-cov-ering ho-lier depths of hap-pi-ness.
we have hope be-cause of per-sons who have known love's lib-er-ty.
we re-mem-ber those whose liv-ing met each mo-ment as a gift.
Thanks to God for those who teach us how to live and how to die!

WORDS: David L. Edwards, 1992
MUSIC: David L. Edwards, 1992; harm. Jean E. Wood-Kobert, 1992

GREENCASTLE
87.87D

♩=96-100

Give Thanks for Life

649

1. Give thanks for life, the meas-ure of our days,
mor - tal, we pass through beau - ty that de - cays, yet
sing to God our hope, our love, our praise,

2. Give thanks for those who made their life a light
caught from the Christ - flame, burst - ing through the night, who
touched the truth, who burned for what is right,

3. And for our own, our liv - ing and our dead,
thanks for the love by which our life is fed, a
love not changed by time or death or dread,

4. Give thanks for hope, that like the wheat, the grain
ly - ing in dark - ness, does its life re - tain in
res - ur - rec - tion to grow green a - gain.

Al - le - lu - ia! Al - le - lu - ia!

WORDS: Shirley Erena Murray, 1986
MUSIC: Ralph Vaughan Williams, 1906

SINE NOMINE
10 10 10 w. alleluias

GOD'S World

650   O God, the Only Source of Life

O God, the only source of life and energy and wealth,
    defend our planet earth.
Teach us to conserve and not to squander the riches of nature,
    to use aright the heritage of former generations,
    and to plan for the welfare of children's children.
Renew our wonder, awaken our concern,
    and make us better stewards and more careful tenants
    of the world you lend us as our home.
Hear us, O Lord, our creator and redeemer,
    in the name of Christ.

          —Timothy Dudley-Smith, 20th-century British hymnwriter

God, Who Stretched the Spangled Heavens 651

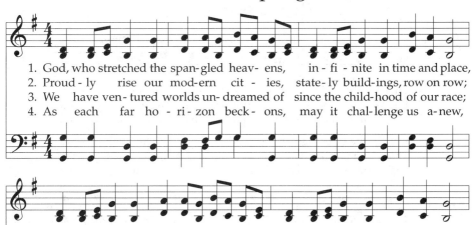

1. God, who stretched the span-gled heav-ens, in - fi - nite in time and place,
2. Proud - ly rise our mod-ern cit - ies, state-ly build-ings, row on row;
3. We have ven-tured worlds un-dreamed of since the child-hood of our race;
4. As each far ho - ri - zon beck-ons, may it chal-lenge us a-new,

flung the suns in burn-ing ra-diance through the si - lent fields of space,
yet their win-dows, blank, un-feel-ing, stare on can-yoned streets be-low,
known the ec - sta - sy of wing-ing through un-trav-eled realms of space;
chil - dren of cre - a - tive pur-pose, serv-ing oth-ers, hon-oring you.

we your chil-dren, in your like-ness, share in-ven-tive powers with you.
where the lone-ly drift un - no-ticed in the cit-y's ebb and flow,
probed the se-crets of the at-om, yield-ing un - i - mag-ined power,
May our dreams prove rich with prom-ise, each en-deav-or well be - gun.

Great Cre - a - tor, still cre - at - ing, show us what we yet may do.
lost to pur-pose and to mean-ing, scarce-ly car-ing where they go.
fac - ing us with life's de-struc - tion or our most tri-um-phant hour.
Great Cre - a - tor, give us guid-ance till our goals and yours are one.

WORDS: Catherine Cameron, 1967
MUSIC: William Moore, 1825

Words © 1967 Hope Publishing Co.

HOLY MANNA
87.87D

♩=100-106

652

En el Principio
(In the Beginning)

WORDS: Carlos Rosas, 1991; tr. Luis Ferrer, 1994
MUSIC: Carlos Rosas, 1991; arr. Susan Adams, 1995

PRINCIPIO
Irr.

Words and music © 1991 Carlos Rosas; tr. and arr. © 1995 Chalice Press

♩.=64-72

Refrain

God, shed your light, let us see your great-ness in hu-man-kind.

God, shed your light, let us see your im-age in all hu-man-kind.

Bread and Justice 653

O God, just as the disciples heard Christ's words of promise and began to eat the bread and drink the wine in the suffering of a long remembrance and in the joy of a hope, grant that we may hear your words, spoken in each thing of everyday affairs;

coffee, on our table in the morning;
the simple gesture of opening a door to go out, free;
the shouts of children in the parks;
a familiar song, sung by an unfamiliar face;
a friendly tree that has not yet been cut down.
May simple things speak to us of your mercy, and tell us that life can be good.

And may these sacramental gifts make us remember those who do not receive them:

who have their lives cut every day, in the bread absent from the table;
in the door of the hospital, the prison, the welfare home that does not open;
in sad children, feet without shoes, eyes without hope;
in war hymns that glorify death;
in deserts where once there was life.
Christ was also sacrificed; and may we learn that we participate in the saving sacrifice of Christ when we participate in the suffering of his little ones.
Amen.

—Rubem A. Alves, 20th-century Brazilian philosopher

654

Here Am I

Unison F♯m Bm7 Esus4 E Dmaj7 A/C♯

1. Here am I, where un-der-neath the brid - ges
2. Here am I, with peo - ple in the line - up,
3. Here am I, where two or three are gath - ered,

Bm7 A/C♯ F♯m E

of our win-ter cit - ies home-less peo - ple sleep.
anx - ious for a hand - out, ach - ing for a job.
read - y to be al - tered, shar - ing wine and bread.

A D/A A Dmaj7 A/C♯

Here am I, where in de - cay - ing hous - es
Here am I, when pen - sion - ers and strik - ers
Here am I, where those who hear the preach - ing

Bm7 A Bm7 D E A

lit - tle chil-dren shiv - er, cry - ing at the cold. Where are you?
sing and march to-geth - er, want - ing some-thing new. Where are you?
change their way of liv - ing, find the way to life. Where are you?

WORDS: Brian Wren, 1982, rev. 1995   HERE AM I
MUSIC: Dan Damon, 1993   3765D.3

♩=86-92

Community of Christ

655

1. Com - mu - ni - ty of Christ, who makes the cross your own,
2. Com - mu - ni - ty of Christ, look past the church - 's door
3. Com - mu - ni - ty of Christ, through whom the word must sound—
4. When men - ace melts a - way, so shall God's will be done,

live out your creed and risk your life for God a - lone:
and see the ref - u - gee, the hun - gry, and the poor.
cry out for jus - tice and for peace the whole world round:
the cli - mate of the world be peace and Christ its sun;

the God who wears your face, to whom all worlds be - long,
Take hands with the op - pressed, the job - less in your street,
dis - arm the powers that war and all that can de - stroy,
our cur - ren - cy be love and kind - li - ness our law,

whose chil - dren are of ev - ery race and ev - ery song.
take towel and wa - ter, that you wash your neigh - bor's feet.
turn bombs to bread, and tears of an - guish in - to joy.
our food and faith be shared as one for ev - er - more.

WORDS: Shirley Erena Murray, 1985
MUSIC: Hebrew melody; arr. Meyer Leoni, 1780

LEONI
66.84D

656 God of Freedom, God of Justice

1. God of free-dom, God of jus-tice, you whose love is
2. Rid the earth of tor-ture's ter-ror, you whose hands were
3. Make in us a cap-tive con-science quick to hear, to

strong as death, you who saw the dark of pris-on,
nailed to wood; hear the cries of pain and pro-test,
act, to plead; make us tru-ly sis-ters, broth-ers

you who knew the price of faith— touch our world of
you who shed the tears and blood— move in us the
of what-ev-er race or creed— teach us to be

sad op-pres-sion with your Spir-it's heal-ing breath.
power of pit-y rest-less for the com-mon good.
ful-ly hu-man, o-pen to each oth-er's need.

WORDS: Shirley Erena Murray, 1980   TREDEGAR
MUSIC: Guthrie Foote (20th century)   87.87.87

Words © 1992 Hope Publishing Co.; music used by permission of Oxford University Press

♩=92-100

God of the Ever-Present Crosses   657

Leader: Remembering that in his life, passion and death Jesus identified with the poor, the oppressed and the marginalized in society, let us join in a litany of intercession for all for whom Christ suffered and died and all for whom he lives today:

Reader 1: Let us pray for all who commit themselves to God's mission to establish human relationships based upon freedom and justice.

Reader 2: Save us from indifference and give us courage to work for justice and responsible freedom.

O God of the ever-present crosses, help your servants.

Reader 1: We pray for the affluent in developed and developing countries that they may not succumb to materialism.

Reader 2: Help us to discover our worth in terms of what we can become as persons rather than in what we own or consume.

O God of the ever-present crosses, help your servants.

Reader 1: We pray for countries where there is exploitation of natural resources, where the earth is desecrated to satisfy the lust for profit.

Reader 2: Save us from misusing what you have given for all to share.

O God of the ever-present crosses, help your servants.

Reader 1: We pray for all tribal and aboriginal peoples threatened with dispossession and the loss of ancestral lands.

Reader 2: Help us to remember that the land is yours and that we hold it in trust for future generations.

O God of the ever-present crosses, help your servants.

Reader 1: We pray for all minority communities faced with the loss of their cultural identity.

Reader 2: Help us to respect each person's way of life.

O God of the ever-present crosses, help your servants.

Reader 1: We pray for refugees forcibly uprooted from their homeland to live as aliens in other lands.

Reader 2: Help us to find human solutions to this human tragedy.

O God of the ever-present crosses, help your servants.

Reader 1: We pray for all peoples separated from one another because of religious or political differences.

Reader 2: Help us to work for tolerance, dialogue and good will among peoples of differing faiths and political convictions.

O God of the ever-present crosses, help your servants.

*—Worship Handbook of the 7th Assembly of the Christian Conference of Asia,
Bangalore, 1981; adapt.*

658 Restless Weaver

1. Rest - less Weav - er, ev - er spin - ning threads of jus - tice
2. Where earth's frag - ile web is rav - eling help us mend each
3. When our vio - lent lust for pow - er ends in lives a -
4. Rest - less Weav - er, still con - ceiv - ing new life— now and

and sha - lom; dream-ing pat - terns of cre - a - tion
bro - ken strand. Bless our ur - gent, bold en - deav - ors
bused and torn, from com - pass - ion's stur - dy fab - ric
yet to be— bind - ing all your vast cre - a - tion

where all crea - tures find a home; gath-ering up life's var - ied
cleans - ing wa - ter, air, and land. Through the Spir - it's in - spi -
fash - ion hope and trust re - born. Where in - jus - tice rules as
in one liv - ing tap - es - try: you have called us to be

fi - bers— ev - ery tex - ture, ev - ery hue: grant us your cre -
ra - tion— of-fering health where once was pain— strength-en us to
ty - rant, give us cour - age, God, to dare live our dreams of
weav - ers. Let your love guide all we do. With your Reign of

WORDS: O. I. Cricket Harrison, 1988, rev. 1993
MUSIC: Attr. B. F. White, 1844; harm. Ronald A. Nelson, 1978

BEACH SPRING
87.87D

♩=70-74

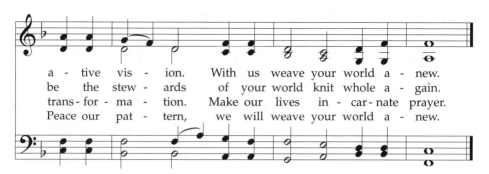

a - tive vis - ion. With us weave your world a - new.
be the stew - ards of your world knit whole a - gain.
trans - for - ma - tion. Make our lives in - car - nate prayer.
Peace our pat - tern, we will weave your world a - new.

Micah 6:6–8

What Does the Lord Require for Praise 659

1. What does the Lord re - quire for praise and of - fer - ing?
2. Peo - ple of earth, give ear! Should you not jus - tice know?
3. How shall our life ful - fill God's law so hard and high?

What sac - ri - fice, de - sire, or trib - ute bid you bring?
Will God your plead - ing hear, while crime and cruel - ty grow?
Let Christ en - due our will with grace to for - ti - fy.

Do jus - tice, love mer - cy, walk hum - bly with your God.
Do jus - tice, love mer - cy, walk hum - bly with your God.
Then just - ly, in mer - cy, we'll hum - bly walk with God.

WORDS: Albert F. Bayly, 1949
MUSIC: Norman L. Warren, 1969

BISHOP TUCKER
66.66.66

Words © Oxford University Press; music © 1973 Hope Publishing Co.

♩=100-104

660 Serving the Poor

Make us worthy, Lord, to serve those throughout the world
who live and die in poverty or hunger.
Give them, through our hands, this day their daily bread;
and by our understanding love, give peace and joy.

—Mother Teresa of Calcutta, 20th-century missionary to the poor

Micah 6:8

661 What Does the Lord Require of You?

What does the Lord re-quire of you? What does the Lord re-
quire of you? What does the Lord re-quire of you?
1. Jus - tice, kind - ness,

WORDS and MUSIC: Jim Strathdee, 1986

MOON
Irr.

♩·=56-60

Matthew 25:31–46

662

Cuando el Pobre
(When the Poor Ones)

Unísono (Unison)

1. Cuan-do el po - bre   na - da tie - ne   y aun re - par - te,
2. Cuan - do su - fre un hom-bre y lo - gra su con - sue - lo,

1. When the poor ones who have noth-ing share with strang-ers,
2. When at last all   those who suf - fer find their com - fort,

cuan-do el hom-bre pa - sa sed   y a-gua nos da,
cuan-do es-pe - ra y no se can - sa de es-pe - rar,

when the thirst-y wa-ter give un - to us all,
when they hope though e - ven hope seems hope-less-ness,

cuan-do el dé - bil a su her-ma-no for - ta - le - ce,
cuan-do a - ma-mos, aun-que el o - dio nos ro-de - e,

when the wound-ed in their weak-ness strength-en oth-ers,
when we love though hate at times seems all a-round us,

WORDS: J. A. Olivar and Miguel Manzano, 1971; tr. George Lockwood, 1980
MUSIC: J. A. Olivar and Miguel Manzano, 1971; arr. Alvin Schutmaat

EL CAMINO
12 11 12 w. refrain

=60

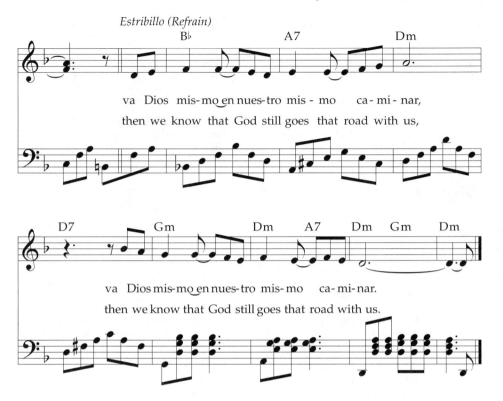

Estribillo (Refrain)

va Dios mis-mo en nues-tro mis - mo ca - mi - nar,
then we know that God still goes that road with us,

va Dios mis-mo en nues-tro mis- mo ca- mi- nar.
then we know that God still goes that road with us.

3. Cuando crece la alegría y nos inunda,
   cuando dicen nuestros labios la verdad,
   cuando amamos el sentir de los sencillos,
   Estribillo

4. Cuando abunda el bien y llena los hogares,
   cuando un hombre donde hay guerra pone paz,
   cuando "hermano" le llamamos al extraño,
   Estribillo

3. When our joy fills up our cup to overflowing,
   when our lips can speak no words other than true,
   when we know that love for simple things is better,
   Refrain

4. When our homes are filled with goodness in abundance,
   when we learn how to make peace instead of war,
   when each stranger that we meet is called a neighbor,
   Refrain

663 Go Down, Moses

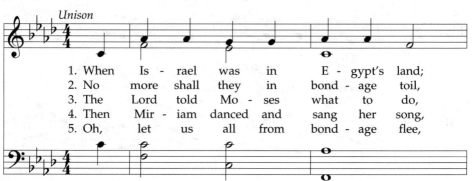

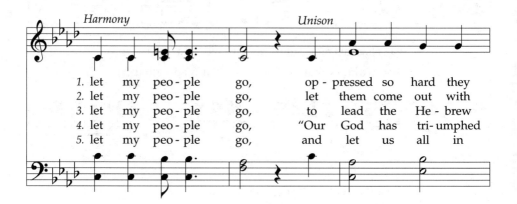

WORDS and MUSIC: African-American spiritual

GO DOWN MOSES
Irr.

♩=60-64

Go down,   Mo- ses,   way down in   E- gypt's land.
go down, Mo- ses,

Go down, go down, Mo- ses,

Tell   old   Pha- raoh,   let   my peo- ple   go.

A Litany for the World   664

Where ignorance, self-love and insensitivity
have fractured life in community,
    give your light, O God of love.

Where injustice and oppression have broken
the spirit of peoples,
    give your light, O God who frees.

Where hunger and poverty, illness and death
have made life an unbearable burden,
    give your light, O God of grace.

Where suspicion and hatred, conflict and fear
have challenged your goodness,
    give your light, O God of peace.

Eternal God,
open the eyes of the nations and peoples
so that they may walk in the light of love:
remove the ignorance and stubbornness of nations and peoples
so that they may drink from the fountains of your goodness.
    Amen.

—John Bell, Iona Community, Scotland

665 Where Cross the Crowded Ways of Life

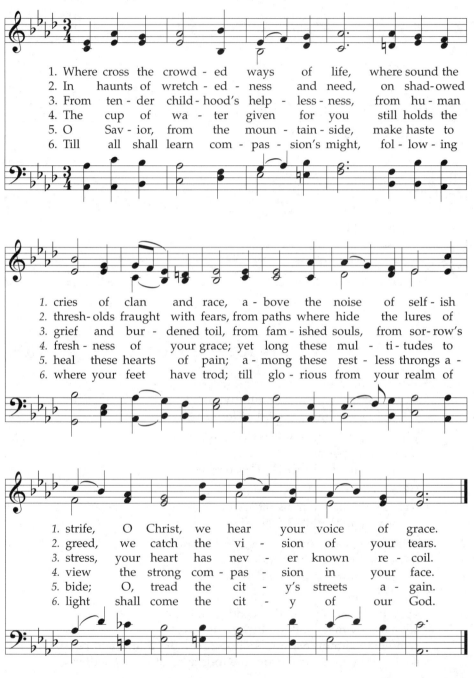

1. Where cross the crowd - ed ways of life, where sound the
2. In haunts of wretch - ed - ness and need, on shad-owed
3. From ten - der child-hood's help - less - ness, from hu - man
4. The cup of wa - ter given for you still holds the
5. O Sav - ior, from the moun - tain - side, make haste to
6. Till all shall learn com - pas - sion's might, fol - low - ing

1. cries of clan and race, a - bove the noise of self - ish
2. thresh-olds fraught with fears, from paths where hide the lures of
3. grief and bur - dened toil, from fam - ished souls, from sor - row's
4. fresh - ness of your grace; yet long these mul - ti - tudes to
5. heal these hearts of pain; a - mong these rest - less throngs a -
6. where your feet have trod; till glo - rious from your realm of

1. strife, O Christ, we hear your voice of grace.
2. greed, we catch the vi - sion of your tears.
3. stress, your heart has nev - er known re - coil.
4. view the strong com - pas - sion in your face.
5. bide; O, tread the cit - y's streets a - gain.
6. light shall come the cit - y of our God.

WORDS: Frank Mason North, 1903; adapt. Ruth Duck, 1981   GERMANY
MUSIC: William Gardiner's *Sacred Melodies*, 1815   LM

The Voice of God Is Calling

666

1. The voice of God is call-ing to wom-en and to men;
2. I hear my peo-ple cry-ing in slum and mine and mill;
3. We heed, O God, your sum-mons, and an-swer: Here are we!
4. From ease and plen-ty save us; from pride of place ab - solve;

the voice once heard in Zi - on, re-sounds on earth a - gain:
no field or mart is si - lent, no cit - y street is still.
Send us up - on your er - rand; let us your ser - vants be.
purge us of low de - sire; lift us to high re - solve;

whom shall I send to suc - cor my peo-ple in their need?
I see my peo-ple fall - ing in dark-ness and de - spair.
Our strength is dust and ash - es, our years a pass-ing hour,
take us, and make us ho - ly; teach us your will and way.

Whom shall I send to loos - en the bonds of shame and greed?
Whom shall I send to shat - ter the fet-ters which they bear?
But you can use our weak - ness to mag-ni - fy your power.
Speak, and, be-hold! we an - swer; com-mand, and we o - bey!

WORDS: John Haynes Holmes, 1913, alt.
MUSIC: William Lloyd, 1840

MEIRIONYDD
76.76D

667 With the Wings of Our Mind

Unison

1. With the wings of our mind on the new wind fly - ing,
2. With the wings of our tears on the new wind flow - ing,
3. With the wings of our song on the new wind ring - ing,

to the si - lent breath - less world our love send - ing,
to the dry and thirst - y earth our love send - ing,
to the drea - ry de - so - late earth our love send - ing,

let the brave jus - tice flag wave high a - bove,
let the foun - tain of love spring forth with joy,
let the vi - sion of light o - pen wide our hearts,

to the heav'ns and the earth free - dom bring - ing.
'til the flow'rs of our hearts ad - vent bloom - ing.
'til the song of our hope free - dom bring - ing.

WORDS: Ik-Wham Mun, Korea; tr. Marion Pope (20th century)
MUSIC: Don-Whan Cho, Korea; alt. Francisco F. Feliciano

TTŪGŌUN MAŪM
Irr.

♩=88-96

For the Healing of the Nations

668

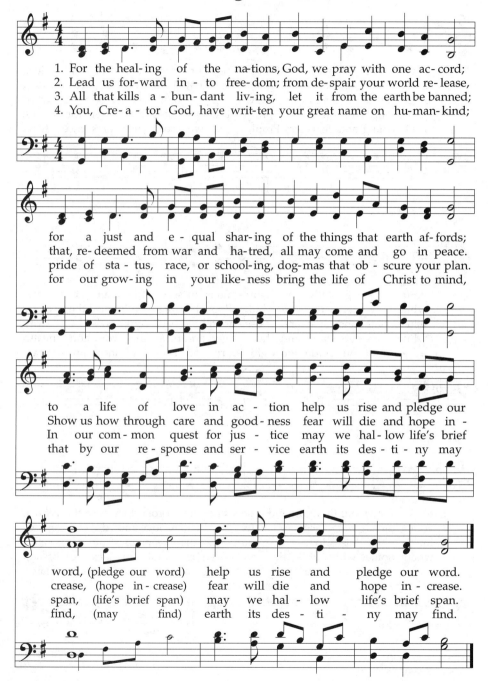

1. For the heal-ing of the na-tions, God, we pray with one ac-cord; for a just and e-qual shar-ing of the things that earth af-fords; to a life of love in ac-tion help us rise and pledge our word, (pledge our word) help us rise and pledge our word.

2. Lead us for-ward in-to free-dom; from de-spair your world re-lease, that, re-deemed from war and ha-tred, all may come and go in peace. Show us how through care and good-ness fear will die and hope in-crease, (hope in-crease) fear will die and hope in-crease.

3. All that kills a-bun-dant liv-ing, let it from the earth be banned; pride of sta-tus, race, or school-ing, dog-mas that ob-scure your plan. In our com-mon quest for jus-tice may we hal-low life's brief span, (life's brief span) may we hal-low life's brief span.

4. You, Cre-a-tor God, have writ-ten your great name on hu-man-kind; for our grow-ing in your like-ness bring the life of Christ to mind, that by our re-sponse and ser-vice earth its des-ti-ny may find, (may find) earth its des-ti-ny may find.

WORDS: Fred Kaan, 1965
MUSIC: John Hughes, 1907

CWM RHONDDA
87.87.877

669   O Young and Fearless Prophet

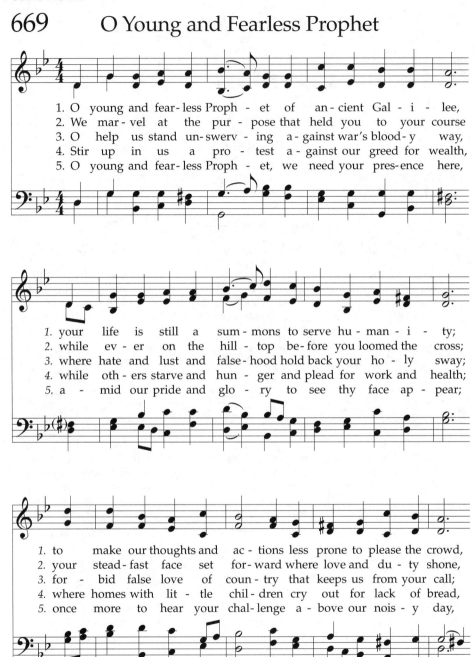

1. O young and fear-less Proph - et of an - cient Gal - i - lee,
2. We mar - vel at the pur - pose that held you to your course
3. O help us stand un-swerv - ing a - gainst war's blood- y way,
4. Stir up in us a pro - test a - gainst our greed for wealth,
5. O young and fear-less Proph - et, we need your pres-ence here,

1. your life is still a sum - mons to serve hu - man - i - ty;
2. while ev - er on the hill - top be - fore you loomed the cross;
3. where hate and lust and false - hood hold back your ho - ly sway;
4. while oth - ers starve and hun - ger and plead for work and health;
5. a - mid our pride and glo - ry to see thy face ap - pear;

1. to make our thoughts and ac - tions less prone to please the crowd,
2. your stead - fast face set for - ward where love and du - ty shone,
3. for - bid false love of coun - try that keeps us from your call;
4. where homes with lit - tle chil - dren cry out for lack of bread,
5. once more to hear your chal - lenge a - bove our nois - y day,

WORDS: S. Ralph Harlow, 1931
MUSIC: Welsh folk melody

LLANGLOFFAN
76.76D

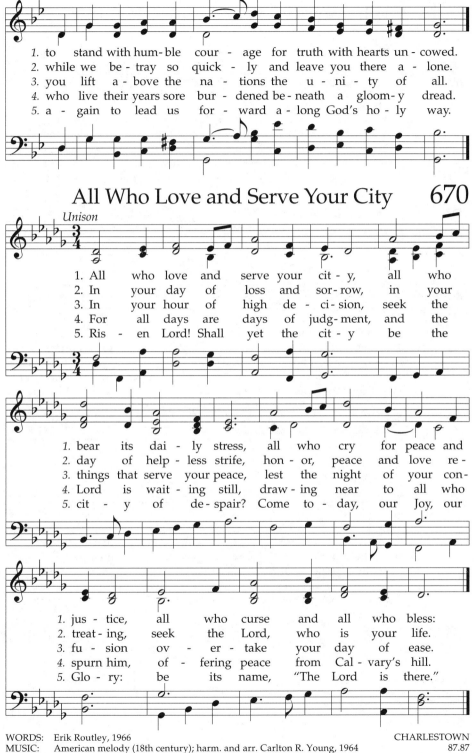

1. to stand with hum-ble cour-age for truth with hearts un-cowed.
2. while we be-tray so quick-ly and leave you there a-lone.
3. you lift a-bove the na-tions the u-ni-ty of all.
4. who live their years sore bur-dened be-neath a gloom-y dread.
5. a-gain to lead us for-ward a-long God's ho-ly way.

All Who Love and Serve Your City 670

Unison

1. All who love and serve your cit-y, all who
2. In your day of loss and sor-row, in your
3. In your hour of high de-ci-sion, seek the
4. For all days are days of judg-ment, and the
5. Ris-en Lord! Shall yet the cit-y be the

1. bear its dai-ly stress, all who cry for peace and
2. day of help-less strife, hon-or, peace and love re-
3. things that serve your peace, lest the night of your con-
4. Lord is wait-ing still, draw-ing near to all who
5. cit-y of de-spair? Come to-day, our Joy, our

1. jus-tice, all who curse and all who bless:
2. treat-ing, seek the Lord, who is your life.
3. fu-sion ov-er-take your day of ease.
4. spurn him, of-fering peace from Cal-vary's hill.
5. Glo-ry: be its name, "The Lord is there."

WORDS: Erik Routley, 1966
MUSIC: American melody (18th century); harm. and arr. Carlton R. Young, 1964

CHARLESTOWN
87.87

Words © 1969 Stainer & Bell Ltd., used by permission of Hope Publishing Co.; harm. © 1965 The
  United Methodist Publishing House

♩=120-126

671   Why Stand So Far Away, My God?

Guitar: capo 1; play Em

1. Why stand so far a - way, my God? Why hide in times of need? The proud, un - bri - dled, chase the poor, and curse you in their greed.
2. Why do you hide when, full of lies, they mur - der and be - tray? They wait to pounce up - on the weak as li - ons stalk their prey.
3. The weak are crushed and fall to earth; the wick - ed strut and preen. Why in these cruel, cha - ot - ic times can - not your face be seen?
4. In a - ges past you heard the voice of those the proud op - press. Re - mem - ber those who suf - fer now, who cry in deep dis - tress.
5. A - rise, O God, and lift your hand; bring jus - tice to the poor. Come, help us stop the flow of blood! Let ter - ror reign no more!

WORDS: Ruth Duck, 1985   MORNING SONG
MUSIC: Wyeth's *Repository of Sacred Music, Part Second*, 1813;   CM
    harm. C. Winfred Douglas, 1940

♩=88-96

Where Restless Crowds Are Thronging 672

1. Where rest-less crowds are throng-ing a - long the cit - y ways,
2. In scenes of want and sor - row and haunts of fla - grant wrong,
3. O Christ, be-hold thy peo - ple; they press on ev - ery hand!

where pride and greed and tur - moil con - sume the fe - vered days,
in homes where kind-ness fal - ters, and strife and fear are strong,
Bring light to all the cit - ies of our be - lov - ed land.

where vain am - bi - tions ban - ish all thoughts of praise and prayer,
in bus - y street of bar - ter, in lone - ly thor-ough - fare,
May all our bit - ter striv - ing give way to vi - sions fair

the peo-ple's spir-its wav - er: but thou, O Christ, art there.
the peo-ple's spir-its lan - guish: but thou, O Christ, art there.
of righ-teous-ness and jus - tice: for thou, O Christ, art there.

WORDS: Thomas Curtis Clark, 1953
MUSIC: William Lloyd, 1840

MEIRIONYDD
76.76D

Words © 1954, renewed 1982, The Hymn Society; used by permission of Hope Publishing Co.

673 Down by the Riverside

1. Gon - na lay down my sword and shield, down by the riv-er-side, down by the riv-er-side, down by the riv-er-side; gon-na lay down my sword and shield, down by the riv-er-side, gon-na stud-y war no more. I ain't gon-na stud-y war no
2. Gon - na lay down my bur - den, down by the riv-er-side, ... lay down my bur - den, ...

WORDS and MUSIC: African-American spiritual

STUDY WAR NO MORE
Irr.

more, ain't gon-na stud-y war no more, ain't gon-na stud-y

war no more, ain't gon-na stud-y war no more, ain't gon-na

stud-y war no more, I ain't gon-na

stud-y war no more, ain't gon-na stud-y war no more.

The Secret Springs That Are Moving Women 674

One of the needs of today is a vision that looks beyond the superficial and extraneous, and sees the secret springs that are moving women in their united efforts for the betterment of our land, and of all the world.

—Ida Withers Harrison, 20th-century Disciples mission executive

675 When Will People Cease Their Fighting?

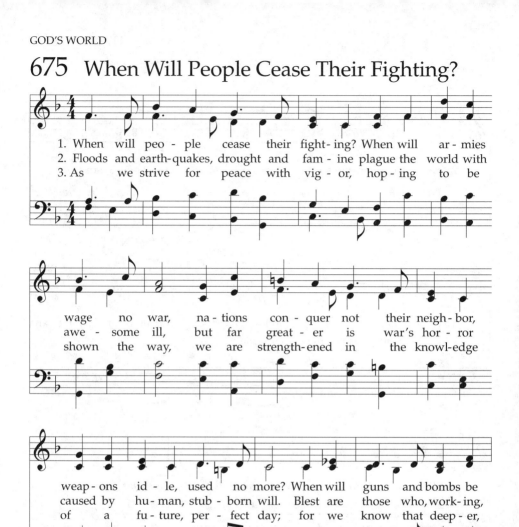

1. When will peo - ple cease their fight- ing? When will ar - mies
2. Floods and earth-quakes, drought and fam - ine plague the world with
3. As we strive for peace with vig - or, hop - ing to be

wage no war, na - tions con - quer not their neigh- bor,
awe - some ill, but far great - er is war's hor - ror
shown the way, we are strength-ened in the knowl-edge

weap - ons id - le, used no more? When will guns and bombs be
caused by hu - man, stub - born will. Blest are those who, work- ing,
of a fu - ture, per - fect day; for we know that deep - er,

si - lent? When will cap - tives be set free? All cre -
pray - ing, pur - pose in their hearts to be in - stru -
rich - er peace is ours when Christ shall reign: then will

WORDS: Constance Cherry, 1986
MUSIC: C. Hubert H. Parry, 1897

RUSTINGTON
87.87D

♩=104-108

Alt. tune: EBENEZER

a - tion groans in long-ing for the world's true lib - er - ty.
ments of peace, com - mit - ted to the na - tions' har - mo - ny.
all our swords be plow-shares and God's chil - dren free from pain.

O God of Love, O Power of Peace 676

1. O God of love, O Power of peace, make
2. Whom shall we trust, O God, but you, where
3. Where saints and an - gels dwell a - bove, all

wars through-out the world to cease. The wrath of hu - man
rest but on your word so true? None ev - er called on
hearts are joined in ho - ly love. O bind us in that

sin re - strain—give peace, O God, give peace a - gain!
you in vain—give peace, O God, give peace a - gain!
heav'n - ly chain—give peace, O God, give peace a - gain!

WORDS: Henry W. Baker, 1861, alt.   CANONBURY
MUSIC: Robert Schumann, 1839, adapt.   LM

677 Let There Be Peace on Earth

Let there be peace on earth, and let it be-gin with me;
let there be peace on earth, the peace that was meant to be.
*With God our cre-a-tor, chil-dren all are we.
Let us walk with each oth-er in per-fect har-mo-ny.
Let peace be-gin with me; let this be the mo-ment now.

Original words: "With God as our Father, brothers all are we. Let me walk with my brother in perfect harmony."

WORDS: Sy Miller and Jill Jackson, 1955
MUSIC: Sy Miller and Jill Jackson, 1955; harm. Charles H. Webb, 1987

WORLD PEACE
Irr.

With ev-ery step I take, let this be my sol-emn vow:
to take each mo-ment and live each mo-ment in peace e-ter-nal-ly.
Let there be peace on earth, and let it be-gin with me.

The Nature of Peace 678

Peace is not the product of terror or fear.
Peace is not the silence of cemeteries.
Peace is not the result of violent repression.
Peace is the generous, tranquil contribution of all to the good of all.
Peace is dynamism. Peace is generosity.
It is right and duty.

—*Oscar A. Romero, 20th-century El Salvadorian archbishop*

679 God the Omnipotent!

1. God the om - nip - o - tent! Bold - ly or - dain - ing
2. God the all - mer - ci - ful! Earth has for - sak - en
3. God the all - righ-teous one! Earth has de - fied you,
4. God the all - prov - i - dent! By your great chas-tening

thun - der and light - ning your strength to dis - play,
all you make ho - ly, and slight - ed your way;
yet to e - ter - ni - ty stands what you say;
earth shall see free - dom and truth hold - ing sway;

bring forth com - pas - sion where vi - o-lence is reign-ing:
bid not your wrath in its ter - rors a - wak - en:
false - hood and wrong shall not tar - ry be - side you:
through the thick cha - os your reign is still has-tening:

give to us peace in our time, we pray.
give to us peace in our time, we pray.
give to us peace in our time, we pray.
you will give peace in your time, we pray.

WORDS: St. 1, 2, Henry F. Chorley, 1842, alt.; st. 3, 4, John Ellerton, 1870, alt.
MUSIC: Alexis Lvov, 1833

RUSSIAN HYMN
11 10.11 9

O God of Every Nation

680

1. O God of ev - ery na - tion, of ev - ery race and land,
2. From search for wealth and pow - er and scorn of truth and right,
3. Keep bright in us the vi - sion of days when war shall cease,

re - deem your whole cre - a - tion with your al - might - y hand;
from trust in bombs that show - er de - struc-tion through the night,
when ha - tred and di - vi - sion give way to love and peace,

where hate and fear di - vide us, and bit - ter threats are hurled,
from pride of race and sta - tion that lures us from your way,
till dawns the morn - ing glo - rious when truth and jus - tice reign,

in love and mer - cy guide us, and heal our strife - torn world.
de - liv - er ev - ery na - tion, e - ter - nal God, we pray.
and Christ shall rule vic - to - rious o'er all the world's do - main.

WORDS: William W. Reid, Jr., 1958, alt.
MUSIC: Finnish folk melody; adapt. and harm. David Evans, 1927

NYLAND
76.76D

♩=52-56

681 O God, We Bear the Imprint of Your Face

1. O God, we bear the im-print of your face: the col-ors of our skin are your de-sign, and what we have of beau-ty in our race as man or wom-an, you a-lone de-fine, who

2. Where we are torn and pulled a-part by hate be-cause our race, our skin is not the same, while some are judged un-e-qual by the state and vic-tims made be-cause they own their name, hu-

3. O God, we share the im-age of your Son whose flesh and blood are ours, what-ev-er skin, in his hu-man-i-ty we find our own, and in his fam-i-ly our prop-er kin: Christ

Original wording in st. 2: we instead of some and they

WORDS: Shirley Erena Murray, 1981, alt.
MUSIC: Dan Damon, 1994

RAUMATI BEACH
10 10.10 10.10 10

Words © 1987, music © 1995 Hope Publishing Co.

♩=66-72

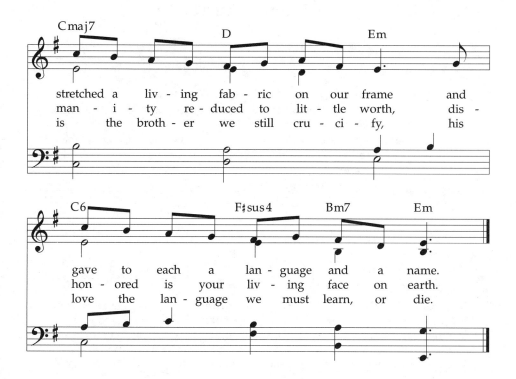

stretched a liv - ing fab - ric on our frame and
man - i - ty re - duced to lit - tle worth, dis -
is the broth - er we still cru - ci - fy, his

gave to each a lan - guage and a name.
hon - ored is your liv - ing face on earth.
love the lan - guage we must learn, or die.

God's Love for All People 682

Eternal God whose image lies in the hearts of all people,
We live among peoples whose ways are different from ours,
    whose faiths are foreign to us,
    whose tongues are unintelligible to us.
Help us to remember that you love all people with your great love,
    that all religion is an attempt to respond to you,
    that the yearnings of other hearts are much like our own
    and are known to you.
Help us to recognize you in the words of truth,
    the things of beauty,
    the actions of love about us.
We pray through Christ,
    who is a stranger to no one land more than another,
    and to every land no less than to another.

—World Council of Churches, Vancouver Assembly, 1983

683

O for a World

1. O   for   a   world   where   ev - ery - one   re -
2. O   for   a   world   where   goods are shared   and
3. We   wel - come   one   world   fam - i - ly   and
4. The   poor   are   rich,   the   weak   are strong,   the
5. O   for   a   world   pre - par - ing   for   God's

1. spects each oth - er's   ways,   where   love   is   lived   and
2. mis - er - y   re - lieved,   where   truth   is   spo - ken,
3. strug - gle with   each   choice   that   o - pens   us   to
4. fool - ish ones   are   wise.   Tell   all   who mourn;   out -
5. glo - rious reign   of   peace,   where   time and   tears   will

1. all   is   done   with   jus - tice and   with   praise.
2. chil - dren spared,   e - qual - i - ty   a - chieved.
3. u - ni - ty   and   gives our   vi - sion   voice.
4. casts be - long,   who   per - ish - es   will   rise.
5. be   no   more,   and   all   but love   will   cease.

WORDS: Miriam Therese Winter, 1987
MUSIC: Carl Gotthelf Gläser, 1828; arr. Lowell Mason, 1839

AZMON
CM

We Cannot Own the Sunlit Sky 684

1. We can-not own the sun-lit sky, the moon, the wild-flow'rs grow-ing,
2. When bod-ies shiv - er in the night and, wea-ry, wait for morn-ing,
3. God calls hu-man-i - ty to join as part-ners in cre - at-ing

for we are part of all that is with-in life's riv - er flow-ing.
when chil-dren have no bread but tears, and war-horns sound their warn-ing,
a fu-ture free from want and fear, life's good-ness cel - e - brat-ing.

With o - pen hands re - ceive and share the gifts of God's cre - a - tion,
God calls hu - man - i - ty to wake, to join in com - mon la - bor,
That new world beck-ons from a - far, in - vites our shared en-deav-or,

that all may have a - bun-dant life in ev - 'ry earth-ly na - tion.
that all may have a - bun-dant life in one-ness with their neigh-bor.
that all may have a - bun-dant life and peace en-dure for - ev - er.

WORDS: Ruth Duck, 1984, 1989
MUSIC: Robert Lowry, 1869, alt.

HOW CAN I KEEP FROM SINGING
87.87D

685 God Made All People of the World

1. God made all peo-ple of the world in-to one big fam-i-ly. Broth-ers and sis-ters all are we, help-ing, work-ing side by side, one in God, build-ing one world, one in God, build-ing one world.

2. Our hearts are full of sin and pride; fear de-stroys our u-ni-ty. Ha-tred and prej-u-dice a-rise; walls di-vide our fam-i-ly; stran-gers now, bro-ken our world, stran-gers now, bro-ken our world.

3. Je-sus has shown us how to love, rec-on-cil-ing hu-man-kind. We live be-liev-ing in his name, find-ing con-fi-dence and love, born in Christ, to a new world, born in Christ, to a new world.

4. Heirs both of glo-ry and of shame, we are peo-ple of this land. Yet we are hop-ing in the Lord, strong in faith and one in love, bring-ing light in-to the world, bring-ing light in-to the world.

WORDS: Hyn Sul Hong, 1967; tr. David Kim and Chang Hee Son
MUSIC: Shin Young Ahn

ONE WORLD
87.87.77

From the *Korean-English Hymnbook*, published by the Korean-English
Hymnbook Publication Commission; used by permission

♩=104-112

Of Women, and of Women's Hopes We Sing 686

1. Of wom-en, and of wom-en's hopes we sing:
2. We praise the God whose im-age is our own,
3. We la-bor for the com-mon-wealth of God,
4. For-giv-ing what is past, we seek the new:

of shar-ing in cre - a-tion's nur-tur-ing,
the mys-ter - y with - in our flesh and bone,
and e-qual as dis - ci-ples, walk the road,
a fin - er jus - tice, and a peace more true,

of bear-ing and of birth-ing new be-lief,
the wom-an-spir - it mov-ing through all time
in work and sta - tus, ask-ing what is just,
the prom-ise of em-power-ing for our day

of pas-sion for the prom-is - es of life.
in proph-e - cy, Mag - nif-i-cat and dream.
for sis - ters of the fam - i - ly of Christ.
when men and wom-en roll the stone a - way.

WORDS: Shirley Erena Murray, 1988
MUSIC: Alfred Morton Smith, 1941

SURSUM CORDA
10 10.10 10

♩=104-112

687 In Christ There Is No East or West

1. In Christ there is no east or west, in him no south or north, but one community of love throughout the whole wide earth.
2. In Christ shall true hearts ev'rywhere their high communion find; his service is the golden cord closebinding humankind.
3. Join hands, disciples of the faith, whate'er your race may be; all children of the living God are surely kin to me.
4. In Christ now meet both east and west in him meet south and north; all loving hearts are one in him throughout the whole wide earth.

WORDS: John Oxenham, 1908, alt.
MUSIC: Alexander R. Reinagle, c. 1830

ST. PETER
CM

688 When, in Awe of God's Creation

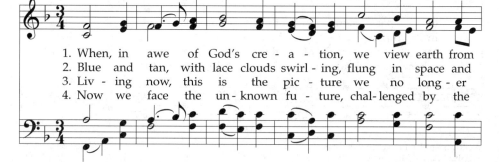

1. When, in awe of God's creation, we view earth from
2. Blue and tan, with lace clouds swirling, flung in space and
3. Living now, this is the picture we no longer
4. Now we face the unknown future, challenged by the

WORDS: Jane Parker Huber, 1991
MUSIC: Rowland H. Prichard, 1844; harm. *The English Hymnal*, 1906

HYFRYDOL
87.87D

out - er space, this mys - te - ri - ous, float - ing mar - ble, strewn with
cir - cling there, ha - bi - tat for myr - iad crea - tures meant for
can de - ny, for we see no an - gry bound-aries when our
work at hand. Still the God of all cre - a - tion sum - mons

clouds and bathed in grace, how can we not pause in
land and sea and air! Must we draw our lines of
view is from the sky: riv - ers, de - serts, for - ests,
us with one com - mand: "Love each oth - er!" Will we

won - der, see - ing earth as one and whole? As we heal our
ha - tred mark-ing nat - ion, class, and race? God, for - give us,
snow-fields, o-ceans, lakes, and moun- tains too, but no fenc - es
do it? "Love each oth - er!" Wars might cease! "Love each oth - er!"

proud di - vi - sions, may earth's heal - ing be our goal.
we en - treat you, for all pride of self and place.
built for bar - ring you from me or me from you.
Jus - tice fol - lows: "Love each oth - er!" There is peace!

689 We Are Not Our Own

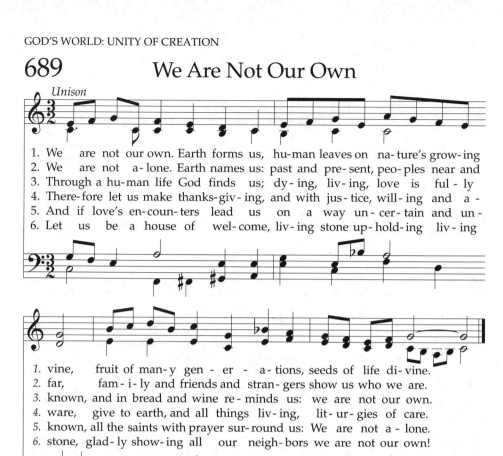

Unison

1. We are not our own. Earth forms us, hu-man leaves on na-ture's grow-ing
2. We are not a-lone. Earth names us: past and pre-sent, peo-ples near and
3. Through a hu-man life God finds us; dy-ing, liv-ing, love is ful-ly
4. There-fore let us make thanks-giv-ing, and with jus-tice, will-ing and a-
5. And if love's en-coun-ters lead us on a way un-cer-tain and un-
6. Let us be a house of wel-come, liv-ing stone up-hold-ing liv-ing

1. vine, fruit of man-y gen - er - a-tions, seeds of life di-vine.
2. far, fam-i-ly and friends and stran-gers show us who we are.
3. known, and in bread and wine re-minds us: we are not our own.
4. ware, give to earth, and all things liv-ing, lit-ur-gies of care.
5. known, all the saints with prayer sur-round us: We are not a-lone.
6. stone, glad-ly show-ing all our neigh-bors we are not our own!

WORDS: Brian Wren, 1987
MUSIC: Brian Wren, 1987; arr. Fred Graham

YARNTON
89.85

© 1989 Hope Publishing Co.

♩=72-76

690 Mountain Brook with Rushing Waters

1. Moun - tain brook with rush - ing wa - ters, ea - gle perched in
2. Pure the wa - ter fresh - ly flow-ing toward its o - cean
3. Wav - ing fields of wheat and bar - ley, gi - ant ap - ples
4. Keep us faith - ful in the strug-gle to con-serve earth's

WORDS: William W. Reid, Jr. 1973
MUSIC: William Rowlands, 1905

BLAENWERN
87.87D

Words © 1973 The Hymn Society, used by permission of Hope Publishing Co.

♩·=46-50

loft - y tree, flower - ing hill - side in the spring - time,
des - ti - ny, clean the air of God's cre - a - tion,
jui - cy red, cat - tle graz - ing in the pas - ture;
threat - ened store as we fight to save the for - est,

white - tailed deer a - lert and free! Beau - ty, beau - ty
rich the soil, the mine, the sea. "Earth is good!" God's
by God's boun - ty we are fed! Well sup - plied the
clean the stream, pro - tect the shore. God and hu - mans

all a - round us! Ju - bi - la - te! Sing for joy! Help us, God, pre-
word pro - claimed it. Ju - bi - la - te! Sing for joy! Save us, God, from
world a - round us! Ju - bi - la - te! Sing for joy! May no greed or
work to - geth - er, Ju - bi - la - te! Sing for joy! Part - ners work - ing

serve earth's splen - dor for to - mor - row's world to see.
waste - ful liv - ing, from pol - lu - tion's trag - e - dy.
war - ring mad - ness scorch the earth or rob our bread.
till as stew - ards we can say, "Earth's good!" once more.

691 We Thank You, God, for Water, Soil, and Air

Unison

1. We thank you, God, for wa - ter, soil, and
2. We thank you, God, for min - er - als and
3. We thank you, God, for price - less en - er -
4. We thank you, God, for weav - ing na - ture's
5. We thank you, God, for mak - ing plan - et

1. air, large gifts sup - port - ing ev - ery -
2. ores— the ba - sis of all build - ing,
3. gy, stored in each at - om, gath - ered
4. life in - to a seam - less robe, a
5. Earth, a home for us and ag - es

1. thing that lives. For - give our
2. wealth, and speed. For - give our
3. from the sun. For - give our
4. frag - ile whole. For - give our
5. yet un - born. Help us to

WORDS: Brian Wren, 1973
MUSIC: William Rowan, 1985

YOGANANDA
10 10.10 9

♩=112-120

1. spoil - ing and a - buse of them. Help
2. reck - less plun - der - ing and waste. Help
3. greed and care - less- ness of power. Help
4. haste, that tam - pers un - a - ware. Help
5. share, con - sid - er, save, and store. Come

1. us re - new the face of the earth.
2. us re - new the face of the earth.
3. us re - new the face of the earth.
4. us re - new the face of the earth.
5. and re - new the face of the earth.

Fashioned for Joy   692

As the hand is made for holding and the eye for seeing,
you have fashioned me for joy.
Share with me the vision that shall find it everywhere:
in the wild violet's beauty;
in the lark's melody;
in the face of a steadfast person;
in a child's smile;
in a mother's love;
in the purity of Jesus.

—A Gaelic prayer

693 Touch the Earth Lightly

Unison

1. Touch the earth light - ly, use the earth
*2. We who en - dan - ger, who cre - ate
3. Let there be green - ing, birth from the
4. God of all liv - ing, God of all

gen - tly, nour - ish the life of the
hun - ger, a - gents of death for all
burn - ing, wa - ter that bless - es and
lov - ing, God of the seed - ling, the

world in our care: gift of great won -
crea - tures that live, we who would fos -
air that is sweet, health in God's gar -
snow and the sun, teach us, de - flect

der, ours to sur - ren - der, trust for the
ter clouds of dis - as - ter— God of our
den, hope in God's chil - dren, re - gen - er -
us, Christ re - con - nect us, us - ing us

* Alternate key signature and accidentals: for st. 2 only

WORDS: Shirley Erena Murray, 1991
MUSIC: Colin Gibson, 1992

TENDERNESS
55.10D

♩.=52-56

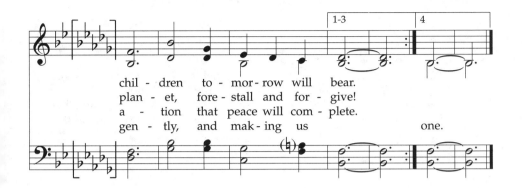

chil - dren   to - mor - row will   bear.
plan - et,   fore - stall and for - give!
a - tion   that peace will com - plete.
gen - tly,   and mak - ing   us   one.

Caring for the Earth 694

(Allow for a period of silent reflection between each section.)

We have faith
in One God, one Source of all life.
One Ground of the whole earth, with all its creatures.

And thus we believe
in the goodness of earth's life,
in the innate worth of all its dependents,
in human partnership in the life of nature.

And thus we believe
that in Christ we have been shown
the special role of the human race
to bear God's likeness
in working and caring for the earth,
in seeking to understand its mysteries and powers,
in gently working with these powers
for the well-being of all children of the earth.

And thus we believe
that God's Spirit will lead us
to sensitive closeness with earth's life,
to that meek, unselfish and compassionate life-style
by which the earth is inherited in peace,
by which its life is transformed
for all creatures to share justly in its bounty.

So be it. Amen.

India, 20th century

695 God of the Fertile Fields

1. God of the fer - tile fields, shap - er of
2. We would be stew - ards true, hold - ing in
3. As grows the hid - den seed to fruit that
4. God of the coun - try - side, dear to the

earth that yields our dai - ly bread; forth from your
trust from you all that you give; help us in
serves our need, your reign yet grows. So let our
Christ who died to make us one; we pledge our

boun - teous hand come gifts your love has planned,
love to share, teach us like you to care
toil be used, no gift of yours a - bused,
lives a - new in faith - ful love to you;

that all in ev - 'ry land be clothed and fed.
for peo - ple ev - ery-where, that all may live.
no hum - ble task re - fused your love be - stows.
guide all we say and do, till life is done.

WORDS: Georgia Harkness, 1955, alt.
MUSIC: Felice de Giardini, 1769

ITALIAN HYMN
664.6664

Words © 1955, renewed 1983, Hope Publishing Co.

Alt. tune: AMERICA

For Beauty of Meadows

696

1. For beau-ty of mead-ows, for gran-deur of trees,
2. As stew-ards of beau-ty re-ceived at your hand,
3. Teach us once a-gain to be gar-deners in peace;

for flow-ers of wood-lands, for crea-tures of seas,
as crea-tures who hear your most ur-gent com-mand,
all na-ture a-round us is ours but on lease;

for all you cre-at-ed and gave us to share,
we turn from our waste-ful de-struc-tion of life,
your name we would hal-low in all that we do,

we praise you, Cre-a-tor, ex-tol-ling your care.
con-fess-ing our fail-ures, con-fess-ing our strife.
ful-fill-ing our call-ing, cre-at-ing with you.

WORDS: Walter H. Farquharson, 1969
MUSIC: Welsh folk melody

ST. DENIO
11 11.11 11

697 Creative God, You Spread the Earth

1. Cre - a - tive God, you spread the earth with life in man - y forms: the deer and elk and col - um - bine, the bee in hum - ming swarms. For - give us for each flow'r and bird now van - ished by our
2. The plan - et teemed with liv - ing things be - fore all hu - man birth, and e - ven fire and beasts of prey re - newed the life of earth. For - give us, that, the last to come, we threat - en sea and
3. O play - ful God, you fill the field with lav - en - der and blue. You paint the bird with in - di - go, with red or tawn - y hue. For - give us that we grieve your heart, de - stroy - ing what you

WORDS: Ruth Duck, 1991
MUSIC: Traditional English melody; harm. Ralph Vaughan Williams

KINGSFOLD
CMD
♩=52-54

hand.   Teach   us   to   treat   with
air.   Teach   us   to   tend   life's
do,   and   teach us   simp -   ler,

lov - ing   care   the   crea - tures   of   the   land.
frag - ile   web   with   wise and   ten - der   care.
gen - tler   ways   to   live on   earth with   you.

Prayer of a Native American   698

O Great Spirit, whose voice I hear in the winds,
    and whose breath gives life to all the world,
    hear me.
I am small and weak.
    I need your strength and wisdom.
Let me walk in beauty
    and make my eyes ever behold
    the red and purple sunset.
Make my hands respect the things you have made.
    Make my ears sharp to hear your voice.
Make me wise so that I may understand
    the things you have taught your people.
Let me learn the lessons you have hidden in every leaf and rock.
I seek strength,
    not to be greater than another,
    but to fight my greatest enemy—myself.
Make me always ready to come to you
    with clean hands and straight eyes.
So when life fades, as the fading sunset,
    my spirit may come to you without shame.

—Anonymous

699 Rejoice, the Lord Is King!

Descant

3. Re - joice in glo - rious hope! For Christ, our Judge, shall come

1. Re - joice, the Lord is King! The ris - en Christ a - dore!
2. God's reign can nev - er fail, Christ rules o'er earth and heaven;
3. Re - joice in glo - rious hope! For Christ, our Judge, shall come

to glo - ri - fy the saints for their e - ter - nal home:

Re - joice, give thanks, and sing, and tri - umph ev - er - more:
the keys of death and hell are to our Je - sus given:
to glo - ri - fy the saints for their e - ter - nal home:

lift up your heart, lift up your voice!

lift up your heart, lift up your voice!

WORDS: Charles Wesley, 1746, alt.
MUSIC: John Darwall, 1770; desc. Sydney H. Nicholson, c. 1945

DARWALL'S 148th
66.66.88

Re - joice, a - gain I say, re - joice!

Re - joice, a - gain I say, re - joice!

O Day of God, Draw Nigh   700

1. O day of God, draw nigh in beau - ty
2. Bring to our trou - bled minds, un - cer - tain
3. Bring jus - tice to our land, that all may
4. Bring to our world of strife your sov - ereign
5. O day of God, draw nigh as at cre -

1. and in power; come with your time - less
2. and a - fraid, the qui - et of a
3. dwell se - cure, and fine - ly build for
4. word of peace, that war may haunt the
5. a - tion's birth; let there be light a -

1. judg - ment now to match our pres - ent hour.
2. stead - fast faith, calm of a call o - beyed.
3. days to come foun - da - tions that en - dure.
4. earth no more, and des - o - la - tion cease.
5. gain, and set your judg - ments on the earth.

WORDS: Robert B. Y. Scott, 1937
MUSIC: *Genevan Psalter*, 1551; arr. William Crotch, 1836

ST. MICHAEL
SM

701 Shall We Gather at the River

1. Shall we gath-er at the riv-er, where bright an-gel feet have
2. On the mar-gin of the riv-er, wash-ing up its sil-ver
3. Ere we reach the shin-ing riv-er, lay we ev-ery bur-den
4. Soon we'll reach the shin-ing riv-er, soon our pil-grim-age will

trod, with its crys-tal tide for-ev-er flow-ing
spray, we will walk and wor-ship ev-er, all the
down; grace our spir-its will de-liv-er, and pro-
cease; soon our hap-py hearts will quiv-er with the

Refrain

by the throne of God?
hap-py gold-en day.
vide a robe and crown.   Yes, we'll gath-er at the riv-er,
mel-o-dy of peace.

the beau-ti-ful, the beau-ti-ful riv-er; gath-er with the

WORDS and MUSIC: Robert Lowry, 1864

HANSON PLACE
87.87 w. refrain

saints at the riv - er that flows by the throne of God.

All Things New

702

RESPONSE

Earth and heaven re - peat the cry, "Glo - ry be to God on high."

R

Then I saw a new heaven and a new earth;
  for the first heaven and the first earth had passed away,
  and the sea was no more.
And I saw the holy city, the new Jerusalem,
  coming down out of heaven from God.
And I heard a loud voice from the throne saying,
"See, the home of God is among mortals.
The LORD will dwell with them as their God;
  they will be God's peoples,
  and God personally will be with them;
God will wipe every tear from their eyes.
Death will be no more;
  mourning and crying and pain will be no more,
  for the first things have passed away."   **R**

And the one who was seated on the throne said,
  "See, I am making all things new."
Also the enthroned one said,
  "Write this, for these words are trustworthy and true."
Then the LORD said to me, "It is done!
  I am the Alpha and the Omega,
  the beginning and the end.
To the thirsty I will give water as a gift
  from the spring of the water of life.
Those who conquer will inherit these things,
  and I will be their God
  and they will be my children.   **R**

WORDS: Revelation 21:1–2a, 3–7; Response, Charles Wesley
MUSIC: Robert Williams; harm. Carlton R. Young, 1992

703   When All Is Ended

1. When all is end - ed, time and troub - les past,
2. As in the night, when light-ning flick - ers free,
3. A - gainst all hope, our wea - ry times have known
4. Then do not cheat the poor, who long for bread,
5. With earth - y faith we sing a song of heaven:
6. With all cre - a - tion, pain and an - ger past,

1. shall all be mend - ed, sin and death out - cast? In
2. and gives a glimpse of dis - tant hill and tree, each
3. wars end - ed, peace de - clared, com - pas - sion shown, great
4. with dream-worlds in the sky or in the head, but
5. all life ful - filled, all loved, all wrong for - given. Christ
6. e - vil ex - haust - ed, love su - preme at last, a -

WORDS: Brian Wren, 1988   SINE NOMINE
MUSIC: Ralph Vaughan Williams, 1906   10 10 10 w. alleluias

1. hope	we	sing,	and hope	to	sing	at	last:
2. flash	of	good	dis - clos - es	what	will		be:
3. days	of	free -	dom,	ty - rants	o -	ver -	thrown:
4. sing	of	slaves	set free,	and	chil -	dren	fed:
5. is	our	sign	of hope,	for	Christ	is	risen:
6. live	in	God,	we'll sing	an	un -	sur -	passed

Al - le - lu - ia! Al - le - lu - ia!

We Are a Christian Movement   704

Ideas of reform, of restoration, of union, and of merger have had their place, but we are fundamentally a Christian movement, and not a restoration movement, nor a merger movement, and it is precisely because we are a Christian movement that we are concerned about Christian unity. But it is Jesus Christ who has been passed on from age to age and whom we received in the teachings of our parents.

—*William B. Blakemore, 20th-century Disciples ecumenist*

705 Mine Eyes Have Seen the Glory

WORDS: Julia Ward Howe, 1861, alt.
MUSIC: American camp-meeting tune (19th century)

BATTLE HYMN OF THE REPUBLIC
15 15 15.6 w. refrain

his truth is march-ing on.
Our God is march-ing on.
while God is march-ing on.
Glo - ry, glo - ry, hal - le-
lu - jah! Glo - ry, glo - ry, hal - le - lu - jah! Glo - ry,
glo - ry, hal - le - lu - jah! His truth is march-ing on.

First Fruits of God's Future   706

You know, O God,
how hard it is to survive captivity without any hope of the Holy City.
Sing to us, God, the songs of the promised land.
Serve us your manna in the desert,
and give us grace to enjoy our day of rest
as an expression of our trust.

Let there be, in some place,
a community of men, women, elderly, children, and new-born babies
as a first fruit, as our appetizer,
and an embrace of the future. Amen.

—*Rubem A. Alves, 20th-century Brazilian philosopher*

707 Marching to Zion

1. Come, we that love the Lord, and let our joys be known; join
2. Let those re-fuse to sing who nev-er knew our God; but
3. The hill of Zi-on yields a thou-sand sa-cred sweets be-
4. Then let our songs a-bound, and ev-ery tear be dry; we're

in a song with sweet ac-cord, join in a song with sweet ac-cord
chil-dren of the heaven-ly King, but chil-dren of the heaven-ly King
fore we reach the heaven-ly fields, be-fore we reach the heaven-ly fields,
march-ing thru Em-man-uel's ground, we're march-ing thru Em-man-uel's ground

and thus sur-round the throne, and thus sur-round the throne.
may speak their joys a-broad, may speak their joys a-broad.
or walk the gold-en streets, or walk the gold-en streets.
to fair-er worlds on high, to fair-er worlds on high.

We're march-ing to Zi-on, beau-ti-ful, beau-ti-ful Zi-on; we're

march-ing up-ward to Zi-on, the beau-ti-ful cit-y of God.

WORDS: Isaac Watts, 1707; refrain Robert Lowry, 1867
MUSIC: Robert Lowry, 1867

MARCHING TO ZION
66.88.66 w. refrain

My Lord, What a Morning

708

My Lord, what a morn-ing; my Lord, what a morn-ing; oh, my Lord, what a morn-ing, when the stars be-gin to fall.

1. You'll hear the trum-pet sound, to wake the na-tions un-der-ground,
2. You'll hear the sin-ner moan, to wake the na-tions un-der-ground,
3. You'll hear the Chris-tian shout, to wake the na-tions un-der-ground,

look-ing to my God's right hand,
look-ing to my God's right hand, when the stars be-gin to fall.
look-ing to my God's right hand,

WORDS: African-American spiritual
MUSIC: African-American spiritual; refrain harm. Verolga Nix, 1981;
  verse and response harm. Larry Sivis, 1993

BURLEIGH
Irr.

Refrain harm. © 1981 The United Methodist Publishing House; verse and response harm. © 1995
  Chalice Press

709 Glorious Things of Thee Are Spoken

1. Glo - rious things of thee are spo - ken,
2. See, the streams of liv - ing wa - ters,
3. Round each hab - i - ta - tion hov - ering,

Zi - on, cit - y of our God; God, whose word can -
spring-ing from e - ter - nal love, well sup - ply thy
see the cloud and fire ap - pear for a glo - ry

not be bro - ken, formed thee for a blest a - bode.
sons and daugh - ters, and all fear of want re - move.
and a cov - ering, show - ing forth that God is near!

On the Rock of A - ges found - ed, what can shake thy
Who can faint, while such a riv - er ev - er flows their
Thus de - riv - ing from their ban - ner light by night and

WORDS: John Newton, 1779, alt.
MUSIC: Franz Joseph Haydn, 1797

AUSTRIAN HYMN
87.87D

sure re - pose? With sal - va - tion's walls sur -
thirst to as - suage? Grace, which like our God, the
shade by day, safe they feed up - on the

round - ed, thou may-est smile at all thy foes.
Giv - er, nev - er fails from age to age.
man - na which God gives them when they pray.

Let the Day Come, Lord 710

Come, Lord Jesus, come!

Let the day come, Lord
  when our world's misery will find your mercy.
Let the day come
  when our poverty will find your riches.

Let the day come
  when our path will find the way to your house.
Let the day come
  when our tears will find your smile.

Let the day come
  when our joy will find your heaven.
Let the day come
  when your church will find the kingdom.

May you be blest, Father, for that day
  when our eyes will find your face!
Throughout all the time of our lives
  you have not ceased to come before us
in your Son Jesus Christ,
  our Savior and our brother.

Come, Lord Jesus, come!

—Lucien Deiss, 20th-century French Catholic liturgist

711 O Day of Peace That Dimly Shines

Unison

1. O day of peace that dim - ly shines
2. Then shall the wolf dwell with the lamb,

through all our hopes and prayers and dreams,
nor shall the fierce de - vour the small;

guide us to jus - tice, truth, and love,
as beasts and cat - tle calm - ly graze,

de - liv - ered from our self - ish schemes.
a lit - tle child shall lead them all.

WORDS: Carl P. Daw, Jr., 1982   CANDLER
MUSIC: Traditional Scottish melody; harm. Carlton R. Young, 1963   LMD

Words © 1982 Hope Publishing Co.; harm. © 1964 The United Methodist Publishing House   ♩=104-112

May swords of hate fall from our hands,
Then en - e - mies shall learn to love,

our hearts from en - vy find re - lease,
all crea - tures find their true ac - cord;

till by God's grace our war - ring world
the hope of peace shall be ful - filled,

shall see Christ's prom - ised reign of peace.
for all the earth shall know the Lord.

A Benediction 712

May the strength of God pilot us.
May the power of God preserve us.
May the wisdom of God instruct us.
May the hand of God protect us, this day and evermore.

—Patrick, 5th-century English missionary in Ireland

713 God of Our Life

1. God of our life, through all the cir - cling years, we trust in you;
2. God of the past, our times are in your hand; with us a - bide.
3. God of the com-ing years, through paths un - known we fol-low you;

in all the past, through all our hopes and fears, your hand we view.
Lead us by faith to hope's true prom-ised land; be now our guide.
when we are strong, Lord, leave us not a - lone; our faith re - new.

With each new day, when morn-ing lifts the veil,
With you to bless, the dark-ness shines as light,
Be now for us in life our dai - ly bread,

we own your mer - cies, Lord, which nev - er fail.
and faith's fair vi - sion chan - ges in - to sight.
our heart's true home when all our years have sped.

WORDS: Hugh T. Kerr, 1916; alt., 1928
MUSIC: Charles Henry Purday, 1860; harm. John Weaver, 1986

SANDON
10 4.10 4.10.10

For the Fruit of All Creation

714

1. For the fruit of all cre-a-tion, thanks be to God;
2. In the just re-ward of la-bor, God's will is done;
3. For the har-vests of the Spir-it, thanks be to God;

for good gifts to ev-ery na-tion, thanks be to God; for the
in the help we give our neigh-bor, God's will is done; in our
for the good we all in-her-it, thanks be to God; for the

plow-ing, sow-ing, reap-ing, si-lent growth while we are sleep-ing,
world-wide task of car-ing for the hun-gry and de-spair-ing,
won-ders that as-tound us, for the truths that still con-found us,

fu-ture needs in earth's safe-keep-ing, thanks be to God.
in the har-vests we are shar-ing, God's will is done.
most of all, that love has found us, thanks be to God.

WORDS: Fred Pratt Green, 1970
MUSIC: Traditional Welsh melody; harm. Luther Orlando Emerson, 1906

AR HYD Y NOS
84.84.888.4

715

Now Thank We All Our God

1. Now thank we all our God with heart and hands and voic- es,
2. O may this boun- teous God through all our life be near us,
3. All praise and thanks to God our Fa - ther and our Moth- er,

who won- drous things has done, in whom the world re - joic - es,
with ev - er joy - ful hearts and bless- ed peace to cheer us,
to Christ and to the One who binds us to each oth - er,

who, from our moth - ers' arms, has blessed us on our way
and keep us full of grace, and guide us when per - plexed,
the one e - ter - nal God, whom earth and heaven a - dore,

with count- less gifts of love, and still is ours to - day.
and free us from all ills in this world and the next.
for thus it was, is now, and shall be ev - er - more.

WORDS: Martin Rinkart, 1636; tr. Catherine Winkworth, 1858, alt.
MUSIC: Johann Crüger, 1647; harm. Felix Mendelssohn, 1840

NUN DANKET
67.67.66.66

A Thanksgiving

The congregation sings the response from the first line of "Now Thank We All Our God" on the facing page.

Now thank we all our God with heart and hands and voices.

O God, we give you thanks for all that you have done for us.
That you have created us, and have given us the gift of life
    and set us to live in this fair earth;
that you have given us work to do, and the strength to do it:

Now thank we all our God with heart and hands and voices.

We give you thanks for all that others have done for us.
For those who taught us when we were children;
for those who in the days of youth gave us the guidance
    that kept us from going astray;
for those who to this day love us and surround us with their care:

Now thank we all our God with heart and hands and voices.

We give you thanks for all that your church has done for us.
For strength and guidance each week for life's way;
for the friendship and the fellowship which we here enjoy;
for the sacraments of your grace, and the prayers of your people:

Now thank we all our God with heart and hands and voices.

We give you thanks for all that you have done for us in Jesus Christ.
That in Christ you have shown us the length and breadth
    and depth and height of your great love for us;
that in Christ you have opened to us a new and living way
    into your presence:

Now thank we all our God with heart and hands and voices.

We give you thanks for everything that has given us
    strength for earth and hope for heaven.
Accept this our sacrifice of praise for your love's sake. **Amen.**

—William Barclay, 20th-century British biblical scholar (adapt.)

Used by permission of Barclay Publications

717

Let All Things Now Living

Descant

2. Ah,_____ O

Unison

1. Let all things now liv - ing a song of thanks - giv - ing to
2. By law God en - forc - es. The stars in their cours - es, the

sun in its or - bit o - be - dient - ly shine. Ah,_____

God our Cre - a - tor tri - um - phant - ly raise; who fash - ioned and
sun in its or - bit o - be - dient - ly shine; the hills and the

the depths of the o - cean pro-

made us, pro - tect - ed and stayed us, by guid - ing us on to the
moun - tains, the riv - ers and foun - tains, the depths of the o - cean pro-

WORDS: Katherine K. Davis, 1939, alt.
MUSIC: Welsh folk melody; desc. Katherine K. Davis, 1939

ASH GROVE
6 6 11.6 6 11D

Matthew 13:24–30

718 Come, Ye Thankful People, Come

Descant

3. These to thee, our God, we owe, source whence our bless-ings flow;

1. Come, ye thank-ful peo-ple, come, raise the song of har-vest home;
2. All the bless-ings of the field, all the stores the gar-dens yield,
3. These to thee, our God, we owe, source whence all our bless-ings flow;

for these our souls raise grate-ful vows and praise. Come, then, ye

all is safe-ly gath-ered in, ere the win-ter storms be-gin;
all the fruits in full sup-ply, rip-ened 'neath the sum-mer sky,
and for these our souls shall raise grate-ful vows and sol-emn praise.

thank - ful peo-ple, come, raise the song of har-vest home;

God, our Mak-er, does pro-vide for our wants to be sup-plied;
all the spring with boun-teous hand scat-ters o'er the smil-ing land,
Come, then, thank-ful peo-ple, come, raise the song of har-vest home;

WORDS: Henry Alford, 1844
MUSIC: George J. Elvey, 1858; desc. O. I. Cricket Harrison, 1994

ST. GEORGE'S WINDSOR
77.77D

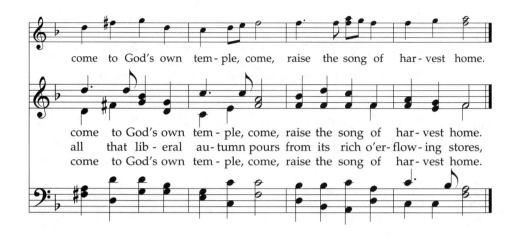

come to God's own tem - ple, come, raise the song of har - vest home.

come to God's own tem - ple, come, raise the song of har - vest home.
all that lib - er - al au - tumn pours from its rich o'er - flow - ing stores,
come to God's own tem - ple, come, raise the song of har - vest home.

Come, Sing a Song of Harvest 719

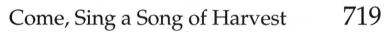

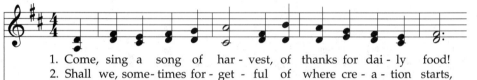

1. Come, sing a song of har - vest, of thanks for dai - ly food!
2. Shall we, some - times for - get - ful of where cre - a - tion starts,
3. May God, the great Cre - a - tor, to whom all life be - longs,
4. And lest the world go hun - gry while we our - selves are fed,

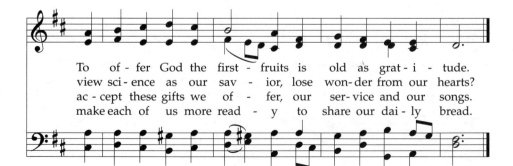

To of - fer God the first - fruits is old as grat - i - tude.
view sci - ence as our sav - ior, lose won - der from our hearts?
ac - cept these gifts we of - fer, our ser - vice and our songs.
make each of us more read - y to share our dai - ly bread.

WORDS: Fred Pratt Green, 1976
MUSIC: Melchior Vulpius, 1609

CHRISTUS, DER IST MEIN LEBEN
76.76

720   O Beautiful for Spacious Skies

1. O beau-ti-ful for spa-cious skies, for am-ber waves of grain,
2. O beau-ti-ful for he-roes proved in lib-er-at-ing strife,
3. O beau-ti-ful for pa-triot dream that sees be-yond the years

for pur-ple moun-tain maj-es-ties a-bove the fruit-ed plain!
who more than self their coun-try loved, and mer-cy more than life!
thine al-a-bas-ter cit-ies gleam, un-dimmed by hu-man tears!

A-mer-i-ca! A-mer-i-ca! God shed full grace on thee,
A-mer-i-ca! A-mer-i-ca! May God thy gold re-fine,
A-mer-i-ca! A-mer-i-ca! God mend thine ev-ery flaw,

and crown thy good with ser-vant-hood from sea to shin-ing sea.
till all suc-cess be no-ble-ness and ev-ery gain di-vine.
con-firm thy soul in self-con-trol, thy lib-er-ty in law.

WORDS: Katherine Lee Bates, 1893
MUSIC: Samuel Augustus Ward, 1882

MATERNA
CMD

My Country, 'Tis of Thee

721

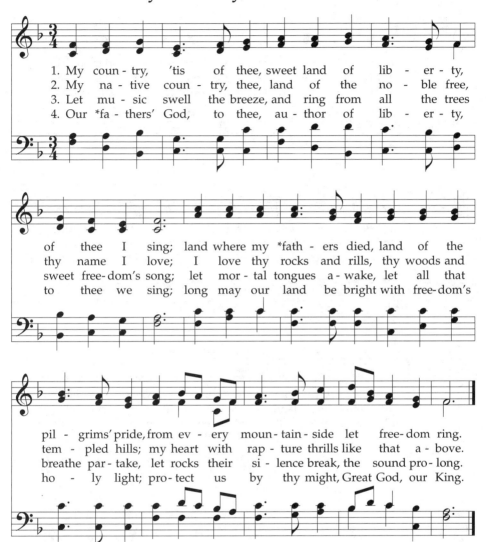

1. My coun-try, 'tis of thee, sweet land of lib-er-ty,
2. My na-tive coun-try, thee, land of the no-ble free,
3. Let mu-sic swell the breeze, and ring from all the trees
4. Our *fa-thers' God, to thee, au-thor of lib-er-ty,

of thee I sing; land where my *fath-ers died, land of the
thy name I love; I love thy rocks and rills, thy woods and
sweet free-dom's song; let mor-tal tongues a-wake, let all that
to thee we sing; long may our land be bright with free-dom's

pil-grims' pride, from ev-er-y moun-tain-side let free-dom ring.
tem-pled hills; my heart with rap-ture thrills like that a-bove.
breathe par-take, let rocks their si-lence break, the sound pro-long.
ho-ly light; pro-tect us by thy might, Great God, our King.

* *Or* parents, parents'

WORDS: Samuel Francis Smith, 1831
MUSIC: *Thesaurus Musicus*, 1744

AMERICA
664.6664

722

This Is My Song

1. This is my song, O God of all the na-tions,
2. My coun-try's skies are blu - er than the o - cean,
3. This is my prayer, O Rul - er of all na-tions:

a song of peace for lands a - far and mine.
and sun - light beams on clo - ver-leaf and pine;
let thy reign come; on earth thy will be done.

This is my home, the coun - try where my heart is;
but oth - er lands have sun - light too, and clo - ver,
In peace may all earth's peo - ple draw to - geth-er,

here are my hopes, my dreams, my ho - ly shrine;
and skies are ev - ery - where as blue as mine.
and hearts u - nit - ed learn to live as one.

WORDS: St. 1, 2, Lloyd Stone, 1934; st. 3, Georgia Harkness, c. 1939, alt.
MUSIC: Jean Sibelius, 1899; arr. *The Hymnal*, 1933

FINLANDIA
11 10.11 10.11 10

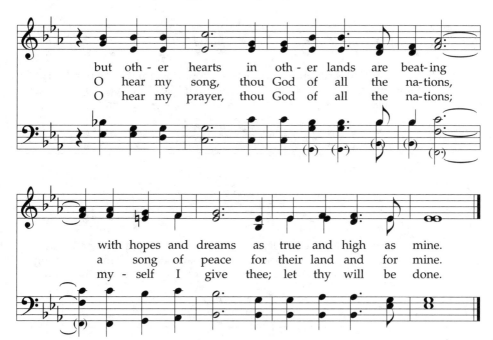

but oth-er hearts in oth-er lands are beat-ing
O hear my song, thou God of all the na-tions,
O hear my prayer, thou God of all the na-tions;

with hopes and dreams as true and high as mine.
a song of peace for their land and for mine.
my-self I give thee; let thy will be done.

A Prayer for the Nation 723

Almighty God,
    you have given us this good land as our heritage.
Make us always remember your generosity
    and constantly do your will.
Bless our land with honest industry,
    truthful education,
    and an honorable way of life.
Save us from violence, discord, and confusion;
    from pride and arrogance
    and from every evil course of action.
Make us who came from many nations
    with many different languages
    a united people.
Defend our liberties and give those
    whom we have entrusted with the authority of government
    the spirit of wisdom,
    that there might be justice and peace in our land.
When times are prosperous, let our hearts be thankful;
    and, in troubled times, do not let our trust in you fail.
We ask all this through Jesus Christ our Lord. Amen.

724   O God of Earth and Altar

1. O God of earth and al - tar, bow down and hear our cry;
2. From all that ter - ror teach - es, from lies of pen and tongue,
3. A - wak-en us to ac - tion and forge us in - to one,

our earth-ly lead-ers fal - ter, our peo-ple drift and die;
from all the eas - y speech - es that soothe us in our wrong,
de - fy - ing sect and fac - tion; O God, your will be done!

the walls of gold en - tomb us, the swords of scorn di - vide;
from sale and prof-a - na - tion of hon - or and the sword,
Op - pres-sive sys-tems snare us; our ap - a - thies in - crease.

take not your thun - der from us, but take a - way our pride.
from sleep and from dam - na - tion, de - liv - er us, O Lord!
Great God, in mer - cy spare us for jus - tice and for peace!

WORDS: St. 1, 2, Gilbert K. Chesterton, 1906, alt.; st. 3, Jane Parker Huber, 1985   LLANGLOFFAN
MUSIC: Welsh folk melody   76.76D

St. 3 © 1985 Jane Parker Huber

God of the Ages, Whose Almighty Hand 725

Trumpets, before
each stanza
(optional)

1. God of the a - ges, whose al - might - y hand
2. Thy love di - vine hath led us in the past;
3. From war's a - larms, from dead - ly pes - ti - lence,
4. Re - fresh thy peo - ple on our toil - some way;

leads forth in beau - ty all the star - ry band
in this free land with thee our lot is cast;
be thy strong arm our ev - er sure de - fense;
lead us from night to nev - er - end - ing day;

of shin - ing worlds in splen - dor through the skies,
be thou our rul - er, guard - ian, guide, and stay,
thy true re - li - gion in our hearts in - crease;
fill all our lives with love and grace di - vine,

our grate - ful songs be - fore thy throne a - rise.
thy Word our law, thy paths our cho - sen way.
thy boun - teous good - ness nour - ish us in peace.
and glo - ry, laud, and praise be ev - er thine.

WORDS: Daniel C. Roberts, 1876, alt.
MUSIC: George W. Warren, 1894

NATIONAL HYMN
10 10.10 10

Psalter

INTRODUCTION

Recently there has been a movement in the church, ecumenical in scope, from simply reading the psalms in worship to a combination of reading and singing. Thus the "responsorial psalm," deeply rooted in early Jewish temple and synagogue worship, is enjoying an amazing revival.

With this renewal of interest, many congregations are rediscovering the power of the psalms as "sung prayer." Their texts contain not only descriptive ancient phrases addressing the concerns and gratitude of the Israelites to God, but colorful and expressive language that conveys the up-and-down feelings of our everyday lives—elements that we as a worshiping people also bring before God.

Traditionally, many of our congregations have used psalms and psalm paraphrases through hymns, calls to worship, benedictions, prayers, scripture litanies, and choral anthems. For that reason, whole psalms or psalm portions were included in the *Hymnbook for Christian Worship* (1970), and in the responsive scripture readings of *Christian Worship: A Hymnal* (1941).

The *Chalice Hymnal* builds upon this traditional use of the psalms and introduces a musical component. Each of the psalms on the following pages is arranged in the familiar "call-response," leader-people format for public reading, using an appropriate music line as a sung response. This response is either a familiar hymn fragment or a brief, easily learned musical phrase, with the text drawn from that psalm or helping to enhance its message. The response is to be repeated at periodic intervals in the reading of the psalm.

This liturgical psalter is based upon the New Revised Standard Version of the book of Psalms. Thirty-nine psalms are included here. They have been selected with a sensitivity to their usage in particular parts of regular Sunday worship; their relation to special seasons and celebrations of the church year; their usefulness in memorial services, services of Christian marriage, and morning and evening prayer; and their frequency of assigned Sunday use in the revised common lectionary.

The responsorial format has also been used for a select group of songs and canticles from the Old and New Testaments, included at appropriate places in the hymnal. The following guidelines apply to the use of those selections as well. They are listed together in the Topical Index under the heading "Canticles."

GUIDELINES

Each psalm text is preceded by a musical phrase marked Response. This is to be sung before and after the psalm is recited, and sometimes at appropriate points within the psalm. Those locations are identified with a bold **R**.

Occasionally a second psalm response is provided. When that psalm is read in worship, the worship bulletin or an announcement should indicate which response is to be used.

Full arrangements of the musical responses are provided, for accompaniment purposes. The congregation may feel more comfortable singing all responses in unison, though portions of familiar hymn tunes lend themselves readily to four-part harmony.

Here is the sequence for putting it all together in worship:
1. A solo voice or members of the choir sing the response.
2. The congregation sings the response together.
3. The first portion—or all—of the psalm is read responsively, with the leader reading lightface type and the congregation reading boldface type.
4. At each location marked with a bold **R**, the congregation sings the musical response again.

The accompanist may wish to play a single lead-in tone at the beginning of each subsequent response.

Other options can be explored. One portion of the congregation may recite the lightface type (e.g., left side, or women) and a second group respond with the boldface type (right side, or men). Also it is possible to use the psalms for responsive reading by themselves, without musical responses.

Psalm 8

Johann J. Schütz; tr. Frances E. Cox
Bohemian Brethren's *Kirchengesänge*

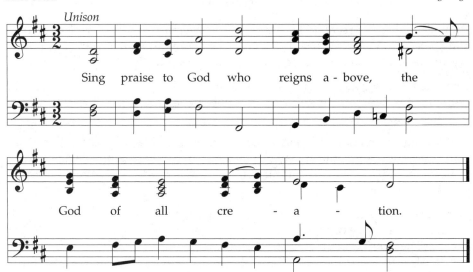

Sing praise to God who reigns a - bove, the

God of all cre - a - tion.

R

1   O L<small>ORD</small>, our God,
    how majestic is your name in all the earth!
    You have set your glory above the heavens.
2   Out of the mouths of babes and infants
    you have founded a bulwark because of your foes,
        to silence the enemy and the avenger.   R

3   When I look at your heavens, the work of your fingers,
        the moon and the stars that you have established;
4   what are human beings that you are mindful of them,
        mortals that you care for them?
5   Yet you have made them a little lower than God,
        and crowned them with glory and honor.   R

6   You have given them dominion over the works of your hands;
        you have put all things under their feet,
7   all sheep and oxen,
        and also the beasts of the field,
8   the birds of the air, and the fish of the sea,
        whatever passes along the paths of the seas.
9   O L<small>ORD</small>, our God,
        how majestic is your name in all the earth!   R

Psalm 15

Amos 5:24
Lon Oliver; harm. Larry Sivis

RESPONSE

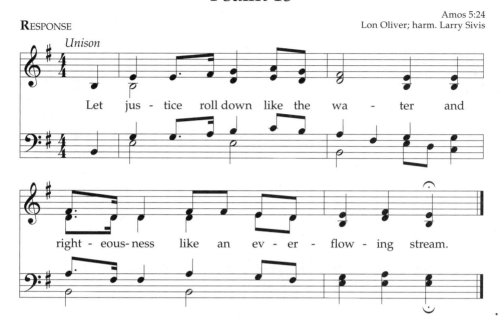

Let jus - tice roll down like the wa - ter and

right - eous-ness like an ev - er - flow - ing stream.

R

1. O God, who may abide in your tent?
    Who may dwell on your holy hill?
2. **Those who walk blamelessly, and do what is right,**
    and speak the truth from their heart;
3. who do not slander with their tongue,
    and do no evil to their friends,
        nor take up a reproach against their neighbors;
4. **in whose eyes the wicked are despised,**
    but who honor those who fear God;
    who stand by their oath even to their hurt;
5. who do not lend money at interest,
    and do not take a bribe against the innocent.
    Those who do these things shall never be moved.   R

Psalm 16:5–11

Fred R. Anderson
Southern Harmony

R~ESPONSE~

Our hearts are glad, our souls re - joice, in God we dwell se - cure.

R

⁵ The L~ORD~ is my chosen portion and my cup;
    you hold my lot.
⁶ **The boundary lines have fallen for me in pleasant places;**
    I have a goodly heritage.
⁷ I bless the L~ORD~ who gives me counsel;
    in the night also my heart instructs me.
⁸ **I keep the L~ORD~ always before me;**
    because God is at my right hand, I shall not be moved.   **R**

⁹ Therefore my heart is glad, and my soul rejoices;
    my body also rests secure.
¹⁰ **For you do not give me up to Sheol,**
    or let your faithful one see the Pit.
¹¹ You show me the path of life.
    In your presence there is fullness of joy;
    in your right hand are pleasures forevermore.   **R**

Psalm 19:1–10

Psalm 19:7
Hebrew melody

RESPONSE

The law of God is just, re - viv-ing all your soul.

R
1   The heavens are telling the glory of God;
         and the firmament proclaims God's handiwork.
2   **Day to day pours forth speech,**
         and night to night declares knowledge.
3   There is no speech, nor are there words;
         their voice is not heard;
4   **yet their voice goes out through all the earth,**
         and their words to the end of the world.
     In the heavens God has set a tent for the sun,
5   which comes out like a bridegroom from his wedding canopy,
         and runs its course with joy and strength.
6   **Its rising is from the end of the heavens,**
         and its circuit to the end of them;
         and nothing is hid from its heat.   R

7   The law of the LORD is perfect,
         reviving the soul;
     the decrees of the LORD are sure,
         making wise the simple;
8   the precepts of the LORD are right,
         rejoicing the heart;
     the commandment of the LORD is clear,
         enlightening the eyes;
9   the fear of the LORD is pure,
         enduring forever;
     the ordinances of the LORD are true
         and righteous altogether.
10   More to be desired are they than gold,
         even much fine gold;
     sweeter also than honey,
         and drippings of the honeycomb.   R

Psalm 22:1–18, 25–31

Psalm 22:27
Gary Alan Smith

RESPONSE

All the ends of the earth shall re - mem - ber and turn un - to God.

> **R**

1 My God, my God, why have you forsaken me?
   Why are you so far from helping me,
   from the words of my groaning?

2 O my God, I cry by day, but you do not answer;
   and by night, but find no rest.

3 **Yet you are holy,**
   enthroned on the praises of Israel.

4 In you our ancestors trusted;
   they trusted, and you delivered them.

5 **To you they cried, and were saved;**
   in you they trusted, and were not put to shame.   R

6 But I am a worm, and not human;
   scorned by others, and despised by the people.

7 **All who see me mock at me;**
   they make mouths at me, they shake their heads;

8 "Commit your cause to the LORD; let him deliver—
   let him rescue the one in whom he delights!"

9 **Yet it was you who took me from the womb;**
   you kept me safe on my mother's breast.

10 On you I was cast from my birth,
   and since my mother bore me you have been my God.

11 **Do not be far from me,**
   for trouble is near
   and there is no one to help.   R

12 Many bulls encircle me,
     strong bulls of Bashan surround me;
13 **they open wide their mouths at me,**
     like a ravening and roaring lion.
14 I am poured out like water,
     and all my bones are out of joint;
    my heart is like wax;
     it is melted within my breast;
15 my mouth is dried up like a potsherd,
     and my tongue sticks to my jaws;
    you lay me in the dust of death.
16 For dogs are all around me;
     a company of evildoers encircles me.
    My hands and feet have shriveled;
17 I can count all my bones.
     They stare and gloat over me;
18 **they divide my clothes among themselves,**
     and for my clothing they cast lots.   **R**

25 From you comes my praise in the great congregation;
     my vows I will pay before those who fear God.
26 The poor shall eat and be satisfied;
     those who seek the LORD shall sing praise .
    May your hearts live forever!
27 All the ends of the earth shall remember and
     turn to the LORD;
    and all the families of the nations
     shall worship before God.
28 For dominion belongs to the LORD,
     who rules over the nations.
29 To God, indeed, shall all who sleep in the earth bow down;
     before God shall bow all who go down to the dust,
     and I shall live for the LORD.
30 Posterity will serve **the LORD;**
     future generations will be told about the Lord,
31 **and proclaim deliverance to a people yet unborn,**
     saying that God has done it.   **R**

Psalm 23

Isaac Watts, alt.
J. L. Macbeth Bain

RESPONSE 1

My Shep-herd, you sup - ply my need and ho- ly is your name.

RESPONSE 2
Unison

Marty Haugen

Shep-herd me, O God, be - yond my wants, be -

yond my fears, from death in - to life.

R

1 The LORD is my shepherd,
    I shall not want.
2 **He makes me lie down in**
    green pastures;
he leads me beside still waters;
3   he restores my soul.
He leads me in right paths
   for his name's sake.
4 Even though I walk through the
    darkest valley,
   I fear no evil;
for you are with me;
   your rod and your staff—
   they comfort me.   **R**

5 You prepare a table before me
   in the presence of my
    enemies;
you anoint my head with oil;
   my cup overflows.
6 Surely goodness and mercy shall
    follow me
all the days of my life,
and I shall dwell in the house of
   the LORD for ever.   **R**

Psalm 24

Fred R. Anderson
Traditional American melody

RESPONSE

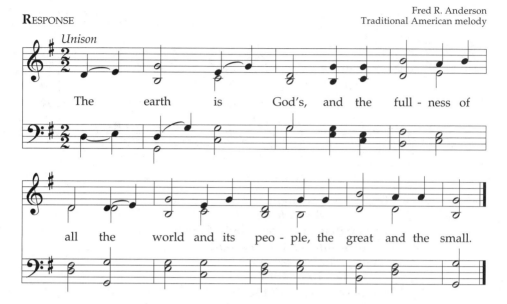

The earth is God's, and the full-ness of all the world and its peo-ple, the great and the small.

R

1 The earth is the LORD's and all that is in it,
   the world, and those who live in it;
2 for God has founded it on the seas,
   and established it on the rivers.
3 Who shall ascend the hill of the LORD?
   And who shall stand in God's holy place?
4 **Those who have clean hands and pure hearts,**
   who do not lift up their souls to what is false,
   and do not swear deceitfully.
5 They will receive blessing from the LORD,
   and vindication from the God of their salvation.
6 **Such is the company of those who seek God,**
   who seek the face of the God of Jacob.   R

7 Lift up your heads, O gates!
   and be lifted up, O ancient doors!
   that the King of glory may come in.
8 Who is the King of glory?
   The LORD, strong and mighty,
   the LORD, mighty in battle.
9 Lift up your heads, O gates!
   and be lifted up, O ancient doors!
   that the King of glory may come in.
10 Who is this King of glory?
   The LORD of hosts, he is the King of glory.   R

Psalm 27:1–6, 13–14

James Montgomery
The Sacred Harp; harm. Austin C. Lovelace

RESPONSE

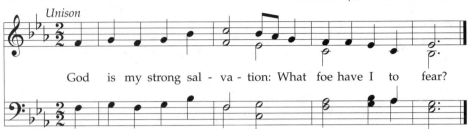

God is my strong sal - va - tion: What foe have I to fear?

R

1 The LORD is my light and my salvation;
    whom shall I fear?
The LORD is the stronghold of my life;
    of whom shall I be afraid?

2 When evildoers assail me
    to devour my flesh—
my adversaries and foes—
    they shall stumble and fall.

3 Though an army encamp against me,
    my heart shall not fear;
though war rise up against me,
    yet I will be confident.

4 One thing I asked of the LORD,
    that will I seek after:
to live in the house of the LORD
    all the days of my life,
to behold the beauty of the LORD,
    and to inquire in God's temple.   **R**

5 God will hide me in a shelter
    in the day of trouble;
will conceal me under the cover of a tent;
    and will set me high on a rock.

6 Now my head is lifted up
    above my enemies all around me,
and I will offer in God's tent
    sacrifices with shouts of joy;
I will sing and make melody to the LORD.

13 I believe that I shall see the goodness of the LORD
    in the land of the living.

14 **Wait for the LORD;**
    be strong, and let your heart take courage.
Wait for the LORD!   **R**

Psalm 29

Charles Wesley
John Hatton

With joy the God of Hosts pro - claim,

ex - tol the great al - might - y name.

R

¹ Ascribe to the LORD, O heavenly beings,
 ascribe to the LORD glory and strength.
² Ascribe to the LORD the glory of his name;
 worship the LORD in holy splendor.
³ The voice of the LORD is over the waters;
 the God of glory thunders,
 the LORD, over mighty waters.
⁴ The voice of the LORD is powerful;
 the voice of the LORD is full of majesty.   **R**

⁵ The voice of the LORD breaks the cedars;
 the LORD breaks the cedars of Lebanon.
⁶ **The LORD makes Lebanon skip like a calf,**
 and Sirion like a young wild ox.
⁷ The voice of the LORD flashes forth flames of fire.
⁸ The voice of the LORD shakes the wilderness;
 the LORD shakes the wilderness of Kadesh.
⁹ The voice of the LORD causes the oaks to whirl,
 and strips the forest bare;
 and in God's temple all say, "Glory!"
¹⁰ The LORD sits enthroned over the flood;
 the LORD sits enthroned as king forever.
¹¹ **May the LORD give strength to God's people!**
 May the LORD bless God's people with peace!   **R**

Psalm 31:1–8

Martin Luther; tr. Frederick H. Hedge
Martin Luther

RESPONSE

A might-y for-tress is our God, a bul-wark nev-er fail - ing.

R

1 In you, O God, I seek refuge;
do not let me ever be put to shame;
in your righteousness deliver me.

2 Incline your ear to me;
rescue me speedily.
Be a rock of refuge for me,
a strong fortress to save me.

3 You are indeed my rock and my fortress;
for your name's sake lead me and guide me,

4 **take me out of the net that is hidden for me,**
for you are my refuge.   R

5 Into your hand I commit my spirit;
you have redeemed me, faithful God.

6 **You hate those who pay regard to worthless idols,**
but I trust in you.

7 I will exult and rejoice in your steadfast love,
because you have seen my affliction;
you have taken heed of my adversities,

8 **and have not delivered me into the hand of the enemy;**
you have set my feet in a broad place.   R

Psalm 32

Psalm 32:11
Gary Alan Smith

RESPONSE

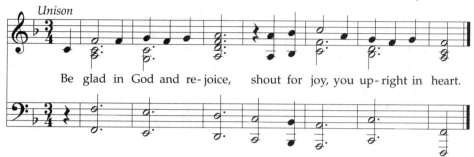

Be glad in God and re-joice, shout for joy, you up-right in heart.

R

1 Happy are those whose transgression is forgiven,
  whose sin is covered.
2 **Happy are those to whom God imputes no iniquity,**
  and in whose spirit there is no deceit.
3 While I kept silence, my body wasted away
  through my groaning all day long.
4 **For day and night your hand was heavy upon me;**
  my strength was dried up as by the heat of summer.
5 Then I acknowledged my sin to you,
  and I did not hide my iniquity;
  I said, "I will confess my transgressions to God,"
  and you forgave the guilt of my sin.   R

6 Therefore let all who are faithful
  offer prayer to you;
  at a time of distress,
  the rush of mighty waters shall not reach them.
7 You are a hiding place for me;
  you preserve me from trouble;
  you surround me with glad cries of deliverance.
8 I will instruct you and teach you the way you should go;
  I will counsel you with my eye upon you.
9 **Do not be like a horse or a mule, without understanding,**
  whose temper must be curbed with bit and bridle,
  else it will not stay near you.
10 Many are the torments of the wicked,
  but steadfast love surrounds those who trust in God.
11 **Be glad in God and rejoice, O righteous,**
  and shout for joy, all you upright in heart.   R

Psalm 40:1–3, 9–11

Psalm 40:11, adapt.
Traditional Dutch melody

RESPONSE

God, your mer-cy is up-on us as we place our trust in you.

R

1 I waited patiently for the LORD,
who inclined to me and heard my cry,

2 **who drew me up from the desolate pit,**
out of the miry bog,
and set my feet upon a rock,
making my steps secure,

3 who put a new song in my mouth,
a song of praise to our God.
Many will see and fear,
and put their trust in the LORD.   R

9 I have told the glad news of deliverance
in the great congregation;
see, I have not restrained my lips,
as you know, O God.

10 I have not hidden your saving help within my heart,
I have spoken of your faithfulness and your salvation;
I have not concealed your steadfast love and your faithfulness
from the great congregation.

11 Do not, O God, withhold
your mercy from me;
let your steadfast love and your faithfulness
keep me safe forever.   R

Psalm 42

Psalm 42:1
Don E. Saliers, alt.

RESPONSE

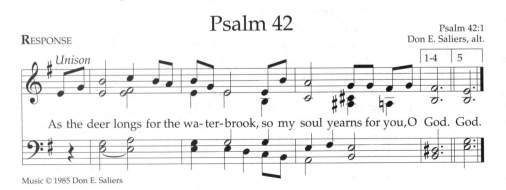

As the deer longs for the wa-ter-brook, so my soul yearns for you, O God. God.

R

1   As a deer longs for flowing streams,
        so my soul longs for you, O God.
2   My soul thirsts for God,
        for the living God.
    **When shall I come and behold
        the face of God?**
3   My tears have been my food
        day and night,
    **while people say to me continually,
        "Where is your God?"   R**

4   These things I remember,
        as I pour out my soul:
    **how I went with the throng,
        and led them in procession to the house of God,**
    with glad shouts and songs of thanksgiving,
        a multitude keeping festival.
5   Why are you cast down, O my soul,
        and why are you disquieted within me?
    Hope in God; for I shall again praise him,
6   **my help and my God.   R**

    My soul is cast down within me;
        therefore I remember you
    **from the land of Jordan and of Hermon,
        from Mount Mizar.**
7   Deep calls to deep
        at the thunder of your cataracts;
    **all your waves and your billows
        have gone over me.**
8   By day you command your steadfast love,
        and at night your song is with me,
        a prayer to the God of my life.   R

9   I say to God, my rock,
        "Why have you forgotten me?
    **Why must I walk about mournfully
        because the enemy oppresses me?"**
10 As with a deadly wound in my body,
        my adversaries taunt me,
    **while they say to me continually,
        "Where is your God?"**
11 Why are you cast down, O my soul,
        and why are you disquieted within me?
    **Hope in God whom I shall again praise,
        my help and my God.   R**

Psalm 46

Martin Luther; tr. Frederick H. Hedge
Martin Luther

RESPONSE

A might-y for-tress is our God, a bul-wark nev-er fail - ing.

R

1   God is our refuge and strength,
         a very present help in trouble.
2   **Therefore we will not fear, though the earth should change,**
         though the mountains shake in the heart of the sea;
3   though its waters roar and foam,
         though the mountains tremble with its tumult.
4   **There is a river whose streams make glad the city of God,**
         the holy habitation of the Most High.
5   God is in the midst of the city; it shall not be moved;
         God will help it when the morning dawns.
6   **The nations rage, dominions totter;**
         God speaks, the earth melts.
7   The LORD of hosts is with us;
         the God of Israel is our refuge.   R

8   Come, behold the works of the LORD,
         who has brought desolations on the earth;
9   **who makes wars cease to the end of the earth;**
         who breaks the bow, shatters the spear;
         and burns the shields with fire.
10   "Be still, and know that I am God!
         I am exalted among the nations,
         I am exalted in the earth."
11   **The LORD of hosts is with us;**
         the God of Israel is our refuge.   R

Psalm 51:1–3, 6–7, 9–13, 15

Psalm 51:10
Carl F. Mueller

RESPONSE

Cre - ate in me a clean heart, O God.

R

1 Have mercy on me, O God,
   according to your steadfast love;
   according to your abundant mercy
   blot out my transgressions.
2 Wash me thoroughly from my iniquity,
   and cleanse me from my sin.
3 **For I know my transgressions,**
   and my sin is ever before me.   R

6 You desire truth in the inward being;
   therefore teach me wisdom in my secret heart.
7 Purge me with hyssop, and I shall be clean;
   wash me, and I shall be whiter than snow.
9 **Hide your face from my sins,**
   and blot out all my iniquities.   R

10 Create in me a clean heart, O God,
   and put a new and right spirit within me.
11 Do not cast me away from your presence,
   and do not take your holy spirit from me.
12 **Restore to me the joy of your salvation,**
   and sustain in me a willing spirit.
13 Then I will teach transgressors your ways,
   and sinners will return to you.
15 **O Lord, open my lips,**
   and my mouth will declare your praise.   R

Psalm 67

Fred R. Anderson
Carlton R. Young

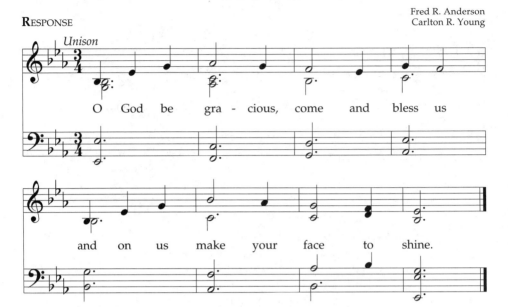

O God be gra - cious, come and bless us
and on us make your face to shine.

R

1   O God, be gracious to us and bless us
        and make your face to shine upon us,
2   **that your way may be known upon earth,**
        your saving power among all nations.
3   Let the peoples praise you, O God;
        let all the peoples praise you.
4   **Let the nations be glad and sing for joy,**
        for you judge the peoples with equity
        and guide the nations upon earth.   R

5   Let the peoples praise you, O God;
        let all the peoples praise you.
6   **The earth has yielded its increase;**
        God, our God, has blessed us.
7   May God continue to bless us;
        let all the ends of the earth revere God.   R

Psalm 84

Arlo D. Duba, alt.
Hal H. Hopson

RESPONSE

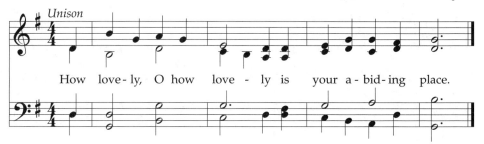

How love-ly, O how love-ly is your a-bid-ing place.

R

1 How lovely is your dwelling place,
   O LORD of hosts!
2 **My soul longs, indeed it faints**
   for the courts of the LORD;
   my heart and my flesh sing for joy
   to the living God.
3 Even the sparrow finds a home,
   and the swallow a nest for herself,
   where she may lay her young,
   at your altars, O LORD of hosts,
   my Sovereign and my God.
4 **Happy are those who live in your house,**
   ever singing your praise.   R

5 Happy are those whose strength is in you,
   in whose heart are the highways to Zion.
6 As they go through the valley of Baca
   they make it a place of springs;
   the early rain also covers it with pools.
7 **They go from strength to strength;**
   the God of gods will be seen in Zion.
8 O LORD God of hosts, hear my prayer;
   give ear, O God of Israel!
9 **Behold our shield, O God;**
   look on the face of your anointed.   R

10 For a day in your courts is better
   than a thousand elsewhere.
   I would rather be a doorkeeper in the house of my God
   than live in the tents of wickedness.
11 For the LORD God is a sun and shield
   who bestows favor and honor.
   No good thing does the LORD withhold
   from those who walk uprightly.
12 **O LORD of hosts,**
   happy is everyone who trusts in you.   R

Psalm 90:1–6, 13–17

Psalm 92:15; 18:2
Johann Crüger; harm. Felix Mendelssohn

RESPONSE

Sing praise to God our rock, in whom we take our ref - uge.

R

1 Lord, you have been our dwelling place
   in all generations.
2 **Before the mountains were brought forth,**
   or ever you had formed the earth and the world,
   from everlasting to everlasting you are God.
3 You turn us back to dust,
   and say, "Turn back, you mortals."
4 **For a thousand years in your sight**
   are like yesterday when it is past,
   or like a watch in the night.
5 You sweep them away; they are like a dream,
   like grass that is renewed in the morning;
6 **in the morning it flourishes and is renewed;**
   in the evening it fades and withers.   R

13 Turn, O Lord! How long?
   Have compassion on your servants!
14 Satisfy us in the morning with your steadfast love,
   so that we may rejoice and be glad all our days.
15 **Make us glad as many days as you have afflicted us,**
   and as many years as we have seen evil.
16 Let your work be manifest to your servants,
   and your glorious power to their children.
17 **Let the favor of the Lord our God be upon us,**
   and prosper for us the work of our hands—
   O prosper the work of our hands!   R

Psalm 95:1–7

Psalm 95:2
Larry Sivis

RESPONSE

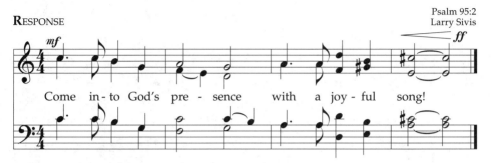

Come in-to God's pre - sence with a joy - ful song!

R

¹ O come, let us sing to the LORD;
    let us make a joyful noise to the rock of our salvation!
² Let us come into God's presence with thanksgiving;
    let us make a joyful noise to God with songs of praise!
³ For the LORD is a great God,
    and a great Ruler above all gods.
⁴ In God's hand are the depths of the earth;
    the heights of the mountains are God's also.
⁵ **The sea belongs to God who made it,**
    and the dry land, which God's hands have formed.   **R**

⁶ O come, let us worship and bow down,
    let us kneel before the LORD, our Maker!
⁷ **For the LORD is our God,**
    and we are the people of God's pasture,
    and the sheep of God's hand.   **R**

Psalm 96

Helen L. Wright, alt.
Hal H. Hopson

RESPONSE

O sing a new song to God, sing to God, sing all the earth.

R

1 O sing to the LORD a new song;
    sing to the LORD, all the earth.
2 **Sing to the LORD, bless God's name;**
    proclaim God's salvation from day to day.
3 Declare God's glory among the nations,
    God's marvelous works among all the peoples.
4 **For great is the LORD, and greatly to be praised;**
    to be revered above all gods.
5 For all the gods of the peoples are idols,
    but the LORD made the heavens.
6 **Honor and majesty are before the LORD;**
    in whose sanctuary are strength and beauty.   R

7 Ascribe to the LORD, O families of the peoples,
    ascribe to the LORD glory and strength.
8 Ascribe to the LORD the glory due that name;
    bring an offering, and come into God's courts.
9 **Worship the LORD in holy splendor;**
    tremble before God, all the earth.   R

10 Say among the nations, "The LORD reigns!
    The world is firmly established; it shall never be moved.
    God will judge the peoples with equity."
11 **Let the heavens be glad, and let the earth rejoice;**
    let the sea roar, and all that fills it;
12 **let the field exult, and everything in it.**
    Then shall all the trees of the forest sing for joy
13 before the LORD, who is coming to judge the earth.
    The LORD will judge the world with righteousness,
    and the peoples with truth.   R

Psalm 97

Folliot S. Pierpoint
Conrad Kocher

Folliot S. Pierpoint
Conrad Kocher

RESPONSE
Unison

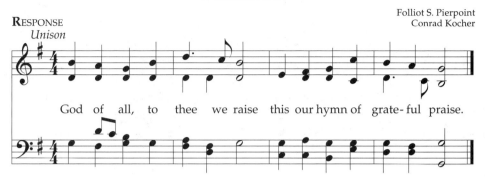

God of all, to thee we raise this our hymn of grate-ful praise.

R

1 The LORD reigns! Let the earth rejoice;
     let the many coastlands be glad!
2 Clouds and thick darkness surround the LORD;
     righteousness and justice are the foundation of God's throne.
3 Fire goes before the LORD,
     and consumes God's adversaries on every side.
4 God's lightnings illumine the world;
     the earth sees and trembles.
5 The mountains melt like wax before the LORD,
     before the Lord of all the earth.
6 The heavens proclaim God's righteousness;
     and all the peoples behold God's glory.   **R**

7 All worshipers of images are put to shame,
     those who make their boast in worthless idols;
     all gods bow down before the LORD.
8 Zion hears and is glad,
     and the towns of Judah rejoice,
     because of your judgments, O God.
9 For you, O LORD, are most high over all the earth;
     you are exalted far above all gods.
10 The LORD loves those who hate evil,
     guards the lives of the faithful
     and rescues them from the hand of the wicked.
11 Light dawns for the righteous,
     and joy for the upright in heart.
12 Rejoice in the LORD, O you righteous,
     and give thanks to God's holy name!   **R**

Psalm 98

Psalm 98:1
David Goodrich

RESPONSE

Sing a new song to the Lord, who has done such mar-vel-ous things.

R

1   O sing to the LORD a new song,
for the Lord has done marvelous things.
God's right hand and holy arm
have gotten the victory.

2   **The LORD has declared victory,
and has revealed vindication in the sight of the nations.**

3   The Lord has remembered steadfast love and faithfulness
to the house of Israel.
**All the ends of the earth have seen
the victory of our God.   R**

4   Make a joyful noise to the LORD, all the earth;
break forth into joyous song and sing praises.

5   Sing praises to the LORD with the lyre,
with the lyre and the sound of melody.

6   **With trumpets and the sound of the horn
make a joyful noise before the LORD who reigns.   R**

7   Let the sea roar, and all that fills it;
the world and those who live in it.

8   Let the floods clap their hands;
let the hills sing together for joy

9   **at the presence of the LORD,
who is coming to judge the earth.
The Lord will judge the world with righteousness,
and the peoples with equity.   R**

Psalm 99:1–5, 9

"A Dios Den Gracias los Pueblos," adapt.
Arr. Jack Fox

RESPONSE

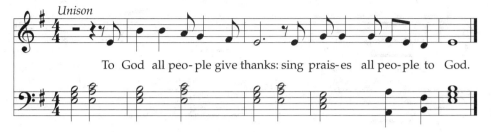

To God all peo-ple give thanks: sing prais-es all peo-ple to God.

R

1 The LORD reigns; let the peoples tremble!
   The LORD sits enthroned upon the cherubim;
   let the earth quake!
2 The LORD is great in Zion,
   and is exalted over all the peoples.
3 **Let them praise your great and awesome name.**
   Holy is the LORD!   R

4 Mighty Ruler, lover of justice,
   you have established equity;
   you have executed justice
   and righteousness in Jacob.
5 Extol the LORD our God;
   worship at God's footstool.
   Holy is the LORD!
9 **Extol the LORD our God,**
   and worship at God's holy mountain;
   for the LORD our God is holy.   R

Psalm 100

Psalm 100:1, 4
Larry Sivis

RESPONSE

Sing for joy. Give thanks and bless God's name.

R

1 Make a joyful noise to the LORD, all the earth.
2 **Serve the LORD with gladness;**
   come into God's presence with singing.
3 Know that the LORD is God.
   It is God who made us, to whom we belong;
   we are God's people, and the sheep of God's pasture. **R**

4 Enter God's gates with thanksgiving,
   and God's courts with praise.
   Give thanks and bless God's name.
5 For the LORD is good;
   God's steadfast love endures forever,
   God's faithfulness to all generations. **R**

Psalm 103:1–5, 11–18

Andraé Crouch

RESPONSE

Bless the Lord, O my soul, and all that is with-

in me, bless God's ho - ly name.

R
1 Bless the LORD, O my soul,
        and all that is within me,
        bless God's holy name.
2 **Bless the LORD, O my soul,**
        and do not forget all God's benefits—
3 who forgives all your iniquity,
        who heals all your diseases,
4 who redeems your life from the Pit,
        who crowns you with steadfast love and mercy,
5 **who satisfies you with good as long as you live**
        so that your youth is renewed like the eagle's.   R

11 For as the heavens are high above the earth,
        so great is God's steadfast love toward those who are faithful;
12 **as far as the east is from the west,**
        so far God removes our transgressions from us.
13 As a father has compassion for his children,
        so the LORD has compassion for the faithful.
14 **For God knows how we were made,**
        and remembers that we are dust.   R

15 As for mortals, their days are like grass;
        they flourish like a flower of the field;
16 **for the wind passes over it, and it is gone,**
        and its place knows it no more.
17 But the steadfast love of the LORD is from everlasting to everlasting
        on those who are faithful,
        and God's righteousness to the children's children,
18 **to those who keep God's covenant**
        and remember to do God's commandments.   R

Psalm 104:1–13

Joachim Neander; tr. Catherine Winkworth, alt.
Erneuerten Gesangbuch

RESPONSE

Praise be to God the Al- might- y, who rules all cre - a - tion.

R

¹ Bless the LORD, O my soul.
  O God, you are very great.
  You are clothed with honor and majesty,
²   wrapped in light as with a garment.
  You stretch out the heavens like a tent,
³   **you set the beams of your chambers on the waters,**
  you make the clouds your chariot,
     you ride on the wings of the wind,
⁴ **you make the winds your messengers,**
     fire and flame your ministers.   **R**

⁵ You set the earth on its foundations,
     so that it shall never be shaken.
⁶ **You cover it with the deep as with a garment;**
     the waters stood above the mountains.
⁷ At your rebuke they flee;
     at the sound of your thunder they take to flight.
⁸ They rose up to the mountains, ran down to the valleys
     to the place that you appointed for them.
⁹ **You set a boundary that they may not pass,**
     so that they might not again cover the earth.   **R**

¹⁰ You make springs gush forth in the valleys;
     they flow between the hills,
¹¹ **giving drink to every wild animal;**
     the wild asses quench their thirst.
¹² By the streams the birds of the air have their habitation;
     they sing among the branches.
¹³ **From your lofty abode you water the mountains;**
     the earth is satisfied with the fruit of your work.   **R**

Psalm 107:1–9, 33–43

James Weldon Johnson
J. Rosamond Johnson

RESPONSE

Lift ev - ery voice and sing, till earth and heav - en ring. Let them re - sound loud as the roll - ing sea.

R

1 O give thanks to the LORD, who is good;
    whose steadfast love endures forever.
2 **Let the redeemed of the LORD say so,**
    those redeemed from trouble
3 and gathered in from the lands,
    from the east and from the west,
    from the north and from the south.
4 Some wandered in desert wastes,
    finding no way to an inhabited town;
5 **hungry and thirsty,**
    their soul fainted within them.
6 Then they cried to the LORD,
    who delivered them from their distress;
7 **and led them by a straight way,**
    until they reached an inhabited town.
8 Let them thank the LORD for steadfast love,
    for wonderful works to humankind.
9 **For the LORD satisfies the thirsty,**
    and fills the hungry with good things. **R**

(Continued on following page)

³³ The LORD turns rivers into a desert,
   springs of water into thirsty ground,
³⁴ a fruitful land into a salty waste,
   because of the wickedness of its inhabitants.
³⁵ The LORD turns a desert into pools of water,
   a parched land into springs of water.
³⁶ And there the LORD lets the hungry live,
   and they establish a town to live in;
³⁷ they sow fields, and plant vineyards,
   and get a fruitful yield.
³⁸ They multiply greatly by the blessing of the LORD,
   who does not let their cattle decrease.
³⁹ When they are diminished and brought low
   through oppression, trouble, and sorrow,
⁴⁰ the LORD pours contempt on despots
   and makes them wander in trackless wastes,
⁴¹ but raises up the needy out of distress,
   and makes their families like flocks.
⁴² The upright see it and are glad;
   and all wickedness stops its mouth.
⁴³ Let those who are wise give heed to these things,
   and consider the steadfast love of the LORD.   **R**

Psalm 116:1–9, 12–17

Psalm 116:13–14, adapt.
David L. Edwards; arr. Charlotte Quarles

R

1   I love the LORD, who has heard
      my voice and my supplications.
2   **Because you listened to me,**
      I will call on you as long as I live.
3   The snares of death encompassed me;
        the pangs of Sheol laid hold on me;
        I suffered distress and anguish.
4   **Then I called on the name of the LORD:**
      "O LORD, I pray, save my life!"
5   Gracious is the LORD, and righteous;
        our God is merciful.
6   **The LORD protects the simple;**
      when I was brought low, God saved me.
7   Return, O my soul, to your rest,
      for the LORD has dealt bountifully with you.
8   For you have delivered my soul from death,
        my eyes from tears,
        my feet from stumbling.
9   **I walk before the LORD**
      in the land of the living.   R

12   What shall I return to the LORD
        for all God's bounty to me?
13   **I will lift up the cup of salvation**
      and call on the name of the LORD,
14   I will pay my vows to the LORD
        in the presence of all God's people.
15   **Precious in the sight of the LORD**
      is the death of the faithful.
16   O LORD, I am your servant;
        I am your servant, the child of your handmaid.
        You have loosed my bonds.
17   **I will offer to you a thanksgiving sacrifice**
      and call on the name of the LORD.   R

Psalm 118:1–4, 14–17, 21–24

Martin Rinkart; tr. Catherine Winkworth
Johann Crüger; harm. Felix Mendelssohn

RESPONSE

Now thank we all our God, with heart and hands and voic - es.

R

1   O give thanks to the LORD, who is good,
    whose steadfast love endures forever!

2   Let Israel say,
    "God's steadfast love endures forever."

3   Let the house of Aaron say,
    "God's steadfast love endures forever."

4   Let those who fear the LORD say,
    "God's steadfast love endures forever."   **R**

14   The LORD is my strength and my might;
     the LORD has become my salvation.

15   There are glad songs of victory in the tents of the righteous:
     "The right hand of the LORD does valiantly;

16   **the right hand of the LORD is exalted;**
         the right hand of the LORD does valiantly."

17   I shall not die, but I shall live,
     and recount the deeds of the LORD.   **R**

21   I thank you that you have answered me
     and have become my salvation.

22   **The stone that the builders rejected**
     has become the chief cornerstone.

23   This is the LORD's doing;
     it is marvelous in our eyes.

24   **This is the day that the LORD has made;**
     let us rejoice and be glad in it.   **R**

Psalm 119:1–8

Amy Grant (Ps. 119:105)
Michael W. Smith; arr. Keith Phillips

RESPONSE

Thy word is a lamp un-to my feet and a light un-to my path.

    R

1 Happy are those whose way is blameless,
     who walk in the law of God.

2 **Happy are those who keep God's decrees,**
     who seek God with their whole heart,

3 who also do no wrong,
     but walk in God's ways.

4 **You have commanded your precepts**
     to be kept diligently.   R

5 O that my ways may be steadfast
     in keeping your statutes!

6 **Then I shall not be put to shame,**
     having my eyes fixed on all your commandments.

7 I will praise you with an upright heart,
     when I learn your righteous ordinances.

8 **I will observe your statutes;**
     do not utterly forsake me.   R

Psalm 121

Jane Marshall

RESPONSE

My help comes from God, the Ma-ker of earth and sky.

R

1 I lift up my eyes to the hills—
from where will my help come?

2 **My help comes from the LORD,**
who made heaven and earth.

3 The LORD will not let your foot be moved;
the LORD who keeps you will not slumber.

4 **The One who keeps Israel**
will neither slumber nor sleep.   R

5 The LORD is your keeper;
the LORD is your shade at your right hand.

6 **The sun shall not strike you by day,**
nor the moon by night.

7 The LORD will keep you from all evil;
he will keep your life.

8 **The LORD will keep**
your going out and your coming in
from this time on and forevermore.   R

Psalm 122

Leona von Brethorst
Arr. Ken Barker

R

¹ I was glad when they said to me,
"Let us go to the house of the Lord!"
² **Our feet are standing
within your gates, O Jerusalem.**
³ Jerusalem—built as a city
that is bound firmly together.
⁴ **To it the tribes go up,
the tribes of the Lord,
as was decreed for Israel,
to give thanks to the name of the Lord.**
⁵ For there the thrones for judgment were set up,
the thrones of the house of David.
⁶ Pray for the peace of Jerusalem:
"May they prosper who love you.
⁷ **Peace be within your walls,
and security within your towers."**
⁸ For the sake of my relatives and friends
I will say, "Peace be within you."
⁹ **For the sake of the house of the Lord our God,
I will seek your good.   R**

Psalm 130

David Goodrich
Gary Chamberlain

RESPONSE

From the depths I cry to you; God, lis-ten to my voice.

R
1   Out of the depths I cry to you, O Lord.
2   **Lord, hear my voice!**
    Let your ears be attentive
        to the voice of my supplications!
3   **If you, O Lord, should mark iniquities,**
        Lord, who could stand?
4   But there is forgiveness with you,
        so that you may be revered.
5   **I wait for you, my soul waits,**
        and in your word I hope.   R

6   My soul waits for the Lord
        more than those who watch for the morning,
        more than those who watch for the morning.
7   O Israel, hope in the Lord!
        For with the Lord there is steadfast love,
        and with God is great power to redeem.
8   **It is God who will redeem Israel**
        from all its iniquities.   R

Psalm 131

RESPONSE 1

John Greenleaf Whittier
Frederick C. Maker, alt.

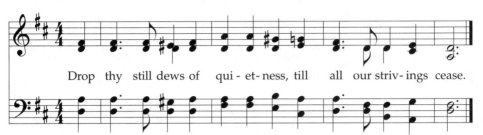

Drop thy still dews of qui - et - ness, till all our striv - ings cease.

RESPONSE 2

Edwin Markham, alt.
Edward Dearle, alt.

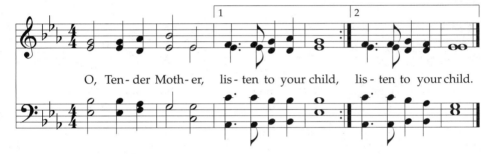

O, Ten - der Moth - er, lis - ten to your child, lis - ten to your child.

R

1. O God, my heart is not lifted up,
   my eyes are not raised too high;
   I do not occupy myself with things
   too great and too marvelous for me.
2. But I have calmed and quieted my soul,
   like a weaned child with its mother;
   my soul within me is like a weaned child.
3. **O Israel, hope in God**
   from this time on and forevermore.   R

Psalm 133

RESPONSE 1

Anonymous
Finnish folk melody; harm. David Evans

U - nite us, God, u - nite   us in your ev-er-last-ing love.

Pablo Sosa; tr. George Lockwood
Pablo Sosa; arr. Alvin Schutmaat

RESPONSE 2

Unison   C   F   G   C

¡Mi - ren qué bue - no,   qué bue - no   es!
O   look and won - der, how good it is!

R

1 How very good and pleasant it is
    when kindred live together in unity!
2 **It is like the precious oil on the head,**
    running down upon the beard,
  on the beard of Aaron,
    running down over the collar of his robes.
3 It is like the dew of Hermon,
    which falls on the mountains of Zion.
  For there God ordained a blessing:
    life forevermore!   **R**

Harm. Response 1 used by permission of Oxford University Press;
  Response 2 © Cancionero Abierto, Buenos Aires, Argentina

Psalm 139:1–12

Psalm 139:23
Martin Luther; adapt. Carlton R. Young

RESPONSE

Search me, O God, and know my heart.

R

1 O God, you have searched me and known me.
2 **You know when I sit down and when I rise up;**
you discern my thoughts from far away.
3 You search out my path and my lying down,
and are acquainted with all my ways.
4 **Even before a word is on my tongue,**
you know it completely.
5 You hem me in, behind and before,
and lay your hand upon me.
6 **Such knowledge is too wonderful for me;**
it is so high that I cannot attain it.   R

7 Where can I go from your spirit?
Or where can I flee from your presence?
8 **If I ascend to heaven, you are there;**
if I make my bed in Sheol, you are there.
9 If I take the wings of the morning
and settle at the farthest limits of the sea,
10 **even there your hand shall lead me,**
and your right hand shall hold me fast.
11 If I say, "Surely the darkness shall cover me,
and the light around me become night,"
12 **even the darkness is not dark to you;**
the night is as bright as the day,
for darkness is as light to you.   R

Psalm 146

Luke 6:20, adapt.
French carol melody; harm. *The English Hymnal*

RESPONSE

Bless-ed are the poor and need-y, for God's jus-tice sure-ly is theirs.

R

1   Praise the LORD!
        Praise the LORD, O my soul!
2   **I will praise the LORD as long as I live;**
        I will sing praises to my God all my life long.
3   Do not put your trust in rulers,
        in mortals, in whom there is no help.
4   **When their breath departs, they return to the earth;**
        on that very day their plans perish.
5   Happy are those whose help is the God of Israel,
        whose hope is in the LORD their God,
6   who made heaven and earth,
        the sea, and all that is in them;
    who keeps faith forever;
7   **who executes justice for the oppressed;**
        who gives food to the hungry.   R

    The LORD sets the prisoners free;
8   and opens the eyes of the blind.
    The LORD lifts up those who are bowed down,
        and loves the righteous.
9   The LORD watches over the strangers,
        and upholds the orphan and the widow,
        but brings to ruin the way of the wicked.
10 **The LORD will reign forever,**
        your God, O Zion, for all generations.
    Praise the LORD!   R

Psalm 147:1–6

Charles Wesley
Robert Williams; harm. Carlton R. Young

RESPONSE

Praise to God who reigns a - bove; Al - le - lu - ia!

R

1   Praise the LORD!
     How good it is to sing praises to our God;
          for he is gracious, and a song of praise is fitting.
2   **The LORD builds up Jerusalem,**
          and gathers the outcasts of Israel.
3   God heals the brokenhearted,
          and binds up their wounds.
4   **God determines the number of the stars,**
          and gives to all of them their names.
5   Great is our Lord, and abundant in power;
          whose understanding is beyond measure.
6   **The LORD lifts up the downtrodden,**
          but casts the wicked to the ground.   R

Psalm 150

Charles Wesley
Henry T. Smart

RESPONSE

Al - le-lu- ia!   Al - le-lu- ia! Praise the Lord re - joice and sing!

> R
>
> 1   Praise God!
>   Praise God in the sanctuary;
>   **praise God in the mighty firmament!**
> 2   Praise God for mighty deeds;
>   **praise God for exceeding greatness!**
> 3   Praise God with trumpet sound;
>   **praise God with lute and harp!**
> 4   Praise God with tambourine and dance;
>   **praise God with strings and pipe!**
> 5   Praise God with clanging cymbals;
>   **praise God with loud clashing cymbals!**
> 6   Let everything that breathes praise God!
>   **Praise God!   R**

An Order for the Lord's Supper with Those Confined

CALL TO WORSHIP

Gathered as a portion of Christ's church, Jesus reminds us of his promise:

> "For where two or three are gathered in my name,
> I am there among them."

We particularly treasure the Lord's Supper in which Christ is made known to us in the breaking of bread. Through sharing of bread and wine in thankful remembrance, we experience afresh the assurance of God's great love and kindness in Christ Jesus. Sustained and nourished within the body of Christ by these emblems, we confidently entrust ourselves to God's future filled with hope and promise.

READING OF SCRIPTURE

An appropriate scripture may be read and briefly applied to particular circumstances. Possible choices include:

> Comfort: Isaiah 40:1–11; 2 Corinthians 1:3–7
> God's Care: Psalms 23, 27, 103
> Promises: Matthew 11:28–30; John 3:16–17
> Help in Trouble: Psalms 46, 91, 121; Romans 8:31–39
> Time of Anxiety: Psalms 37:1–11; Matthew 6:25–34
> Repentance and Confession: Psalm 51; 1 John 5:14–15
> Christian Love: 1 Corinthians 13
> Growth in Grace: Ephesians 3:13–21; Philippians 3:7–14

WORDS OF INSTITUTION

We recall that the Lord Jesus on the night when he was betrayed took a loaf of bread, and when he had given thanks, he broke it and said, "This is my body that is for you. Do this in remembrance of me." In the same way he took the cup also, after supper, saying, "This cup is the new covenant in my blood. Do this, as often as you drink it, in remembrance of me." For as often as you eat this bread and drink the cup, you proclaim the Lord's death until he comes.

COMMUNION PRAYER

The prayer or prayers of thanksgiving and remembrance may be spoken freely or given as follows:

Our gracious God, we thank you for loving the world into existence and sustaining all of life by your goodness. With gratitude we recall that you revealed yourself through prophets and teachers and most fully in the life, death, and resurrection of Jesus, our Lord and Savior. Through the power of your Spirit, let us know afresh the joy of Christ's living presence, the strength to face every circumstance of life, and the knowledge that nothing can ever separate us from your love. Amen.

PARTAKING OF BREAD AND CUP

Being sensitive to the communicant's condition, one or both elements may be served in whatever manner is deemed fitting. If partaking is impossible, touch the elements to the lips in an act of intention, giving assurance of Christ's presence.

SERVING BREAD AND CUP

Sharing the bread, say:

> The body of Christ,
> the bread of heaven.

Or: Take and eat this in remembrance that
Christ died for you, and be thankful.

Sharing the cup, say:

> The blood of Christ,
> the cup of salvation.

Or: Drink this in remembrance that Christ's blood
was shed for you, and be thankful.

BENEDICTION

> May God bless you and keep you.
> May God's face shine upon you
> and be gracious to you.
> May God look upon you with kindness
> and give you peace. Amen.

Basic Resources
for Sunday Worship

To assist worship leaders in their responsibilities, examples are given of ways to express the various elements in a worship service. Additional resources will be found throughout the hymnal and are indexed for easy reference.

GREETING

> O come, let us sing to our God;
> > let us make a joyful noise to the rock of our salvation!
> We come, O God, into your presence with thanksgiving,
> > rejoicing with songs of praise! (Psalm 95:1–2)

> *Or:*

> Friends in Christ,
> we are gathered to give thanks
> for all we have received from God's good hands:
> to praise God's holy name;
> to acknowledge and confess our sins;
> to hear God's holy word;
> and to ask those things needful for life.
> Let us draw near to God in all humility
> and celebrate God's infinite goodness and mercy.

OPENING PRAYER

> Gracious God, gentle in your power and strong in your tenderness,
> you have brought us forth from the womb of your being
> and breathed into us the breath of life.
> We know that we do not live by bread alone
> but by every word that comes from you.
> Feed our deep hungers with the living bread
> that you give us in Jesus Christ.
> May Jesus' promise, "Where two or three are gathered in my name,
> there am I in the midst of them," be fulfilled in us.
> Through the Holy Spirit, make us a joyful company of your people
> so that with the faithful in every place and time
> we may praise and honor you, God Most High. Amen.

> *Or:*

> Almighty God, we come seeking you
> in the midst of our joy and our brokenness,

as individuals and as a community.
Move among us during this hour of worship.
By the power of your Holy Spirit,
turn us from our foolishness to your truth
in our thoughts, prayers, and songs and in all our living.
For we pray in the name of Jesus Christ. Amen.

Or a Confession of Sins:

Most merciful God, we humbly admit that we need your help.
We confess that we have wandered from your way:
we have done wrong, and we have failed to do what is right.
You alone can save us.
Have mercy on us:
wipe out our sins and teach us to forgive others.
Bring forth in us the fruit of the Spirit
that we may live as disciples of Christ.
This we ask in the name of Jesus our Savior. Amen.

CALL TO DISCIPLESHIP

Believe the good news of God's abounding love in Jesus Christ. Persons desiring to make their confession of faith in Christ and be baptized into his body, or to transfer membership to this congregation, or to renew their Christian commitment, may come forward as the congregation sings a hymn of dedication.

Upon welcoming persons by name, ask them individually to affirm (or upon transfer of membership, to reconfirm) the church's faith:

Do you believe that Jesus is the Christ, the Son of the living God,
and do you accept him as Lord and Savior?

Or:

Do you believe in Jesus the Christ, born of God in the Spirit,
and do you accept Christ as your Sovereign and Savior?

Or:

Do you believe in Jesus the Christ, Word of the living God,
and do you commit yourself to the way of Christ,
through the grace of God and the power of the Holy Spirit?

PRAYERS OF THE PEOPLE

Leader: Be mindful, O Lord, of us your people who are present
together here in this place, and
of those who are absent
through age, frailty, or sickness.

Left:	We commend the children to your care,
Right:	the young to your guidance,
Left:	the married to your enriching,
Right:	the aged to your support,
Left:	the faint-hearted to your strengthening power,
Right:	the scattered to your shepherd's love, and
Left:	the wandering to your call to repent and be forgiven.
Leader:	Journey with all travelers; help the bereaved; release the addicted; heal the sick.
Left:	Bring assurance to all who are passing through trouble, need, or anxiety.
Right:	Remember for good all who love us, those who care nothing for us, and those who have asked us (unworthy as we are) to pray for them.
Leader:	There are surely some whom we have forgotten, but you, Lord, will surely remember them;
All:	For you are the Helper of the helpless, the Saver of the lost, the Refuge for the wanderer, and the Healer of the sick. Since you know each one's need, and hear every prayer, we commend each one to your merciful grace and your everlasting love. Grant to us that together we may praise your great name, now and for ever. Amen.

THE INVITATION TO COMMUNION

This is the Lord's Table and Christ invites you to share this meal of grace.
Christ recognizes you and looks upon you with favor.
Christ befriends you and wants you within his circle.
Count yourself among Christ's disciples
by partaking in this feast of fellowship.

OFFERTORY SENTENCE

Let us present with joy our offerings of commitment and support
for the work of Christ's church.

OFFERTORY PRAYER

Wondrous Creator, you provide for our strength and gladness through the privilege of human creativity and labor. You supply all that is needful to bring forth bread and drink from the earth. With grateful hearts we offer you these signs of our work and this bread and wine, that you may use them all to glorify your name in us and in all creation. Amen.

PRAYERS AT THE TABLE

When only one prayer is offered:

With grateful hearts, O God, we come to Christ's Table:
remembering that you spoke creation into existence and
pronounced it good;
remembering that you called servants to make your word known
and declared your reign;
remembering that you effected salvation through Jesus Christ
and reconciled us to you.
Be known to us now, through the gift of your Spirit,
in the breaking of bread and the drinking of cup:
renew your image within us;
restore our trust in your love;
refresh our spirits for caring service.
Join us with all your people everywhere in joyous praise for your
everlasting love.

Or:

Prayer over the Bread

With grateful hearts, O God, we remember the gift of your love in Jesus Christ, who for our sakes was broken that we may be made whole. Bind us together in Christian love. Grant that Christ may be made known afresh to us in the breaking of this bread. Empower us with your Spirit so to eat of this bread that we are sustained to share bread with all the world.

Prayer over the Cup

We celebrate with all your people, O God, the sacrificial gift of Jesus Christ whose life was poured out for many for the forgiveness of sins. As we partake of your cup of salvation, may we receive it as from the hand of Christ who loves us as we are, and bids us share his eternal fellowship. Receive us. Renew us. Refresh us. Fill us with the joy of your Spirit.

WORDS OF INSTITUTION AND BREAKING OF THE BREAD

Let us recall "that the Lord Jesus on the night when he was betrayed took a loaf of bread, and when he had given thanks, he broke it and said, 'This is my body that is broken for you. Do this in remembrance of me.' In the same way he took the cup also, after supper, saying, 'This cup is the new covenant in my blood. Do this, as often as you drink it, in remembrance of me.' For as often as you eat this bread and drink the cup, you proclaim the Lord's death until he comes" *(1 Corinthians 11:23–26, NRSV).*

LORD'S PRAYER

Or:

Our Father, who art in heaven,
    hallowed be thy Name,
    thy kingdom come,
    thy will be done,
       on earth as it is in heaven.
Give us this day our daily bread.
And forgive us our sins,
    as we forgive those
      who sin against us.
And lead us not into temptation,
    but deliver us from evil.
For thine is the kingdom,
    and the power, and the glory,
    for ever and ever. Amen.

Our Father in heaven,
    hallowed be your Name,
    your kingdom come,
    your will be done,
       on earth as in heaven.
Give us today our daily bread.
Forgive us our sins
    as we forgive those
      who sin against us.
Save us from the time of trial,
    and deliver us from evil.
For the kingdom, the power,
    and the glory are yours,
    now and for ever. Amen.

PASSING OF THE PEACE

As the risen Christ greeted his beloved disciples with the greeting, "Peace be with you," let us now turn and greet one another in mutual love.

PRAYER AFTER COMMUNION

O God, we thank you for uniting us by baptism in the body of Christ
    and by this meal filling us with joy and hope.
Grant that in the days ahead
    our lips which have sung your praises may speak the truth,
    our eyes which have seen your love may look with compassion
      on the needs of the world,
    our hands which have held this loaf and cup
      may be active in your service.
We ask it in the name of Jesus Christ. Amen.

BENEDICTION

May God bless you and keep you.
May God's face shine upon you and be gracious to you.
May God look upon you with kindness and give you peace. Amen.

Or:

COMMISSIONING/ BENEDICTION

Go forth into the world to serve God with gladness;
be of good courage; hold fast to that which is good;
render to no one evil for evil; strengthen the fainthearted;
support the weak; help the afflicted;
honor all people; love and serve God,
rejoicing in the power of the Holy Spirit.

The grace of Jesus Christ, the love of God,
and the communion of the Holy Spirit be with you all. Amen.

Daily Worship

A Three-Year Cycle of Daily Devotion
Prepared by Colbert S. Cartwright

INTRODUCTION

To grow as Christians we need a disciplined awareness of the loving God in daily living. God is always present with us, but becomes alive and real for us only as we consciously attend to God's Spirit in our hearts and world. Too often we center our lives upon God on Sunday but make little vital connection between that God and what we do in the thick of daily living. Consciousness of the Divine can illumine our daily existence with the reality of God and a transforming awareness of self, neighbor, and world. This is the life of Christian faith.

Setting aside a brief time each day to praise God, to invite God afresh to be with us during the day, to feed on Holy Scripture, and open our hearts to God in prayer, helps us grow in faith and life. We can do this either individually or in a larger setting.

Such a daily discipline need not be lengthy or burdensome. Rather, the approach should be one of lighthearted earnestness, seeking to be authentically in touch with God. Although a suggested outline is given, it need not always be followed through to the end. When the spark of God's Spirit kindles and warms our hearts, our objective has been fulfilled. St. Teresa of Avila suggests that too often a Christian seeks to kindle the divine spark by collecting wood, driving oneself crazy with blowing on the fire and rearranging the wood, yet all one's efforts only put out the fire more and more. The object is not to follow a prescribed discipline or set order but to be in touch with God.

Each day's discipline may include these elements:

1. Attending to God.
2. Praising God Through Use of a Hymn of the Day
3. Praying a Psalm of the Week, Seeking to Make It Our Own
4. Reading and Meditating upon a Scripture Passage
5. Formulating a Thought or Prayer for the Day
6. Praying to God

The first three acts could be done aloud so as to hear them more forcefully. Here are some guidelines for following this discipline.

1. **Attending to God.** This may be as simple as alerting ourselves to God's presence. It may be stimulated by a call to worship such as:

> O God, you are my God, I seek you,
> my soul thirsts for you;
> my flesh faints for you,
> as in a dry and weary land where there is no water.

So I have looked upon you in the sanctuary,
    beholding your power and glory.
Because your steadfast love is better than life,
    my lips will praise you.   —Psalm 63:1–3, NRSV

2. **Praising God Through Use of a Hymn of the Day.** Worship is primarily centering upon God. We start with attending to God and not by focusing upon ourselves. Our purpose in worship is to focus upon God so that God's love rebounds back to inscribe God's image upon our lives. In loving God, God's love enters our hearts to make us more loving. As Saint Augustine said, "One loving spirit sets another on fire." A hymn of the day is assigned by number according to this hymnal's listings. It may be sung or read.

3. **Praying a Psalm of the Week, Seeking to Make It Our Own.** The Psalms express to God the heartfelt feelings of the people of God in all the diverse circumstances of life. Sometimes they are extravagant with praise; at other times they are filled with complaints and supplications. Always, they are fully human in honest dialogue with the God of steadfast but severe mercy. The Psalms poetically enable us to express ourselves honestly before God.

The daily discipline over a three-year period includes the reading of nearly all the psalms. Some readings have been reduced in length to accommodate daily usage.

We read the psalm of the week each day, letting it grow in familiarity till at week's end we know it well, perhaps by memory.

4. **Reading and Meditating upon a Scripture Passage.** In some vital sense God speaks to the believer through Holy Scripture. Through encounter with these human words, persons of faith hear God's voice. This divine word often reassures, but also convicts and converts.

The daily discipline over the three-year period includes the reading of the entire New Testament. Each year centers upon one of the four Gospels—Mark and John being combined in the second year. This focusing upon the Gospels is intended to emphasize that Christians first know God through Jesus the Christ. When we speak of attending to God within our lives, we do this in the knowledge that it is Christ, the fullness of God, who dwells within us. In all that we do we seek to have the mind of Christ.

For Christians the Hebrew Scriptures are a vital heritage that speaks of God's dealing with Israel long before Jesus Christ was born. Therefore, classic passages from these scriptures are utilized in alternate weeks with the New Testament. They testify to the mighty deeds of God as well as furnish us with rich spiritual food.

The scriptural materials are presented consecutively so as to maintain continuity of thought. In order to include the entire New Testament, the Old Testament passages have been limited in number but not to the degree of diminishing their richness. The verses are numbered as they appear in the New Revised Standard Version of the Holy Bible.

5. **Formulating a Thought or Prayer for the Day.** This formulation is at the heart of daily disciplined worship. In reading the hymn, the psalm, and the scripture, we do so with the thought in mind of hearing a special word from God for each day. We may capture a thought, a phrase, a promise, an affirmation, a supplication, or a prayer—something we can hold easily in mind and heart for the day. It will be God's word to call to mind as we walk along each day's journey of life.

Some days the word will come quickly and we do not necessarily need to complete all the reading. At other times we may want to read the same passage over several times till we sense a word from God. Often our thoughts will be shaped by the particular issues of life facing us that day.

Here is an example of how such formulations are made: Look at Year A, 3rd Week, Friday. The daily hymn is "Help Us Accept Each Other (Kaan)." The psalm is 40:1–10. The daily scripture is Matthew 5:43–48.

From the hymn of the day we may choose to formulate a phrase such as:

- Help us accept each other as Christ accepted us.
- Help me to do the truth in love.
- Grant, O God, that I may practice your acceptance, until I know by heart the table of forgiveness and laughter's healing art.

Or from the reading of the psalm we might formulate a phrase such as:

- O Lord, put a new song in my mouth, a song of praise to you.
- I delight to do your will, O my God.
- Let me not conceal your steadfast love, O God, from those I meet.

From the passage in Matthew we could formulate some words such as:

- Christ, let me love my enemies today and pray for those who misuse me.
- Praise be to you, O God, for sending the rain on the just and the unjust.
- God let me know what this means: "You, therefore, must be perfect, as your heavenly Father is perfect."

Those having trouble remembering their formulation may want to write it down on a piece of paper and refer to it during the day. The words could be posted on a mirror for easy reference.

6. **Praying to God.** This prayer can take many forms: thanking God for the gift of the day; asking God's blessing upon friends and loved ones; asking divine help for someone in difficult circumstances; seeking strength and wisdom for the specific tasks of the day; making intercession on behalf of the weak and dispossessed; and offering supplication for peace and justice in the world.

The purpose of such worship is to enter into an intimacy with God. Prayer is talking with God as friend to friend. We respond to God's friendship through trusting affection, open honesty to the one whose love for us is unbreakable, and thoughtful reflection upon the marvels of being embraced by such love. Our desire is for God and to know more fully God's Messiah, Jesus, who is for us the Way, the Truth, and the Life. Ultimately, our gaze is directed toward God who ever graces us with glimpses of unbounded love.

Year A

Matthew, Genesis—Esther, Jude, Romans, Galatians, Ephesians,
1 and 2 Thessalonians, 1 and 2 Timothy, Titus, Philippians, 2 Peter, Colossians

		Psalm for Week	Sunday	Monday
1st Week	Scripture	91	MT 1:1—2:12	3:1–12
	Hymn		144	142
2nd Week	Scripture	8	GEN 1:1–27	1:28—2:4
	Hymn		64	690
3rd Week	Scripture	40:1–10	MT 5:13–20	5:21–26
	Hymn		478	487
4th Week	Scripture	105:1–15	GEN 8:6–12	8:20—9:17
	Hymn		631	288
5th Week	Scripture	17	MT 6:5–15	6:16–21
	Hymn		575	173
6th Week	Scripture	143	GEN 18:16, 22–33	21:1–7
	Hymn		73	244
7th Week	Scripture	29	MT 7:15–20	7:21–28
	Hymn		439	537
8th Week	Scripture	4	GEN 32:22–32	37:12–36
	Hymn		13	512
9th Week	Scripture	6	MT 9:1–8	9:9–13
	Hymn		431	233
10th Week	Scripture	77	EX 2:11–23	3:1–12
	Hymn		467	666
11th Week	Scripture	119:73–88	MT 10:26–33	10:34–39
	Hymn		82	559
12th Week	Scripture	78:1–8	EX 15:1–18	15:19–21
	Hymn		215	13
13th Week	Scripture	1	MT 12:15–21	12:22–32
	Hymn		700	244
14th Week	Scripture	138	EX 32:1–24	LEV 19:1–2, 9–18
	Hymn		249	572
15th Week	Scripture	119:1–16	MT 13:24–30	13:31–43
	Hymn		595	77
16th Week	Scripture	7	DEUT 4:32–40	6:1–9
	Hymn		725	362
17th Week	Scripture	104:24–35	MT 14:22–36	15:1–9
	Hymn		539	635
18th Week	Scripture	18:1–19	JOSH 20:1–9	JUDG 4:4–9
	Hymn		77	12

Tuesday	Wednesday	Thursday	Friday	Saturday
3:13–17 *248*	4:1–11 *180*	4:12–17 *540*	4:18–25 *337*	5:1–12 *573*
2:5–25 *254*	3:1–24 *556*	4:1–16 *512*	6:5–22 *679*	7:1–12 *58*
5:27–30 *619*	5:31–37 *568*	5:38–42 *242*	5:43–48 *487*	6:1–4 *719*
11:1–9 *681*	12:1–9 *489*	15:1–6 *542*	17:1–22 *24*	18:1–15 *552*
6:22–24 *669*	6:25–34 *354*	7:1–6 *579*	7:7–11 *302*	7:12–14 *173*
22:1–14 *86*	25:19–34 *306*	28:1–22 *577*	29:15–28 *330*	32:9–12 *276*
8:1–17 *503*	8:18–20 *344*	8:21–22 *474*	8:23–27 *629*	8:28–34 *247*
42:1–25 *3*	45:1–15 *500*	45:16—46:4 *576*	50:15–21 *620*	EX 2:1–10 *686*
9:14–17 *426*	9:18–34 *188*	9:35–38 *506*	10:1–15 *666*	10:16–25 *572*
3:13–15, 21–28 *12*	6:1–13 *663*	8:1–10 *630*	12:1–14 *228*	14:10–31 *632*
10:40–42 *424*	11:1–6 *403*	11:7–19 *168*	11:20–30 *353*	12:1–14 *584*
16:1–21 *419*	17:1–7 *559*	20:1–21 *594*	24:12–18 *333*	25:10–22 *502*
12:33–37 *265*	12:38–45 *215*	12:46–50 *486*	13:1–17 *586*	13:18–23 *289*
NUM 6:22–27 *446*	11:10–25 *86*	20:1–13 *622*	27:12–23 *454*	DEUT 4:1–9 *463*
13:44 *610*	13:45–53 *195*	13:54–58 *596*	14:1–12 *71*	14:13–21 *321*
8:11–18 *277*	18:15–22 *669*	26:1–11 *458*	30:15–20 *5*	34:1–12 *648*
15:10–20 *691*	15:21–31 *352*	15:32–39 *538*	16:1–12 *17*	16:13–20 *273*
11:29–40 *545*	16:23–31 *686*	RUTH 1:1–18 *420*	2:1–13 *714*	3:1–5; 4:13–17 *618*

YEAR A—WEEKS 19-35

		Psalm for Week	Sunday	Monday
19th Week	Scripture	131	MT 16:21–28	17:1–13
	Hymn		*344*	*595*
20th Week	Scripture	84	1 SAM 1:21—2:10	3:1–20
	Hymn		*285*	*452*
21st Week	Scripture	103:1–14	MT 18:15–22	18:23–35
	Hymn		*392*	*408*
22nd Week	Scripture	3	2 SAM 1:1, 17–27	5:1–12
	Hymn		*17*	*707*
23rd Week	Scripture	24	MT 21:1–11	21:12–27
	Hymn		*192*	*570*
24th Week	Scripture	105:1–10, 24–28	2 SAM 11:26—12:13	12:14–24
	Hymn		*21*	*265*
25th Week	Scripture	5	MT 22:34–46	23:1–12
	Hymn		*611*	*602*
26th Week	Scripture	9:1–11	1 K 3:16–28	8:22–43
	Hymn		*266*	*274*
27th Week	Scripture	46	MT 24:15–31	24:32–35
	Hymn		*65*	*676*
28th Week	Scripture	34	2 K 2:1–12	4:8–17
	Hymn		*643*	*53*
29th Week	Scripture	136:1–4, 10–26	MT 26:1–5	26:6–13
	Hymn		*86*	*188*
30th Week	Scripture	148	2 CHR 36:15–23	EZRA 3:8–13
	Hymn		*119*	*38*
31st Week	Scripture	26	MT 27:1–2	27:3–10
	Hymn		*576*	*274*
32nd Week	Scripture	14	ROM 1:1–7	1:8–17
	Hymn		*476*	*533*
33rd Week	Scripture	11	ROM 3:21–31	4:1–12
	Hymn		*610*	*537*
34th Week	Scripture	10:1–14	ROM 7:1–6	7:7–13
	Hymn		*381*	*253*
35th Week	Scripture	95	ROM 9:19–29	9:30—10:4
	Hymn		*20*	*280*

Tuesday	Wednesday	Thursday	Friday	Saturday
17:14–23	17:24–27	18:1–5	18:6–9	18:10–14
535	*69*	*431*	*511*	*69*
8:4–20	16:1–13	16:14–23	17:32–49	24:1–22
721	*135*	*7*	*554*	*632*
19:1–15	19:16–30	20:1–16	20:17–28	20:29–34
190	*132*	*23*	*490*	*20*
6:1–15	7:1–17	7:18–28	9:1–13	11:1–15
290	*584*	*552*	*383*	*608*
21:28–32	21:33–46	22:1–14	22:15–22	22:23–33
339	*275*	*665*	*720*	*228*
18:1–15	18:24–33	19:1–8	23:1–7	1 K 3:3–15
276	*639*	*502*	*138*	*464*
23:13–15	23:16–24	23:25–36	23:37–39	24:1–14
593	*633*	*287*	*83*	*484*
17:1–16	17:17–24	18:20–39	19:1–15	21:1–22
718	*598*	*634*	*594*	*140*
24:36–44	24:45–51	25:1–13	25:14–30	25:31–46
93	*383*	*586*	*695*	*183*
5:1–16	1 CHR 17:16–27	22:6–16	29:10–20	2 CHR 34:22–33
371	*289*	*275*	*382*	*686*
26:14–25	26:26–35	26:36–46	26:47–56	26:57–75
23	*408*	*196*	*724*	*350*
9:5–15	NEH 1:1–11	7:73b—8:12	ESTH 4:8–17	7:1–10; 9:20–22
22	*306*	*618*	*634*	*703*
27:11–26	27:27–44	27:45–56	27:57–66	28:1–20
208	*202*	*203*	*156*	*222*
1:18–32	2:1–16	2:17–29	3:1–8	3:9–20
59	*73*	*265*	*87*	*724*
4:13–25	5:1–11	5:12–21	6:1–14	6:15–23
216	*161*	*546*	*221*	*225*
7:14–25	8:1–17	8:18–30	8:31–39	9:1–18
546	*265*	*251*	*73*	*671*
10:5–21	11:1–10	11:11–24	11:25–32	11:33–36
308	*707*	*275*	*4*	*321*

YEAR A—WEEKS 36-52

		Psalm for Week	Sunday	Monday
36th Week	Scripture *Hymn*	115	ROM 12:1–8 *609*	12:9–21 *487*
37th Week	Scripture *Hymn*	117	ROM 15:1–6 *490*	15:7–13 *703*
38th Week	Scripture *Hymn*	113	GAL 1:1–10 *39*	1:11–24 *666*
39th Week	Scripture *Hymn*	43	GAL 3:19—4:7 *681*	4:8–20 *472*
40th Week	Scripture *Hymn*	53	EPH 1:1–2 *348*	1:3–14 *546*
41st Week	Scripture *Hymn*	102:1–12	EPH 4:1–16 *272*	4:17–24 *463*
42nd Week	Scripture *Hymn*	52	JUDE 1:1–2 *10*	1:3–4 *635*
43rd Week	Scripture *Hymn*	50:7–15	1 TH 1:1–10 *244*	2:1–8 *65*
44th Week	Scripture *Hymn*	76	1 TH 5:1–11 *497*	5:12–28 *517*
45th Week	Scripture *Hymn*	94:12–22	2 TH 3:6–18 *631*	1 TIM 1:1–11 *538*
46th Week	Scripture *Hymn*	128	1 TIM 6:1–10 *515*	6:11–21 *88*
47th Week	Scripture *Hymn*	119:137–144	2 TIM 3:1–9 *287*	3:10–17 *322*
48th Week	Scripture *Hymn*	85	2 PET 1:1–15 *644*	1:16–21 *105*
49th Week	Scripture *Hymn*	18:20–30	COL 1:1–10 *88*	1:11–14 *514*
50th Week	Scripture *Hymn*	28	COL 2:20–23 *77*	3:1–11 *390*
51st Week	Scripture *Hymn*	31:9–16	PHIL 1:3–11 *517*	1:12–18a *108*
52nd Week	Scripture *Hymn*	135:1–14	PHIL 3:2–11 *195*	3:12–16 *606*

Tuesday	Wednesday	Thursday	Friday	Saturday
13:1–7 *720*	13:8–10 *138*	13:11–14 *231*	14:1–12 *616*	14:13–23 *453*
15:14–29 *719*	15:30–33 *579*	16:1–16 *476*	16:17–23 *434*	16:25–27 *333*
2:1–10 *403*	2:11–14 *21*	2:15–21 *100*	3:1–14 *200*	3:15–18 *4*
4:21—5:1 *135*	5:2–15 *600*	5:16–21 *69*	5:22–26 *270*	6:1–18 *207*
1:15–23 *241*	2:1–10 *340*	2:11–22 *685*	3:1–13 *322*	3:14–21 *200*
4:25—5:2 *2*	5:3–20 *457*	5:21—6:9 *453*	6:10–20 *613*	6:21–23 *441*
1:5–7 *717*	1:8–13 *26*	1:14–16 *266*	1:17–23 *635*	1:24–25 *218*
2:9–16 *9*	2:17—3:5 *356*	3:6–13 *527*	4:1–12 *573*	4:13–18 *645*
2 TH 1:1–4 *576*	1:5–12 *118*	2:1–12 *476*	2:13–17 *542*	3:1–5 *88*
1:12–20 *66*	2:1–15 *345*	3:1–16 *259*	4:1–16 *690*	5:1–24 *450*
2 TIM 1:1–7 *379*	1:8–18 *454*	2:1–7 *613*	2:8–13 *550*	2:14–26 *618*
4:1–8 *478*	4:9–22 *276*	TIT 1:1–16 *514*	2:1–15 *62*	3:1–15 *365*
2:1–10a *250*	2:10b–22 *463*	3:1–7 *247*	3:8–13 *565*	3:14–18 *39*
1:15–20 *150*	1:21–23 *205*	1:24—2:5 *335*	2:6–7 *715*	2:8–19 *376*
3:12–17 *7*	3:18—4:1 *656*	4:2–6 *570*	4:7–18 *433*	PHIL 1:1–2 *461*
1:18b–30 *610*	2:1–11 *117*	2:12–13 *257*	2:14–18 *478*	2:19—3:1 *164*
3:17—4:1 *612*	4:2–7 *699*	4:8–9 *668*	4:10–20 *25*	4:21–23 *43*

Year B

Mark, John, Job—Ezekiel, 1 and 2 Corinthians

		Psalm for Week	Sunday	Monday
1st Week	Scripture	2	MK 1:1–8	1:9–11
	Hymn		121	176
2nd Week	Scripture	31:1–8	JOB 1:1a; 2:1–13	3:1–26
	Hymn		453	306
3rd Week	Scripture	32	MK 1:35–39	1:40–45
	Hymn		558	564
4th Week	Scripture	47	JOB 38:1–23; 40:1–2	40:6–14
	Hymn		59	12
5th Week	Scripture	147:1–11	MK 3:7–12	3:13–19a
	Hymn		672	357
6th Week	Scripture	118:1–18	PROV 4:1–18	6:16–22
	Hymn		596	500
7th Week	Scripture	56	MK 4:26–29	4:30–34
	Hymn		604	478
8th Week	Scripture	82	ECC 2:1–13	SONG 1:1–17
	Hymn		276	499
9th Week	Scripture	44:1–19	MK 6:6b–13	6:14–29
	Hymn		452	635
10th Week	Scripture	89:1–18	IS 6:1–8	9:1–7
	Hymn		666	673
11th Week	Scripture	119:89–104	MK 7:24–30	7:31–37
	Hymn		9	559
12th Week	Scripture	71:1–21	IS 26:16–19	28:23–29
	Hymn		645	714
13th Week	Scripture	6	MK 9:1–13	9:14–29
	Hymn		176	628
14th Week	Scripture	22	IS 35:1–10	40:1–11
	Hymn		212	122
15th Week	Scripture	18:19–29	MK 10:32–45	10:46–52
	Hymn		621	101
16th Week	Scripture	29	IS 43:18–25	44:1–8
	Hymn		709	212
17th Week	Scripture	37:8–22	MK 12:13–17	12:18–34
	Hymn		725	18
18th Week	Scripture	25:1–15	IS 51:12–16	52:7–10
	Hymn		489	454

Tuesday	Wednesday	Thursday	Friday	Saturday
1:12–13	1:14–15	1:16–20	1:21–28	1:29–34
570	*140*	*342*	*186*	*471*
5:1–27	7:1–21	19:13–29	23:1–17	29:1–25
212	*510*	*225*	*618*	*636*
2:1–12	2:13–17	2:18–22	2:23–28	3:1–6
431	*337*	*272*	*212*	*328*
42:1–6, 10–11, 17	PROV 1:20–33	2:1–15	3:1–12	3:21–35
66	*573*	*464*	*305*	*9*
3:19b–30	3:31–35	4:1–9	4:10–20	4:21–25
586	*714*	*289*	*324*	*322*
8:1–12, 22–31	9:1–6	13:1–15	15:1–17	22:1–9
258	*534*	*605*	*724*	*475*
4:35–41	5:1–20	5:21–34	5:35–43	6:1–6a
550	*39*	*188*	*556*	*669*
IS 1:1–10	1:18–20	2:1–17	5:1–7	5:8–23
683	*340*	*675*	*659*	*119*
6:30–44	6:45–52	6:53–56	7:1–13	7:14–23
581	*339*	*502*	*287*	*589*
10:1–4	10:12–19	11:1–10	12:1–6	25:1–9
86	*88*	*160*	*39*	*542*
8:1–10	8:11–13	8:14–21	8:22–30	8:31–38
321	*293*	*586*	*356*	*344*
29:13–24	30:8–16	30:19–26	32:1–8	32:11–20
132	*266*	*247*	*554*	*700*
9:30–41	9:42–50	10:1–12	10:13–16	10:17–31
269	*463*	*498*	*113*	*174*
40:18–31	41:17–20	42:1–9	42:14–20	43:1–13
25	*696*	*475*	*618*	*558*
11:1–11	11:12–19	11:20–26	11:27–33	12:1–12
193	*61*	*504*	*143*	*562*
45:18–19	49:1–7	49:8–18	50:4–9	51:1–8
54	*461*	*20*	*86*	*67*
12:35–40	12:41–44	13:1–8	13:9–31	13:32–37
652	*382*	*613*	*482*	*679*
52:13–53:12	54:4–13	55:1–11	57:14–21	58:3–9a
210	*583*	*66*	*405*	*422*

YEAR B—WEEKS 19-35

		Psalm for Week	Sunday	Monday
19th Week	Scripture	139:1–12, 23–24	MK 14:1–11	14:12–21
	Hymn		518	295
20th Week	Scripture	9:13–20	IS 60:1–7	61:1–11
	Hymn		239	95
21st Week	Scripture	22:1–8, 22–24	MK 15:1–15	15:16–32
	Hymn		210	198
22nd Week	Scripture	108	JER 1:4–10	2:1–13
	Hymn		14	679
23rd Week	Scripture	87	JN 1:6–9	1:10–13
	Hymn		540	144
24th Week	Scripture	119:145–160	JER 4:11–18	4:19–28
	Hymn		88	73
25th Week	Scripture	104:1–15	JN 2:1–12	2:13–22
	Hymn		176	289
26th Week	Scripture	72	JER 8:4–7	8:8–13
	Hymn		538	386
27th Week	Scripture	42	JN 3:22–30	3:31–36
	Hymn		565	168
28th Week	Scripture	103:15–22	JER 14:19–22	15:10–21
	Hymn		44	586
29th Week	Scripture	36	JN 5:1–9a	5:9b–18
	Hymn		371	210
30th Week	Scripture	33:1–12	JER 28:5–9	29:1–9
	Hymn		679	670
31st Week	Scripture	78:9–32	JN 6:22–40	6:41–46
	Hymn		414	351
32nd Week	Scripture	38	EZEK 17:22–24	18:1–9
	Hymn		642	579
33rd Week	Scripture	51:10–19	JN 7:25–31	7:32–36
	Hymn		515	463
34th Week	Scripture	69:13–18	1 COR 1:1–9	1:10–17
	Hymn		649	494
35th Week	Scripture	146	JN 8:31–38	8:39–47
	Hymn		630	527

Tuesday	Wednesday	Thursday	Friday	Saturday
14:22–31	14:32–42	14:43–52	14:53–65	14:66–72
612	*196*	*211*	*165*	*210*
62:10–12	63:7–9	63:16–64:8	65:17–25	66:10–14
5	*93*	*588*	*711*	*116*
15:33–41	15:42–47	16:1–13	16:14–20	JN 1:1–5
202	*333*	*188*	*482*	*492*
2:14–32	2:33–37	3:11–20	3:21–25	4:1–4
95	*387*	*594*	*411*	*720*
1:14–18	1:19–28	1:29–34	1:35–42	1:43–51
399	*177*	*160*	*339*	*709*
5:1–5	5:20–31	6:13–15	6:16–21	7:1–15
321	*475*	*164*	*672*	*654*
2:23–25	3:1–10	3:11–15	3:16	3:17–21
17	*376*	*646*	*39*	*651*
8:18–9:9	9:23–24	10:11–16	12:1–13	13:15–17
501	*195*	*58*	*697*	*586*
4:1–15	4:16–26	4:27–30	4:31–42	4:43–54
409	*461*	*16*	*477*	*555*
17:5–13	18:1–11	20:7–13	22:13–17	23:1–6
615	*588*	*455*	*668*	*154*
5:19–29	5:30–38	5:39–47	6:1–15	6:16–21
97	*542*	*321*	*410*	*85*
31:1–14	31:27–34	33:14–16	LAM 3:19–33	EZEK 2:1–5
707	*327*	*552*	*86*	*450*
6:47–51	6:52–59	6:60–71	7:1–9	7:10–24
428	*124*	*323*	*633*	*348*
18:25–32	33:1–20	34:11–24	36:22–28	37:1–14
452	*122*	*80*	*54*	*250*
7:37–39	7:40–53	8:1–11	8:12–20	8:21–30
709	*669*	*5*	*322*	*581*
1:18–31	2:1–5	2:6–16	3:1–15	3:16–23
548	*195*	*213*	*253*	*129*
8:48–59	9:1–12	9:13–34	9:35–41	10:1–10
130	*469*	*546*	*339*	*558*

YEAR B—WEEKS 36-52

		Psalm for Week	Sunday	Monday
36th Week	Scripture	81:5b–16	1 COR 4:1–13	4:14–21
	Hymn		*695*	*632*
37th Week	Scripture	23	JN 10:11–21	10:22–42
	Hymn		*558*	*646*
38th Week	Scripture	86	1 COR 8:1–13	9:1–27
	Hymn		*572*	*110*
39th Week	Scripture	22:25–31	JN 12:1–11	12:12–19
	Hymn		*188*	*191*
40th Week	Scripture	88	1 COR 12:1–11	12:12–26
	Hymn		*269*	*378*
41st Week	Scripture	19	JN 13:12–19	13:20
	Hymn		*461*	*301*
42nd Week	Scripture	31:17–24	1 COR 15:12–25	15:26–34
	Hymn		*216*	*538*
43rd Week	Scripture	80	JN 14:15–17	14:18–24
	Hymn		*266*	*324*
44th Week	Scripture	119:49–64	2 COR 1:1–2	1:3–7
	Hymn		*335*	*502*
45th Week	Scripture	30	JN 16:4b–11	16:12–15
	Hymn		*269*	*266*
46th Week	Scripture	119:33–48	2 COR 3:7–18	4:1–6
	Hymn		*264*	*105*
47th Week	Scripture	133	JN 17:14–19	17:20–26
	Hymn		*385*	*503*
48th Week	Scripture	37:23–28	2 COR 5:16–21	6:1–10
	Hymn		*513*	*415*
49th Week	Scripture	142	JN 18:38b—19:16	19:17–24
	Hymn		*213*	*548*
50th Week	Scripture	149	2 COR 8:16–24	9:1–15
	Hymn		*7*	*714*
51st Week	Scripture	66:1–12	JN 20:19–23	20:24–29
	Hymn		*254*	*220*
52nd Week	Scripture	140	2 COR 11:30–33	12:1–10
	Hymn		*622*	*528*

Tuesday	Wednesday	Thursday	Friday	Saturday
5:1–13	6:1–11	6:12–20	7:1–24	7:25–40
254	*588*	*689*	*509*	*464*
11:1–16	11:17–27	11:28–37	11:38–44	11:45–57
545	*79*	*199*	*5*	*78*
10:1–22	10:23—11:1	11:2–22	11:23–26	11:27–34
395	*517*	*393*	*420*	*397*
12:20–26	12:27–36a	12:36b–43	12:44–50	13:1–11
230	*108*	*143*	*540*	*385*
12:27–31	13:1–13	14:1–25	14:26–40	15:1–11
245	*526*	*255*	*507*	*543*
13:21–30	13:31–35	13:36–38	14:1–7	14:8–14
60	*494*	*618*	*278*	*39*
15:35–49	15:50–58	16:1–4	16:5–12	16:13–24
109	*218*	*606*	*474*	*611*
14:25–31	15:1–11	15:12–17	15:18–27	16:1–4a
296	*15*	*585*	*159*	*635*
1:8–11	1:12—2:4	2:5–11	2:14–17	3:1–6
85	*565*	*242*	*233*	*588*
16:16–24	16:25–28	16:29–33	17:1–5	17:6–13
699	*527*	*620*	*562*	*84*
4:7–15	4:16–18	5:1–5	5:6–10	5:11–15
617	*599*	*646*	*713*	*610*
18:1–11	18:12–14	18:15–18	18:19–27	18:28–38a
346	*292*	*495*	*210*	*278*
6:11–13	6:14—7:1	7:2–16	8:1–7	8:8–15
667	*572*	*576*	*606*	*655*
19:25–30	19:31–37	19:38–42	20:1–10	20:11–18
197	*204*	*198*	*220*	*196*
10:1–6	10:7–18	11:1–11	11:12–15	11:16–29
69	*195*	*472*	*168*	*629*
20:30–31	21:1–14	21:15–19	21:20–23	21:24–25
323	*321*	*349*	*545*	*480*
12:11–18	12:19–21	13:1–4	13:5–10	13:11–14
487	*69*	*14*	*136*	*438*

Year C

Luke, Daniel—Zechariah, Hebrews, Philemon,
1 Peter, Acts, James, 1, 2, and 3 John, Revelation

		Psalm for Week	Sunday	Monday
1st Week	Scripture	97	LK 1:1–25	1:26–38
	Hymn		*190*	*127*
2nd Week	Scripture	100	DAN 3:8–28	4:28–37
	Hymn		*554*	*27*
3rd Week	Scripture	111	LK 2:22–40	2:41–52
	Hymn		*444*	*184*
4th Week	Scripture	98	HOS 11:1–11	14:4–9
	Hymn		*290*	*143*
5th Week	Scripture	25:16–22	LK 4:14–30	4:31–44
	Hymn		*140*	*186*
6th Week	Scripture	57	MIC 4:1–5	5:1–6
	Hymn		*673*	*144*
7th Week	Scripture	41	LK 6:1–11	6:12–19
	Hymn		*594*	*570*
8th Week	Scripture	12	MIC 7:18–20	AMOS 5:6–15
	Hymn		*86*	*55*
9th Week	Scripture	116	LK 6:43–45	6:46–49
	Hymn		*573*	*618*
10th Week	Scripture	119:65–72	OBAD 1:1–4	JON 3:1—4:11
	Hymn		*608*	*670*
11th Week	Scripture	107:23–32	LK 8:4–15	8:16–18
	Hymn		*381*	*478*
12th Week	Scripture	127	ZEPH 1:1, 12–18	2:1–4
	Hymn		*578*	*402*
13th Week	Scripture	132	LK 9:7–17	9:18–20
	Hymn		*422*	*356*
14th Week	Scripture	73:1–20, 27–28	ZECH 9:9–12	14:20–21
	Hymn		*191*	*111*
15th Week	Scripture	96	LK 9:57–58	9:59–62
	Hymn		*612*	*465*
16th Week	Scripture	110	HEB 2:14–18	3:1–11
	Hymn		*585*	*453*
17th Week	Scripture	119:105–125	LK 10:38–42	11:1–4
	Hymn		*612*	*463*
18th Week	Scripture	99	HEB 6:9–20	7:1–19
	Hymn		*625*	*14*

Tuesday	Wednesday	Thursday	Friday	Saturday
1:39–45 *139*	1:46–56 *130*	1:57–80 *16*	2:1–7 *144*	2:8–21 *148*
7:9–18 *17*	9:1–10,17–19 *679*	HOS 2:14–20 *88*	4:1–11 *697*	6:1–6 *632*
3:1–14 *177*	3:15–38 *365*	4:1–4 *337*	4:5–8 *25*	4:9–13 *180*
JOEL 2:12–17a *7*	2:21–27 *690*	2:28–32 *595*	MIC 2:1–11 *703*	3:1–8 *249*
5:1–11 *342*	5:12–16 *564*	5:17–26 *503*	5:27–32 *337*	5:33–39 *272*
5:7–9 *542*	6:1–8 *659*	6:9–16 *651*	7:1–7 *638*	7:8–10 *637*
6:20–26 *70*	6:27–31 *623*	6:32–36 *73*	6:37–38 *382*	6:39–42 *586*
5:18–24 *461*	6:1–8 *670*	7:1–9 *672*	8:1–10 *652*	8:11–14 *324*
7:1–10 *555*	7:11–17 *598*	7:18–35 *461*	7:36–50 *188*	8:1–3 *686*
NAH 1:1–9 *77*	HAB 1:1–4 *642*	2:1–14 *537*	2:20 *124*	3:17–19 *622*
8:19–21 *486*	8:22–25 *566*	8:26–39 *594*	8:40–56 *445*	9:1–6 *459*
3:1–7 *651*	3:11–20 *292*	HAG 2:1–9 *125*	ZECH 7:1–10 *661*	8:1–17 *153*
9:21–27 *346*	9:28–36 *182*	9:37–45 *669*	9:46–48 *133*	9:49–56 *669*
MAL 3:1–7 *618*	3:8–18 *606*	HEB 1:1–14 *114*	2:1–4 *582*	2:5–13 *90*
10:1–6 *494*	10:7–12 *632*	10:13–20 *39*	10:21–24 *58*	10:25–37 *600*
3:12–19 *534*	4:1–11 *95*	4:12–16 *502*	5:1–10 *543*	5:11—6:8 *517*
11:5–13 *354*	11:14–23 *326*	11:24–26 *259*	11:27–32 *102*	11:33–36 *586*
7:20–28 *196*	8:1–13 *212*	9:1–22 *39*	9:23–28 *402*	10:1–18 *416*

YEAR C—WEEKS 19-35

		Psalm for Week	Sunday	Monday
19th Week	Scripture *Hymn*	49	LK 11:37–54 *391*	12:1–3 *665*
20th Week	Scripture *Hymn*	62	HEB 10:19–25 *601*	10:26–39 *254*
21st Week	Scripture *Hymn*	66:13–20	LK 12:35–40 *257*	12:41–48 *383*
22nd Week	Scripture *Hymn*	50:16–23	HEB 13:1–6 *75*	13:7–16 *537*
23rd Week	Scripture *Hymn*	79	LK 13:10–17 *506*	13:18–21 *604*
24th Week	Scripture *Hymn*	64	JAS 2:1–7 *284*	2:8–13 *453*
25th Week	Scripture *Hymn*	119:161–176	LK 14:25–33 *344*	14:34–35 *491*
26th Week	Scripture *Hymn*	130	JAS 5:1–12 *638*	5:13–18 *540*
27th Week	Scripture *Hymn*	51:1–9	LK 16:19–31 *679*	17:1–10 *22*
28th Week	Scripture *Hymn*	145	1 PET 1:13–21 *572*	1:22–25 *2*
29th Week	Scripture *Hymn*	40:11–17	LK 18:18–34 *417*	18:35–43 *300*
30th Week	Scripture *Hymn*	55:12–22	1 PET 4:12–19 *470*	5:1–14 *65*
31st Week	Scripture *Hymn*	35:1–8, 22–28	LK 20:1–8 *177*	20:9–19 *382*
32nd Week	Scripture *Hymn*	68:32–35	ACTS 2:43–47 *719*	3:1–10 *570*
33rd Week	Scripture *Hymn*	39	LK 22:1–13 *385*	22:14–23 *400*
34th Week	Scripture *Hymn*	69:1–8, 30–36	ACTS 4:32–37 *245*	5:1–11 *383*
35th Week	Scripture *Hymn*	22:9–21	LK 22:63–71 *165*	23:1–12 *669*

Tuesday	Wednesday	Thursday	Friday	Saturday
12:4–7	12:8–12	12:13–15	12:16–21	12:22–34
82	*266*	*672*	*351*	*59*
11:1–3	11:4–22	11:23–40	12:1–13	12:14–29
64	*533*	*635*	*637*	*572*
12:49–53	12:54–56	12:57–59	13:1–5	13:6–9
236	*329*	*598*	*507*	*536*
13:17–25	JAS 1:1–8	1:9–16	1:17–18	1:19–27
206	*464*	*349*	*715*	*470*
13:22–30	13:31–35	14:1–6	14:7–14	14:15–24
687	*550*	*461*	*391*	*386*
2:14–26	3:1–12	3:13–18	4:1–12	4:13–17
383	*662*	*136*	*582*	*562*
15:1–7	15:8–10	15:11–32	16:1–13	16:14–18
450	*74*	*329*	*695*	*265*
PHILE 1:1–7	1:8–25	1 PET 1:1–2	1:3–9	1:10–12
476	*403*	*448*	*99*	*510*
17:11–19	17:20–37	18:1–8	18:9–14	18:15–17
531	*632*	*585*	*542*	*147*
2:1–10	2:11–25	3:1–12	3:13–22	4:1–11
273	*587*	*498*	*391*	*461*
19:1–10	19:11–27	19:28–40	19:41–44	19:45–48
654	*556*	*141*	*670*	*289*
ACTS 1:1–11	1:12–26	2:1–13	2:14–28	2:29–42
233	*565*	*236*	*198*	*431*
20:20–26	20:27–47	21:1–19	21:20–28	21:29–38
724	*649*	*719*	*482*	*12*
3:11–16	3:17–26	4:1–12	4:13–22	4:23–31
463	*288*	*479*	*450*	*266*
22:24–30	22:31–38	22:39–46	22:47–53	22:54–62
579	*576*	*194*	*484*	*213*
5:12–16	5:17–42	6:1–7	6:8–15	7:1–22
29	*334*	*22*	*263*	*330*
23:13–25	23:26–31	23:32–43	23:44–49	23:50–56
210	*196*	*402*	*188*	*198*

YEAR C—WEEKS 36-52

		Psalm for Week	Sunday	Monday
36th Week	Scripture *Hymn*	123	ACTS 7:23–43 *663*	7:44–53 *273*
37th Week	Scripture *Hymn*	150	LK 24:1–12 *226*	24:13–35 *231*
38th Week	Scripture *Hymn*	67	ACTS 9:19b–25 *146*	9:26–31 *245*
39th Week	Scripture *Hymn*	112	1 JN 2:7–11 *491*	2:12–17 *630*
40th Week	Scripture *Hymn*	70	ACTS 10:34–48 *91*	11:1–18 *259*
41st Week	Scripture *Hymn*	90:1–12	1 JN 3:18–24 *494*	4:1–6 *67*
42nd Week	Scripture *Hymn*	65	ACTS 13:34–52 *5*	14:1–20 *59*
43rd Week	Scripture *Hymn*	15	2 JN 1:1–3 *287*	1:4–13 *688*
44th Week	Scripture *Hymn*	27	ACTS 15:30–41 *416*	16:1–10 *461*
45th Week	Scripture *Hymn*	13	REV 2:8–11 *124*	2:12–17 *277*
46th Week	Scripture *Hymn*	107:1–16	ACTS 17:16–33 *500*	18:1–17 *618*
47th Week	Scripture *Hymn*	37:1–9	REV 5:1–10 *234*	5:11–14 *110*
48th Week	Scripture *Hymn*	61	ACTS 20:17–38 *272*	21:1–16 *722*
49th Week	Scripture *Hymn*	48	REV 11:1–19 *693*	12:1–17 *33*
50th Week	Scripture *Hymn*	63	ACTS 24:1–23 *215*	24:24—25:12 *627*
51st Week	Scripture *Hymn*	126	REV 18:1–24 *39*	19:1–21 *234*
52nd Week	Scripture *Hymn*	121	ACTS 27:1–12 *6*	27:13–26 *85*

Tuesday	Wednesday	Thursday	Friday	Saturday
7:54—8:3 *187*	8:4–13 *368*	8:14–25 *265*	8:26–40 *431*	9:1–19a *620*
24:36–49 *296*	24:50–53 *233*	1 JN 1:1–4 *323*	1:5–10 *442*	2:1–6 *431*
9:32–35 *461*	9:36–43 *722*	10:1–8 *556*	10:9–23a *485*	10:23b–33 *288*
2:18–27 *321*	2:28 *573*	2:29—3:3 *165*	3:4–10 *517*	3:11–17 *345*
11:19–30 *420*	12:1–17 *635*	12:18–25 *618*	13:1–12 *454*	13:13–33 *135*
4:7–12 *205*	4:13–16 *517*	4:17–21 *641*	5:1–12 *214*	5:13–21 *590*
14:21–23 *629*	14:24–28 *528*	15:1–11 *73*	15:12–21 *61*	15:22–29 *491*
3 JN 1:1–8 *561*	1:9–14 *253*	REV 1:1–8 *97*	1:9–20 *562*	2:1–7 *463*
16:11–15 *686*	16:16–34 *277*	16:35–40 *450*	17:1–9 *84*	17:10–15 *464*
2:18–29 *173*	3:1–6 *250*	3:7–13 *715*	3:14–22 *304*	4:1–11 *4*
18:18–28 *257*	19:1–10 *177*	19:11–20 *503*	19:21–41 *666*	20:1–16 *408*
6:1–17 *708*	7:1–17 *413*	8:1–13 *566*	9:1–21 *693*	10:1–11 *713*
21:17–26 *130*	21:27–39 *613*	21:40—22:29 *373*	22:30—23:11 *464*	23:16–35 *637*
13:1–8 *25*	14:1–20 *705*	15:1–8 *4*	16:1–21 *680*	17:1–18 *684*
25:13–27 *13*	26:1–11 *161*	26:12–18 *484*	26:19–23 *452*	26:24–32 *343*
20:1–15 *400*	21:1–8 *658*	21:9–27 *200*	22:1–7 *701*	22:8–21 *104*
27:27–38 *545*	27:39–44 *546*	28:1–10 *465*	28:11–16 *490*	28:17–31 *467*

Index of Copyright Owners

Permissions have been obtained for *Chalice Hymnal* with the restriction that its distribution is limited to North America. Some items showing no copyright information may have copyright protection in other countries. Every effort has been made to trace the owner(s) and/or administrator(s) of each copyright. The Publisher regrets any omission and will, upon written notice, make the necessary correction(s) in subsequent printings.

Scripture, unless otherwise indicated, is adapted from the *New Revised Standard Version Bible*, © 1989 by the Division of Christian Education of the National Council of Churches of Christ in the USA, and is used by permission.

Items in *Chalice Hymnal* that are not in public domain may be reproduced only by permission from the respective copyright owner(s). Addresses of copyright owners of three (3) or more items in the book are listed below. Other addresses are given in the index under the appropriate listing.

2   Descant: © 1995 Chalice Press.

3   Adaptation: © 1991 Austin C. Lovelace, 7522 E. Bates Drive, Denver CO 80231.

4   Descant: © 1995 Chalice Press.

7   Words: © 1972 by Hope Publishing Co. All rights reserved. Used by permission.

8   Words, Music: © 1987 Sacred Music Press, div. of The Lorenz Corp., Dayton OH. All rights reserved. Reproduced by permit #239149.

9   © 1982 by Hope Publishing Co. All rights reserved. Used by permission.

10   Words, Music: © 1989 by Hope Publishing Co. All rights reserved. Used by permission.

11   From Women Pray – Second National Meeting of United Church of Christ Women. Copyright 1986 The Pilgrim Press. Used by Permission.

12   Words: © 1987 Oxford University Press.

13   Words, Music: © 1986 by Hope Publishing Co. All rights reserved. Used by permission.

14   Words: © 1992 GIA Publications, Inc. All rights reserved.

15   Stanza 5: © 1981 Ruth Duck.

20   Harmonization: © 1964 The United Methodist Publishing House.

25   Translation, stanza 4: © 1989 The United Methodist Publishing House. Descant from *20 Hymn Tune Descants* by C. S. Lang. Reprinted by permission of Novello & Company, Inc.

26   Words, Music: Used by permission of Asian Institute for Liturgy and Music.

27   Descant: Copyright © 1965 (Renewed) by Shawnee Press, Inc. (ASCAP). International Copyright Secured. All Rights Reserved. Reprinted by Permission.

28   Words, Music: © 1986 by Sandi's Songs (adm. by Addison Music Co., P.O. Box 1425, Anderson IN 46015) (BMI) / Gaither Music Co. (ASCAP) / River Oaks Music Company (a division of The Sparrow Corp.). All rights on behalf of River Oaks Music Company administered by The Sparrow Corp. All rights reserved. Used by permission.

29   Translation: © 1995 Chalice Press.

30   Words, Music: Used by permission of Lumko Institute, P.O. Box 5058, Delmenville 1403, South Africa.

32   Words, Music: © 1974 New Song Ministries, R.R. 1 Box 454, Erin TN 37061.

33   Words, Music: © 1953, renewed 1981, Manna Music, Inc.

34   Music: © 1979 Les Presses de Taizé. Used by permission of GIA Publications, Inc. All rights reserved.

37   Music: © 1995 Elaine Clemens Berkenstock, 3027 Thayer Street, Evanston IL 60201.

38   Words, Music: © 1972 Communiqué Music, Inc. (a division of The Sparrow Corp.). All rights administered by The Sparrow Corporation. All rights reserved. Used by permission.

39   Words, Music: © 1971 Communiqué Music, Inc. (a division of The Sparrow Corp.). All rights administered by The Sparrow Corporation. All rights reserved. Used by permission.

40   Translation: Used by permission of I-to Loh, 117 Tung-men Road, Section 1, Tainan, Taiwan.

43   Words, Music: © 1995 Chalice Press.

45   Words, Music: Used by permission of Pablo Fernández Badillo, P.O. Box 744, San Antonio PR 00690.

50   Adaptation: © 1989 The United Methodist Publishing House.

53   Words: © 1957 Eleanor Farjeon. Used by permission of Harold Ober Associates, Inc., 425 Madison Avenue, New York NY 10017. Arrangement: © 1987 CRC Publications, 2850 Kalamazoo Avenue SE, Grand Rapids MI 49560.

54   Words, Music: © 1985 Oxford University Press.

55   Words: © 1950 Oxford University Press. Music: © 1963 The United Methodist Publishing House.

58   Harmonization: © 1986 GIA Publications, Inc. All rights reserved.

60   Words, Music: © 1976 Resource Publications, Inc., 160 E. Virginia Street #290, San Jose CA 95112. Translation: © 1989, The United Methodist Publishing House. Arrangement: © 1983, The United Methodist Publishing House.

62   Words: © 1980 Jane Parker Huber.

63   Words, Music: © 1981 Meadowgreen Music Company (a division of The Sparrow Corp.). All rights administered by The Sparrow Corporation. All rights reserved. Used by permission.

65   Adaptation: © 1981, 1990, Ruth Duck.

67   Descant: © 1990 by Hope Publishing Co. All rights reserved. Used by permission.

69   Words: © 1989 The United Methodist Publishing House. Arrangement: © 1969 Concordia Publishing House, 3558 S. Jefferson Avenue, St. Louis MO 63118.

70   Words: © 1983 Jaroslav J. Vajda. Music: © 1983 GIA Publications, Inc. All rights reserved.

71   Translation: © 1974 by Hope Publishing Co. All rights reserved. Used by permission. Music: © 1963 The United Methodist Publishing House.

73   Harmonization: © 1989 The United Methodist Publishing House.

74   Words: © 1990 Jaroslav J. Vajda. Music: © 1991 GIA Publications, Inc. All rights reserved.

75   Words, Music: © 1985 John Ylvisaker, New Generation Publishers, 303 6th Street SW, Waverly IA 50677.

76   Harmonization: © 1929 Oxford University Press.

77   Words, Music: © 1979, 1991, New Dawn Music. All rights reserved. Used with permission.

79   Words: Adaptation copyright © 1992 The Pilgrim Press. Harmonization: © 1934 Oxford University Press.

81   "Listen, Lord—A Prayer" (first twelve lines), from *God's Trombones* by James Weldon Johnson. Copyright 1927 The Viking Press, Inc., renewed © 1955 by Grace Nail Johnson. Used by permission of Viking Penguin, a division of Penguin Books USA Inc.

83   Words: © 1991 Jean Janzen. Music: © 1995 Chalice Press.

84   Words, Music: Used by permission of Asian Institute for Liturgy and Music. Arrangement: © 1995 Chalice Press.

86   Words, Music: © 1923, renewed 1951, by Hope Publishing Co. All rights reserved. Used by permission.

88   Stanza 3: © 1989 by Hope Publishing Co. All rights reserved. Used by permission.

90   Harmonization: Used by permission of Oxford University Press.

95   Descant: © 1985 Wm. B. Eerdmans Publishing Co., 255 Jefferson Avenue SE, Grand Rapids MI 49503.

104 Harmonization: © 1940 The Church Hymnal Corp.

105 Translation: © 1978 *Lutheran Book of Worship*. Reprinted by permission of Augsburg Fortress.

106 Words, Music: © 1972, 1978, Manna Music, Inc.

107 Translation: © 1995 Chalice Press.

108 Words, Music: © 1974 by Hope Publishing Co. All rights reserved. Used by permission.

109 Translation: © 1982, 1989, The United Methodist Publishing House.

110 Words: Alterations © 1993 The Pilgrim Press. Descant: Used by permission of Oxford University Press.

111 Arrangement: © 1990 Iona Community. Used by permission of GIA Publications, Inc. All rights reserved.

112 Words, Music: © 1983 Meadowgreen Music Company (a division of The Sparrow Corp.) / Songchannel Music. All rights administered by The Sparrow Corp. All rights reserved. Used by permission.

114 Words, Music: © 1963, 1975, renewed 1991, Fred Bock Music Company, P.O. Box 570567, Tarzana CA 91357.

115 Words, Music: © 1970, 1995, William J. Gaither ASCAP. All rights reserved. Used by permission.

116 Words, Music: © 1948 Martin & Morris Music, Inc. All rights administered by Unichappell Music, Inc. All rights reserved. Arrangement: © 1992 The Pilgrim Press.

117 Arrangement: © 1986 by Word Music (a division of WORD, INC.). All Rights Reserved. Used By Permission.

118 Words, Music: © 1982 Bob Jay Music Co., c/o Garrett Johnson, 443 W. 151st Street #3D, New York NY 10031.

120 Used by permission of the Church of the Province of Southern Africa (Anglican), c/o The Publishing Committee, P.O. Box 61394, Marshalltown 2107, S. Africa.

121 Music: © 1984 Les Presses de Taizé. Used by permission of GIA Publications, Inc. All rights reserved.

127 Translation: © 1940, 1943, renewed 1971, The Church Hymnal Corp.

128 Words: © 1995 Chalice Press.

130 Words: © 1978, 1987, Medical Mission Sisters. Harmonization: © 1989 The United Methodist Publishing House.

131 Words: © 1978, 1987, Medical Mission Sisters. Harmonization: © 1989 The United Methodist Publishing House.

132 Words, Music: © 1989 by Hope Publishing Co. All rights reserved. Used by permission.

133 Words, Music: © 1993 by Hope Publishing Co. All rights reserved. Used by permission.

134 Words, Music: © 1976 C. A. Music (division of Christian Artists Corp.), 209 Chapelwood Drive, Franklin TN 37064. All Rights Reserved. Used By Permission.

135 Words: © 1973 by Hope Publishing Co. All rights reserved. Used by permission. Music: © 1983 by Hope Publishing Co. All rights reserved. Used by permission.

136 Words: © 1995 Chalice Press.

137 Words Response: © 1973 by Hope Publishing Co. All rights reserved. Used by permission. Music © 1983 by Hope Publishing Co. All rights reserved. Used by permission.

138 Words, Music: © 1983 GIA Publications, Inc. All rights reserved.

139 Words, Music: © 1972 Alberto Taulè, c/o The National Association of Pastoral Musicians, 225 Sheridan Street NW, Washington DC 20001. Translation: © 1989 The United Methodist Publishing House. Harmonization: Used by permission of Juan Francisco Chávez, Arenal 48, Depto. 10, 01050 México (San Angel), D.F., Mexico.

141 Words: "A Christmas Hymn" from *Advice to a Prophet and Other Poems*, copyright © 1961 and renewed 1989 by Richard Wilbur, reprinted by permission of Harcourt Brace & Company, 6277 Sea Harbor Drive, Orlando FL 32887. Music: © 1984 GIA Publications, Inc. All rights reserved.

142 Words: © 1957 Eleanor Farjeon. Used by permission of Harold Ober Associates, Inc., 425 Madison Avenue, New York NY 10017. Harmonization: Used by permission of Oxford University Press.

146 Translation: © 1978 *Lutheran Book of Worship*. Reprinted by permission of Augsburg Fortress.

147 Harmonization: © 1978 *Lutheran Book of Worship*. Reprinted by permission of Augsburg Fortress.

148 Descant: © 1961 Oxford University Press.

150 Descant: Copyright © 1976 Paragon Music Corp./ASCAP. All Rights Reserved. Used by permission of Benson Music Group, Inc., c/o Commercial Licensing, 365 Great Circle Road, Nashville TN 37228.

151 Descant: Used by permission of Oxford University Press.

155 Harmonization: © 1964 The United Methodist Publishing House. Descant: © 1979 by Hope Publishing Co. All rights reserved. Used by permission.

156 Words Response: © 1992 GIA Publications, Inc. All rights reserved.

157 From *Come, Lord Jesus* by Lucien Deiss. Copyright 1976, 1981, by Lucien Deiss. All rights reserved. Used by permission of World Library Publications, 3825 N. Willow Road, Schiller Park IL 60176.

158 Words: © 1989 by Hope Publishing Co. All rights reserved. Used by permission. Music © 1983 by Hope Publishing Co. All rights reserved. Used by permission.

161 Words, Music: Copyright © 1934, 1944 (Renewed) by G. Schirmer, Inc. (ASCAP). International Copyright Secured. All Rights Reserved. Reprinted by Permission.

163 Music Adaptation: Used by permission of Rosalind Rusbridge, 9 Springfield House, Cotham Road, Bristol BS66DQ, U.K.

164 Harmonization: © 1955, renewed 1983, Westminster John Knox Press.

166 Translation: © 1927 The Frederick Harris Music Company, 529 Speers Road, Oakville, Ontario L6K 2G4, Canada. Harmonization: © 1978 *Lutheran Book of Worship*. Reprinted by permission of Augsburg Fortress.

167 Arrangement: © 1989 The United Methodist Publishing House.

168 Words: © 1968 by Hope Publishing Co. All rights reserved. Used by permission. Arrangement: © 1924 (Renewed) by J. Curwen & Sons. Administered by G. Schirmer, Inc. (ASCAP). International Copyright Secured. All Rights Reserved. Reprinted by Permission.

171 Words, Music: © 1985 Malcolm Music (BMI), a division of Shawnee Press, Inc. International Copyright Secured. All Rights Reserved. Reprinted by Permission.

173 Words Alterations: © 1993 The Pilgrim Press.

174 Harmonization: © 1987 GIA Publications, Inc. All rights reserved.

175 Words, Music: © 1990 Asian Institute for Liturgy and Music.

176 Words: © 1990 by Hope Publishing Co. All rights reserved. Used by permission.

177 Words: © 1975 by Hope Publishing Co. All rights reserved. Used by permission. Harmonization: © 1986 by Hope Publishing Co. All rights reserved. Used by permission.

178 From *World Call*, June, 1972. © 1972 Christian Board of Publication.

181 Words: © 1991 GIA Publications, Inc. All rights reserved.

182 Words: © 1991 GIA Publications, Inc. All rights reserved.

183 Words: © 1968 by Hope Publishing Co. All rights reserved. Used by permission. Music © 1989 The United Methodist Publishing House.

186 Words, Music: © 1984 Oxford University Press.

187 Words: © 1990 Mennonite World Conference, 50 Kent Avenue, Kitchener, Ontario N2G 3R1, Canada.

188 Words: © 1983 by Hope Publishing Co. All rights reserved. Used by permission. Music: © 1995 Chalice Press.

192 Descant: © 1995 Chalice Press.

193 Words: © 1985 Oxford University Press.

198 Music Adaptation and Arrangement: © 1989 The United Methodist Publishing House.

201 From *Come, Lord Jesus* by Lucien Deiss. Copyright 1976, 1981, by Lucien Deiss. All rights reserved. Used by permission of World Library Publications, 3825 N. Willow Road, Schiller Park IL 60176.

203 Words: © 1973, 1995, by Hope Publishing Co. All rights reserved. Used by permission.

206 Words, Music: © 1966 Manna Music, Inc.

208 Arrangement: © 1994 Floyd Knight, Jr., 9601 Monrovia, Apt. 104, Lenexa KS 66215.

209 © 1987 Chalice Press.

211 Arrangement: © 1995 Chalice Press.

212 Words: © 1987 Elinor F. Johns, 38 Ruttan Bay, Winnipeg, Manitoba R3P 0H6, Canada.

213 Words: © 1988 Iona Community. Used by permission of GIA Publications, Inc. All rights reserved.

216 Descant: Copyright © 1965 (Renewed) by Shawnee Press, Inc. (ASCAP). International Copyright Secured. All Rights Reserved. Reprinted by Permission.

218 Translation, Harmonization: © The World Student Christian Federation, 5, Route des Morillons, 1218 Grand-Saconnex, Geneva, Switzerland.

219 From *The Glory of Christian Worship* by G. Edwin Osborn. © 1960 Christian Theological Seminary, 1000 W. 42nd Street, Indianapolis IN 46260.

220 Translation: © 1995 Ruth Duck.

326 Words, Music: © 1984 Meadowgreen Music Company (a division of The Sparrow Corp.) / Bug & Bear Music. All rights reserved. International copyright secured. Used by permission.

327 Music: © 1990 by Hope Publishing Co. All rights reserved. Used by permission.

328 Words, Music: © 1986 GIA Publications, Inc. All rights reserved.

329 Words, Music: © 1989 by Hope Publishing Co. All rights reserved. Used by permission.

330 Words: © 1995 Chalice Press. Music Adaptation: Used by permission of Rosalind Rusbridge, 9 Springfield House, Cotham Road, Bristol BS66DQ, U.K.

331 Words: © 1981 The Hymn Society. All rights reserved. Used by permission of Hope Publishing Co.

332 © 1995 Chalice Press.

333 Words: © 1989 by Hope Publishing Co. All rights reserved. Used by permission. Music: © 1995 Chalice Press.

334 Words: © 1983 by Hope Publishing Co. All rights reserved. Used by permission. Music © 1983 Ann Loomes, 19 Chapel Road, Llanharan, Pontyclun mid Glamorgan, CF7 9QA, U.K.

335 Words: © 1979 The Hymn Society. All rights reserved. Used by permission of Hope Publishing Co.

341 By Colbert S. Cartwright. © 1995 Chalice Press.

342 Words, Music: © 1979, 1987, Cesareo Gabaraín. Published by OCP Publications. All rights reserved. Used with permission. Translation: © 1989 The United Methodist Publishing House. Harmonization: Used by permission of Juan Francisco Chávez, Arenal 48, Depto. 10, 01050 México (San Angel), D.F., Mexico.

347 From *The Great Commitment* by Lin D. Cartwright. © 1962 Chalice Press.

350 Music: Used by permission of Fleming H. Revell Co., P.O. Box 6287, Grand Rapids MI 49516.

351 Words, Music: © 1964 by Sacred Songs (a division of WORD, INC.). All Rights Reserved. Used By Permission.

352 Words, Music: © 1979 Mercy Publishing, c/o Music Services, 209 Chapelwood Drive, Franklin TN 37064.

353 Words: © 1991 GIA Publications, Inc. All rights reserved. Music: © 1993, Selah Publishing Co., Inc., P.O. Box 3037, Kingston NY 12401. Used by permission. All rights reserved.

354 Words, Music: © 1972 Marathana! Music (Administered by The Copyright Company). All Rights Reserved. International Copyright Secured. Used by Permission.

356 Words Adaptation: © 1995 Chalice Press.

357 Words: © 1995 Chalice Press.

358 Used by permission of The United Church of Canada, 85 St. Clair Avenue East, Toronto, Ontario M4T 1M8, Canada.

361 Used by permission of The United Church of Christ, 700 Prospect Avenue, Cleveland OH 44115.

362 Words: © 1995 Chalice Press.

364 Used by permission of the Consultation on Church Union, Research Park, 151 Wall Street, Princeton NJ 08540.

365 Words: © 1987 GIA Publications, Inc. All rights reserved. Harmonization: © 1958, renewed 1986, Broadman Press. Assigned to Van Ness Press, 127 9th Avenue N., Nashville TN 37234.

366 Words: © 1987, 1991, Oxford University Press. Music: © 1995 Chalice Press.

368 Words: © 1995 Chalice Press. Harmonization: © 1990 John Weaver, Madison Avenue Presbyterian Church, 921 Madison Avenue, New York NY 10021.

369 By Ronald J. Allen and Colbert S. Cartwright. © 1995 Chalice Press.

372 From *Mid-Stream*, Jan., 1985. Used by permission of the Council on Christian Unity, P.O. Box 1986, Indianapolis IN 46206.

373 Words: © 1995 Chalice Press. Music: © 1987 by Hope Publishing Co. All rights reserved. Used by permission.

374 Words, Music: © 1984 GIA Publications, Inc. All rights reserved.

375 Words: © 1993 by Hope Publishing Co. All rights reserved. Used by permission. Music: © 1989 The United Methodist Publishing House.

376 Words: © 1969 John Brownlow Geyer, 335 Blackness Road, Dundee DD2 1SN, Scotland, U.K. Music: © 1967 Chalice Press.

378 Words: © 1980 Jane Parker Huber. Harmonization: © 1943, renewed 1971, The Church Hymnal Corp.

379 Words: © 1995 Chalice Press.

381 Words, Music: © 1992 by Hope Publishing Co. All rights reserved. Used by permission.

385 Words: © 1974 by Hope Publishing Co. All rights reserved. Used by permission. Harmonization: © 1990 John Weaver, Madison Avenue Presbyterian Church, 921 Madison Avenue, New York NY 10021.

386 Words: © 1984 by Hope Publishing Co. All rights reserved. Used by permission.

391 Words, Music: © 1989 Iona Community. Used by permission of GIA Publications, Inc. All rights reserved.

392 Words: Used by permission of Oxford University Press. Music: © 1957 (renewed) H. W. Gray Co. All rights reserved. Used by permission of Warner Brothers Publications, Inc., P.O. Box 4340, Miami FL 33014. Music Adaptation: © 1967 Chalice Press.

393 Words, Music: © 1978, John B. Foley, S.J. and New Dawn Music. All rights reserved. Used with permission.

395 Words, Music: © 1987 Ekklesia Music, Inc., P.O. Box 22967, Denver CO 80222.

396 Words, Music: © 1973, Cesareo Gabaraín. Published by OCP Publications. All rights reserved. Used with permission. Translation: © 1989 The United Methodist Publishing House. Harmonization: Used by permission of Juan Francisco Chávez, Arenal 48, Depto. 10, 01050 México (San Angel), D.F., Mexico.

397 Words: © 1931 Oxford University Press. Music: © 1948 United Reformed Church, 86 Tavistock Place, London WC1H 9RT, U.K.

400 Words, Music: © 1988 David L. Edwards. Arrangement: © 1995 Chalice Press.

403 Words, Music: © 1972 Broadman Press. Assigned to Van Ness Press, 127 9th Avenue N., Nashville TN 37234.

408 Words, Music: © 1984 Fred Bock Music Company, P.O. Box 570567, Tarzana CA 91357.

410 Words, Music: © 1995 Chalice Press.

412 From *The Untold Story: A Short History of Black Disciples.* © 1976 Chalice Press.

413 Words, Music: © 1966 Joe Wise. Used by permission of GIA Publications, Inc. All rights reserved.

414 Words, Music: © 1984 Les Presses de Taizé. Used by permission of GIA Publications, Inc. All rights reserved.

415 Words, Music: © 1969 by Hope Publishing Co. All rights reserved. Used by permission.

419 Words: © 1991 GIA Publications, Inc. All rights reserved.

420 Words: © 1971 by Hope Publishing Co. All rights reserved. Used by permission. Harmonization: © 1989 The United Methodist Publishing House.

421 Words, Music: © 1991 Carlos Rosas, 2427 W. Huisache, San Antonio TX 78228. Translation: © 1995 Chalice Press. Arrangement: © 1995 The United Methodist Publishing House.

422 Words, Music: © 1975 by Hope Publishing Co. All rights reserved. Used by permission.

423 Words: © 1972 Westminster John Knox Press.

424 Arrangement: Copyright © 1980 by G. Schirmer, Inc. (ASCAP). International Copyright Secured. All Rights Reserved. Reprinted by Permission.

425 Arrangement: © 1965 The United Methodist Publishing House.

426 Words, Music: © 1994 by Hope Publishing Co. All rights reserved. Used by permission.

427 Words: © 1982 by Hope Publishing Co. All rights reserved. Used by permission.

428 Words: © 1988 by Hope Publishing Co. All rights reserved. Used by permission.

429 Words, Music: © 1977 Archdiocese of Philadelphia, 222 N. 17th Street, Philadelphia PA 19103.

430 Words (Stanzas 1, 4, 5, 6, 7), Music: © 1988 Iona Community. Used by permission of GIA Publications, Inc. All rights reserved.

431 Words: © 1983 Jaroslav J. Vajda. Harmonization: © Oxford University Press.

432 Words: © 1995 Chalice Press.

435 Words, Music: Copyright © 1940 by Unichappell Music Inc. (BMI). Copyright Renewed, Assigned to Chappel & Co. International Copyright Secured. All Rights Reserved.

436 Words: © 1983 The United Methodist Publishing House. Harmonization: © 1989 The United Methodist Publishing House.

437 Words, Music: © 1976 Hinshaw Music, Inc., P.O. Box 470, Chapel Hill NC 27514. Used by permission.

438 Translation: © 1982 The United Methodist Publishing House.

440 Music: © 1983, 1990, Swinging Door Music, RD 1, Box 489, West Hurley NY 12491.

441 Words, Music: © 1995 Chalice Press.

442 Words, Music: © 1984 Utryck. Used by permission of Walton Music Corporation, 170 NE 33rd Street, Ft. Lauderdale FL 33334.

443 From *The Untold Story: A Short History of Black Disciples.* © 1976 Chalice Press.

444 Words Adaptation, Music Adaptation: © 1961 Concordia Publishing House, 3558 S. Jefferson Avenue, St. Louis MO 63118.

445 Words, Music: © 1982 Barber L. Waters, 60 Johnson Circle, N. Andover MA 01845, and Kenneth E. White, 83 Main Street, Brewster NY 10509.

447 Words, Music: © 1984 Utryck. Used by permission of Walton Music Corporation, 170 NE 33rd Street, Ft. Lauderdale FL 33334.

448 Words, Music: © 1987 Medical Mission Sisters.

449 From *All Desires Known* by Janet Morley. © 1988 Morehouse Publishing Co., 871 Ethan Allen Highway, Ridgefield CN 06877.

450 Words: © 1989 by Hope Publishing Co. All rights reserved. Used by permission.

451 Adapted from New Testament texts by Colbert S. Cartwright. © 1995 Chalice Press.

452 Words, Music: © 1981, Daniel L. Schutte and New Dawn Music. All rights reserved. Used with permission.

453 Words: © 1981 Jane Parker Huber.

454 Words, Music: © 1993 by Hope Publishing Co. All rights reserved. Used by permission.

455 Words, Music: © 1983 David L. Edwards. Arrangement: © 1995 Shalom Publications, 7225 Berkridge Drive, Hazelwood MO 63042.

457 Words, Music: © 1993 by Hope Publishing Co. All rights reserved. Used by permission.

458 Words, Music: © 1979 Julian B. Rush, 700 Pennsylvania #101, Denver CO 80203.

459 Words: © 1978 by Hope Publishing Co. All rights reserved. Used by permission. Music: © 1942, renewed 1970, by Hope Publishing Co. All rights reserved. Used by permission.

460 Adapted from "General Principles and Policies" of the Division of Overseas Ministries, Christian Church (Disciples of Christ). Used by permission.

461 Words: © 1961 Oxford University Press. Harmonization: © 1978 *Lutheran Book of Worship.* Reprinted by permission of Augsburg Fortress.

462 Words Response Adaptation, Music: © 1989 The United Methodist Publishing House.

463 Words: © 1960 Judson Press, P.O. Box 851, Valley Forge PA 19482.

465 Words, Music: © 1978 Desert Flower Music.

466 Used by permission of Kenneth L. Teegarden, 7013 Serrano Drive, Ft. Worth TX 76126.

467 Words, Music: © 1992 David L. Edwards. Arrangement: © 1995 Chalice Press.

469 Words, Music: © 1969 Desert Flower Music.

470 Words © 1969 by Hope Publishing Co. All rights reserved. Used by permission. Music: Used by permission of Oxford University Press.

471 Words © 1974 by Hope Publishing Co. All rights reserved. Used by permission. Music © 1985 GIA Publications, Inc. All rights reserved.

472 Stanza 2 Adaptation: © 1995 Ruth Duck.

473 From *Something Beautiful for God: Mother Teresa of Calcutta* by Malcolm Muggeridge. Copyright © 1971 by The Mother Teresa Committee. Reprinted by permission of HarperCollins Publishers, Inc.

474 Words, Music: From the *Korean-English Hymnbook,* published by the Korean-English Hymnbook Publication Commission. Used by permission of Tukyul Andrew Kim, 29148 Fairfax Street, Southfield MI 48076. Translation © 1995 Chalice Press.

475 Words: © 1971 by Hope Publishing Co. All rights reserved. Used by permission.

476 Words: © 1973, 1980, by Hope Publishing Co. All rights reserved. Used by permission.

477 Words, Music: © 1969 Bud John Songs, Inc. (a division of The Sparrow Corp.). All rights administered by The Sparrow Corporation. All rights reserved. Used by permission.

478 Words, Music: © 1979 Cesareo Gabaraín. Published by OCP Publications. All rights reserved. Used with permission. Translation: © 1989 The United Methodist Publishing House. Harmonization: Used by permission of Juan Francisco Chávez, Arenal 48, Depto. 10, 01050 México (San Angel), D.F., Mexico.

485 Words: © 1992 GIA Publications, Inc. All rights reserved.

486 Words, Music: © 1992 by Hope Publishing Co. All rights reserved. Used by permission.

487 Words: © 1974 by Hope Publishing Co. All rights reserved. Used by permission. Music: © 1977 by Hope Publishing Co. All rights reserved. Used by permission.

488 From *Thankful Praise.* © 1987 Chalice Press.

489 Words: © 1991 GIA Publications, Inc. All rights reserved. Harmonization: © 1983, used by permission of Gracia Grindal, Luther Theological Seminary, 2481 Como Avenue, St. Paul MN 55108.

490 Words, Music: © 1977 Scripture in Song (Administered by Maranatha! Music, c/o The Copyright Company). All Rights Reserved. International Copyright Secured. Used by Permission.

491 Words: © 1992 GIA Publications, Inc. All rights reserved. Music: © 1983 by Hope Publishing Co. All rights reserved. Used by permission.

492 Translation, Music: © 1986 Verbum Fölag AB. Used by permission of GIA Publications, Inc. All rights reserved. Harmonization: © 1995 Chalice Press.

493 Translation: © 1995 Chalice Press.

494 Words, Music: © 1966 FEL Publications, assigned to The Lorenz Corp. All rights reserved. Reprinted by permit 238291.

495 Words, Music: © 1979 Rosemary Crow, 33 Deerhaven Lane, Asheville NC 28803.

496 Words, Music: © 1983 Benjamín Villanueva, 1102 75th Street, Houston TX 77011. Translation: © 1983 George Lockwood, P.O. Box 220, Oroville WA 98844. Arrangement: © 1983 Esther Frances, 829 Congress Street, Apt. #1, Portland ME 04102.

497 Words, Music: © 1983 Desert Flower Music.

498 Words: © 1968 by Hope Publishing Co. All rights reserved. Used by permission.

499 Words, Harmonization: © 1983 by Hope Publishing Co. All rights reserved. Used by permission.

500 Words: © 1991 Oxford University Press.

501 Arrangement: © Faith and Life Press, 722 Main Street, Newton KS 67114.

503 Words: © 1969 by Hope Publishing Co. All rights reserved. Used by permission.

504 Words: © 1982 by Hope Publishing Co. All rights reserved. Used by permission.

505 From *Services for Occasions of Pastoral Care*. © 1990 Westminster John Knox Press.

506 Words, Music: © 1991 GIA Publications, Inc. All rights reserved.

507 Words: © 1993 Mary R. Bittner, 104 Robin Hill Drive, Naperville IL 60540.

508 From *Meditations of the Heart* by Howard Thurman. © 1953 Howard Thurman Educational Trust, 2020 Stockton Street, San Francisco CA 94133.

509 Words: © 1988, 1991 Oxford University Press. Music: © 1980 Floyd Knight, Jr., 9601 Monrovia, Apt. 104, Lenexa KS 66215.

510 Words: © 1992 GIA Publications, Inc. All rights reserved. Music: © 1988 Ann MacKenzie, 225 High Street, Walpole MA 02081.

511 Words, Music: © 1993 by Hope Publishing Co. All rights reserved. Used by permission.

512 Words: © 1994 by Hope Publishing Co. All rights reserved. Used by permission.

513 Words, Music: From the *Korean-English Hymnbook*, published by the Korean-English Hymnbook Publication Commission. Used by permission of Tukyul Andrew Kim, 29148 Fairfax Street, Southfield MI 48076.

514 Words: © 1939 J. W. Gilchrist, 10 Wychwood Park, Toronto, Ontario M6G 2V5, Canada.

518 Words: © 1983 by Hope Publishing Co. All rights reserved. Used by permission. Music: © 1987 by Hope Publishing Co. All rights reserved. Used by permission.

519 Words, Music: © 1995 Chalice Press.

522 Translation: © 1995 Chalice Press.

523 Words, Music: © Les Presses de Taizé. Used by permission of GIA Publications, Inc. All rights reserved.

526 Words, Music: © 1972 by Hope Publishing Co. All rights reserved. Used by permission.

528 Words, Music: © 1978 Integrity's Hosanna! Music, Inc. P.O. Box 16813, Mobile AL 36616. All rights reserved. International copyright secured. Used by permission.

529 Harmonization: © 1977 Richwood Music, 107 Hemlock Court, Hendersonville TN 37075.

531 Harmonization: © 1981 The United Methodist Publishing House.

533 Words, Music: © 1965 Manna Music, Inc.

534 Words: © 1971 by Hope Publishing Co. All rights reserved. Used by permission.

535 Translation: © 1976 by Hope Publishing Co. All rights reserved. Used by permission. Music: © 1959 The United Methodist Publishing House.

536 Translation: © 1989 The United Methodist Publishing House.

538 Words: © 1954, renewal 1982 by The Hymn Society. All rights reserved. Used by permission of Hope Publishing Co. Music: © 1963 The United Methodist Publishing House.

539 Words, Music: © 1950 by Unichappell Music Inc. Copyright Renewed. International Copyright Secured. All Rights Reserved.

547 Composed by Reinhold Niebuhr in 1943.

553 From *The Faith We Affirm* by Ronald E. Osborn. © 1979 Chalice Press.

554 Words, Music: © 1981 Maranatha! Music (Administered by The Copyright Company). All Rights Reserved. International Copyright Secured. Used by Permission.

555 Words, Music: © 1971 Manna Music, Inc.

562 Words, Music: © 1971, 1995 William J. Gaither ASCAP. All rights reserved. Used by permission.

564 Words, Music: © 1963, 1995 William J. Gaither ASCAP. All rights reserved. Used by permission.

565 Words Stanza 2: © 1978 *Lutheran Book of Worship*. Reprinted by permission of Augsburg Fortress.

566 Arrangement: © 1933, renewed 1961, Presbyterian Board of Christian Education. Used by permission of Westminster John Knox Press.

567 From *The Way of Prayer* by Peter Ainslie, 1930.

568 Arrangement: © 1984 Margaret W. Mealy, 1404 Summit Road, Berkeley CA 94708.

569 Music: © 1981 Les Presses de Taizé. Used by permission of GIA Publications, Inc. All rights reserved.

575 Words, Arrangement: © 1992 by Hope Publishing Co. All rights reserved. Used by permission.

579 Arrangement: © 1989 The United Methodist Publishing House.

583 Words, Music: © 1953 by Doris Akers. Copyright Renewed. All Rights Administered by Unichappell Music Inc. International Copyright Secured. All Rights Reserved.

584 Arrangement: © 1979. Used by permission of J. Jefferson Cleveland Estate, c/o William McClain, Wesley Theological Seminary, 4500 Massachusetts Avenue NW, Washington DC 20016.

589 Harmonization: © 1995 Chalice Press.

591 From *Meditations of the Heart* by Howard Thurman. © 1953 Howard Thurman Educational Trust, 2020 Stockton Street, San Francisco CA 94133.

592 Music Adaptation and Arrangement: © 1989 The United Methodist Publishing House.

595 Harmonization: © 1964 The United Methodist Publishing House.

596 Words, Music: © 1989 Medical Mission Sisters.

597 From *WomanWisdom: A Feminist Lectionary and Psalter: Women of the Hebrew Scriptures: Part One* by Miriam Therese Winter. Copyright © 1991 by Medical Mission Sisters. Reprinted by permission of The Crossroad Publishing Company, 370 Lexington Avenue, New York NY 10017.

598 Arrangement: © 1995 Floyd Knight, Jr., 9601 Monrovia, Apt. 104, Lenexa KS 66215.

599 Music: Copyright © 1971 by Range Road Music Inc., Quartet Music, Inc., and New Cadenza Publishing Corp. Administered by Hal Leonard Publishing Corp. International Copyright Secured. All Rights Reserved. Used by Permission.

600 Words, Music: © 1969 by Hope Publishing Co. All rights reserved. Used by permission. Harmonization © 1989 by Hope Publishing Co. All rights reserved. Used by permission.

604 Words, Music: © 1928 Grand View College, Des Moines IA 50316. Harmonization: © 1966 Judson Press, P.O. Box 851, Valley Forge PA 19482.

605 Words: © 1976 The Hymn Society. All rights reserved. Used by permission of Hope Publishing Co. Harmonization: © 1964 The United Methodist Publishing House.

606 Words © 1961, renewal 1989 by The Hymn Society. All rights reserved. Used by permission of Hope Publishing Co.

607 Words, Music: Used by permission of Asian Institute for Liturgy and Music.

610 Words, Music: © 1917 by Heidelberg Press. © Renewed 1945 by C. Harold Lowden. Assigned to The Rodeheaver Company (a division of WORD, INC.). All Rights Reserved. Used by Permission.

614 Arrangement: © 1995 Chalice Press.

616 Words: © 1975 by Hope Publishing Co. All rights reserved. Used by permission. Music: © 1995 Chalice Press.

617 Words, Music: © 1954 Singspiration Music/ASCAP. All Rights Reserved. Used by permission of Benson Music Group, Inc., c/o Commercial Licensing, 365 Great Circle Road, Nashville TN 37228. Translation: © 1995 Chalice Press.

620 Words, Music: © 1943 by Unichappell Music Inc. Copyright Renewed. International Copyright Secured. All Rights Reserved.

624 From *A Book of Public Prayers* by Harry Emerson Fosdick. Copyright © 1959 by Harry Emerson Fosdick. Reprinted by permission of HarperCollins Publishers, Inc.

627 Harmonization: © 1981 The United Methodist Publishing House.

628 Words, Music: © 1938 by Unichappell Music Inc. Copyright Renewed. International Copyright Secured. All Rights Reserved.

629 Arrangement: © 1995 Floyd Knight, Jr., 9601 Monrovia, Apt. 104, Lenexa KS 66215.

630 Music Adaptation: © 1989 The United Methodist Publishing House.

631 Words, Music: © 1921 by Edward B. Marks Music Company. Copyright Renewed. Administered by Hal Leonard Publishing Corp. International Copyright Secured. All Rights Reserved. Used by Permission.

633 Words: © 1992 GIA Publications, Inc. All rights reserved.

638 Words, Music: © 1986 by Hope Publishing Co. All rights reserved. Used by permission.

639 Words: © 1983 by Hope Publishing Co. All rights reserved. Used by permission.

640 Words Response: © 1963 Ladies of the Grail (England). Used by permission of GIA Publications, Inc. All rights reserved. Music: © 1979 GIA Publications, Inc. All rights reserved.

641 Arrangement: © 1989 Shalom Publications, 7225 Berkridge Drive, Hazelwood MO 63042.

642 Words: © 1991 Oxford University Press. Music: © 1995 Chalice Press.

643 Arrangement: © 1995 Chalice Press.

645 Music: © 1992 Unitarian Universalist Association, 25 Beacon Street, Boston MA 02108.

646 Words: © 1972 The Hymn Society. All rights reserved. Used by permission of Hope Publishing Co.

648 Words, Music: © 1992 David L. Edwards. Harmonization: © 1995 Chalice Press.

649 Words: © 1987 by Hope Publishing Co. All rights reserved. Used by permission.

650 © 1982 by Hope Publishing Co. All rights reserved. Used by permission.

651 Words: © 1967 by Hope Publishing Co. All rights reserved. Used by permission.

652 Words, Music: © 1991 Carlos Rosas, 2427 W. Huisache, San Antonio TX 78228. Translation, Arrangement: © 1995 Chalice Press.

653 Reprinted from *I Believe in the Resurrection of the Body* by Rubem A. Alves. Translation copyright © 1986 Fortress Press. Used by permission of Augsburg Fortress.

654 Words: © 1983 by Hope Publishing Co. All rights reserved. Used by permission. Music: © 1995 by Hope Publishing Co. All rights reserved. Used by permission.

655 Words: © 1992 by Hope Publishing Co. All rights reserved. Used by permission.

656 Words: © 1992 by Hope Publishing Co. All rights reserved. Used by permission. Music: Used by permission of Oxford University Press.

657 © 1981 Christian Conference of Asia, Pak Tin Village, Mei Tin Road, Shatin, N.T., Hong Kong.

658 Words: © 1995 Chalice Press. Harmonization: © 1978 *Lutheran Book of Worship*. Reprinted by permission of Augsburg Fortress.

659 Words: © Oxford University Press. Music: © 1973 by Hope Publishing Co. All rights reserved. Used by permission.

661 Words, Music: © 1986 Desert Flower Music.

662 Words, Music: © 1971, J. A. Olivar, Miguel Manzano and San Pablo Internacional – SSP. All rights reserved. Sole U.S. Agent: OCP Publications. Used with permission. Translation: © 1980 The United Methodist Publishing House.

664 © WGRG, Iona Community, 416 Great Western Road, Glasgow G49HZ, Scotland.

667 Words, Music: Used by permission of Asian Institute for Liturgy and Music.

668 Words: © 1968 by Hope Publishing Co. All rights reserved. Used by permission.

670 Words: © 1969 by Stainer & Bell Ltd. Used by permission of Hope Publishing Co. All rights reserved. Used by permission. Harmonization: © 1965 The United Methodist Publishing House.

671 Words: © 1992 GIA Publications, Inc. All rights reserved. Harmonization: © 1940 The Church Hymnal Corp.

672 Words: © 1954, renewal 1982 The Hymn Society. All rights reserved. Used by permission of Hope Publishing Co.

675 Words: © 1990 Constance Cherry, 1025 Oakdale Drive, Findlay OH 45840.

677 Words, Music: © 1955, renewed 1983, Jan-Lee Music, P.O. Box 1517, Honokaa HI 96727.

678 From *The Violence of Love* by Archbishop Oscar Romero, edited by James R. Brockman and Henri Nouwen. Copyright © 1988 by Chicago Province of the Society of Jesus. Reprinted by permission of HarperCollins Publishers, Inc.

680 Words: © 1958, renewal 1986 by The Hymn Society. All rights reserved. Used by permission of Hope Publishing Co. Music Adaptation, Harmonization: Used by permission of Oxford University Press.

681 Words: © 1987 by Hope Publishing Co. All rights reserved. Used by permission. Music: © 1995 by Hope Publishing Co. All rights reserved. Used by permission.

682 Reprinted by permission of the World Council of Churches, 150 Route de Ferney, 1211 Geneva 2, Switzerland.

683 Words: © 1990 Medical Mission Sisters.

684 Words: © 1992 GIA Publications, Inc. All rights reserved.

685 Words, Music: From the *Korean-English Hymnbook*, published by the Korean-English Hymnbook Publication Commission. Used by permission of Tukyul Andrew Kim, 29148 Fairfax Street, Southfield MI 48076.

686 Words: © 1992 by Hope Publishing Co. All rights reserved. Used by permission.

688 Words: © 1992 Jane Parker Huber.

689 Words, Music: © 1989 by Hope Publishing Co. All rights reserved. Used by permission.

690 Words: © 1973 by The Hymn Society. All rights reserved. Used by permission of Hope Publishing Co.

691 Words: © 1975 by Hope Publishing Co. All rights reserved. Used by permission. Music: © 1985, Selah Publishing Co., Inc., P.O. Box 3037, Kingston NY 12401. Used by permission. All rights reserved.

693 Words, Music: © 1992 by Hope Publishing Co. All rights reserved. Used by permission.

694 Reprinted from *Worship in an Indian Context*, edited by Eric J. Lott (UTC Publications, Bangalore, India).

695 Words: © 1955, renewal 1983 by Hope Publishing Co. All rights reserved. Used by permission.

696 Words: © 1971 Walter Farquharson, Box 58, Saltcoats, Sask. S0A 3R0, Canada.

697 Words: © 1992 GIA Publications, Inc. All rights reserved. Harmonization: Used by permission of Oxford University Press.

699 Descant: © 1947 by Hope Publishing Co. All rights reserved. Used by permission.

702 Harmonization: © 1992 The United Methodist Publishing House.

703 Words: © 1989 by Hope Publishing Co. All rights reserved. Used by permission.

704 From *The Panel of Scholars Reports*, *Vol. 3*. © 1963 Chalice Press.

708 Refrain harmonization: © 1981 The United Methodist Publishing House. Verse and Response Harmonization: © 1995 Chalice Press.

Unified Index of Authors, Translators, Composers, Arrangers, and Sources

Topical Index of Hymns

Index of Worship Materials by Category

Scripture References

This index identifies only those hymns that have a direct relationship to a specific
biblical text, as indicated on the hymn page.

Metrical Index

Index of Tune Names

Index of First Lines and Titles

Hymns and other musical selections are listed both by first line and commonly known title (as shown on the hymn page). Titles of worship materials are in italics.